Margaretha Adriana Alt
Mother of the Indonesian Pentecostal Mission

Christianity came here because our *ndoro* brought the Gospel to the poor, especially to the poor.
— Joenoes, Gambang Waluh, 1957.

Sister Alt became known far and wide as 'Mother Alt' to those who came under her godly influence.
— Harold Carlblom
Assemblies of God missionary to Indonesia, 1979.

MARGARETHA ADRIANA ALT

MOTHER OF THE INDONESIAN PENTECOSTAL MISSION

CORNELIS VAN DER LAAN

CPT

CPT Press
Cleveland, Tennessee

Margaretha Adriana Alt
Mother of the Indonesian Pentecostal Mission

Published by CPT Press
900 Walker ST NE
Cleveland, TN 37311
USA

email: cptpress@pentecostaltheology.org
website: www.cptpress.com

ISBN-13: 978-1-935931-83-6

Originally published in Dutch by Uitgeverij Van Wijnen, Franeker, The Netherlands under the title: *Moesje Alt: 50 jaar zendelinge in Nederlands-Indië* by Cornelis van der Laan, Copyright © 2016, and in Indonesian by Penerbit Gandum Mas, Malang, Indonesia, under the title: *Moesje Alt: Pelopor Gerakan Pentakosta di Indonesia* by Cornelis van der Laan, Copyright © 2016.

The author gratefully acknowledges Bart Sigmond-de Vrij, Ella Koetsier-de Vrij, Ruth Groeneveld, Hans Groeneveld, Christine van Abkoude, R.E.O. Ekkart, Alief Handojo, and Suus Boef for permission to use photographs from their collections.

CONTENTS

PREFACE

To explain why I have written this book I will go back to 1973, the year I experienced a spiritual renewal in my own life. I joined the Pentecostal church in Amsterdam where I became acquainted with *Glorieklokken* (*Bells of Glory*) the song-book of 'Sister Alt'. With a full heart I sang along: 'I am walking in the light with Jesus'. The songs gave words to what I was feeling inside.

Later I developed an interest in the history of the Pentecostal movement. As I delved into the past, once again I encountered Sister Alt. Without exception, people who had known her spoke with great affection of 'Moesje Alt' ('Mother Alt'). Obviously she was an inspiration for many. By reading her autobiography and her periodical *Gouden Schoven* (*Golden Sheaves*) I became convinced of the importance of her life story.

I have tried to reconstruct her personality, her motivation, her working environment, her relationships with people, her social and cultural world, her influence on others, and what she has to say to us today. This book is the result of my quest.

I have received much help from people willing to share their memories or materials with me. In particular I mention here: Bart Sigmond-de Vrij, Ella Koetsier-de Vrij, Ruth and Hans Groeneveld, Rudi Ekkart, Henk Sleebos, and Evert van der Molen. I am indebted to Alle Hoekema, Tom van den End, and Paul van der Laan for their valuable remarks while reading the manuscript and to George Thomassen and Peter Kay for correcting my Dutch-English. I am thankful to all these and others who have helped me.

I hope this book will do justice to the life of this outstanding woman. Often she had to fight against rejection based on her gender. In the words of the apostle Paul, her defence has always been that God has chosen to use the weak and those who count as nothing in the world (cf. 1 Cor. 1.27–28).

Cornelis van der Laan, January 2019

ABBREVIATIONS

BPM	Bataafsche Petroleum Maatschappij
CAMA	Christian and Missionary Alliance
DZV	Doopsgezinde Zendingsvereeniging
ECK	Evangelisch Christelijke Kerk
GKN	Gereformeerde Kerken in Nederland
GPdI	Gereja Pantekosta di Indonesia
GSJA	Gereja Sidang-sidang Jamaat Allah
GUP	Gereja Utusan Pantekosta
GS	*Gouden Schooven, Gouden Schoven*
KWI	Konferensi Waligereja Indonesia
NGZV	Nederlandsche Gereformeerde Zendingsvereeniging
NHK	Nederlandse Hervormde Kerk
NZG	Nederlandsch Zendingsgenootschap
NZV	Nederlandsche Zendingsvereeniging
PGI	Persekutuan Gereja-gereja di Indonesia
PGNI	Pinkstergemeente in Nederlandsch-Indië
PGPI	Persekutuan Gereja-gereja Pentakosta Indonesia
PII	Persekutuan Injili Indonesia
SA	Salvation Army
SDA	Seventh-Day Adventists
SDB	Seventh-Day Baptists
TEAM	The Evangelical Missionary Alliance
UZV	Utrechtsche Zendingsvereeniging

1

INTRODUCTION

I was twelve years old, when one evening at The Hague I heard a Christian choir singing the familiar mission song: 'Do you hear that voice, calling from afar, begging for salvation, it is a cry of sorrow'.

Although still not converted and rather indifferent to spiritual matters, this song hit me like an arrow deep in my heart. In my spirit I saw dark figures rising, stretching their hands upwards, begging. In a moment I decided: 'When I grow up, I will go to the gentiles as a missionary to tell them about Jesus'.[1]

This book is about the life of Margaretha Adriana Alt (1883–1962), known as Margot, but better known as Sister Alt or Moesje Alt. For her early years I will refer to her as Margot, thereafter Moes or Moesje, meaning mother. Shortly before her death, she completed her autobiography *Herinneringen uit mijn leven* (*Memories from My Life*). In the preface she addressed her readers: 'Do not set your expectations too high. This is just the story of a very ordinary human being, who has known struggle and hardship like you, yet one who was allowed to have victory by the grace of Christ in me'.[2] She wrote at the request of her co-workers in the hope that that it would prove helpful to her readers in their life of faith.

The preface is typical of her approach: modest and at the same time authoritative. She does not want to force herself upon the reader, yet she knows she is a witness of Christ. The tale of her life

---

[1] M.A. Alt, 'Mag de vrouw spreken in de gemeente?', *GS* 9.6 (March 1933), pp. 4-7 (6).

[2] M.A. Alt, *Herinneringen uit mijn leven* (Velp: Pinksterzending, 1963), p. 5.

story is interwoven with spiritual and moral lessons. This is how she always wrote, preached and lived.

In this introduction I outline the sources I have used, followed by a sketch of the Dutch East Indian background, where Moesje Alt lived for fifty-eight years without interruption. Next I describe the situation of the mission on Java at the beginning of the twentieth century. Chapters two to fourteen portray her life story in chronological order. The last four chapters illuminate her songs, writings, theology, and draw some conclusions as to her significance.

Sources

For this research, above all, I have made use of all available publications written by Moesje Alt herself. Of most importance is the autobiography she finished shortly before her death in 1962. It has been published as *Herinneringen uit mijn leven* in 1963, including the appendix *Raadgevingen en persoonlijke ervaringen* (*Counsel and Personal Experiences*). A second (unchanged) printing in 1971 is amplified with the inclusion of the reprint of *Ons Kampleven* (*Our Life in the Camps*). I have traced and studied nearly all the publications of Alt including the complete thirty-one volumes (12,000 pages!) of *Gouden Schoven (Golden Sheaves)*, the periodical she edited from 1928 to 1962. All her articles and letters from 1910 to 1922 in the periodical *De Boodschapper (The Messenger)* have also been consulted.

Next to these published sources, many handwritten documents have been found. Most important among these are the collection of poems from the period 1899 to 1906; the diary from the period 1910 to 1919; the diary from the period 1945 to 1961 and the handwritten autobiography of 1943. Out of the thousands of letters she must have written, some fifty have been found. Also of help have been the three Bibles with handwritten notes in the margins and with pasted in sheets with sermon notes; a sermon notebook, as well as a number of books that have been important for Alt with many of her underlinings and notes in the margins.

I have researched the historical background of The Hague around the beginning of the twentieth century, as well as parallel developments in the Dutch Indies in the first half of that century. I have paid special attention to the situation of the Christian mission and the rise of the Pentecostal movement on Java. Using genealogical research I have been able to complement the available data about the family. Where possible I have contacted descendants of family members or relatives. Dozens of people with memories of Alt have been interviewed, among whom are co-workers, church members, and (grand) children of foster daughters.

Literary and archival research, interviews, the diaries, a volume of poems, and letters form an important addition to the sources already published by Alt. Many times it is as if we are granted a look behind the curtain. This way I can present a more complete picture of the life of this remarkable woman. I briefly describe the historical context before launching into Moesje Alt's life story. As the scene is mainly set during Dutch rule, the geographical names of that period are used (for instance Batavia instead of Jakarta).

In publications about the history of the Indonesian Pentecostal movement, up to now very little original research has been done into the initial period. The majority of references are to the short, previously existing accounts, but which also include their inaccuracies. On the whole, Dutch sources have been completely neglected, while Dutch was the official language at the time. The most important periodical *Gouden Schoven* has never been used. The same goes for the periodical *Dit is Het* (*This is It*), published since 1923, as well as consultation of the mission archives and the secular newspapers. Until 1934 Moesje Alt was part of Indonesian mainstream Pentecostalism. Because the history of the formative period needs addition and correction, ample attention is paid to this initial phase. However, in the interests of better readability some parts of this history have been worked out in appendices.

This research too has a limited scope. Although I have used many primary sources that have not been used before, for the most parts these are Dutch sources. The focus is on Moesje Alt, a Dutch missionary. I make no apology for this; after all it is her biography. To do justice to the initial period of the Pentecostal movement would require more research into the contribution of the Chinese and Indonesian evangelists utilizing more primary sources in the Indonesian languages.

Historical background of Indonesia

During the course of history many peoples from the Asian mainland moved to the archipelago we today know as Indonesia. With new arrivals the existing inhabitants on the coast were often pushed into the interior where life was harder. As a result of this continued migration hundreds of ethnic groups developed with as many languages being spoken. In the eighth century Hinduism and Buddhism from India took firm root. Kingdoms came and went. Each dynasty established a new capital. During the fifteenth and sixteenth century, Islam was embraced, except on Bali that remained Hindu. Owing to trade relations, Malay became the *lingua franca*, of which modern Indonesian (*Bahasa Indonesia*) is a variant.[3]

After a century of Portuguese influence, the Dutch more or less took over control in the seventeenth century. These Europeans introduced Christianity, first the Catholic then the Protestant version. Except for a short period around the turn of the nineteenth century when the British were ruling the Indonesian waves, Dutch dominion continued until the Japanese occupation in 1942.

The five largest islands were Java, Sumatra, Borneo (Kalimantan), Celebes (Sulawesi), and New Guinea (Papua Barat/Papua). There was a great distinction between Java (including the small island Madura) and the other islands, called the 'outer areas'. The Dutch mainly settled along the coast of Java, where they cultivated sugar, coffee, tea, and tobacco. The larger plantations were situated in the less populated outer areas, which also included mines and oil fields. Batavia (Jakarta) on Java became the centre of power. Java had three provinces: West-, Middle-, and East-Java. The capitals were respectively: Bandung, Semarang, and Surabaya. Each province was divided into a number of residentships, mostly named after the capital of the residentship concerned. For instance, Kediri was the capital of the residentship Kediri in East-Java. Each residentship was ruled by a governor called Resident. The highest official in the Dutch Indies, the Governor General, resided in Batavia.

East- and Middle-Java was mainly inhabited by Javanese, while in the South of West-Java the Sundanese had a strong presence. The

---

[3] Frank L. Cooley, *Indonesia: Church & Society* (New York: Friendship Press, 1968), p. 10.

Europeans and Chinese lived mostly in the cities, where next to Dutch and Chinese also Malay, the trade language, was spoken.

Although Java (including Madura) only covered seven percent of the total land, it hosted two thirds of the population. For our story the last census under Dutch rule is important. During that census of 1930 out of a total of 60.9 million inhabitants, 41.7 million (68 percent) lived on Java. These consisted of four groups: 1. Indonesians ('Inlanders') 59.1 million (97.4 percent); 2. Europeans 240,000 (0.4 percent); 3. Chinese 1.2 million (2 percent); and 4. other Asians (mainly Arabs) 115,000 (0.2 percent).[4]

The society had different social layers with a strong hierarchy. The privileged upper layer was formed of a small group of Dutch and other Europeans; then the Orientals (Chinese and Arabs) and finally the large group of Indonesians called 'Inlanders'. Among the Indonesians there was a huge distinction between the aristocracy and the common people. The Indonesian royals and rulers stood far above the people. The colonial rulers kept these distinctions in place, using it to serve their own commercial interest.[5] One section of the Dutch viewed their stay overseas as temporary. These import-Dutch were also called 'movers'.[6] The Dutch that came to regard the Indies as their home or had been born there, were the 'stayers'. A special group among the stayers was formed of the Indo-Europeans, or Indos. They were the children and their descendants from mixed marriages or sexual liaisons with concubines. If they were acknowledged by the European father, they were registered as Europeans. If not, they were

---

[4] *Volkstelling 1930 Deel VIII Overzicht voor Nederlands-Indië* (Batavia: Landsdrukkerij, 1936), pp. 7–8. The category Europeans also include North-Americans, Egyptians, Japanese, Armenians, Turks, and others put on a par like indigenous women married to Europeans. As to religion, the figures of the census are incomplete. Only the Europeans, Ambonese, Batak, and Menadonese have been questioned about their religion, not the other Indonesians and the Chinese. The number of Christians was 911,000 (1.5 percent); for Java/Madura alone 185,000 (0.44 percent). According to the annual report *Indisch Verslag* of 1936 there were 2 million Christians in 1935 (3 percent). 'Het aantal Christenen in Nederlandsch Oost-Indië', *Nederlands Zendingsblad* 20 (1937), pp. 153–54. These figures were based upon statistics from churches and mission organizations. The Pentecostal movement counted 3,446 baptized members.

[5] Wim F. Wertheim, *Indonesië van vorstenrijk tot neo-kolonie* (Mepel: Boom, 1978), p. 41. Cf. Ulbe Bosma, Remco Raben and Wim Willems, *De Geschiedenis van de Indische Nederlanders* (Amsterdam: Bert Bakker, 2008), pp. 27–28.

[6] Hans Meijer, *In Indië geworteld: De twintigste eeuw* Amsterdam: Bert Bakker, 2004), pp. 9–10.

counted as Indonesians. In practice there was a clear distinction between the 'totok' (full blood white) European and the Indo-European, often determined by physical characteristics, exemplified in the
saying: 'the more pigment, the less payment'.[7] Top positions in indus-
trial life were mostly restricted to full blooded Europeans. The subordinates were mainly Indos. The government offered better chances
for Indos to gain higher positions. To gain promotion it was important to have had an education in The Netherlands. In a class-ori-
entated society so strongly dictated by descent, it was better not to
have social interactions with subordinates of a different colour.[8]

Among the middle class and in-between traders were a lot of Chinese, but also Arabs. The Chinese distinguished between 'singkeh' or
'totok' (full blooded, first generation Chinese), and the 'peranakan'
(child of the land, those born in the Dutch Indies, often of mixed
blood). In 1930 of the 580,000 Chinese on Java 80 percent belonged
to the peranakan.[9] By government regulation the Chinese lived in
their own quarters, had no access to government positions and had
to travel with passes.[10] Each quarter was under the supervision of a
Chinese Captain. The Captain was from the Chinese elite and responsible for order and security in the quarters and for collecting taxes.

Around 1900 the Dutch developed their own form of imperialism
called 'ethical policy'. In theory the motivation was ethical rather than
economic, paying more attention to the interest of the indigenous
population. It involved efforts to 'uplift' the inhabitants of the Indies
in the direction of a measure of self-government under Dutch rule.[11]
Improvements became visible in education, health care, irrigation
works, and in building roads and railways.

Allowing more private enterprise was optimistically presented as
beneficial for the population. Western example and Western leadership would stimulate the 'slow Javanese' to make up for the deficit in

---

[7] Wim F. Wertheim, 'Koloniaal racisme in Indonesië: Ons onverwerkt verleden?', *De Gids* 154 (1991), pp. 367–85 (369).

[8] Meijer, *In Indië geworteld*, p. 28.

[9] W. Dharmowijono, *Van koelies, klontongs en kapiteins: Het beeld van de Chinezen in
Indisch-Nederlands literair proza 1880–1950* (PhD thesis, Faculty of Humanities, University of Amsterdam, 2009, p. 46; http://dare.uva.nl/record/1/319403).

[10] Dharmowijono, *Van koelies*, pp. 77–81.

[11] H.W. van der Doel, *Afscheid van Indië: De val van het Nederland imperium in Azië*
(Amsterdam: Prometheus, 2000), pp. 19, 21. Cf. E.H. Kossmann, *The Low Countries
1780–1940* (Oxford History of Modern Europe; Oxford: Clarendon Press, 1978),
pp. 398–412.

their developmental opportunities.[12] Mission societies made a significant contribution by founding schools and hospitals. The Indo-Europeans, however, viewed this development as a threat to their vulnerable in-between position.[13] Some of the measures had an unfavourable outcome for the Chinese. Running pawnshops and the selling of opium, usually done by Chinese, were now taken over by the government.[14]

Western education gradually produced a new class of educated Indonesians. Their pursuit of equal chances would in time give birth to a nationalistic movement. The broadly felt dissatisfaction already expressed itself in the establishment of Sarekat Islam (Islamic Society) in 1912. Initially directed against the economic power of the Chinese, it was transformed into a political movement aimed at throwing off the colonial yoke. The government granted the population some consultation by the institution of a People's Council, but the nationalistic tide would not be turned back. From 1926 the Partai Nasional Indonesia (National Party of Indonesia) with Chairman Sukarno (1901–1970) campaigned for complete independence. The government reacted by arresting and later expelling Sukarno. The authorities failed to remove the distrust among the population. When the Japanese attacked the Dutch Indies, the antipathy against the Dutch was so strong, that many welcomed the occupying force with enthusiasm.[15]

Europeans and some of the Indos were interned in Japanese camps. In August 1945, right after the capitulation of Japan, the Republic of Indonesia was proclaimed. The Dutch who were released from the camps did not comprehend why the Indonesian population had turned so hostile. Because The Netherlands was not ready to give up the colony, years of violence and bloodshed followed. During the period from 1945 to 1947 many Dutch were interned in republican camps. In December 1949 the Dutch finally complied with a transfer of sovereignty to the new republic. Only New-Guinea (Papua) would remain under Dutch rule until 1962.

---

[12] Wertheim, *Indonesië*, p. 63.
[13] Meijer, *In Indië geworteld*, p. 18.
[14] Dharmowijono, *Van koelies*, p. 74.
[15] Leslie Palmier, *Indonesia* (London: Thames & Hudson, 1965), p. 104.

Mission on Java at the beginning of the twentieth century

The census of 2000 showed that 88 percent of the 206 million inhabitants were Muslim, making Indonesia the country with the largest Muslim population in the world.[16] The same census counted eighteen million Christians, or 9 percent of the population. Others have arrived at higher numbers of Christians.[17] The 3 percent of Christians on Java was much lower than the national percentage.[18]

Mission activities on Java really began to advance when halfway through the nineteenth century mission societies started to send missionaries. Up till then there were hardly any indigenous Javanese Christian communities. The Protestant Church in the Dutch Indies (Indische Kerk) was under tutelage and defrayment by the State. European Protestants in the larger cities usually belonged to this church. The government carried out a policy of 'peace and order', therefore mission to the Muslim population was discouraged. Church ministers and missionaries needed permission to operate in particular districts.

The ethical policy advocated by the State in the beginning of the twentieth century brought a more positive attitude towards mission. It became possible to operate in some of the former closed areas and to receive more State subsidy for education and medical care run by the churches. The Roman Catholic Church had been present since the time of Portuguese rule in the sixteenth century, but from the nineteenth century missionaries were again permitted. The Jesuits were active in education. From 1900 the number of Dutch

---

[16] Leo Suryadinata, Evi Nurvidya Arafin and Aris Ananta, *Indonesian Population: Ethnicity and Religion in a Changing Political Landscape* (Indonesian Population Series 1; Singapore: Institute of South East Studies, 2003), p. 104.

[17] David B. Barrett, George T. Kurian and Todd M. Johnson in *Word Christian Encyclopedia* (Oxford: Oxford University Press, 2001), 1:104, calculate the number of Christians for mid-2000 at nearly twenty-eight million, making 13.1 percent of a total population of 212 million. Of the 28 million, nearly 9.5 million are Pentecostal/Charismatic. Mainly responsible for the difference is the category crypto-Christians in the latter publication. These are hidden Christians in areas of strong Muslim hostility. Patrick Johnstone and Jason Mandryk in *Operation World 21ˢᵗ Century Edition* (Gerards Cross: WEC Int., 2001), p. 339, estimate 34 million Christians (16 percent), among whom 10.8 million are Pentecostal/Charismatic. A more recent publication by Jan S. Aritonang and Karel Steenbrink speaks of 17 million Protestants among whom six million are Pentecostal, excluding the Charismatics in the mainline churches. Jan S. Aritonang and Karel Steenbrink (eds.), *A History of Christianity in Indonesia* (Leiden: Brill, 2008), p. 882.

[18] Aritonang and Steenbrink, *History Christianity Indonesia*, p. 639.

immigrants grew significantly. In all the large cities Protestants and Catholics built huge church buildings, schools and hospitals, initially meant for the Europeans and Indo-Europeans.

The Nederlandsch Zendelinggenootschap (NZG, Dutch Missionary Society) sent missionaries to the Moluccas, Minahasa, and Timor. In 1851 Jelle Jellesma was the first to go to East-Java. Dissatisfaction with the influence of Modernism in the NZG led to the establishment of four orthodox mission societies during the period from 1855 and 1859: the Java-Comité (Java Committee), the Nederlandsche Gereformeerde Zendingsvereeniging (NGZV, Dutch Reformed Mission Society), the Nederlandsche Zendingsvereeniging (NZV, Dutch Mission Society) and the Utrechtsche Zendingsvereeniging (UZV, Utrecht Mission Society). During this period the Mennonites founded their Doopsgezinde Zendingsvereeniging (DZV, Mennonite Mission Society).[19]

From 1863 the NZV sent missionaries to West Java.[20] The Sundanese in West Java were not very receptive to the gospel, yet a small Sundanese church came into being. Converts were generally from among the poor. In order to help them find a living, land was acquired which gave rise to Christian settlements. Later this policy was changed as it isolated Christians from society. The Chinese were more open to the gospel, but formed a separate church.

Middle Java had a cultural centre in Djokjakarta in the South, but Semarang in the North was the economic centre. The NGZV was active in Middle Java as from 1861.[21] In 1894 their work was largely taken over by the Gereformeerde Kerken Nederland (GKN, Reformed Churches in the Netherlands, founded in 1892). The

---

[19] The Dutch language has two words for Reformed: 'Hervormd' and 'Gereformeerd'. Gereformeerd was the original designation. In 1816 the name of the Gereformeerde Kerk changed to Nederlandse Hervormde Kerk (Netherlands Reformed Church). The secessions in the nineteenth century continued under the old name Gereformeerd as a symbol of being the true heirs of the original church. The same is visible in the names of the mission societies.

[20] M. Lindenborn, *West-Java als zendingsterrein der Nederlandsche Zendingsvereeniging* (Onze Zendingsvelden III; Utrecht: Zendingsstudieraad, [1922]). Th. van den End, *De Nederlandse Zendingsvereniging in West-Java 1858–1963* (Oegstgeest: Raad voor de Zending, 1991).

[21] D. Pol, *Midden-Java ten zuiden* (Onze Zendingsvelden IV; Utrecht Zendingsstudieraad, 1922). H. Reenders, *De Gereformeerde Zending in Midden-Java 1859–1931*. Chr.G.F. de Jong, *De Gereformeerde Zending in Midden-Java 1931–1975* (Zoetermeer: Boekencentrum, 1997).

remaining part went with the Salatiga Mission. The Salatiga Mission was a joint enterprise of the Ermelosche Zendingsgemeente (Ermelo Mission) and the German Neukirchener Mission.

The GKN only accepted academically trained and fully ordained ministers as missionaries, while the other mission societies employed those with a lower educational standard. Governor-General A.W.F. Idenburg, the highest authority in the colony and representative of the ethical policy, was a committed Christian and sympathetic towards the GKN.[22] Some missionaries like H.A. van Andel pled for a separate approach for the mission among the Chinese, as they were not Muslim.

The Mennonite DZV obtained permission to labour in the North of Middle Java, in the Jepara residence. Their first missionary was Pieter Jansz (1820–1904), whose daughter Marie we will come across later. Jansz translated the Bible into Javanese. His strategy of using agriculture as a means of evangelization was like the one the NZV had tried in West Java. His son Pieter Anthonie Jansz put this in practice with the land colony Mergaredja (Way to Prosperity), North of Taju. The number of Christians grew, but so did their isolation in society. But the fact that missionaries were both spiritual leaders and landlords had negative results.[23]

In the second part of the nineteenth century the Javanese Christian, Sadrach Surapranata, a converted Muslim, led a large indigenous movement of about 5,000 followers. At first he cooperated with missionaries of the NGZV. After a rupture with them in 1891 he became the apostle of the Irvingian Apostolic Church. Sadrach attempted to clothe Christianity in a Javanese coat. After his death most of his followers joined the existing churches.

The Salvation Army (Bala Keselamatan) arrived in 1894.[24] Their first officers paid a visit to Sadrach in Karangjoso. Semarang was their headquarters from 1895–1913; after that, it was Bandung. They were also active in Magelang, Rembang, Pati and Kudus. In 1902 the colony Salib Putih (White Cross), near Salatiga, was founded for victims

---

[22] Aritonang and Steenbrink, *History Christianity Indonesia*, p. 677. Idenburg was Governor-General during 1909–1916.

[23] Th.E. Jensma, *Doopsgezinde zending in Indonesië* (The Hague: Boekencentrum, 1968), pp. 41–52.

[24] Melattie Brouwer, *History of the Salvation Army in Indonesia 11894–1949* (Hawthorn, Victoria: Citadel Press, 1996).

of floods and volcanic eruptions. In 1915 they opened an eye clinic in Semarang, in addition to many other social activities. Initially the Salvation Army was viewed with skepticism by the other missionaries, as they operated where others were already working. Missionaries were also cautious of Johannes van der Steur, better known as Pa van der Steur, who cared for Indo-European orphans in Magelang from 1892.[25] He had been sent out by the small Seventh-Day Baptist Assembly in Haarlem, but on the field he had chosen an independent path.

Usually the groups in the above subsection were designated as sects, together with the Pentecostals. From1929–1942 S.C. Graaf van Randwijck was mission consul in the Dutch Indies. In his standard work on mission *Handelen en denken in dienst der zending* (1981 – *Acting and Thinking in the Service of Mission*) only one paragraph is dedicated to the 'sects'. His justification is that from the point of view of the mission they are 'their hostile brothers, not prepared to respect the work of other mission societies'.[26] Next he blames the sects for consciously working among already Christians and for not trying to understand the culture or learning another language than Malay. Also H.D.J. Boissevain, secretary of the Zendingsstudie-Raad (Mission Study Council), in his overview of mission *De zending in Oost en West* (1943 – *The Mission in East and West*) sees no place for the Pentecostals:

> Aside from that it is uncertain that these movements will have sufficient viability to survive, one may also question whether they belong in a book about Protestant Mission. For the most part they do not help to spread the Gospel, but rather make propaganda for their own particular views concerning certain texts or pericopes from the Bible. By doing so they often hinder the actual and full preaching of the Gospel.[27]

On both counts (no viability and no contribution) Boissevain was proved wrong. These examples are typical of the great gap that existed for many decades between the established mission churches and

---

[25] Vilan van de Loo, *Johannes 'Pa' van der Steur (1865–1945): Zijn leven, zijn werk en zijn Steurtjes* (The Hague: Stichting Tong Tong, 2015).

[26] M.C. Graaf van Randwijck, *Handelen en denken in dienst der zending: Oegstgeest 897–1942* (2 vols.; The Hague: Boekencentrum, 1981), p. 211.

[27] H.D.J. Boissevain, *De Zending in Oost en West: Verleden en Heden 2* (Zeist: Zendingstudie-Raad, 1945), p. 252.

the upcoming Pentecostal Movement, a gap to which the Pentecostals themselves also contributed. It explains why in so many descriptions of the mission in the Dutch Indies there is little or no interest in the Pentecostals. This book contributes to a broader understanding by paying full attention to the 'hostile brothers'.

Margot Alt was a missionary in Middle and East Java for more than forty years. The last ten years she worked in Papua. She started in 1910 as a missionary nurse of the Seventh-Day Baptists and later joined the Pentecostals. To a large extent these affiliations determined her position in relation to other mission societies in a time when distrust from both sides prevailed. How did she deal with these limitations? Even more importantly, how did she relate to the local people and their culture? Did she walk in new ways or was she treading the known paths? These and other questions will be addressed in the following chapters.

2

BACKGROUND

My older brother (by two years) and I saw the light of day at The Hague. At my birth in 1883 I received the name Margaretha. I was the only girl among three boys in the house of our grandparents, who had lovingly taken us in as motherless children. Two nephews, brothers, about our age, who had also lost their mother, were brought up together with us. Our fathers who worked elsewhere paid for our upkeep.[1]

This chapter describes the environment in which Moesje Alt, known at this time as Margot, grows up. First we will acquaint ourselves with the parents Jan Alt and Anna Wigleven and with the grandparents on both sides of the family, as well as with the aunts and nephews that played a role in Margot's life. This is followed by a sketch of The Hague around 1900.

Johannes David Alt (1853–1934)

Johannes David (called Jan), Margot's father, is born on 28 August 1853, in Leiden and is the son of a carpenter.[2] He is the fifth generation of the Alt family in Leiden – the family having migrated from Germany in the eighteenth century. At the age of twelve he becomes fatherless. Jan is the only one of the six children in the family that survived childhood. A year and a half later his mother remarries and

---

[1] M.A. Alt, *Herinneringen uit mijn leven* (Velp: Pinksterzending, 1963), p. 8.
[2] Data about the family Alt found in the City Archives in Leiden, The Hague, Rotterdam, and Amsterdam.

becomes the wife of a widower, Anthonie Molenaar (1816–1900), who is a shoemaker at Leiden.[3] Jan now acquires a younger step-brother and two younger step-sisters.[4] He becomes a cabinet-maker. At age twenty-seven he moves to The Hague where he marries Anna Wigleven who is five years younger than himself.

Jan finds work as a postman in The Hague. Two children are born. Abraham (nicknamed Bram), born 24 March 1881,who is named after his grandfather on his father's side and Margaretha Adriana (nicknamed Margot), born 22 August 1883, who is named after her grandmother on her mother's side. Because of Jan Alt's adultery the marriage ends after six years. Jan leaves the house and temporarily lives in Amsterdam. At the request of Anna the marriage is officially dissolved by the court on 17 January 1887.[5] Jan moves to Laecken, near Brussels, in March 1887, where he marries Carolina Lange in October of the same year.[6] Anna dies on 2 August 1887, and the two children go to live with their grandparents. Jan's second marriage breaks up in January 1895.[7] One year later he marries Johanna de Jong and moves to Amsterdam.[8] On 7 February 1934, at the age of 80, he dies of a cerebral haemorrhage. His second and third marriages are childless.

Margot's diary reveals the effort she made to get in contact with her father. In late 1913 she finally obtains his address. She gets an answer to her letter and longs to get a photograph of him. One year later we read of a 'dear letter' from her father who has found work at the same factory. Unfortunately no further data or a photo of Jan

---

[3] Anthonie Molenaar was twice a widower. He was born in Hoogland and died 14 October 1900 in Leiden.

[4] Gerrit (1854), Jacoba (1857) and Celia Johanna (1863). Population Register 1860–1870 buurt 23 folio 70. City Archive Leiden.

[5] Divorce certificate No. 117 in BS DH 1883–1892. City Archive The Hague. The Population Register records the departure of Jan Alt to Brussels on 5 March 1887.

[6] Carolina Philippina Lange (born 6 November 1863 in The Hague) had been married before to Johannes Alexander Kroesen (1857–1936) born in Semarang. Their marriage was dissolved on 22 November 1886. The Kroesens had lived for several years in the Dutch Indies. Their son Tiemen C.J. Kroesen (born 1 November 1881 in Batavia) is a surgeon in Semarang in 1927. Tiemen and Margot may have met each other there.

[7] Divorce certificate No. 4, 23 January 1895 s1003v. City Archive Rotterdam. The verdict of the court dated 12 December 1894, is based on adultery committed by Jan Alt.

[8] Marriage on 23 March 1896 in Rotterdam to Johanna Wilhelmina de Jong, born 22 August 1864 at Ellemeet, sewing-woman in Rotterdam. Marriage Cerficate No. 396, 1896 d008. City Archive Rotterdam.

has been found. Thanks to his military conscription at age twenty, we know he had blond hair, blue eyes, and was 1,63 meters tall.[9] It is apparent that Margot inherited her dark brown eyes and dark hair from her mother. In her many publications Margot often refers to people who have been influential in her life, but never mentions her father. Clearly his role in her life has been marginal. It seems that after she turns three he is basically absent, which makes her feel she is an orphan. When Margot in 1910 looks back after the death of her mother, she refers to herself and her brother as 'orphans'.[10] Perhaps we find here a reason why as an adult she shows so much compassion for orphans.

Johanna Margaretha Wigleven (1858–1887)

My mother was a godly woman and of handsome appearance. She loved her children dearly.[11]

In spite of a short life, her mother Anna Wigleven made a lasting impression on Margot: 'The memory of my dear mother with her profound belief in God has not left me all my life. She possessed a solid faith, by which she maintained a serene rest under much suffering in soul and body.'[12] In her times of personal struggle and pain Margot often has the image of her mother in her mind and prays: 'Lord give me her courage and perseverance'.[13] Every time the strong faith and pure walk of her mother is brought to mind: 'She had a lovely appearance and walked with God. Her pure and unselfish life, as described to us by others, was an example to her children.'[14] The Bible which Margot inherits from her mother is worn out by its heavy use and has underlining on nearly every page.[15] Later, Margot would name her first foster child after her mother.

---

[9] Militie register. Vol: 0516, Period: 1874, Leiden, inventory no. 0516, 1873, 1816–1929, deed no. 321. City Archive Leiden.

[10] M.A. Alt, 'Mijn vrede geef Ik u', *De Boodschapper* (October 1910), pp. 182-87 (182).

[11] M.A. Alt, 'Autobiografie 1943', p. 1.

[12] Alt, *Herinneringen*, p. 7.

[13] Alt, *Herinneringen*, p. 7

[14] Alt, *Herinneringen*, p. 7

[15] M.A. Alt, 'Allerlei uit Israël: De Bijbel als aanklager', *GS* 21.8 (August) 1952), p. 10.

The parents of Anna are Gerardus Willem Wigleven (1832–1906) and Margaretha Adriana Homberg (1837–1905).[16] They have six daughters: Anna (1858–1887), Marie (1860–1934), Margot (1861–1885), Sophie (1863–1913), Tine (1865–1913), and Paulowna (1867–1878). Marie becomes a teacher and remains unmarried. Margot marries a teacher Gerrit de Haas (1855–1929) in 1882. On Margot Alt's second birthday (22 August 1885), her aunt Margot dies. The two children from this marriage, Gerard and Fer, will later be brought up by the grandparents for an extended period, together with Bram and Margot.[17] In April 1887 the widower Gerrit de Haas marries Sophie Wigleven, the sister of his first wife.[18] Tine marries the bookkeeper, Willem Kok in 1896.[19] Paulowna, the youngest, dies aged eleven of tuberculosis. So, as she grows up Margot has three aunts: Marie, Sophie, and Tine. Because of the weak health (kidney disease) of Margot's grandmother, it is Aunt Tine, 'a strong nice looking young woman', who takes care of the housekeeping.[20]

We lack details of the youth of Margot's mother Anna. At the age of twenty she moved to Leiden.[21] It is likely she met Jan Alt during this period, perhaps in church. The church records in Leiden reveal that both transferred their membership to the Reformed Church in The Hague on the same day in May 1880.[22] Six weeks later they marry on 16 June 1880 in The Hague. Both children, Bram and Margot, are baptized in the Reformed Church.[23] Anna shares the same strong

---

[16] R.E.O. Ekkart, 'Het Geslacht Wigleven in Nederland', *Gens Nostra* 20 (1965), pp. 353–66.

[17] The Population Register records on the address of the grandparents the names of Bram and Margot, but not those of the nephews Gerrit Willem (born 1883) and Paul Ferdinand de Haas (born 1885). On 1 April 1887, G.W.C. de Haas remarries Sophie Wigleven. At the end of December Sophie gives birth to a twin. To relieve Sophie the two oldest children move to the grandparents for a prolonged period.

[18] A poetry album that G.W.C. de Haas gave to Sophie Wigleven is preserved and referred to in K. Thomassen (ed.), *Alba Amicorum: Vijf eeuwen vriendschap op papier gezet* (The Hague: 1990), pp. 107–108. On 19 June 1886, her sister Anna wrote a page in this album. Later Sophie sends this page to Margot, who keeps the handwriting of her mother as a treasure in her Bible.

[19] Ekkart, 'Geslacht Wigleven'.

[20] Alt, 'Autobiografie 1943', p. 4.

[21] Her stay in Leiden: 16 April 1878 until 4 December 1879. Population Registers Leiden and The Hague.

[22] Index 'Attestaties NH 1620–1889', dated 2 May 1880. City Archive Leiden.

[23] Alt, *Herinneringen*, p. 19. Margot's confirmation is in 'the church where I was baptized as a baby'.

faith as her mother and appears to have prophetic gifts. At night while sick in bed, Anna sees in a vision that God cuts the life thread of her sister Margot with a pair of scissors. The next morning her mother informs her that Margot has died unexpectedly in childbirth.[24] In the last years of her life, Anna, the only one in her family to do so, joins the so-called 'small church', a designation for a secession from the Reformed Church by believers unsatisfied with the liberalism in the church.[25] By then Anna possibly is already suffering from tuberculosis, the illness from which she would die after a long struggle. On the night of 2 August 1887, the night that Anna dies, grandmother Wigleven feels a hand on each of her shoulders. It is as if God speaks to her to take both children into her home. Up to that point the family had been planning to place the children in an orphanage.[26]

The decision of the grandparents to take custody of the two children is decisive for their further development. The grandparents live in the centre of The Hague, right across from the monumental tower of Saint Jacob's Church, the city's main church. The grandfather is caretaker and later director of the city's washing and bathing house. The family lives on the second floor of the building. Margot speaks with affection of the time with her grandparents. The two nephews, Gerard and Fer, will have stayed a considerable time together with Bram and Margot, as Margot writes that they were all raised together. When in 1903 Margot leaves for the Dutch Indies by boat, both her nephews are there to say goodbye.

The Hague around 1900

In my youth the social-democrats began to gain more and more ground, especially among the labour class, but the middle class kept aloof. 'The reds' were fiercely combatted. They were called

---

[24] Alt, 'Autobiografie 1943', p. 3.

[25] Early 1887 a part of the Reformed Church in The Hague joined the secession called 'Doleantie' led by Abraham Kuyper and established the Gereformeerde Kerk. Probably Anna joined this group. Three other options in the period 1880–1887 are continuations of an earlier secession of the Reformed Church called 'Afscheiding', they too used the designation Gereformeerde Kerk. Cf. Ch. Dumas, *Waar Hagenaars kerkten: Geschiedenis van de Haagse kerken gebouwd voor 1900* (The Hague: Boekencentrum, 1983). Research in the fragmentary church archives did not produce results as to the membership of Anna Wigleven.

[26] Alt, 'Autobiografie 1943', pp. 1–2.

demanding, unsatisfied and ungrateful and in the churches they were admonished to act with meekness and submission. In my childhood years there was an enormous gap between poor and rich; there was great poverty in the back-streets. By the grace of God this is all turned to the good. The societal circumstances have improved greatly.[27]

The Hague, known as the location of the residence of the royal family and of the seat of the national government, experiences a rapid growth in the second half of the nineteenth century. The population increases from 70,000 in 1850 to 206,000 in 1900.[28] The mortality rate drops as living conditions improve, due to healthier nutrition, the construction of a sewerage system, a water system, and better medical care. An agricultural crisis drives many from the rural areas to the cities. A large number of repatriates from the Dutch East Indies settle in The Hague, giving the society an East Indian flavor.[29] As the residence of the government, it is an attractive location for banks and insurance companies. Around 1900 The Hague together with Amsterdam constitutes the financial-economical centre of the country. A large number of companies have connections with the Dutch Indies. Writers and artists settle in the city. New suburbs are built, and the life of the city modernizes at a fast rate. In 1899 the first Peace Conference convenes. It is the beginning of The Hague as an international capital for Peace and Justice. Many rich people choose to live in The Hague. The upper class areas have a lot of green space, along with an intensive cultural life, including a play-house, theatre, concert hall, societies, and a zoo. The welfare system develops too, but not everyone profits.

Typically for this period, there is sharp contrast between poor and rich. Around 1850 three classes can be distinguished: nobility, middle class, and labourers. There are separate schools for the poor and for the more wealthy. Children of the elite receive tutelage at home or at boarding schools. Children of the middle class go to the civil schools, as Margot did. The children of the labourers go to the schools for the poor that are free or to the school for 'those of less fortune'

---

[27] Alt, *Herinneringen*, p. 42.

[28] The data of this section are mainly taken from: T. de Nijs and J. Sillevis (eds.), *Den Haag Geschiedenis van de stad 3* (Zwolle: Waanders, 2005).

[29] H.E. van Gelder, *'s-Gravenhage in zeven eeuwen* (Amsterdam: Meulenhof, 1937), pp. 282, 324.

where there are modest tuition fees. The city authorities are responsible for providing elementary school as well a basic secondary school. Usually a few years of extended schooling is added to the elementary school. In 1865 a high school for boys is started and from 1879 also for girls.

Gradually the rigid class orientation that so strongly characterized society loses its hold. The labour movement holds demonstrations in favour of general voting rights and better social conditions. It emphazises the needs of the labourers, expressed in labour unions, educational provision, and social legislation. Ferdinand Domela Nieuwenhuis, Lutheran pastor in The Hague, leaves the church to become leader of the socialist movement. On the annual Prince's Day, the third Tuesday in September, he organizes Red Tuesday.

The Netherlands Reformed Church is a prominent presence in the city. In comparison with the rest of the country, it loses fewer members to the several secessionary movements that took place in the nineteenth century.[30] Right opposite the large tower of the Saint Jacob's Church in the centre of The Hague is the home of the Wigleven grandparents where our main character is raised.

Bram and Margot Alt

---

[30] The census in 1899 showed 61% Protestant, 31% Roman-Catholic 3.2% Jewish and 2.7% Unchurched.

3

YOUTH IN THE HAGUE 1883–1903

My very first memories from my childhood are closely connected with the sick-bed of my mother. In the dim glow of a distant memory – I was not even four years old when God took her to Himself after a long illness – I see a young woman with beautiful dark hair lying on a bed and I hear a friendly, soft voice speaking to my older brother and me. In my later years I was told that in the last hours before her departure, my dying mother laid hands upon us blessed us and with her weak voice dedicated us to the Lord.[1]

The dramatic events that take place in her third year engrave them-selves in Margot's memory. In that year (1887) the marriage of her parents is dissolved due to her father's adultery. Then come the sick-ness and tragic death of her mother, resulting in her moving with her brother Bram to her grandparents' house. Shortly after her fourth birthday her father remarries in Belgium.

In her writings, Margot does not mention her parents' divorce and the remarriage of her father. It is most likely this was kept from her at the time. The only information we read about her father is that he works elsewhere and pays for her upbringing with her grandparents. Of the two nephews who grow up with her, she finds Gerard to be dull, so Margot plays more with Fer, who is two years younger. She does not get along very well with her brother Bram, who she finds bossy and combative.[2] We can follow the developments of her youth

---

[1] M.A. Alt, *Herinneringen uit mijn leven* (Velp: Pinksterzending, 1963), p. 7.
[2] Alt, 'Autobiografie 1943', p. 3.

in terms of her school years, her first job as a nanny, her spiritual development, and her departure for the Dutch Indies.

Elementary School

Shortly after the death of her mother, Margot goes to the neighbouring Christian nursery school, 'Light, Love and Life'. Of this Margot writes: 'The ladies were sweet to us little ones, but the only thing I remember well is that the girls from the backstreets who acted as helpers, drank our milk and ate the filling from our sandwiches, which had so lovingly been given me from home'.[3]

Elementary School in 1892
Margot sitting in the middle row in black dress, age 9

For her elementary education she goes to the Public Civil School for boys and girls in the Korte Lombardstraat. Accompanied by a slightly older girl from next door, Margot walks to school every morning and afternoon. Susanna Reijs, three years older than Margot, is in the same school. She characterizes the school as cozy and attributes much praise to the head master Hofman, who is like a father to everyone. For the little ones, no day is complete unless they have not

---

[3] Alt, *Herinneringen*, p. 10.

seen him.[4] Susanna's claim, 'No one ever forgot him, not even when they had grown up', is confirmed when Margot seventy years later connects Hofman's name with the school. Susanna's father is a gymnastic instructor at this school and her younger brother Herman is in the same class as Margot. Thanks to him a beautiful class photo taken in 1892 has been kept. On the left we see Charles Hofman seated; in the middle, nine-year-old Margot looks at us in an enigmatic way. The Public Civil School offers six years of regular elementary education and three years of basic secondary education. From 1894, after six years of elementary education, Margot takes choir lessons at the Music School. It is not clear whether she combines the choir classes with the basic secondary education at the Civil School.

Music School

As both Bram and Margot love music, they go to the Royal Music and Singing School in the Korte Beestenmarkt. The school, founded in 1826, has a Music department to train professional musicians, but also a Singing department for choir members and soloists.[5] (The Singing department being a stepping stone to the Music department). Along with music and singing, there are classes in Dutch, French, Italian and recitation.

Bram is a great talent. He plays violin, piano, and organ. Already during his years at the Music School he receives all kinds of invitations to play in small gatherings and churches. Margot has a good voice and plays a small violin. Together with Bram she plays and sings at parties and for relatives. She writes: 'I started to become proud, because the adults flattered me. How careless to uplift a child of that age in such a way.'[6]

From 1894 to 1897 Margot attends the choir classes. In these years the number of students is always above 300, with more girls than boys and the majority in the Singing department. The first two annual student reports classify Margot as a diligent student, but in the third

---

[4] Nannie van Wehl [pseudonym for Susanna Reijs], *Verhalen van mijn jongen* (Arnhem: H. ten Brink, 1922), pp. 102–24.

[5] [G.A. Haeften (ed.)], *Koninklijk Conservatorium voor Muziek te 's-Gravenhage 1828-1926* (The Hague: Mouton, 1926), p. 29. Cf. Annual Reports in National Archive The Hague, inventaris No. 49.

[6] Alt, *Herinneringen*, p. 17.

year her diligence wanes and her progress is modest.[7] Margot wants to become a famous singer, but by the time she has to be assessed to see whether she meets the entry requirements for the solfeggio class (specialization for solo singers), her voice has declined in quality and she fails the audition. According to *Herinneringen* she is sixteen when she leaves the Music School, but in the lists of pupils her name does not appear after 1897 when she was fourteen.

Margot Alt at Age 18 (1901)

Bram graduates in 1901. He gives music lessons in The Hague, becomes church organist at Voorburg, then Heusden, and from 1910 in the Martine Church at Bolsward. In 1915 he marries Trijntje (Tine) Wesseling (1897–1964) at Harlingen, but they have no children. He becomes known for his organ concerts and also as a choir director. He travels extensively giving lectures about opera, using gramophone records and slides. 'Colourful as a musician and as a man, Abraham

---

[7] Annual reports present in the National Archive in The Hague.

Alt was someone with a joyful demeanour. His artistic qualifications varying from *organist of great renown* to *magician*'.[8] Like his father he dies of a cerebral haemorrhage, at Bolsward on 16 December 1941, when he was sixty years old.

Domestic Science School

The rejection for the solfeggio is a big disappointment for Margot. As teachers are often praising her poems and stories and allowing her to recite them before class, she decides she now wants to study to become a writer. But her education takes a different direction.

> My wise 'old fashioned' grandmother however, was of the opinion, that a girl of my age had to diligently learn how to do housekeeping and learn to sew, so that I would later become a good 'helper for my husband,' because who knows?[9]

Against her will Margot is sent to the Domestic Science School for girls. A two year training course in housecraft forms the basis of a program to become a cookery school teacher, but there are also courses in handicraft. In 1896 the school moves to a new building in the Eerste van den Boschstraat. Margot will have studied here in the period 1898–1900.[10] In these years she is deeply in love with Dirk de Visser Smits (1881–1974). The book of poems she starts in this time reveals she cannot get him out of her mind. When in 1915 she turns over the pages of an 'old dairy' (this book of poems?) she sighs: 'Oh, how I was an overexcited child in love – but my love was clean and pure'.[11] Dirk is to figure significantly in a later chapter.

At the age of seventeen Margot obtains the certificate to teach handicraft. It is not known whether she ever stood before a class, but it clear that she is not interested in the position: 'Becoming a handicraft teacher horrified me. The salary was so minimal that I was not even able to buy my clothing and I liked to go out well dressed with

---

[8] http://www.martinikerkbolsward.nl/joomla/index.php?option=com_conte nt &task=view&id=121&Itemid=196.

[9] Alt, *Herinneringen*, p. 17.

[10] For the history of the school see Rosa Bilkes, *De Spinazie-academie: 125 jaar Haags huishoudonderwijs* (The Hague: Haags Historisch Museum, 2012). The very fragmentary school archive present in the National Archive contains no data of Alt as a student.

[11] M.A. Alt, 'Dagboek 1910–1919', 1 May 1915 [p. 141].

my friends.'[12] Now and then she joins her brother at the opera or at a concert.

Growing up in The Hague almost naturally gives Margot a love for the royal family. In Saint Jacob's Church she regularly sees Queen Emma together with Princess Wilhelmina, three years older than Margot. At the age of seven, standing beside her grandfather, she watches the funeral procession of King Willem III passing by. The crowning of Wilhelmina as Queen in 1898 is a feast: 'The beautiful clothing of the Indian royals riding through The Hague in chariots and the stories that circulated about the wealth and beauty of Dutch Indies, were perhaps in part the reason , that I started to long to see that promised land of milk and honey once for myself'.[13] The marriage of Wilhelmina to Prince Hendrik on 7 February 1901, 'was the most wonderful national fetival that I ever witnessed in my homeland'.[14] The seventeen-year-old Margot enjoys it to the full.

In those days, as she writes in *Herinneringen*, she lives far away from God, although she is not indifferent to the faith. She is young, energetic, and healthy, and she wants to make something of her life. Life in the home of her grandparents is too monotonous and no longer appeals to her. The Dutch Indies attract her: 'In my eyes it was a land of magic, full of mysteries as in the fairy tales of A Thousand and One Nights'.[15]

Nursery Governess

Margot keeps at a distance from her grandparents: 'When I was eighteen, I went into the world to make my own living. Soon I got a position as nursery governess to a Dutch Indies family with four children'.[16] In May 1903 she will accompany this family to the Dutch Indies, the land of her dreams. In *Herinneringen* she explains that the journey was the reason for her to take the job: 'A head engineer family from Banka, on furlough in Holland, offered to pay for the trip if I would take care of the children in conjunction with the lady of the

---

[12] Alt, *Herinneringen*, p. 17.

[13] Alt, *Herinneringen*, p. 18.

[14] Alt, *Herinneringen*, p. 18.

[15] Alt, *Herinneringen*, p. 18.

[16] M.A. Alt, 'Mijn vrede geef Ik u', *De Boodschapper* (October 1910), pp. 182-87 (183).

house. As I was fond of children, I accepted it with both hands.'[17] The family is that of Jan de Koning Knijff (1867–1924) and Jenny Jacobson (1874–1916).[18] De Koning Knijff has been in the Netherlands on sick leave since September 1900. In 1903 he is fit enough to return to Java, where he will become Chief Mining Engineer stationed in Batavia. (In 1915 he will become professor of mining at the Technical University at Delft.)[19]

For four and a half years Margot works in this family.[20] As her period ends halfway through 1906, she must have started in the end of 1901 or at the beginning of 1902, which is about one year and a half before the actual departure. In mid 1902 the four children, Marie, Eduarda, Aart and Jenny are aged about nine, five, three and two years.[21] The poems in her book show that Margot travels to several places in this period: Valkenberg (August 1902), Nauheim near Frankfurt (October 1902), and then Nijmegen (November 1902 until April 1903). Valkenberg and Nauheim perhaps refer to a day out, but Nijmegen is a longer stay. In a poem from August 1902 Margot in a witty fashion tells that her life as governess is not really pleasant: 'small salary, hard words' and 'kissing the hand that beats you'.[22]

Spiritual Development

> In my grandmother – God bless her memory – we found a second mother, who gave us a Christian upbringing ... At an early age we were sent to Sunday School and Children's Church, in the parish hall of the old Rev. Knottnerus, close to our neighbourhood. Together with my grandmother I later faithfully visited the great St.-Jacobs Church, one of The Hague's most impressive buildings ... Leaving the service accompanied by the mighty waves of sound

---

[17] Alt, *Herinneringen*, p. 20.

[18] The passengers list of the s.v. Sindoro groups Margot together with the family J. de Koning Knijff. *Bataviaasch Nieuwsblad* 29 June 1903, No. 175, appendix.

[19] A.H. van Lessen, 'Ter herdenking: Prof.ir. J. de Koning Knijff', *De Ingenieur* 40 (1925), pp. 363–64.

[20] Alt, 'Mijn vrede geef Ik u', p. 183.

[21] Marie (1893–1988), Eduarda Elisabeth (1897–?), Aart Willem (1899–1944) and Jenny (1900–1924). Names and dates of birth come from the Population Register in The Hague where the family registered in August 1915.

[22] Alt, 'Kinderjuffrouw (In Holland)', 'Gedichtenbundel 1899–1906', Valkenberg, August 1902, [pp. 12–13].

from the great church organ, I felt uplifted to a higher sphere and it took a moment for me to realize I was still upon the earth.[23]

Margot wrote that both her mother and grandmother possessed prophetic gifts. At the age of forty, her grandmother had experienced a conversion. Of the children, Anna and Marie followed her in that experience. Grandfather only goes to church once a year, on New Year's Eve, which always elicits grandmother's remark: 'Grandpa is paying his account for a year'.[24]

Grandmother teaches the children to pray, before and after the meal; in the morning and in the evening, but for the children it is nothing more than a routine. Every week Margot visits Sunday School, where she always has to repeat the phrase: 'The Lord Jesus died on the cross for our sins'. She puzzles over these words, but does not understand them: 'I had a rather introverted character and for my age I reflected very deeply about things'.[25] Too shy to talk about it with her grandmother, there is a struggle inside:

> In fear of death because of my naughtiness I began to place myself under the Law around my sixth or seventh year and to live more or less like a saint ... Already in my childhood years my repeated spiritual failings were a cause of fear and remorse. Only much later I understood that the Lord from early on had worked in my heart. I had a tender conscience and could not bear untruth in myself.[26]

The high demands that Margot lays upon herself, resulting in an unrelenting cycle of failure, will trouble her all her life. Margot characterizes the pastors in St. Jacob's Church as 'distinguished, stiff, untouchable persons'.[27] An exception is Rev. F. van Gheel Gildemeester, who is jovial and gets along with the youngsters. Grandmother often takes Margot to a small hall where evangelist Daniël Wilkens (1834–1931) preaches every week about the future of the Jewish people.[28] Wilkens is also a family friend and 'in many ways my grandmother's

---

[23] Alt, *Herinneringen*, p. 8.
[24] M.A. Alt, 'Autobiografie 1943', p. 2.
[25] Alt, *Herinneringen*, p. 13.
[26] Alt, *Herinneringen*, p. 14.
[27] Alt, *Herinneringen*, p. 12.
[28] M.A. Alt, 'Een evangelist bij de gratie Gods: Br. Daniel Wilkens', *GS* 7.8 (April 1931), pp. 9–11.

spiritual mentor'.[29] Frequently she watches Wilkens standing on a bench, dressed in black, evangelizing in the great market. When Margot is about nine-years-old, she is sick in bed with typhus, Wilkens comes to visit her. He takes her hand saying: 'Child, if you were to die this night, would you be prepared to go to Jesus?'[30] Margot does not answer, for she is not at all prepared, but it leaves a great impression on her. Around this age she attends a meeting of the Salvation Army. Their female preachers were a virtually unheard of phenomenon in those days. Margot admires their courage because they have to wear 'these horrible hats and are mocked by everyone'.[31]

When Margot is eleven or twelve a missionary speaks in the Children's Church. As she enters the hall, the choir is already in action. The song is about 'heathens' who lift up their bound hands to heaven for help. Margot stands at the threshold, rooted to the spot.

> And while I stood there listening, suddenly a wonderful, happy feeling set tremors though me – (did I receive my calling to be an evangelist at that moment?) – and in my own mind I made a decision: 'When I grow up I will go to the Indies and preach the Gospel.[32]

It is a firm decision, but other matters are given priority in Margot's life and the calling fades into the background. Looking back, when she is older she understands that in that moment God had called her for her life's mission.[33] But the initial outcome is that as she grows older, her faith becomes weaker, partly under the influence of her friends, 'who mocked everything that was holy, so that in the end I was ashamed of the childish faith held by my grandmother and it annoyed me when she admonished us'.[34] At the age of eighteen, Margot is confirmed as a member of the Reformed Church by Rev.

---

[29] Alt, 'Evangelist bij de gratie Gods', p. 9.

[30] Alt, 'Evangelist bij de gratie Gods', p. 10.

[31] Alt, *Herinneringen*, p. 13.

[32] M.A. Alt, 'Van Sabbat tot Pinksteren 1', *GS* 17.2 (February 1948), pp. 6-7. In *Herinneringen* (p. 16) the designation 'Indies' is omitted in the description of this moment.

[33] Alt, *Herinneringen*, p. 16.

[34] Alt, 'Mijn vrede geef Ik u', pp. 182–83.

Karres. It is more to please her grandmother and to ease her conscience: 'my faith was highly superficial'.[35]

Her brother Bram investigates all kinds of religious and spiritual
movements: 'Theosophy, Spiritism, Mormonism, and Rosicrucian,
etc. Like so many he was looking for truth, but God's Word remained
a closed book for him'.[36] He speaks a lot with Margot about a 'so
called Christian occultism'.[37] It influences Margot to read 'foolish and
damaging' literature. On 23 March 1903, she once more visits the
grave of her mother, where she used to pray to God for protection:

> *I thought, on my way there, how long it has been*
> *Since I last visited that place of death –*
> *Since I had last prayed on mother's grave stone*
> *That God might keep me in the struggle of life.*[38]

As the time of departure for the Indies approaches, Margot makes
the effort to say goodbye to her pastor. He wishes her a good journey,
but deep in her heart Margot has expected something else.[39] Margot
then goes to evangelist Wilkens and asks him to pray for her. Wilkens
is touched by this request. He kneels next to her and blesses her. In
fact, he is not only a spiritual mentor for Margot's grandmother.
When in 1908 Margot experiences a conversion, she immediately
shares her joy with Wilkens. They will keep in contact until his death.

On 28 May 1903, Margot departs from Rotterdam on the steam
vessel Sindoro, waving goodbye to family members. Parting from her
grandparents is hard. They do not understand what drives her to go
to such a distant land. Was it not good being with them? 'They did
not yet understand that the hand of God was leading me to go, because He had prepared a task for me over there.'[40] She promises to
return soon, in accordance with her plans, but it will turn out differently.[41] She will never see her father, grandparents and brother again.

---

[35] Alt, 'Van Sabbat tot Pinksteren 1', p. 6. In her article 'Waarom ik mij bij de
Pinkstergemeente heb aangesloten', *GS* 5.4 (April 1929), pp. 3-6, she is seventeen
years when she does confirmation.

[36] Alt, *Herinneringen*, p. 19.

[37] Alt, 'Mijn vrede geef Ik u', p. 183.

[38] M.A. Alt, 'De Wereld in', 'Gedichtenbundel 1899-1906', The Hague, 23
March 1903, [pp. 22–23].

[39] Alt, *Herinneringen*, p. 20.

[40] Alt, *Herinneringen*, p. 20.

[41] Alt, 'Van Sabbat tot Pinksteren 1', p. 6.

At the farewell she writes a poem:

Farewell my dear fatherland
Farewell my sea and white dunes
I will no longer play at your beach
Or frolic at your tops
I will go to the land that God is showing me;
Over there, where the sun rises! [42]

---

[42] M.A. Alt, 'Vaarwel!', 'Gedichtenbundel 1899-1906', Rotterdam, 28 May 1903 [pp. 30–31].

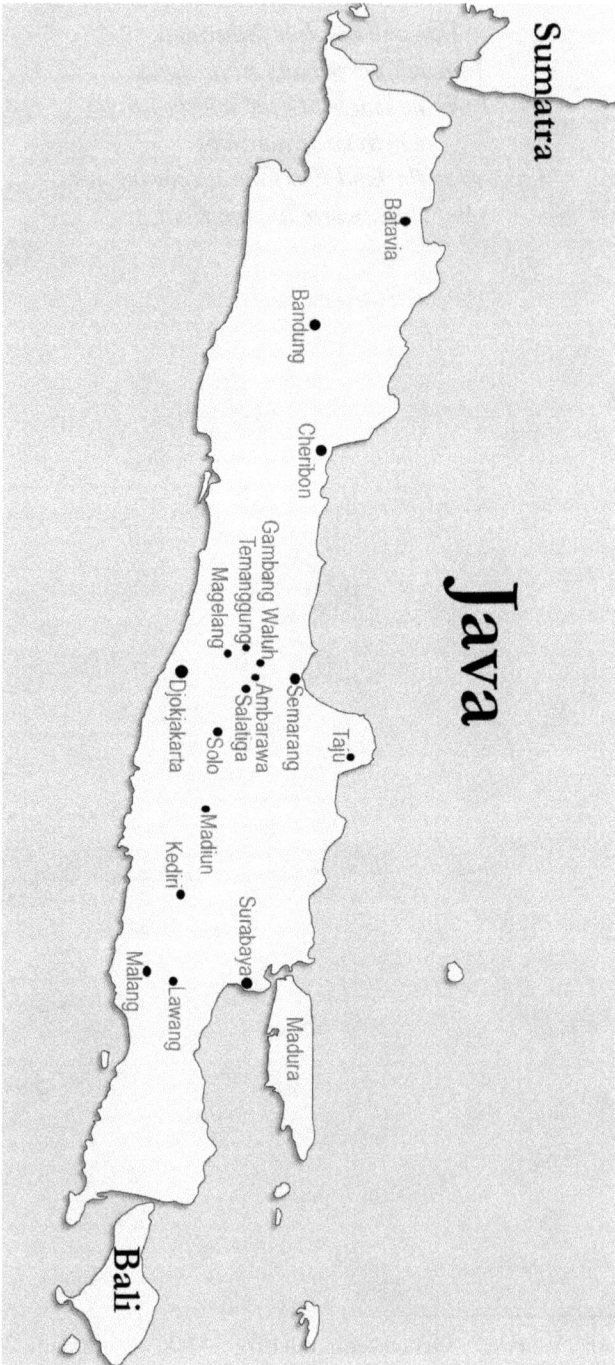

Sumatra

Batavia

Bandung

Cheribon

Gambang Waluh
Temanggung
Magelang
Ambarawa
Salatiga
Semarang

Djokjakarta

Solo

Taju

Madiun

Kediri

Surabaya

Malang
Lawang

Java

Madura

Bali

4

JAVA 1903–1910

And still my eyes peer towards the fatherland
Where I once saw all my love glimmering
Until with the coast that forever disappears
Also the light of my soul is getting lost.
Still the stars are shining and the sun is beaming,
The day has gone and come
And as I turn, then I stand alone
Alone! with my grief and my dreams.[1]

Nursery governess at Weltevreden

On 3 July 1903, the Sindoro arrives in the harbor of Tandjong Priok
at Batavia. During the following three years, Margot will stay with the
engineer's family in the Willemslaan, near the station in Weltevreden,
the European suburb of Batavia. These are difficult years for Margot.
The poem 'Kinderjuffrouw' ('Governess') indicates that the work oppresses her and she feels imprisoned. Many poems reveal a gloomy
mood. She is homesick and mourns her separation from her loved
ones far away. From the day of her arrival, she also has to fight against
malaria: 'But I forced my way through it and did not want to surrender, nor to the strong feeling of homesickness that so plagued me
the first years'.[2] Tormented by malaria in August 1903, she is so

---

[1] M.A. Alt, 'Afscheid', 'Gedichtenbundel 1899-1906', on board Sindoro, 30 May
1902 [pp. 32–33].
[2] M.A. Alt, *Herinneringen uit mijn leven* (Velp: Pinksterzending, 1963), p. 20.

desperate that she asks God to take her life, at the same time the
fatherland pulls:

> *I feel the fever glow in my veins*
> *A burning red covers my cheek*
> *I am sick and feeling so scared*
> *I hear the green palms rustle*
> *And I feel the burning hot wind*
> *My heart is pulled to the cool North*
> *Because I am a child of Holland*[3]

On 22 August 1903, nearly recovered, she celebrates her first birthday
on Java. Her thoughts are drawn home, to the living room of her
grandparents; because God has answered her grandmother's prayer:

> *The tower clock rings with the sound of its full voice:*
> *It's time for church – It's time for church – draw near to Him!*
> *The hour has come for confession and prayer –*
> *Release now your hearts from sin and stain.*
> *And grandmother sends her prayer up,*
> *With lips trembling, a tear in her eye*
> The bell-ringing is silenced and sweet granny keeps knitting –
> But God has answered her supplication for her grandchild.[4]

In November 1904, Margot is at the point of dying in the Tjikini
hospital (Batavia), but again she recovers:

> *And softly he came slipping my way*
> *The Bleak Death;*
> *A grinning smile answers my supplications*
> *And dying distress.*
>
> ...
>
> *Quickly his hand, cool, cold and icy*
> *Touches my forehead*
> *And from the doctors lips it rustles:*
> *'It will be over soon'.*
>
> ...
>
> *And I lift up my hands to heaven,*

---

[3] M.A. Alt, 'Ziek', 'Gedichtenbundel 1899-1906', Weltevreden, 18 August 1903
[pp. 48–49].

[4] M.A. Alt, 'Hollandsch Binnenhuisje', 'Gedichtenbundel 1899-1906', Weltevreden, 22 August 1903 [pp. 50–51].

Yes — God is great —
And softly he slips away
The Bleak Death! [5]

On 30 October 1905, grandmother dies. The message of her death strikes Margot a painful blow, but her life as governess allows her little time for mourning. Above her poem she writes a phrase from Victor Hugo: 'C'est l'âge sans pitié' ('It is the time without compassion'):

Then they brought me a note
I read it hastily — at once
It contained sad news
The paper fell to the ground.
The little ones stopped playing
Amazed at my grief
I quickly escaped their touching
Too painful for my heart.
Yet in the quiet of my room
The slumbering sorrow awakened
No tears offered me relief —
The stroke hit me deep and cruel! [6]

The next day she writes:

There is a time for coming
There is a time for going —
God has taken much from me
Yet I have to go forward! [7]

In 1910 she thinks back to her grandmother: 'She has been a loyal Christian and had a long life of struggle and grief behind her. On the stone that covers her grave, the words that led to her conversion were engraved, namely Hebrews 9:27. "It is appointed unto men once to die, but after this the judgement"!' [8] Margot's spiritual life is going

---

[5] M.A. Alt, 'De Dood', 'Gedichtenbundel 1899-1906', Tjikini, 30 November 1904 [pp. 79–81].

[6] M.A. Alt, 'Het leven', 'Gedichtenbundel 1899-1906', 26 November 1905, Weltevreden [p. 99].

[7] M.A. Alt, [no title], 'Gedichtenbundel 1899-1906', 27 November 1905 [p. 100].

[8] M.A. Alt, 'Mijn vrede geef Ik u', *De Boodschapper* (October 1910), pp. 182-97 (183).

more and more downhill. Two weeks after the message of her grandmother's death, she writes a poem about losing her childhood here:

> *I searched for God – and I thought: I have found Him*
> *In struggle and believing, in love and delight*
> *Yet everything passes away, flowers and people alike –*
> *Even the child's faith in the existence of a God!*[9]

Her contract as governess ends in early 1906. The doctors advise her
to return to the Netherlands or to move to a cooler climate. Margot
has started to love the Indies and opts for the latter.

Margot Alt at Age 21 in Batavia (1904)

Nurse at Lawang

Margot applies for a position as apprentice-nurse in the psychiatric
hospital known as Sumber Porong at Lawang, East-Java and is accepted: 'An unconscious longing to make myself useful drove me to
it – an inner pressure to do something that would add value to my
life'.[10] Lawang is South of Surabaya. Because of its altitude it has a

---

[9] M.A. Alt, 'God', 'Gedichtenbundel 1899-1906', 8 December 1905 [pp. 102–
103].
[10] Alt, *Herinneringen,* p. 21.

comfortable, cool climate. It is a modern hospital that practises re-straint-free care for psychiatric patients. Contrary to closed psychiatric institutions in cities, it combines a hospital with a farm colony. A relatively small central institution for the more disturbed patients is surrounded by simple lodgings for the quieter patients who find occupation in agricultural activities.[11]

On her way from Batavia to Lawang, Margot stops in Magelang where she visits the work of Van der Steur. In 1892 Johannes van der Steur (1865–1945) had been sent out as a missionary by the Seventh-Day Baptist (SDB) church at Haarlem.[12] He feels called to care for the abandoned children of mixed blood, who are usually the progeny of a Dutch soldier as father and a Javanese mother. He houses these children in Home Orange Nassau at Magelang, Middle-Java. He leaves the SDB early in 1896; later he will join the Dutch Indies Protestant Church. After some time Van der Steur manages to obtain financial support from the government. He becomes known as 'Pa van der Steur'. Over the years he cares for 7,000 children, who are called Steurtjes (little Steurs). Margot has great respect for Van der Steur, and their paths will cross again later.[13]

In early 1906, she is warmly welcomed into the hospital. She undergoes the training with pleasure. During the four and a half years she works there, she obtains two diplomas: general nurse and psychiatric nurse. Caring for the psychiatric patients fills her life. It is a relief compared with the period before: 'In this time I more or less awoke from the dormant, indifferent state I was in'.[14]

From her youth Margot has loved reading. Books by Elise van Calcar and Marie Corelli tickle her fancy but also make her uneasy. In these days she does not possess a Bible. As in the case of her brother previously, she shows interest in Spiritism and Theosophy. A fellow nurse holds spiritistic séances. Margot participates several times. Evening by evening they sit holding hands and waiting for the spirits.

---

[11] S. Lijkles, *Verslag omtrent het Gouvernements Krankzinnigengesticht Lawang (Residentie Pasoeroean) vanaf de opening op 23 June 1902 tot ultimo 1905* (Batavia: Landsdrukkerij, 1906).

[12] G. Velthuijsen Jr., 'De inzegening van Joh. van der Steur als zendeling onder de kolonialen in Indië', *De Boodschapper* (December 1892), pp. 189–92.

[13] M.A. Alt, 'Iets over Pa van der Steur', *GS* 9.5 (March 1936), p. 17. Alt dates her first visit around thirty years before, therefore I assume this was in 1906 on her way to Lawang.

[14] Alt, 'Mijn vrede geef Ik u', p. 183.

Margot even believes she has conversations with the spirits of her mother and grandmother.[15] Later she will describe these séances in detail in an article written as a warning for the periodical *De Boodschapper* (*The Messenger*).[16]

Margot Alt, Age 22
Shortly Before Departure to Lawang (February 1906)

The doctors warn the nurses about nervous overexertion. An older colleague suddenly becomes insane; screaming loudly, she is taken away. The incident has a deep impact on Margot, causing her nervous system to suffer. Fear of becoming insane haunts her day and night, making her incapable of eating or sleeping. The doctor gives her sick leave and prescribes means to build up her strength. She continues to lose weight and suffers from anemia and palpitations of the heart.[17] 'God entered into judgement with me. For hours I wandered around the mountains behind the institution where I worked. As in a film my sins and thousands of my shortcomings

---

[15] Alt, 'Mijn vrede geef Ik u', p. 183.
[16] M.A. Alt, 'Het Spiritisme', *De Boodschapper* (February 1910), pp. 25–27.
[17] Alt, 'Van Sabbat tot Pinksteren 1', *GS* 17.2 (February 1948), pp. 6–7 (6).

flashed through my mind.'[18] The idea of having to return to the Netherlands in a wretched condition brings her to her knees.

Conversion

I made, at that spot, in that holy hour,
With Jesus, my Saviour, an eternal covenant,
And I said: 'My all, my life, my time,
Be now forever dedicated to my King'.[19]

Margot is twenty-four years when she reaches this turning point: 'A serious illness that overcame me in the midst of a light-hearted worldly life, and took away all my energy and physical strength, made me return to the God of my childhood'.[20] One evening in July 1908 she kneels in her room, for the first time in years, and starts to pray:

> I begged the Lord to forgive my worldly attitude and all my other sins; I was in such a weak and emaciated condition that I wept and my whole body trembled. For a long time I was on my knees: 'Lord,' I spoke, 'let me not continue as a wretch. Raise me up and I promise you with all my heart: I will begin a new life and serve you from now on.'[21]

After a lengthy time of prayer, Margot goes to bed. For the first time in months, she sleeps soundly. On awakening, she feels completely well, and then it dawns on her: 'Jesus has forgiven my sins and I have become a child of God'. She starts to give thanks, and 'at the same moment the room was filled with a beam of light, and a sweet and lasting, peace descended as balm upon my miserable heart'.[22] At last she is in possession of the peace she had been searching for. It is as if she is now living in a different world! The same day she resumes her duties.

For seven days she lives on a cloud, but then the shining joy fades away. She cannot explain it. Did she grieve the Lord? She is condemned in her spirit because of her sins and defects of character, but, 'Then I glanced through the open window and looked to heaven

---

[18] Alt, 'Autobiografie 1943', p. 11.
[19] M.A. Alt, 'Wedergeboren', *GS* 17.2 (February 1948), p. 3.
[20] Alt, 'Van Sabbat tot Pinksteren 1', p. 6.
[21] Alt, *Herinneringen,* p. 23.
[22] Alt, *Herinneringen,* p. 23.

for help. The same moment my eyes discovered a dark cross, sharply standing out against the clear sky and a voice speaking to me: "My child, your sins are nailed to the cross".[23] She understands that her sins no longer burden her. She knows she is born again by the Holy Spirit. Evangelist Wilkens, whom she has written to for advice, explains 'that after the first abundant joy, the Holy Spirit will always show us, that "the just will live by faith" and not by feelings'.[24]

There is a clear effect on her work. She also breaks completely with Spiritism. Instead of the dance music she used to play at nights on the piano for her colleagues, she now only plays classical music and sings the spiritual songs of Ira D. Sankey. She burns the books that have alienated her from God: all kinds of novels, but also Willem Kloos, Frederik van Eeden, Multatuli and a whole series of Marie Corelli books. Naturally this provokes consternation among her colleagues. Her fellow-nurses call her a fanatic, but gradually some show sympathy. The Bible, given to her by a fellow nurse, always accompanies her to the ward and is kept open in the medicine cupboard for regular consultation. Margot now reads books by Charles Spurgeon and Andrew Murray. Next to the Bible, the *Imitation of Christ* by Thomas à Kempis is dearest to her. Her conversion, writes Margot, took place without the intervention of other believers. Yet, there is someone in her work community who has prayed for her conversion.

Seventh-Day Baptism

> One of the nurses I worked with, a Seventh-Day Baptist, spoke to me about keeping God's commandments. From God's Word she showed that the fourth command has not changed, in the same way that the eighth or ninth have not changed – that the law consisting of decrees has not been abolished by the coming of Jesus, but that the Ethical law, that is the Ten Commandments, according to the witness of Jesus will remain unchanged, until all will be fulfilled.[25]

---

[23] Alt, *Herinneringen*, p. 23.

[24] Alt, *Herinneringen*, p. 26.

[25] Alt, 'Mijn vrede geef Ik u', p. 186. I follow the story as Margot wrote it in 1910. Later versions (1948 and 1962) are written after Margot left the SDB and tell the story from that perspective.

Cornelia Slagter is Seventh-Day Baptist. Three years before, she was
sent to Java as missionary nurse by her home church in Haarlem. The
past year she and Margot have been colleagues. The two do not get
along together very well. Among the nurses, Slagter is the only one
who testifies of her faith. Once she tries to convert Margot, but the
latter decidedly turns her down. Slagter distributes a brochure from
Pieter Jansz warning against Spiritism, after which the spiritistic séances stop. On 10 November 1908, she writes in a letter to home
about Margot: 'One who for a long time was a *free thinker*, sought her
satisfaction in Spiritism, is now by the Spirit of God born again. She
is a very educated girl … participated in everything that the world
considers worthwhile, is highly appreciated in her environment'.[26]

Slagter informs Margot that worshipping on Sunday instead of
the Sabbath, just like infant baptism, is instituted by men and therefore sinful in the eyes of God.[27] More conversations follow with
some Bible study. Margot brings the matter of the Sabbath to God
in prayer. In a dream she receives the text 'For whosoever will keep
the whole law and yet offend in one point, he is guilty of all' (Jas
2.10): 'Of course I considered this dream as an answer to my prayer
and did not hesitate any longer, but immediately became a Sabba-
tarian'.[28]

On 19 December 1908, Margot celebrates her first Sabbath together with Slagter.[29] On 30 December, Margot writes her first letter
to the pastor of the SDB church at Haarlem. Keeping the Sabbath is
not easy, as Saturday is the busiest day of the week in the hospital.
Margot is in a constant state of self-accusation, because she must
often break the Sabbath. Usually the two can withdraw on Sabbath
evening (Friday). On Sunday evening they go together with three
other colleagues to a Bible reading in Lawang.[30] In this period Margot
becomes a total abstainer from alcohol, as is common in the SDB
church. She also passes her hospital exams.

---

[26] C. Slagter, "Van Zr. Slagter te Lawang," *De Boodschapper* (January 1909), p. 10.

[27] Alt, 'Mijn vrede geef Ik u', p. 186.

[28] Alt, 'Mijn vrede geef ik u', p. 186. The dream, also mentioned in her letter
of 30 December 1909, is left out in later versions describing her switch to the SDB,
there the answer comes directly to prayer: M.A. Alt, 'Van Sabbat tot Pinksteren 2',
GS 17.3 (March 1948), p. 5, and Alt, *Herinneringen*, p. 38.

[29] C. Slagter, 'Van Zr. Slagter', *De Boodschapper* (February 1909), p. 29.

[30] C. Slagter, 'Van Zr. Slagter', *De Boodschapper* (April 1909), p. 90.

Water Baptism

> It is with great joy in my heart that I can report that I have received
> the Holy Baptism on the Sabbath, March 12, [1910,] at Gambang
> Waluh.[31]

In her first letter to the SDB church, Margot is already in agreement
with the teaching of baptism for believers by immersion, nevertheless
she wants to wait some time:

> Yet I would rather await God's approval. Perhaps you find this
> strange, as I am convinced, but baptism has not yet been a cause
> of struggle or deep thought in me. So, in this matter I wish to
> trustingly wait, if the Lord also wants to reveal His will to me.[32]

Some months later Margot is ready to be baptized. As Pa van der
Steur no longer belongs to the SDB church, Do Graafstal is the only
male representative on Java. Therefore a long journey to Gambang
Waluh must be undertaken. A few times the trip has to be postponed,
but finally in March 1910 Margot and Slagter manage to take a two-
week furlough.[33] On their way they visit the work of Pa van der Steur
in Magelang. Again Margot is impressed with what she sees, especially
the little children. From there they travel to Gambang Waluh in the
mountains, where Marie, sister of Pa van der Steur, lives with her
husband Do Graafstal.

Since 1893, Marie van der Steur (1868–1962) has been her
brother's loyal co-worker at Magelang. In 1903 she marries Sergeant
Dominicus Graafstal (1870–1927).[34] Unlike her brother, Marie and

---

[31] M.A. Alt, 'De doop van Zr. Alt', *De Boodschapper* (May 1910), p. 87. According
to M.A. Alt, 'Van Sabbat tot Pinksteren 2', *GS* 17.3 (March 1948), God's Spirit
opened her eyes to the 'Biblical Baptism' several months after her conversion,
which would be somewhere in the autumn of 1908. In *Herinneringen* (37) published
in 1963, she confirms that her eyes were opened to the 'Biblical Baptism by immersion' before she decided to join the SDB-church.

[32] M.A. Alt, 'Geachte heer Velthuijsen', *De Boodschapper* (February 1909), p. 31.
Letter dated 30 December 1908.

[33] The name Gambang Waloh becomes Gambang Waloeh in 1928, after inde-
pendence spelled Gambang Waluh (at present Gambangwaluh). In a letter of 20
July 1909 Margot explains that because of different circumstances the journey to
Gambang Waluh has been constantly postponed. M.A. Alt, 'Uit Insulinde', *De
Boodschapper* (September 1909), p. 165.

[34] Marie and Do met one another on Java, but married during a furlough in the
Netherlands. Shortly before the marriage Do became a member of the SDB church
at Haarlem.

her husband remain in the SDB church. They become the leaders of the land colony Gambang Waluh. The property had been let by the government on a long lease to Van der Steur. Later the Graafstals will act as intermediaries when Margot moves to this place.

The last part of the journey up the mountain is by tandu (carriage chair). Margot and Slagter celebrate the Sabbath on Friday evening in the home of the Graafstal family. The next morning the whole company, including the children, walks to the small river nearby. Graafstal gives a short explanation of water baptism: 'After I had confessed my faith, I underwent the baptism under God's blue heaven and friendly sun shine while all present were singing on the bank'.[35] Back home all sing: 'May the Lord's blessing descend upon you!' and they celebrate the Lord's Supper. Margot is now officially a member of the SDB church in Haarlem.

This church is led by G. Velthuijsen, Sr. (1834–1910). Velthuijsen had left the Reformed Church in 1869 and founded a Baptist church in Haarlem. Brochures from the North American Seventh-Day Baptists convince him to keep the Sabbath. In 1877 he and the majority of his church leave the Baptist church and constitute the first SDB assembly in the Netherlands. The congregation can be typified as a Baptist church which observes the Sabbath. More churches are founded in Groningen, Rotterdam, Amsterdam, and The Hague.[36] Since sending Johannes and Marie van der Steur to Java, the Haarlem church is actively involved with the mission in the Dutch Indies, which will only become stronger. Since her conversion in 1908, Margot feels called to mission work. She is, however, not free to go. She has vowed to marry the love of her youth. It is hard for her to break that promise.

---

[35] Alt, 'De doop van Zr. Alt', p. 87.

[36] G. Zijlstra, 'Historie der Zevendedags-Baptiste Gemeenten' (Lecture presented to the Conference at Haarlem on 7 July 1951). J.A. Nieuwstraten, *Geschiedenis van de Zevendedags Baptiste Gemeenten in Nederland* (Haarlem: ZDB-Gemeente, 1977).

5

ENGAGEMENT

The Lord had clearly called me to His wonderful service and I wanted nothing else than to follow Him as servant of the Gospel. However, in my life there was a serious obstacle obstructing the fulfilment of this longing.[1]

In *Herinneringen uit mijn leven* we read that Margot is engaged at the time of her conversion in July 1908. She has made plans to return to the Netherlands in order to be married there. The conversion has radically changed her life. How is she to proceed? She tries to ease her anxiety with the thought that the man in question will be converted once they are together, but it does not give her peace. This issue is partly responsible for the postponing of the baptism: 'My intention to return to Holland, which it seems does not have the approval of the Lord, has also for a short while kept me from being baptised'.[2]

Repeatedly Margot is reminded of the text 'She is at liberty to be married to whom she will; only in the Lord' (1 Cor. 7.39). She takes this to mean that God does not approve of a marriage with someone not converted.[3] The text hurts her like a knife wound in her heart and it haunts her day and night. She believes God is requiring her to make

---

[1] M.A. Alt, *Herinneringen uit mijn leven* (Velp: Pinksterzending, 1963), p. 31.

[2] M.A. Alt, 'Uit Insulinde', *De Boodschapper* (September 1909), p. 165.

[3] This is also the reason why she records the episode in *Herinneringen*: 'When I describe this delicate subject here in a few lines, I do so with the sincere intention to warn our young readers against a thoughtless marriage. Two souls so closely connected cannot but become deeply unhappy when the one does not understand the other in spiritual matters. I have seen many sad examples of it' (32).

this sacrifice for him. In the end she breaks the engagement: 'After much correspondence I decided to terminate the bond that had been there between us since our childhood'.[4]

What is also at stake is that Margot feels called as a messenger of the Gospel: 'In those days I was very aware of the fact that God had not called me to marriage, but to His special service, and that gave me unspeakable joy – a joy so great, that it pushed aside all human feelings'.[5] In her she feels that same fire burning as the apostle Paul speaks of to the Corinthians (1 Cor. 9.16): 'Woe is unto me, if I preach not the gospel!'[6]

Dirk de Visser Smits

Courtship

In *Herinneringen* Margot does not mention the name of her fiancé and in her diary only his first name Dirk appears, but research identifies

---

[4] Alt, *Herinneringen*, p. 32.
[5] Alt, *Herinneringen*, p. 32.
[6] Alt, *Herinneringen*, p. 32.

him as Dirk de Visser Smits (1881–1976).[7] The book of poems, the diary, and her correspondence show how strong their love has been and how giving up the engagement felt like a 'sacrifice'.

Dirk was born at Zetten on 29 September 1881. His father J.D. de Visser Smits (1853–1919) is (who was also born at The Hague), is at the time of Dirk's birth teaching at the Gymnasium at Zetten.[8] In 1886 Dirk's mother dies and the family moves to The Hague, where his father becomes the first director of the Christian Teachers Academy.[9] Later this school will be named after him. Father remarries and more children are born. Dirk and two other children follow their father's footsteps and also become teachers.

Margot speaks of a bond since their childhood but does not disclose how they met. Her diary reveals she was deeply in love with him at the age of fourteen, in 1897–1898, the year she moves from the Music School to the Domestic Science School. Her book of poems commences in 1899 and is dedicated to Dirk with a short poem:

To D. de V.S.
To You my soul – to You my heart
To You my joy and grief
To You are my highest thoughts devoted
From this warfare till eternity.
Margot A.

The next poem 'Herfstklanken' ('Autumn Sounds') is dated October 1899. The text does not speak of love but is written in the 'we'-form. Then follows 'Verlangen' ('Longing') in February 1900, when Margot is sixteen. It appears that the relationship has ended or has cooled down. After that there is silence for about a year. The fourth poem is from March 1901 and is about a sunny corner in the cold temple of life. In the fifth poem 'Schemeren' ('Twilight') in December 1901, Margot mourns her first love that has been short lived:

---

[7] After having identified Dirk, I traced the grandchildren, who were unaware that their grandfather had been engaged to another woman before he married their grandmother. When they checked a box with documents from their grandfather, they were stunned to find a book of poems and a letter from Margot Alt in which she breaks off the engagement.

[8] A Gymnasium is a secondary school preparing pupils to qualify as university students.

[9] 'J.D. de Visser Smits', newspaper cutting from 1911, Collection Veenhuijzen, Centraal Bureau voor Genealogie, The Hague.

...

The spreading dusk brings a comfortable warmth into the room.
I stare absorbed in my musing into the fire,
I think as always of my first love,
'The first rose of love' but of such short-duration!

...

The game of flames is sweetly dying down
It gets so dark in my soul and around me
The last spark of the fire is soon gone,
Just like the love disappeared from his heart.

Book of Poems

The book of poems is started especially for Dirk. Its continuation must have been in question when the relationship seems to break up. It is even more so when Margot (early in 1902) decides to go to the Dutch Indies as a governess, and lives away from The Hague. It isn't until August 1902 that the sixth poem ('Kinderjuffrouw', 'Governess') appears. From then onwards Margot picks up the book more often. The first six poems take three years, while the next three and a half years produce fifty-three poems. In January and April 1903, two more poems are written for Dirk which anticipate the farewell in July. Dirk is first going to finish his studies in Botany and does not want to bind Margot until he has achieved his goal. Afterwards, they agree, they will get engaged. 'We separated from each other as loyal friends. We were both unconverted and wholly in the world.'[10] Margot keeps thinking of Dirk and regularly he is present in her poems. In August 1905, she once more looks back in 'Listen – do you still remember?':

Listen, do you still remember, how you have loved me
In those days, long flown
When I read love in God's nature
And love in your eyes?
When you were completely mine
My heart belonged to you
And nothing in our first joy of love
disturbed our pure happiness.

---

[10] M.A. Alt, 'Autobiografie 1943', p. 6.

...

The beautiful dream is long gone
My deepest grief worn away
Listen, do you still remember how you have loved me?
Or have you already forgotten?

The book of poems is completed in February 1906. The last pages are dedicated to love. The poem compares what is usually seen as love with what real love is. The date is 8 February 1906. Her time as governess is ending. She does not return to the Netherlands but decides to stay in the Indies. Margot's photo in the beginning of the book is dated 20 February 1906 in Batavia. Did she send the book to Dirk at that time or was it given to him at a later stage?[11] No doubt many letters were exchanged between the two. In the beginning of 1908, both Margot and Dirk have passed their exams, and Dirk announces their engagement. He wants her to return to the Netherlands, but Margot prefers to stay in the Dutch Indies. In the end she agrees, but then her conversion jeopardizes the plan. She tries to bring him to conversion without success. He promises to always allow her freedom in her spiritual aspirations. In an attempt to find the will of God, she places an advertisement offering to accompany a patient to the Netherlands in return for travel expenses. Usually such offers find a quick response. But not this time! Finally someone reacts. Margot is overjoyed; it is God's will after all to marry! Everything is prepared, but a few days before departure she receives a disappointing message. The sick lady can be accompanied by her own husband. It is as if Margot's whole world collapses: 'Frightful days came and went. Nights of tears and grief. But I knew enough of God's will to know what I had to do.'[12] After a year and a half of struggle and much correspondence, she decides to break the engagement in February 1910:

> My dear, do not try to get me back, we are standing too far apart from each other. God himself has come in between and would erect a shadow between us were we to marry against His will. There would never be that intimate affinity between you and me that so beautifully unites husband and wife, as I would not be able

---

[11] Dirk has always kept the farewell letter and the poem book. Both documents have been kindly donated by the grandchildren.

[12] Alt, 'Autobiografie 1943', p. 19.

to speak to you about holy, spiritual things. We would become alienated from each other; for certain fear would snare us when specific matters came up for discussion. My darling you would become unhappy and so would I. Try to resign yourself to it and forgive me.[13]

Diary

In Margot's diary, which she starts in September 1910, Dirk is mentioned as many as twenty-six times up to September 1918. Initially Margot cherishes the hope that Dirk will come to conversion and be called as a missionary to Java to help her in the work. Together with Marie Jansz she earnestly prays for this to happen. There is more correspondence between the two in 1910. Around his birthday, she orders a book for him. In November 1910 Margot hears from a friend that Dirk has become engaged. It is a heavy blow. Reading the message she is 'as if in a stupor' (Diary, 14 November 1910). Shortly afterwards she writes that the Lord has taken away the sorrow about Dirk. When in March 1911 her aunt Marie confirms that Dirk is engaged, her reaction is: 'May God bless him! Our ways are far apart. I can think of him with a heart at rest – the Lord has called me to another work' (3 November 1911). However the unrest returns when aunt Sophie reports in June 1912, that Dirk is getting married and will go to Batavia as a teacher of Botany! For her it is 'hard that he comes here with his wife' (27 June 1912). A week later she has a dream about Dirk. She has to burn everything of Dirk's: his letters, his so-often-kissed photos. She sells the medallion and his ring to benefit the mission work (3 July 1912). She hopes never to meet him again (27 July 1912).

On 8 August 1912, 30-year old Dirk marries 24-year Jenneke (Jennie) Karolina van Nieukerke, daughter of a bicycle manufacturer. In September the couple arrive in Batavia, where Dirk has an assignment with the Willem III Gymnasium. The situation becomes more complicated, when in 1915 Dirk moves to Semarang, close to Margot. In September 1916 Margot is at Semarang for a five-day conference. During a walk she sees Dirk passing on the other side of the street. He greets her with a tip of his hat, while she looks straight

[13] Margot Alt to Dirk de Visser Smits, Lawang 13 February 1910.

ahead (28 October 1916). In August 1918, Margot receives a note from Jennie, who appears to have divorced Dirk. Jennie would like Margot and Dirk to meet again, but Margot is not inclined to do so. Using a bit of deception, Jennie gets Margot and Dirk together in her house, without their knowing it. When Jennie is alone with Margot, she asks Margot if she still loves him. Margot answers: 'Yes – I still love him, but we do not fit together – he is of the world and I am not of the world. Moreover a Christian cannot marry a divorced man' (2 September 1918). Dirk, unaware of Margot's presence, joins them. When Jennie leaves them alone, Margot trembles heavily and calls after Jennie: 'I do not want to speak to him'. In spite of their meeting being the fruit of manipulation, they have a relaxed conversation in the front veranda in the presence of the three children. For the first time after fifteen years they speak to each other as old friends. Yet, a new relation is impossible. Margot writes: 'Dirk abused the name of God repeatedly. I would never be happy with him as long as he would not serve God' (2 September 1918). One week later: 'The temptation has passed. For several days I had a heavy battle. Dirk's image was constantly before my spirit, but upon my urgent prayer the Lord has taken it all away from me' (9 September 1918). It is the last reference to Dirk in her diary. Years later he sends her a copy of his dissertation with the written note: 'Out of friendship and respect'.[14]

Jesus is my bridegroom

Soon afterwards, Jennie returns to the Netherlands with the children. In The Hague she becomes co-founder of the Free School. In August 1923 Dirk leaves Semarang to pursue doctoral studies at Utrecht University.[15] On 29 June 1925, he is awarded a doctorate in mathematics and physics. Dirk returns to the Dutch Indies with the children and marries D.M.F. Stave on 21 December 1925. He becomes teacher at the STOVIA medical training school in Batavia. From 1927 he is at the NIAS medical training school in Surabaya. In 1932 he is Dean of Students of the students' home in Batavia. One year later he retires but remains in Batavia until in 1948 he returns home and settles in Oegstgeest. His two great interests are freemasonry and

---

[14] Alt, 'Autobiografie 1943', p. 20.
[15] Title dissertation: *Invloed der temperatuur op de permeabiliteit van het protoplasma bij beta vulgaris L.*

medicinal herbs. On Java he collects herbs and plants. He writes articles about their curative power, but the book he wants to write is
never completed.[16] For many years he is member of the Executive
Committee of the Freemasons in the Dutch Indies and editor of
their periodical, *Indisch Maçonniek Tijdschrift*. In 1931 he publishes a
history of masonry: *Vrijmetselarij: Geschiedenis, maatschappelijke betekenis
en doel* (*Freemasonry: History, social significance and purpose*).[17]

The diary, the farewell letter, and the autobiography all demonstrate how emotional the affair has been for Margot. On the basis of
Bible verses, prayer, and the last-minute cancellation of the journey,
she is convinced of the need to break off the engagement. One year
and a half after her conversion she acts accordingly. Her arguments
in the farewell letter are quite rational: God's Word does not allow
her to marry him; they would stand in each other's way; they would
be alienated, and there would be fear to discuss certain issues. Her
feelings however, remain unchanged: she keeps on loving him. She is
very open-hearted about this in her diary. She acknowledges her feelings, but she does not want to be led by them. Giving up Dirk at first
seems impossible to her, 'and yet I did it voluntary when the Lord
required that I give him up' (13 October 1910). In tears she writes:
'Now the Lord Jesus is my bridegroom!' (27 July 1912).

Other men who make advances are turned down.[18] Sometimes she
longs for someone stronger than herself and to have a child of her
own (19 June 1917). Much to her regret, she will never become a
mother. Yet, as foster mother and as missionary she will become a
spiritual mother for many. Besides 'Sister Alt' it will become common
to address her as 'Moes' or 'Moesje', meaning mother, which in Malay
is 'Ibu'. From now on the name Moes will be used.

---

[16] His article 'Excursie in de omgeving van Batavia', was published in *De Tropi-
sche Natuur* 3 (1914), pp. 88–91; 107–11. In 1950 a provisional agreement was made
with the publisher W. van Hoeve for the publication of: 'De geneeskrachtige
planten van Indonesië in vergelijking met die van India, China, de Philippijnen en
andere gebieden' ('The curative power of plants in Indonesia in comparison with
those in India, the Philippines and other areas').

[17] Cf. Th. Stevens, *Vrijmetselarij en samenleving in Nederlands-Indië en Indonesië 1764–
1962* (Hilversum: Verloren, [1994], with on page 140 a picture of Dirk de Visser
Smits.

[18] The diary gives two examples in 1910 and 1917.

6

PANGUNGSEN AT TAJU 1910–1914

I resigned as a nurse. The fact that the doctors only reluctantly let me go made the farewell less hard than I had thought. I started my duties as a mission nurse in a colony for the poor at Taju. The head of this colony belonged to the Seventh-Day Baptist church, just as I did.[1]

After her conversion, Margot is a different person. Her faith has not made her 'grumpy and gloomy ... the people in my environment know that I am generally cheerful, yet calm. To be true, I am more secluded from the world but more simple and tolerant than before and, as I heartily hope, more upright.'[2] Simultaneously with this change, an inner calling grows in her to preach the gospel. Once she has broken her engagement, the way to becoming a mission nurse is open to her. Without knowing where she will go, she submits her resignation. Among her contacts within the Seventh-Day Baptists (SDB), the work of Marie Jansz catches her eye. Within the stipulated three month period for working out her resignation, she feels this to be her new location. It is a big step with many uncertainties. Compared with what might await her, she has been living in relative luxury with an assured income. Before her lies a hard life in a lonely spot, without salary, and fully depending of gifts.

The SDB periodical *De Boodschapper (The Messenger)* reports in November 1910 about Moes: 'After serious considerations, she has decided to leave her job as nurse in the Governmental Psychiatric

---

[1] M.A. Alt, *Herinneringen uit mijn leven* (Velp: Pinksterzending, 1963), p. 40.
[2] M.A. Alt to Dirk de Visser Smits, Lawang, 13 February 1910.

Hospital at Lawang in order to dedicate herself, together with Sister Jansz, to evangelization and works of charity in dark Java'.[3] We will first become better acquainted with Jansz, after which we will take up Moes' story again.

Marie Jansz

Marie Jansz (1864–1945) is the daughter of Pieter Jansz (1820–1904), Mennonite missionary. Just like the other nine children in the family, Marie is born in Java. Her father is known for translating the Bible into Javanese. Marie Jansz becomes a Seventh-Day Baptist, but for a period she is also officer in the Salvation Army. For some time, she also cooperates with the Seventh-Day Adventists (SDA). Although reared as Mennonite, she starts to observe the Sabbath in 1893.[4] At that time she lives with her parents at Pati, Middle-Java. Late in 1893, she meets Marie van der Steur, when Marie arrives in Semarang.[5] Around this time Marie Jansz is baptized by immersion by Johannes van der Steur.[6] In her letters in *De Boodschapper,* she advocates keeping the Sabbath. Her father, Pieter Jansz, also sends in letters, but he argues for Sunday observance.[7] Possibly in this period there was no formal tie with the SDB-church at Haarlem, at least in the eyes of Marie Jansz, because shortly hereafter she joins the Salvation Army (SA).

Late in 1894, the first Salvation Army officers from the Netherlands arrive in the Dutch Indies: they are Jacob Brouwer and Adolf van Emmerik. They start in Middle-Java and quickly make Semarang

---

[3] 'Belangrijk nieuws uit Indië', *De Boodschapper* (November 1910), p. 212.

[4] M. Jansz, 'Een veilige weg,' *De Boodschapper* (August 1893), pp. 155–56. In this first letter dated 20 June 1893, Jansz writes she has been thinking about the Sabbath more than a year and has started to observe the Sabbath. In 1907 P.T. Skadsheim writes in 'Country Life in Java', *The Signs of the Times* 22.20 (20 May 1907), pp. 314–15, that Jansz has already been keeping the Sabbath for fourteen years. Cf. Milton Hook, *An Oriental Foster Child: Adventism in South-East Asia before 1912* (Wahroona, Australië: Adventist Education, n.d.), pp. 13–14.

[5] Poldi Carlos, *Johannes van der Steur. Een Haarlemse diamant in de Gordel van Smaragd* (1998), pp. 75–76.

[6] C. Slagter, 'Een vrucht van 'De Boodschapper', *De Boodschapper* (October 1905), p. 685.

[7] Pieter Jansz, 'Een pleidooi voor den Zondag', *De Boodschapper* (December 1893), pp. 236–38; answered by G. Velthuijsen Jr. in 'Antwoord'. In 1894–1895 more letters follow and as many replies.

their headquarters.[8] In 1902, Van Emmerik starts a house for home-
less Javanese in the colony of Salib Putih (White Cross) near Salatiga.
Initially Pieter Jansz is critical of the SA, but later he becomes sympathetic. He even translates a number of their documents into Javanese. His daughter Marie becomes the first Salvation Army officer
born in Indonesia.[9] Her letters in *De Boodschapper* witness to her increasing activities as evangelist in and around Pati but do not mention
her connection with the SA.[10] Jansz speaks Malay, but now she also
has to learn Javanese.

Margot Alt, Age 27,
Starting as Missionary Nurse (1910)

[8] Melattie Brouwer, *History of the Salvation Army in Indonesia 1 1894–1949* (Hawthorn, Victoria: Citadel Press, 1996).
[9] According to Brouwer (p. 18) Marie Jansz is an officer in 1898 and when Jansz
later becomes a teacher at Djokjakarta and in Magelang she remains loyal to the
Salvation Army.
[10] Perhaps the repeated rejections of the Salvation Army in *De Boodschapper* is
the reason Marie Jansz keeps silent. In a letter dated 7 May 1904, Jansz writes that
about the time in Pati she worked together with an officer of the Salvation Army.
M. Jansz, 'Van Pangoengsen', *De Boodschapper* (July 1904), pp. 382–83.

In 1901 and 1902, the area is struck by floods, a volcanic eruption, crop failure, and cholera. Following the example of Van Emmerik, these disasters stimulate Marie Jansz to begin a relief work. In March 1902, she starts to care for refugees in her home village of Pati.[11] She takes in hundreds of refugees, at first in a house, but soon in sheds allocated by the local government. She is now recognized as a missionary of the SDB church in Haarlem.[12] The church supports her personally, but the relief work is paid for by the local government.

Jansz does not want to offer just temporary help, but she also wants to provide more structured aid. The people need a piece of land and the means to cultivate it. The government is prepared to lend out land in the Muria Mountains, near Taju, on a long-term basis, but the work will have to be self-supporting. By regular newsletters in secular newspapers, such as *Bataviaasch Nieuwsblad, Soerabaijasch Handelsblad, De Locomotief,* and *Nieuws van den dag voor Nederlandsch-Indië,* Jansz motivates readers to donate money for the project. Every month she gives an account of the income and expenditure. For her own maintenance she can rely on the SDB-church.[13] With large gifts from individuals, some bamboo houses are built and equipment is acquired for the land colony. During 1902, the first groups of colonists, under the leadership of Jansz, move to the colony. The colony of the poor is named Pangungsen (Place of Refuge).

Nearly every year the storms cause great damage to buildings and crops. A typhus epidemic takes away half of the people in the colony. Sometimes there are two or three funerals on a single day. The colony is very remote. Everything has to be transported along a steep and rough mountain path. Besides a house for the sick, they also build a pharmacy, a school, and a church. Of the 180 residents, about a third, mostly children, depend on Jansz for their support. The others receive a piece of land to cultivate so that they can provide their own living. Upon arrival, all the residents are Muslim. There is no pressure to become Christian, but some are converted. The meetings led by

---

[11] M. Jansz, 'Pangoengsen', *Pniël: Weekblad voor het christelijk gezin* 28.1416 (25 February 1919), pp. 49–56. See also *Pniël* 28.1449 (2 August 1919), pp. 241–44 and *Pniël* 29.1474 (27 March 1920), pp. 97–99.

[12] To support Marie Jansz the 'Pieter-Hendrik Fonds' is established in Haarlem, named after the son of pastor Velthuijssen who shortly before had tragically died. Joh. P. Schouten, 'Donker Java', *De Boodschapper* (April 1902), pp. 70–71.

[13] M. Jansz, 'Pangoengsen', *De Locomotief* 13 (December 1902).

Jansz on the Sabbath are open to all without obligation.[14] However, she is rather alone in her work for the colony. During 1904, she temporarily gets help from her niece, H. Jansz.[15] In September 1904, she has four baptismal candidates, but, in a letter to the SDB church, she wonders, who will baptize them? Jansz longs to celebrate the Lord's Supper with them, but they must first be baptized. In April 1905, she repeats her question to the SDB-church at Haarlem. Finally, she herself baptizes Mertadjaja, the Javanese helper, on 9 September 1905, after which Mertadjaja baptizes the other nine converts.[16] A baptism performed by a woman is controversial for the readers of De Boodschapper. In January 1906, the editor explains to the readers that 'in an emergency laws may be broken'.[17]

In Haarlem, on the day of the first baptism in Pangungsen, Cornelia Slagter is sent out as mission nurse to assist Jansz.[18] Slagter, a farmer's daughter from the province of Groningen, joined the SDB in 1892.[19] In 1905, she resigns as nurse from the psychiatric hospital 'De Brinkgreve' at Deventer in obedience to the call of God. Her mission work in Taju gets off to a bad start. Because she does not know the language and culture, she feels lonely and of little use. On top of that, her relationship with Jansz is difficult.[20] Eighteen months later Slagter is ill and has to leave the colony.[21] After a year of recovery with Graafstal in Gambang Waluh, she becomes a psychiatric nurse at Lawang, where she meets Moes.

---

[14] M. Jansz, 'Pangoengsen', *Bataviaasch Nieuwsblad* (15 August 1904).

[15] M. Jansz, 'Pangoengsen', *Bataviaasch Nieuwsblad* (19 July 1904). Probably referring to H.J.W. Jansz (1884–1977).

[16] M. Jansz in *De Boodschapper*, 'Aan de Gemeente', (November 1904), pp. 465–66; 'Aan de Gemeente' (July 1905), pp. 622–23; 'Van Pangoengsen' (November 1905), p. 706.

[17] 'Doopbediening door een vrouw', *De Boodschapper* (January 1906), pp. 17–19. After his baptism Mertadjaja receives the self-chosen name Johanan. M. Jansz, 'Van Pangoengsen', *De Boodschapper* (March 1906), p. 49.

[18] Joh. P. Schouten, 'Inzegening en Afvaardiging van Zuster Cornelia Slagter', *De Boodschapper* (October 1905), pp. 674–81. Slagter is born on 4 February 1866 at Zeerijp (Loppersum).

[19] C. Slagter, 'Een vrucht van De Boodschapper', *De Boodschapper* (October 1905), pp. 683–85.

[20] C. Slagter, 'Van Zuster Slagter', *De Boodschapper* (February 1907), pp. 32–34. C. Slagter, 'Van Lawang', *De Boodschapper* (August 1908), pp. 147–49.

[21] Slagter arrives in November 1905 and stays until June 1906. M. Jansz, 'Pangoengsen', *Bataviaasch Nieuwsblad* (20 December 1905). In 1922 Slagter will take over the work in Pangungsen from Jansz .

In November 1906, the first missionaries of the Seventh-Day Adventists (SDA) arrive on Java. Sent out from Australia, they settle in Surabaya. As soon as they find out that Marie Jansz observes the Sabbath, they seek to make contact.[22] In March 1907, they make their first visit to Pangungsen.[23] Because of her poor health and the heavy work load, Jansz is in need of help. A consultation with the Mennonite missionaries, J. Fast, J. Hübert, and N. Thiessen, does not come to anything.[24] The matter becomes more urgent when Jansz also has to take care of her sick mother. Late in 1908, she hands over the work to the SDA.[25] Jansz keeps the house that had been built at her expense, in order to stay at the colony at her convenience. She has a good relationship with the SDA, although she does not agree with all their teachings.[26] The SDB-church at Haarlem no longer wants to support the colony now led by the SDA and redirects the donations to the work of Graafstal in Gambang Waluh.[27] Under the new

---

[22] The first letter from Jansz in answer to the letter of the SDA is published in: G. Teasdale, 'Java', *Union Conference Record* 11.14 (8 April 1907), p. 2.

[23] P.T. Skadsheim, 'Pangoengsen, Tajoe, Java', *Union Conference Record* 11.19 (13 May 1907), pp. 2–3.

[24] M. Jansz, 'Van Pangoengsen', *De Boodschapper* (November 1907), pp. 209–10; 'Pangoengsen', *De Boodschapper* (January 1908), p. 7. E-mail Alle Hoekema to the author, 18 September 2012, citing from the Minutes of the Missionary Conference, 3–4 December 1907 in Margaredja.

[25] M. Jansz, 'Pangoengsen', *Soerabaijasch Handelsblad* (24 December 1908). Jansz writes that she has to quit the work for some time.

[26] P.T. Skadsheim in 'More News from Java', *Union Conference Record* 11.21 (27 May 1907), pp. 5–6, reports about Jansz: 'She wholly agrees with the Spirit of Prophecy, tithes and the Second Coming of Christ. She already had believed in the Sabbath and baptism. The state of death will be the most difficult for her, as she so often spreaks about those who are in heaven.' In April 1907 the missionaries Jones and Gates visit her and conclude: 'When we found out that she did not agree with some of our teachings, we thought it better not to take it [Pangoengsen] over'. P. Tunheim, 'Java Mission', *Union Conference Record* 12.36 (7 September 1908), p. 25. Tunheim is the same as the one previously called Skadsheim. One year later the SDA reconsiders and decides to take over the colony after all: 'Although she does not agree with us in everything, she is moving in our direction and as I hope will accept it soon'. J.E. Fulton in 'A Letter', *North Pacific Union Gleaner* 3.39 (20 January 1909), p. 2. In December 1908 Jansz can finally hand over th keys to Tunheim. P. Tunheim, 'Back to Pangoengsen', *Union Conference Record* 13.7 (15 February 1909), p. 3. In February 1909 missionary George Wood becomes the leader of the agricultural work. G. Teasdale, 'Our Mission to Sourabaya', *The Signs of the Times* 24.17 (26 April 1909), p. 268.

[27] A. Bakker, 'Pieter Hendrik Fonds', *De Boodschapper* (January 1909), p. 11.

leadership, the Pangungsen project deteriorates.[28] After the death of her mother, Jansz starts another colony near Pangungsen, but at the foot of the mountain. She builds some houses, a school, and a sick-bay. As this project is independent of the SDA, it is eligible for support from the SDB. This is the location where Moes will come. The work is supported with donations from individuals from the Dutch Indies and also from the North American SDB Missionary Society, while Moes gets her support from Haarlem.[29]

Pangungsen

> O may the Lord help and equip me. I know He does not forget His child and yet it is sometimes as if He is another Jesus than my sweet Saviour that I had at Lawang. What foolishness! My home-sickness was terrible during the first days, but now the Lord has helped me through. To Him is the honour.[30]

On 22 September 1910, Moes arrives in the new location called Bethel (later New Pangungsen). After four days of homesickness, she starts a diary that will run until March 1919. For a long time she feels useless not speaking Javanese. She also finds it hard not to have someone of her age-group to talk to. Working with children and treating patients give her much satisfaction. She sows blackberries, gooseberries, and raspberries, but, as she also loves flowers, she plants asters and pinks in pots.

Jansz is sad because of the decline of old Pangungsen. When the Adventists do not succeed in obtaining a license from the government, the leadership of the whole colony is returned to Jansz in the beginning of December 1910.[31] Around this time the Graafstals leave Gambang Waluh and settle at Temanggung. Their support from the SDB mission fund now becomes available as support for Moes.[32] In December 1910, Moes travels to Batavia to speak to the Governor-

---

[28] M. Jansz, 'Een oude bekende aan het hoofd van Pangoengsen', *Bataviaasch Nieuwsblad* (27 December 1910).

[29] G. Velthuijsen Jr., 'Donker Java', *De Boodschapper* (August 1911), pp. 113–14.

[30] M.A. Alt, 'Dagboek 1910–1919' ('Diary 1910–1919'), 26 September 1910.

[31] M.A. Alt, 'Goede tijding', *De Boodschapper* (March 1911), pp. 31–32. 'Dagboek 1910–1919', 16 December 1910. Cf. 'The Work in the Australasian Field', *Australasian Record* 15.13–14 (27 March 1911), p. 13; 'Sabbath-school Department Report', *Australasian Record* 15.48 (4 December 1911), p. 6.

[32] G. Velthuijsen Jr., 'Belangrijk bericht', *De Boodschapper* (February 1911), p. 28.

General (GG). For both Jansz and Moes, it is important to be recognized as mission nurses; but other missionaries have urged the GG not to grant this permission.[33] In March 1911, Jansz herself goes to the GG, who receives her warmly. However, he makes it clear that it is difficult for the government to allow women to baptize.[34] In May 1911, Moes travels to Sumber Waras (Source of Blessing), the rehabilitation centre of the SDA at Prigen, sixty-five kilometer outside of Surabaya. On her way, she visits her former work place in Lawang: 'I have visited my patients; all still recognized me'.[35] In later years, she will visit the institution several times.

Her relationship with Jansz who is nineteen-years-older than her is good but at the same time rather complicated. In the beginning, Moes feels inferior in everything and greatly looks up to Jansz, whom she calls 'Aunt'. She makes a big effort to please 'Aunt', but always thinks she finds her fickle and weak. Jansz has a very simple life style. She eats the same very basic meals as the Javanese, drinks black coffee to economize on milk, and walks barefooted to save money on slippers. Knowing how Jansz lives, the pastor of the Haarlem church pleads that Moes would receive nourishing food, 'in order that her strength does not decrease'. However, from the money they send, Moes only takes a little for herself.[36]

Moes, just like Jansz, gets up every morning around four o'clock and dedicates one hour to God. She prays for deliverance from pride and dishonesty. Several times she writes in her diary that she has entered into full liberty but a few days later that freedom proves to have been shortlived. Now and then she asks God for a sign and then opens her Bible at random for a text. She reads books by Andrew Murray, believes strongly in divine healing, and longs for the fullness of the Holy Spirit. Sometimes she lays hands on the sick for healing.

Once when Jansz was absent, a seriously ill patient shows no improvement after her prayer. She decides to fast until healing is achieved. After eight days Jansz returns and firmly reprimands the weakened Moes. The patient is brought to Semarang and dies after a

---

[33] Alt writes in her diary 25 March [1911]: 'The missionaries and dr. Bervoets at Margaredja do everything to get us away from here. To them it is a splinter in the eye, that we are here and that the Sabbath is celebrated here'.

[34] Alt, 'Dagboek 1910–1919', 16 April 1911.

[35] Alt, 'Dagboek 1910–1919', 5 May 1911.

[36] G. Velthuijsen Jr., 'Donker Java', *De Boodschapper* (August 1911), p. 114; M. Jansz, 'Donker Java', *De Boodschapper* (October 1911), p. 150.

few months. Moes experiences a shock to her nervous system, and for a time she is afraid she is losing her mind. She realizes her foolishness and learns not to act upon feelings, voices, nor spur of the moment decisions, because 'the devil can present himself as an angel of light'.[37] For a short while, the event places the relation between Jansz and Moes under pressure.

Diary 1910-1919, First Page

---

[37] Alt, 'Dagboek 1910–1919', 16 September 1911.

In *De Boodschapper* of August 1911, Moes writes about a baptismal ceremony in the river. Who performs the baptism is not mentioned (perhaps on purpose). When Moes later looks back on this period, she writes about Jansz: 'In the church she founded, she baptized believers and administered the Lord's Supper, as there were no brothers present'.[38]

Since the work is spread over two locations, it often occurs that Jansz is in the old section and Moes visits the sick and leads the meetings on her own. Gradually she learns the Javanese language thoroughly. Halfway though 1911, she is in full partnership with Jansz. From then on, both their names appear under the monthly reports in the newspapers.[39] On her birthday in 1911, Moes receives the book of daily devotions *Lichtstralen op den Levensweg* (*Light Beams on the Life Journey*) from Jansz, with a text from the Bible for every morning and evening. Moes uses the book for her daily devotions. In the margin, she regularly writes a note with a date.[40] Now and then she receives letters and sometimes visits from Slagter.

In 1912, Slagter is on furlough in the Netherlands and brings reports of the mission work to the SDB-church at Haarlem. Pangungsen is described as a native village with forty bamboo houses with thatched roofs . In the middle stands the bamboo house of the sisters. The church, erected in 1906, is the only building of wood. Every morning there is a short prayer meeting, with much singing accompanied by an organ. Jansz and Moes both have good voices. The colony can partially support itself with djagung (corn) and with the proceeds of the milk from cows and goats. Necessary alterations are made to the second hand clothing they receive under the supervision of Moes, and some is sold in the market.[41]

From November 1911, Moes spends nearly three months in Salatiga, caring for Hanna, a sick niece of Jansz.[42] This period brings

---

[38] M.A. Alt, 'De Melaatschen-Kolonie Dana Radja', *GS* 8.8 (August 1932), pp. 4–7 (7).

[39] From July 1911 until June 1913. Hereafter the reports are unsigned until January 1915.

[40] It concerns: *Lichtstralen op den Levensweg*, translated from English by C. Kuyper (Amsterdam: Egelings' Boekhandel, 1903), 800 pages. Moes made 659 notes, of which 579 refer to the period 1921–1927, a period in which few other sources are available.

[41] Pieter-Hendrikfonds, 'Donker Java', *De Boodschapper* (October 1912).

[42] Probably Johanna Betist-de Boer (1874–1936), daughter of J.M.E. de Boer-Jansz (1852–1931).

her some relief. It is as if there is more room in her heart, and she constantly has more light and peace. Back in Pangungsen she is happy and content. On 29 February 1912, she writes: 'I feel as if I am only now starting to live for the Lord'. In this period Jansz and Moes issue a small monthly paper under the title *Heiligmaking* (*Sanctification*), not about the work, but about a sanctified life.[43] In April 1912, Moes comes across a girl who is almost three years old in Magelang, who has been rejected by her unmarried Javanese mother. Moes takes her as her foster child and calls her Annie, after her own deceased mother. Later, the Javanese mother seeks contact with her daughter, and after one year, the mother actually joins the work at the colony.

In June 1912, Moes reads the Dutch Pentecostal periodical *Spade Regen* (*Latter Rain*) and prays for the promise of the Holy Spirit. She corresponds with Gerrit Polman of the Pentecostal church in Amsterdam. During this time, Dr. Boon, her previous leader at Lawang and now general director of the hospital at Buitenzorg, offers her a job as head-nurse. She finds it a great honour. However, she also sees it as a temptation to become proud, so she turns it down.[44]

Her constantly recurring malaria exhausts her and causes a lasting stomach complaint. In February 1914, she goes to Temanggung to recover, but she is so weakened that she needs to be admitted to the military hospital at Magelang.[45] After six weeks, she is strong enough to return to Temanggung.[46] At the same time, Marie Graafstal is seriously ill and needs to go to the hospital. Moes now takes care of the housekeeping and looks after the patients. The cooler climate and the kind reception by Do and Marie Graafstal are beneficial to her. At this time she hears that the plantation at Gambang Waluh is deserted. In June, she revisits the place, where she had been baptized four years previously. In this deserted place, she hears the voice of the Lord: 'This will be your field of labour'. Marie Graafstal returns from the

---

[43] In November 1912 they have issued this paper for one year, of which no copies have been found. With the proceeds they hope to support the ministry. M. Jansz and M.A. Alt, 'Pangoengsen', *Bataviaasch Nieuwsblad* (16 November 1912). In *Gouden Schooven* Moes will later repeatedly reprint articles from *Heiligmaking;* for instance M.A. Alt, 'Vrijheid', *GS* 10.12 (June 1934), pp. 5–7.

[44] Alt, 'Dagboek 1910–1919', 5 September 1912.

[45] In May/June 1913 Moes also had stayed three weeks to recover at Temanggung. During her time in the hospital the *De Boodschapper* reports that she probably can no longer return to Pangungsen. 'Donker Java', *De Boodschapper* (July 1914), p. 109.

[46] Alt, 'Autobiografie 1943', p. 33.

hospital but is still weak. Therefore, it is decided that Moes will take the mentally deficient patients with her to Gambang Waluh. In August 1914, she makes a last visit to the colony in Taju to say good-bye to Jansz. By the end of October, she has started an independent work at Gambang Waluh.

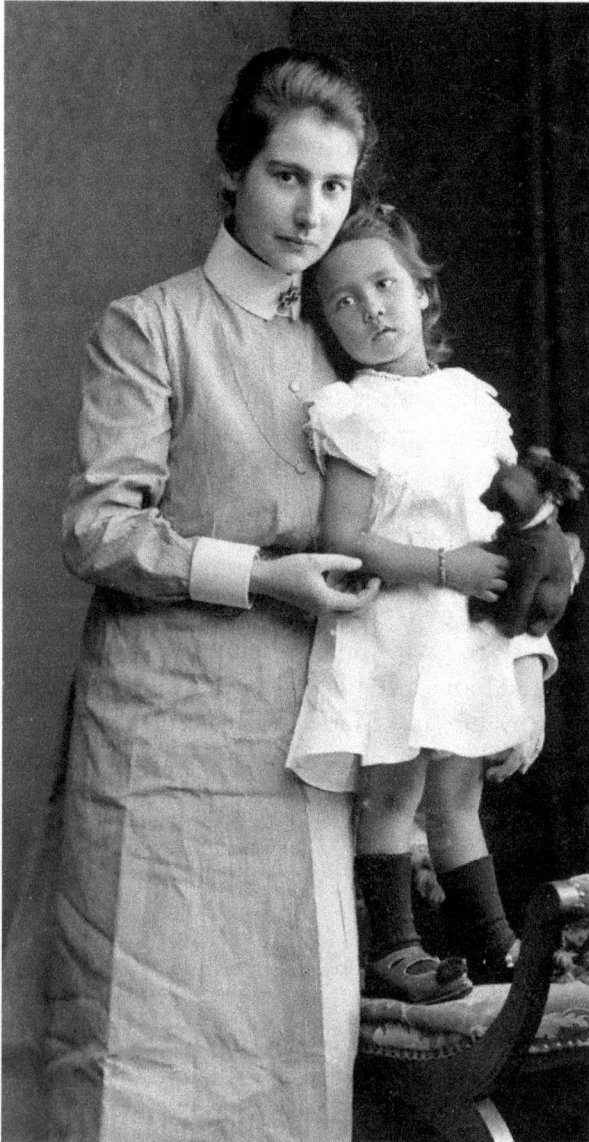

Margot with Foster Child Annie (1914)

In spite of her physical weakness, Jansz continues the work in Pangungsen, assisted by Javanese helpers, for another eight years. In 1922, some of the residents in need of help are brought to an institution for Javanese beggars led by Rev. A. Merkelijn at Magelang. The colony at Pangungsen is carried on by Cornelia Slagter.[47] Jansz takes a few of the orphans and starts the Javanese orphans' colony 'New Matrix' at Magelang.[48] Slagter, who still does not speak Javanese, gets support from Georg Vizjak who speaks the language and takes on the leadership of the church.[49] The work is supervised by a society for Christian Philanthropy, of which Marie Graafstal-van der Steur is the treasurer.[50]

---

[47] C. Slagter, 'Een aandoenlijke ontboezeming en een roepstem', *De Boodschapper* (November 1928), pp. 159–63.

[48] M. Jansz, 'Javaansche Weezenkolonie' in *Bataviaasch Nieuwsblad* (20 October 1922) and (20 March 1923). M. Jansz, 'Zorg voor Inl. weezen', *Nieuws van den dag voor Nederlandsch-Indië* (18 October 1922).

[49] 'Pangoengsen', *Utrechts Nieuwsblad* (1 March 1927); M[arie] G[raafstal], 'Zuster Slagter's feestdag', *Indische Courant* (5 November 1930); 'Zuster C. Slagter: Een onderscheiding', *Indische Courant* (2 March 1936).

[50] 'Pangoengsen', *Utrechts Nieuwsblad* (March 1927). A later report indicates that Old Pangungsen is led by Mr. Leimena and New Pangungsen by Slagter. The society is called: Vereeniging Christelijke Philantropie voor Inlanders tot hun zedelijke opheffing. S.M. Graafstal-van der Steur, 'Christelijke Philanthropie', *Nieuws van den dag voor Nederlandsch-Indië* (7 October 1939).

7

GAMBANG WALUH 1914

After I had visited the plot once more, my decision was made. It was as if I heard the voice of the Lord in my soul: 'This will be your field of labour'. In that moment a wide perspective opened before my eyes – I felt my calling, received when I was twelve, would now be fulfilled and joy filled my soul.[1]

Former Coffee Plantation

Gambang Waluh is a former coffee plantation of nearly 200 hectares. It is situated on one of the offshoots of the Ungaran Mountains between Temanggung and Ambarawa, Middle Java. Eleven hundred meters above sea level, it is relatively cool; but even here malaria lies in wait. Five desas (village communities) surround the plantation. The population is Muslim, but the folk Islam is mixed with spirit and ancestor worship. No longer profitable as a coffee plantation, the government leases the plot to Pa van der Steur in 1901 as a land colony for the boys from Orange Nassau. The young men are trained to run small-scale farms. The colony is led by Albert and Anna Binkhuijzen, but in 1904 Do and Marie Graafstal take over the leadership. It is not easy to make the enterprise self-supporting. By the end of 1907, Van der Steur considers the experiment a failure. The location is unfavourable, it makes a loss, and the youth decline intellectually.[2] The Graafstals, who are unwilling to give up, transform it into a 'Home of Mercy' for mentally deficient children from Orange Nassau. By growing coffee, tobacco, vanilla, coco-nuts, and later running a dairy-

---

[1] M.A. Alt, *Herinneringe uit mijn leven* (Velp: Pinksterzending, 1963), p. 42.
[2] 'Het werk der liefde', *Bataviaasch Nieuwsblad* (1 October 1907).

farm, Graafstal tries to generate income, but without success.[3] When their own children reach school age, the family eventually moves to Temanggung. They continue to care for a number of mentally deficient children. For this work the Zendingsonderneming Temanggung (Mission enterprise Temanggung) is founded with Rev. R.J. Horstman as its secretary.[4] From 1901 Reginus Johannes Horstman (1856–1924) directs a secondary school in Temanggung for children of the Javanese elite.[5] Except for the Javanese caretaker, the plot at Gambang Waluh remains deserted until 1914.

Gambang Waluh (1917), Moes with a child on her knee in the midst of patients and fosterchildren. Sitting next to her is Cornelia Slagter and standing at the back row on the left is Georg Vizjak.

---

[3] Poldi Carlos, *Johannes van der Steur. Een Haarlemse diamant in de Gordel van Smaragd* (1998), p. 123. Zevendedags-Baptiste Gemeente, *Zevendedags-Baptiste Zending* (Haarlem: ZDB-gemeente, 1935), p. 3.

[4] M.A. Alt, 'Gambang Waloeh', *GS* 5.6 (June 1929), pp. 17–19.

[5] H. Reenders, *De gereformeerde zending in Midden-Java 1853–1931* (Zoetermeer: Boekencentrum, 2001), p. 863. Horstman is born in Amsterdam and since 1884 a missionary on Java, first of the Neukirchener Mission and then of the NGZV and until 1897 of the GKN. After the death of his first wife he remarries in 1897 the Javanese Christine Thomas. Several children from this marriage will become leaders in the Pentecostal Movement.

Life in the rural areas is characterized by the desas, subdivided in kampongs (suburbs). Religious and social life are interwoven. It is difficult for Javanese converts to remain Christians, especially in an environment that is almost completely Muslim. For this reason, Pieter Jansz, the father of Marie Jansz, had advocated for the formation of land colonies where Christians could establish their own communities. His son and successor, Pieter Antonie Jansz (1853–1943), realized this by founding the nearby colony Margaredja.[6] The disadvantages of such a scheme are that Christians are isolated from their environment, and the missionary functions as landlord, causing spiritual and business matters to be mingled. Whilst taking into account and seeking to remedy these disadvantages, Moes has something similar in mind for Gambang Waluh.

A village is born

> For a good fifteen years, I was allowed to live and work among these plain people, and those were the happiest years of my life, although I suffered a lot from malaria there and had to combat financial need. Yet, never, not a single day, has the Lord abandoned us and countless were His blessings and deliverances. With these I could fill a book.[7]

On 28 October 1914, while the Great War rages in Europe, Moes moves to Gambang Waluh to bring a message of peace to the people. At the age of 31, she will now be in charge of a new work, a role that will suit her well. The four years with Jansz have given her an excellent preparation for what is awaiting her. Her main goal is to evangelize among the Javanese. To relieve the still-weak Marie Graafstal, she takes over the care of the mentally deficient patients.[8] With only seven guilders cash, she has to rely on donations and the lodging allowance she receives for the patients. All her life she will refuse any

---

[6] Harold S. Bender, W.F. Golterman, and Leo Laurense, 'Doopsgezinde Zendingsraad' (1990), *Global Anabaptist Mennonite Encyclopedia Online* (http:// gameo.org/index.php? title=Doopsgezinde_Zendingsraad).

[7] M.A. Alt, 'Berichten van het arbeidsveld', *GS* 19.6 (June 1950), p. 17.

[8] G. Velthuijsen Jr., 'Donker Java', *De Boodschapper* 39 (January 1915), p. 6. The patients are nursed by Moes. One of the boys is lame on both legs, another 'totally crazy' and cannot talk, a third boy suffers from nervous cramps. M.A. Alt, 'Uit een brief van Zr. Alt', *De Boodschapper* 39 (March 1915), p. 60.

subsidy from the government for the evangelization work. Following George Müller, the founder of orphanages in England, she wants to rely completely upon God.[9] *De Boodschapper* frequently publishes letters from Moes and the incoming donations for 'Dark Java' are accounted for. Moes now is the main missionary of the little SDB assembly.

Upon arrival in Gambang Waluh, writes Moes, she finds 'only two or three residents, real heathens, who still sacrifice at the river and upon the graves and hardly understand anything of the Islamic faith'.[10] There are two buildings which are in a ruinous state. The large house, where Binkhuijzen and Graafstal have lived before, becomes home for Moes and her companions. It is the only stone house. It has five rooms and a large dining room. None of the windows is intact, and no door can be locked. The other house, which is being used as a stable, is in even worse shape. On the first night, Moes, sitting on a large rock in front of the house, reads: 'In all places where I record My name, I will come unto thee and I will bless thee.' (Exod. 20.24b). She is reminded of the text she read when she started in Taju: 'They that sow in tears shall reap in joy. He that goes forth and weeps, bearing precious seed, shall doubtless come again with rejoicing, bringing his sheaves with him' (Ps. 126.5–6).[11]

On 31 October 1914, she celebrates her first Sabbath, together with the five patients, her foster child, Annie, and Roesminah, a Javanese teenage girl who has followed her since Taju. More patients will come. On 1 December, she starts a Javanese evening school, where the people of the surrounding desas learn to read and write, without having to pay tuition. A few days before Christmas, Pa van der Steur sends Moes a two year old girl who has been abandoned. Moes accepts her as her second foster child and calls her Dora or Sis. Although Moes will take in dozens of (orphan) children, she considers these two (Annie and Sis) to be her own.[12]

---

[9] The Mission EnterpriseTemanggung will later receive subsidy for the mentally deficient patients. M.A. Alt, 'Een brief van Zuster Alt', *De Boodschapper* 21 (November 1921), p. 281.

[10] M.A. Alt, 'Hoe Gods Geest op Gambang Waloeh viel 1', *GS* 17.5 (May 1948), p. 4.

[11] M.A. Alt, 'Autobiografie 1943', p. 37.

[12] Annie's official name is: Johanna Margaretha Vetter (1909–1974). Later she will marry Albertus de Frètes and have six children. Dora or Sissie's official name is: Christine Carolina Fickel (1912–1996). For some years she will do secretarial

At first the people from the desas are suspicious. One day, the caretaker comes to Moes with a man from a neighbouring desa, named Kromo, who has cut grass on the plot to feed his goats. As the land is government property, he ought to be punished. Kromo falls on his knees and begs for mercy, but the caretaker wants Moes to punish the thief. Moes explains to Kromo that in the eyes of God theft is a sin; but she sends him away with a kind rebuke and allows him to keep his bundle of grass.[13] Through her conduct, Moes wins the confidence of the people. On 22 August 1915, she celebrates her thirty-second birthday. The neighbouring Javanese are invited to the party. A hundred come to see the magic lantern (predecessor of the slide projector).[14] Later Kromo comes to live on the plot, together with his family, and becomes a Christian. Just as in Pangungsen, people start coming for medicines or treatment of their wounds. The people of the desas may be given a piece of land by Moes on the condition that the whole family comes to church on the Sabbath. The former coffee plantation gradually becomes a village.

From September 1915, a simple building constructed from plaited bamboo serves as a school. Classes can now be held during day time. The children sit on the bamboo floor and write at long tables in rows of five.[15] The walls are decorated with Biblical pictures. Moes starts every class with prayer and singing. For some parents, this is a reason to keep their children at home, but Moes does not want to compromise on this point. On Sabbath evening, she holds kumpulan (meetings), where some young people from the desas attend. If weather permits, she walks to the surrounding desas on Sabbath afternoon to evangelize. Some open their houses for meetings with the magic lantern. In January 1916, there are twenty mentally deficient patients, and nearly all of them come along.[16] Moes usually travels on foot, but

---

work for the periodical *Gouden Schooven*. Sometimes she writes a piece under the name Tine Fickel. Later she will marry Willem Frederik Karel Oetgens van Waveren Pancras Clifford (1910–1945) and have six children. Moes considers all these children as her grandchildren. This information comes from a granddaughter of Annie (Anne Louise Barbier) and from a daughter of Sissie (Maud Severijn-Clifford).

[13] Alt, *Herinneringen,* p. 43.

[14] M.A. Alt, 'Dagboek 1910–1919', 23 August 1915.

[15] M.A. Alt, 'Uit Gambang Waloh', *De Boodschapper* 39 (February 1916), pp. 45–46.

[16] M.A. Alt, 'Een blik op het werk van Zr. Alt', *De Boodschapper* 39 (May 1916), pp. 134–35.

for some years she has an old horse, which makes travelling to Temanggung (twenty kilometres away) easier. Visitors are often carried
up hill in a tandu (carrying-chair) by four carriers.

Initially parents only send their sons to school. Among the first
are five boys from Porot, the nearest desa (village), about twenty
minutes walking distance. In November 1915, two of them are converted, the first fruits of a year of labour, and more will follow.[17] In
December 1915, Moes leads her first marriage service and gives her
blessing to two couples. On 24 April 1916, the first two converts are
baptized in the river by Do Graafstal in the presence of some Muslims who had been very hostile before.[18] Contrary to Jansz, Moes will
never baptize anyone herself. There is a six-month probation period
before converts are baptized, during which they are taught about the
Sabbath. At their baptism, they receive a Biblical name which they
themselves choose. The two boys, Ribin and Wagi, are about nine-
teen, and from then on are called Iskaq and Joenoes (Isaac and John).
Later they will become leaders in the church.

The school runs so well and is so popular that Moes can no longer
admit new pupils. The parents now ask Moes to accept their daughters. Since it is a real miracle that they are prepared to send their
daughters to school, Moes admits them.[19] Halfway through 1916,
Moes has sixty pupils. Twice a week, after school hours, the girls also
have a sewing-class. Adults also want an education. In addition to the
children in the morning and the adults in the afternoon, Moes has
separate classes for her foster children in the evening.[20] Later a Javanese teacher will take over the language classes, but Moes keeps the
introductory prayer, singing, and Scripture reading for herself.

Of her bouts of malaria, she writes in early 1915: 'The malaria still
has not left me. If I had stayed in Taju, I would, humanly speaking,
have died there. There I received *the* set-back. Malaria is the most
resistant disease that I know, because it so undermines the constitution.'[21] Especially in her first year, she is often sick and takes a lot of
quinine.

---

[17] Alt, 'Uit Gambang Waloh', (February 1916), pp. 45–46. 'Dagboek 1910–
1919', 12 December 1915; *Herinneringen*, p. 44.

[18] M.A. Alt, 'Van Zr. Alt', *De Boodschapper* 39 (August 1916), p. 238.

[19] Alt, 'Van Zr. Alt', p. 239.

[20] C. Slagter, 'Hoe het thans gaat op Gambang Waloh', *De Boodschapper* 40 (April
1917), pp. 113–16.

[21] M.A. Alt, 'Uit een brief van Zr. Alt', *De Boodschapper* 39 (March 1915), p. 60.

In August 1916, Cornelia Slagter comes to assist in the work.[22] Moes can use her help. Although their relationship requires a lot of hard work, Slagter takes care of nearly all the adult patients, cares for the pharmacy, and treats those with wounds. Moes concentrates on the young patients, the school, housekeeping, and evangelization.[23] More and more families settle at Gambang Waluh and attend the meetings.

In February 1917, Georg Vizjak visits the work.[24] Georg Vizjak (1871–1937) is born in Croatia and is an officer in the Salvation Army. In July 1913, he is sent from Switzerland to Java.[25] He works as a nurse in the clinic for eye diseases at Semarang.[26] The project at Gambang Waluh is so appealing to him that he joins the work in May 1918 and also becomes a member of the SDB. In Semarang, Moes also meets the German nurse, Klara Keil, who works in the hospital of the Salatiga Mission.[27] The two become friends. Moes writes in her diary on 21 March 1917: 'I have such a feeling that one day we will work together, although at the moment it is not in the least likely'. In June, Keil comes over for a ten-day visit. For Moes these are 'days of sunshine and joy'. Keil accepts the Sabbath and baptism upon confession of faith. She resigns from the hospital, and in October 1917, she joins the work in Gambang Waluh.[28] From now on, Moes is called director. Just like Moes, Slagter, Vizjak, and Keil regularly fall ill. In 1918, Slagter even has to take long-term sick leave caused by a nervous breakdown.[29]

---

[22] Slagter, 'Hoe het thans gaat', pp. 113–16.

[23] M.A. Alt, 'Uit Gambang Waloh', *De Boodschapper* 40 (April 1917), pp. 142–45.

[24] In 'Ein Brief aus Java von Kapitän Vizjak', *Der Kriegsruf* (3 July 1915) Vizjak calls himself Croatian. According to the SA officers registration in Switzerland he has Austrian nationality.

[25] The SA Officers Registration in Switzerland reveals that Vizjak from 1908–1913 served in Switzerland. 'Reisebericht der kapitäne Vieverglet und Vizjak aus Java', *Der Kriegsruf* (20 September 1913).

[26] Vizjak, 'Ein Brief aus Java von Kapitän Vizjak' (14 March 1914).

[27] Klara Keil is born in 1878 and is a missionary of the Neukirchener Mission. On Java it cooperates with the Ermelosch Zendingsgenootschap in the Salatiga Mission. Cf. Bernd Brandl, *Die Neukirchener Mission: ihre Geschichte als erste deutsche Glaubensmission* (Keulen: Rheinland Verlag, 1998), pp. 215, 354.

[28] C. Slagter, 'Zeer verblijdend nieuws uit Gambang Waloh', *De Boodschapper* 41 (February 1918), pp. 53–54.

[29] M.A. Alt, 'Goed nieuws uit Gambang Waloh', *De Boodschapper* 41 (June 1918), pp. 205–206.

Moesje with Some of the Orphans in Gambang Waluh (1920)

In 1917, a third house (made of wood) is built for the male patients. A beautiful photograph from 1917 has survived showing
Vizjak, Slagter, and Moes with two foster daughters and fourteen patients. In March 1918, Moes reports that about fifty people attend the
meetings on Sabbath morning: the residents of the plot, some of the
school pupils, and the Christians.[30] There is a need for a separate
church building, but there is no money to build it. In October 1918,
eight persons are baptized by Do Graafstal, among whom are Keil
and a couple of twelve-year-old Javanese boys. After four years of
labour, there are now thirteen baptized Javanese. Four baptized
Christians live in the desa Porot. Through the witness of the first two
baptized boys, Iskaq and Joenoes, many are drawn to Christ. Meetings are held in the home of Joenoes.[31] Late in 1922, there is a small
house church, which, Moes writes, is mainly the result of the faithful
labour of the two evangelists.[32] Around 1920, she receives the commission to issue a Javanese hymn book, although she does not have
the money to pay for it:

---

[30] Alt, 'Goed nieuws'.
[31] M.A. Alt, 'Brief van Zr. Alt', *De Boodschapper* 42 (February 1919), p. 54. M.
Alt, 'Een treffend schrijven van Zr. Alt', *De Boodschapper* 42 (May 1919), pp. 144–
47.
[32] M.A. Alt, 'Uit Gambang Waloh', *De Boodschapper* 47 (March 1922), pp. 63–64.

On the command of the Lord, I had made a Javanese song book for my continually growing church. I had translated many songs from Johan de Heer into Javanese and added a number of others. The book was neatly printed by Van Dorp and became popular. But alas, when the bill was presented, I had no money. Where would I get 600 guilders? I had made the book completely in faith, knowing I was in the will of the Lord …

One afternoon Miss J[onker], a teacher from Temanggung, came walking up the hill. Shortly before, she had found the Lord, and full of joy, we talked together about the things of God. Just before her departure, she suddenly said to me: 'I have 600 guilders in my savings account, and because I am alone and live very simply, I do not know what to do with that money. Therefore I feel a strong urge to give it to you for the work of the Lord'. Tears of joy and thankfulness welled up in my eyes. What a wonderful, lovely Saviour we have![33]

Late 1918, the terribly dangerous Spanish fever and a dreadful epidemic strike Middle Java. Whole kampongs die out. All the surrounding desas are infected. People from the area bring babies whose parents have died to Gambang Waluh. In spite of the risks, Moes takes more than forty of these orphans. Every night the whole church gathers to pray for protection. Moes and Keil are infected by the fever but survive. Not one of the housemates or church members dies. After the epidemic, Moes also receives some neglected Indo-European children. *De Boodschapper* of April 1920 publishes a picture of Moes with some of the young orphans. In May 1920, there is another picture of the Indo-European patients and the three nurses, Moes, Slagter, and Keil, as well as a picture of the Javanese patients in national dress.[34] These are mentally deficient, blind, deaf and dumb, crippled, and psychiatric patients. In early 1920, there are seventy-five patients, excluding the orphans.[35] With so many patients to care for, there is little room to evangelize; but this will soon change.

[33] Alt, 'Autobiografie 1943', pp. 42–43.
[34] G. Velthuijsen Jr., 'Laat het U een blijdschap zijn te helpen dragen!', *De Boodschapper* (May 1920), pp. 121–25.
[35] In a letter from October 1920 Moes speaks of a family of 110 persons. M.A. Alt, 'Uit Gambang Waloh', *De Boodschapper* 45 (February 1921), pp. 36–37.

One day at Gambang Waluh

In January 1921, the daily newspaper, *Soerabaijasch Handelsblad,* publishes a long report of a visit to Gambang Waluh by Mrs. S. Grullemans-Velthuijsen. It gives us a splendid inside view of every day life there :

> For two-and-a-half hours we go uphill, along high steep hills and more rolling valleys. Finally in a very isolated location, we see the goal of our journey, the three houses in Gambang Waluh, ahead of us ... How lovely and friendly it looks here! After wandering through the always beautiful, yet austere mountains, with their endless clumps of overgrown reed-grass, we see a garden with roses! Sister Alt, director of the institution, with a sweet earnest appearance, who immediately wins you over, invites us inside. We enter the main building, an old tumbled-down house with bamboo walls and holes in the ground because of old age. But all this one only sees later, because using the simplest means it is all made as cozy as possible, as only a woman of taste can do. A seat made of rotan sitting, a cupboard with books, an old piano, a writing table, a few tables with portraits, texts and pictures on the walls, is all the furniture in the large room; but one feels at home there. Asked by our friendly host whether we want something to eat, we gladly say yes. As we take refreshment and while we are eating the simple meal, we listen as Sister Alt shares details of her work.

> She and two other nurses care for the mentally deficient – poor things, who can in no way survive in normal society and – that hard expression must be used here – are not crazy enough for the psychiatric institution. Not only the mentally deficient are admitted here, but also the lame and the blind and those who suffer from fainting fits or epilepsy, all these abandoned ones thrown away by society. No one is ever turned away. And this work of charity is united by the sisters with the work of the mission. Once a week the Javanese from neighbouring desas assemble to hear the Word of God. Sister Alt addresses them in Javanese.

> When an epidemic was raging in the neighbouring desas, she went inside the houses and encouraged the dying and the bereaved. The Javanese have an unlimited confidence in their 'ndoro-nona' [mistress-miss]. The children from the desas who belong to no one are

brought to her; sometimes new-born babies, whose mothers have died, sometimes blind poor souls. Also [Indo-] European children, who were alone and abandoned in this world, have been taken in by Sister Alt … Some very young babies are lying in the neo-natal ward in some improvised cradles. Even though she takes the responsibility for the whole institution, this is the ward Sister Alt personally looks after. She teaches the small ones to play and sing and gives the older ones a more formal education. The mentally deficient are separated from the normal ones …

The evening has long fallen. Supper is ready. All the abandoned children enter the dining room and seat themselves at the long table, on which the smoky flames from paraffin lamps form the only light. The plate with rice pap is hungrily emptied. That too is one of the gifts of Sister Alt; she knows how to feed all these people out of a very shallow purse. Then a chapter from the Bible is read. It is a surprising feeling to us in this strange company … three Dutch women, who left their homeland years ago, have buried themselves in the isolated interior of a country they did not know with a bunch of abandoned children. From where do they draw the courage to perform their work of charity year in and year out? Sister Alt reads: 'My help comes from the Lord, who made heaven and earth. He will not suffer thy foot to be moved: He that keeps you will not slumber'.[36]

Home visitation

In a letter dated 19 February 1922, Moes takes us along on a home visitation:

Come, let me invite you today to join me on such a trip. Perhaps it will give you a clearer picture of the circumstances over here.

---

[36] S. G[rullemans].-V[elthuijsen], 'Gambang Waloh', *Soerabaijasch Handelsblad* (25 January 1921), cited in *De Boodschapper* 45 (April 1921), pp. 86–89. Also published in *Algemeen Handelsblad* (10 March 1921). The author S.L. Grullemans-Velthuijsen works for the *Soerabaijasch Handelsblad*. With her husband she visited Gambang Waluh in 1920. Because her husband got ill, they stayed longer enabling the author to write several articles. Another article about a visit to the desa Porot was later reprinted by Moes in *Gouden Schooven*: S.L.G.-V., 'Koempoelan in de desa', *GS* 6.29 (November 1930), pp. 15–17 and repeated in *GS* 10.21 November 1937.

It is eight o'clock in the morning. Breakfast with the children is finished, the bell for school has rung, and they have all just taken their seat on the benches. Suddenly I receive the message that one of my pupils, the son of a lurah (head of a desa), has died and is already buried. I have my horse saddled, take leave of the children, and commence the five kilometer trip to the village where the child has died. It is beautiful, clear weather. I ride along the small mountain trails, overgrown on both sides with hedges full of fragrant wild roses. The trails are full of mud, as we are in the rainy season, but my horse is keen to ride whether uphill or downhill.

Here and there I meet politely squatted or friendly greeting Javanese. They all know the ndoro nona suster (mistress-miss-sister) from Gambang Waluh and according to local custom ask: 'Where are you going to?' It is a polite greeting, something like our: 'How are you?' …

Small, naked children and mothers with sucklings in the slendang (carriage towel), and men ready to go to the djagung (corn) field with two baskets attached to a stick on their shoulders assemble at the entry of the kampong.

I ask for the house of the lurah and someone kindly shows me the way. I descend and leave my horse in the custody of the boy that came with me. On foot, I enter the kampong – now, that means something in the rainy season. For the first time in my life, I come to think that high heels under my shoes might be of use, because here and there I sink into the mud! Slipping now and then, I slowly wrestle my way ahead, holding onto the hedge alongside the path and finally I arrive at the reason for my journey – a fairly large house, surrounded by a big yard …

A rather young woman, yet already the mother of eight big children, with tousled hair and a tear-stained face appears. She is the mother of the deceased child. She points me to a seat on the couch and silently squats at my feet. As I cautiously start to talk about the little boy, the far-away look in her eyes disappears and she softly cries. She sits there, looking so helpless and hunched up, with her head resting on her knees – an image of misery. Then she starts to speak, slowly and monotonously. He was such a nice lad, quick and clever and not at all proud … Always good and kind to his lonely mother – and now he was dead. *Tuan Allah* (the Lord God) had punished her badly. But why? She did not know. She was a pure woman who never sinned. For already eleven years, she had been loyal to her husband, who because of murder, has been banished to Celebes for fifteen years. She never wronged a person, had always cared for her child during the short period of his illness, and had given him all the obat [medicine] prescribed by the dukuns [tradional healer] – and now Allah punished her. She did not understand it, but the will of Allah is good, very good.

I tried to comfort her, but the words seem to slide over her. She had eyes only for the child before her, lying on the bench, who has died suddenly – and she did not know why. But, the will of Allah was good – *langkung dening sahé* (very good!)

I peer outside and pray to God to inspire me what to say. Poor, subjected, slavish souls! What do they understand of the will of God? ... I start to talk to her about the life after this life, about the love of God revealed in His Son, Jesus Christ. She really listens attentively. Her eldest son enters and also squats on his knees.

I ask permission to pray. *'Oh inggih – sahé!'* ('O yes that is good.')

In the middle of the prayer, she calls with a loud voice to her daughter who has appeared at the door: 'Come in and bring the coffee here for ndoro'.

Used as I am to such disturbances, I calmly close my prayer ... . Then, I say goodbye, and the whole family sees me off. The mother heartily thanks me for the love shown to her and her child. Then I ride back the same way thinking about the big problem: 'How can one win these poor souls, quite set in their old ways , sunk in sins, for the Saviour?' And then my Bible gives only one answer: 'God be praised, who always gives us victory in Christ'. Yes, that is how it is!

We slowly approach Gambang Waluh. My horse smells the barn and starts to trot. Underneath us, in a valley, are the buildings with their sink roofs, surrounded by high dark trees shining in the bright sunlight – a lovely, picturesque spot on God's earth. The children see us approaching, and rejoicing, they rush towards us.

I lift up one onto the horse, and with a cheerful command, the horse heads home[37]

Changes

In the course of 1921, big changes come into being. The work among the mentally deficient becomes eligible for subsidy.[38] A Government advisor, Dr. Engelhard, inspects the colony and finds the situation untenable. The buildings do not meet governmental requirements, and raising new buildings in such an isolated place with no electricity and water is not recommended. He also criticizes the selection policy employed by Moes, who accepts anyone in need, believing that the means will be provided. In the inspector's eyes, this is a big mistake.[39] Since Moes wants to remain for the sake of the Javanese, the Committee of the Mission Enterprise decides to split the work.[40] The subsidized part will move to Temanggung in November 1921. This consists of the work among the mentally deficient and the Indo-European patients. Vizjak and Keil will go to Temanggung.[41] Slagter finds temporary employment elsewhere and, from June 1922, will take over the work of Jansz in Pangungsen.[42] Moes is to remain with the Javanese orphans in order to dedicate herself fully to the work among the Javanese. The old house, where she lived with the children for seven years, is in such a deplorable state that it must be torn down.

---

[37] M.A. Alt, 'Uit Gambang Waloh', *De Boodschapper* 47 (April 1922), pp. 92–96.

[38] For the pioneer labour of the House of Mercy at Gambang Waluh the Mission Enterprise is eligible to receive a contribution of 3/4 of the running costs. In the Budger 1921 the Minister of Colonies has already made a provison: 'Begrooting van Nederlandsch-Indie voor het dienstjaar 1921, 4.10', *Handelingen der Staten-Generaal. Bijlagen 1920–1921*, appendix B, p. 77.

[39] D.J.B. Wijers, 'Mijn Brief IX', *De Vredebode* 8.339 [October or November 1921], p. 3. R.J. Horstman is still secretary and D. Graafstal is chairman.

[40] M.A. Alt, 'Een brief van Zuster Alt', *De Boodschapper* 45 (November 1921), pp. 281–83. Klara Keil, 'De Uittocht uit Gambang Waloh', *De Boodschapper* 47 (June 1922), pp. 155–58. In *Lichtstralen op den levensweg* Moes writes on 12 July 1921 to have decided to stay, solely for the Javanese.

[41] Keil with the female patients are housed in the former home of Wijers who is moving to Padalarang. Vizjak and the male patients for the time being go to the new home of chairman Graafstal. Wijers, 'Mijn Brief IX'.

[42] Vizjak and Keil marry on 6 August 1923 and in 1925 settle in Pangungsen to assist Slagter. The characters of Vizjak and Slagter do not match. In 1926 the couple Vizjak moves to the old Pangungsen, while Slagter remains in the new Pangungsen. Velthuijsen Jr., 'Nadere berichtgeving van het Indische Arbeidsveld', *De Boodschapper* 52 (January 1927), pp. 150–51.

During the demolition, it becomes apparent that they have been pro-
tected from disaster for years.[43] Moes and her children move to the
other house, a little higher up, that had been in use as a barn. The
bamboo walls are repaired. It is large enough to serve as an orphanage. Moes has thirty-six Javanese orphans under eight years of age
she wants to raise, among whom are five blind children.[44]

Yet Moes is not only occupied with the work on the mountain, as
is shown by a remarkable letter found in the library of the University
of Amsterdam. With much fear, and after long delay, Moes dares to
send a letter to the well-known writer, psychiatrist, and world-re-
former, Frederik Willem van Eeden (1860–1932). She has read several of his books. As a young girl she 'raved about' his philosophical
fairy-tale *De kleine Johannes* (*Little John*). She apologizes profusely for
her letter. Each time she tries to sideline it, the Holy Spirit insistently
prompts her to continue. The message she has for him from God is
in three words: 'Become a child'. She ends with excuses and 'No mor-
tal knows anything about this letter, it is something between me and
God'.[45] The letter comes in a period that Van Eeden is wrestling with
spiritual truths and experiences a conversion. On 18 February 1922,
he becomes a member of the Roman Catholic Church. Perhaps Moes
has written more such letters to people who have been influential in
her life.

In December 1921, Moes brings one of the orphans to the hospital at Ambarawa. The child dies of plague. The Committee against
Plague takes action. The house where the children live must be
cleared. The children move temporarily to the Slagter's former, much
smaller, home. A charity foundation donates money to make the

---

[43] Alt, 'Autobiografie 1943', p. 50.

[44] Alt, 'Een brief van Zuster Alt', (November 1921), pp. 281–83.

[45] M.A. Alt to F.W. van Eeden, Temanggung, 30 December 1921. Present in the
library of the University of Amsterdam under HSS-mag XXIV C1/Brief M.A. Alt
aan F.W. van Eeden. Nowhere in her writings is a reference to this letter. Moes does
sometimes quote a poem from Van Eeden such as 'Ik ben herkend' ('I have been
recognized') in *GS* 11.23 (December 1935), pp. 5–6, or 'De waterlelie' ('The water-
lily') in *GS* 17.3 (March 1948), p. 4, but under the heading 'The reborn heart'. In
March 1948 Moes ends her brochure about what happens to unborn children, 'Wat
geschiedt er met ongeboren kinderen?', with Van Eeden's poem 'Toen ons kindje
glimlachte' ('When our little child was smiling'). In the publication of Van Eeden's
diaries no reference to Alt's letter has been found. Frederik van Eeden, *Dagboek
1878–1923 Volume 4 1919–1923* (ed. H.W. van Tricht; Culemborg: Tjeenk Will-
ink/Noorduijn, 1971).

houses suitable for living. Moes, who has not asked anyone but the Lord for help, sees this as a confirmation that her calling is in Gambang Waluh.[46]

Moes now has more time to do home visitations. In a letter of February 1922, she gives the vivid description of such a visit cited above.[47] It is the last report of Moes in *De Boodschapper*. A handwritten note in her devotional book *Lichtstralen* reveals that her decision to renounce the Sabbath is made on 22 February 1922.[48] The Saturday that weekend, she writes, is for the first time a normal working day, and the church assembles on Sunday. Probably around this time she lays down her uniform as nurse. From August 1922, the designation for the donations in *De Boodschapper* is no longer 'for the labour at Gambang Waluh,' but 'for the labour of the Sisters at Temanggung'. In the December issue the editor explains:

> To our deep regret Sister Alt has completely separated herself from our assembly. Her work is no longer consistent with the practices of our assembly, which is the reason why we *as assembly* can no longer support her ...
> We are not at all hostile against her, although we think she errs.[49]

It is a terrible blow for the Haarlem SDB-church, because the work of Moes has always been warmly supported. The annual report of 1922, presented in March 1923, mentions:

> How we were so powerfully shaken awake in the beginning of 1922 by the message that came to us that Sister Alt had left the Sabbat and had taken with her the whole assembly of Javanese Christians ... A sharp pain was felt by us all, not least by our pastor, who so gladly called the labour of Sister Alt a treasure of the assembly.[50]

---

[46] M.A. Alt, 'Uit Gambang Waloh', *De Boodschapper* 47 (March 1922), pp. 48, 62–63 (62-63).

[47] M.A. Alt, 'Uit Gambang Waloh', *De Boodschapper* 47 (April 1922), pp. 92–96.

[48] C. Kuyper (trans.), *Lichtstralen op den Levensweg* (Amsterdam: Egelings Boekhandel, 1903), a tiny format book providing a Bible text for each day, morning and evening. Moes makes notes in the margin.

[49] De Redactie, 'Donker Java', *De Boodschapper* 47 (December 1922), p. 326.

[50] M. v.d. S., 'Jaarverslag van de Gemeente van Zevendedags Baptisten te Haarlem over 1922', *De Boodschapper* 49 (March 1923), p. 42. However in her letter of 16 January 1922, Moes still mentions meetings on Sabbath morning. M.A. Alt, 'Uit Gambang Waloh', *De Boodschapper* 47 (March 1922), p. 48.

At the annual Conference of the Union of SDB in August 1923, the pastor adds: 'Sister Alt has joined the so-called Pentecostal church and has taken the inland assembly along with her in the renouncing of the Lord's Sabbath'.[51] The next chapter describes how Moes came to this transition, but starts with a sketch of the beginning of the Pentecostal Movement.

Gambang Waluh Panoramic View (1920)
Living Quarters on the Left

---

[51] G. Velthuijsen Jr., 'Een waarlijk vruchtbaar leven en de gevaren die het bedreigen', *De Boodschapper* 48 (March 1923), p. 42. According to Slagter, who had already left Gambang Waluh when it happened, Moes became very ill and at that time when her body was weak she adopted the teaching of Johan de Heer about leaving the Sabbath. C. Slagter, 'Een aandoenlijke ontboezeming en een roepstem', *De Boodschapper* 53 (November 1928), p. 161.

8

TRANSITION TO THE PENTECOSTAL MOVEMENT

Faster and louder the words came from my lips. I was not accustomed to praying that loud, but then it was as if I could do nothing else. My praise changed into the words: 'glory' and 'hallelujah' – and lo and behold, there the power of God suddenly came upon me. No one had prayed with me; no one had laid hands upon me. Just as at my conversion, it was only the precious Holy Spirit himself who touched me and filled me with himself.[1]

Beginning of the Pentecostal Movement

The Pentecostal Movement emerged at the beginning of the twentieth century. Its chief characteristic is the emphasis on the work of the Holy Spirit. Believers are called to seek a 'baptism with the Holy Spirit'. It is a revival of the gifts of the Holy Spirit as seen at the time of the New Testament. Prophecy, healing, speaking in tongues, and deliverance from evil spirits are reckoned to be in operation today. This 'outpouring of the Holy Spirit' is seen in the context of an imminent second coming of Christ which, in turn, gives a strong impulse to missionary endeavors. The gospel must be carried around the world. The Azusa Street revival in Los Angeles in1906 is of great importance to the development of the movement. Within a few years of Azusa Street, there are Pentecostal missionaries on all continents.

---

[1] M.A. Alt, 'Autobiografie 1943', p. 61.

In the Netherlands, the Pentecostal Movement starts in 1907 under the leadership of Gerrit and Wilhelmine Polman.

Johan and Anna Maria Thiessen
With Orphans in Pakantan, Sumatra (1912)

From the Dutch Pentecostal movement, several lines run to Java. Wilhelmine Polman-Blekkink was born and raised in Middle Java (Wonosobo), where her father was a teacher. Her sister, Marie, originally serves as a missionary on Java of the Salvation Army. Later, she serves with her husband, William Bernard, as missionaries of the Pentecostal movement. From 1912, Elise Scharten, from Amsterdam, is a Pentecostal missionary to China. Her brother-in-law and sister, Johannes and Jenneke Pik, are missionaries of the NZG in East Java. On her way to China or on the return journey, Elise occasionally makes a stopover on Java and gives lectures. In 1911, the ophthalmic surgeon, Dr. Piet Pilon, is a medical missionary of the Salatiga Mission in Middle Java. During his prepatory medical study in Amsterdam, he has attended the Pentecostal church for three years and received the baptism with the Holy Spirit.[2] Polman has been sending his Pentecostal periodical to the Dutch Indies since 1909. In 1920, the paper publishes a request from believers in the Dutch Indies to send Pentecostal missionaries to Java. In that year, Polman founds the Dutch Pentecostal Missionary Society. One year later, the first Pentecostal missionaries arrive in the Dutch Indies.

In 1921, Johan Thiessen (1869–1953) settles with his family at Bandung. In the same year, the unmarried Anna Gnirrep goes to Batavia. A year later, William and Marie Bernard-Blekkink (the sister of Wilhelmine Polman), along with their four daughters and Mina Hansen (from Denmark) settle in Temanggung.[3] They work together with the Reformed minister, Rev. R.J. Horstman and focus on the Javanese and Chinese population.[4] All these newcomers are missionaries of the Dutch Pentecostal Missionary Society. Also in 1921, two couples, Dik and Christine van Klaveren and Cornelis and Mies Groesbeek, are sent to Bali. They are former SA officers of Dutch origin sent by Bethel Temple, an independent Pentecostal Church in Seattle, Washington, led by W.H. Offiler (1875–1957). They feel called to Bali. However, in 1922, the government, afraid of unrest, compels them to move to Java.[5] Initially, all these Pentecostal missionaries work together on Java.

---

[2] Cornelis van der Laan, *Sectarian Against His Will* (Metuchen, NJ: Scarecrow, 1991), p. 243. 'A Dutch University Student´s Pentecost', *Cloud of Witnesses to Pentecost in India* 8 (August 1908), pp. 25–26.

[3] William Bernard (1866–1945), an English businessman, had lost his first wife in 1912. On 20 June 1914 he married Marie Henriette Blekkink (1882–1932), sister of Mrs. Polman. They left for Java in August 1922 together with Miss Mina Hansen (1893–1839) who had stayed about a year with the Polmans in Amsterdam. A.A. Boddy, 'Pentecostal Items', *Confidence* 5.2 (February 1912), p. 43. G.R.Polman, 'Uit den arbeid', *Spade Regen* 15.3 (June 1922), p. 46.

[4] Letter from Bernard in *Spade Regen* (November 1922), p. 128; Wm. Bernard, 'Java never had revival', *Things Old and New* 3.1 (April 1923), p. 7. Marie Bernard-Blekking, like her sister Wilhelmine born and raised in the Dutch Indies (Wonosobo), could speak Javanese.

[5] D. van Klaveran [sic] and C.L. van Klaveran, *Messengers of the Cross to the Peoples, Tribes, Nations of the Dutch East-Indies* (Seattle, Washington: Bethel Temple, [1926]).

Thiessen is born in Ukraine. After his studies in Switzerland and the Netherlands, he is the first missionary of the Dutch Mennonite Mission (DZV) in North Sumatra from 1902–1912. Back in the Netherlandst he lives in Apeldoorn for several years, where he is active in the Maranatha City Mission of Rev. J.H. Gunning. Gunning is a Reformed pastor and editor of the periodical *Pniël*. During this period, Thiessen joins the Pentecostal movement. On Java, Thiessen initially cooperates with the emeritus Reformed minister D.J.B. Wijers (1864–1923) and with the missionary C.J. Hoekendijk (1873–1948). Wijers wants to open a rest home in Bandung for those seeking rest and spiritual guidance. He sees in Thiessen the right person to lead the project. However, only few residents come, so the project fails. Thiessen often accompanies Hoekendijk on his evangelistic journeys. Hoekendijk has been a missionary of the NZV up to 1917. In the eyes of the NZV, he focuses too much on the Dutch and Indo-Europeans.[6] Therefore, together with Wijers, he establishes the 'Union of Evangelization' with the aim of reaching the Europeans with the gospel. Hoekendijk becomes an evangelist on behalf of the Union. He holds revival meetings throughout Java, organizes conferences, and edits the periodical *Vredebode* (*Messenger of Peace*). When Thiessen joins him on a journey, he witnesses to him of his Pentecostal experience.

Missionaries on Java have been warned against the Pentecostal movement, based on negative reports from Germany. The following events show how sensitive this issue is. At the Whitsuntide Conference of the Union of Evangelization in 1922 at Bandung, Hoekendijk preaches about the need for the baptism with the Holy Spirit and prays for a Pentecostal revival. When Polman publishes the sermon in his Pentecostal periodical *Spade Regen*, it leads Gunning in *Pniël* to draw the premature conclusion that Hoekendijk has joined the Pentecostal Movement.[7] The Evangelicals in the Netherlands

---

Van Klaveren had to leave Bali in April 1922 within three days. Groesbeek was allowed to stay until December. A.J.C. Kraft in 'Een bezoek aan Bali', *Nederlandsch Zendingsblad* 5.11 (1922), pp. 168–69, calls Groesbeek a Dutchman who speaks Malay.

[6] Th. van den End (ed.), *Bladen uit mijn levensboek: Autobiografie van Ds. C.J. Hoekendijk (1873–1948)* (The Hague: Boekencentrum, 1993).

[7] *De Vredebode* no. 371 (June 1922); 'Uit den Arbeid', *Spade Regen* 15.5 (August 1922), 77; J.H. Gunning JHz., 'De doop des Heiligen Geestes', *Pniël* 31.1604 (23 September 1922), pp. 301–302.

quickly explain that Gunning has made an unfortunate mistake.[8] In August 1922, Thiessen optimistically believes he has taken away some of the prejudices:

> By false reports and writings from the Netherlands, there were reservations against Pentecostalism. Among the missionaries, one was warned from Surabaya to Batavia against the dangerous Pentecostal spirit. Due to the many meetings that I held in the conferences, the opinion has changed. At present, there is a cry from Surabaya to Batavia in many small circles of believers: 'Oh God, give us a Pentecostal baptism'.[9]

In the meantime, the other Pentecostal missionaries have arrived in Java. Through Thiessen, Hoekendijk meets Van Klaveren, Groesbeek, and Bernard. For the first time he hears someone speaking in tongues.[10] Hoekendijk is cautious and remains aloof. Others inside the Union are more open to the Pentecostal message, like the Treasurer and head teacher, Derk H.W. Weenink van Loon (1870–1944)[11] and the Chairman Dr. Frederik M. Baron van Asbeck (1889–1968).[12] Hoekendijk, on the contrary, has more and more doubts. The cooperation breaks up after the events in Tjepu.

In 1923, a small circle of believers, led by Groesbeek, starts meeting at Tjepu in the house of George van Gessel, who works for the Batavian Petrol Company (BPM). On 29 March 1923, which is Good

---

[8] A. Winckel, 'Br. Hoekendijk', *Ons Orgaan* 17.271 (1 November 1922), p. 191. P.N. van der Laan, *The Question of Spiritual Unity: The Dutch Pentecostal Movement in Ecumenical Perspective* (PhD thesis, University of Birmingham, 1988), pp. 188–89.

[9] 'Letter from J. Thiessen', Bandung, 20 August 1922, *Spade Regen* 15.8 (November 1922), pp. 126–27.

[10] Van den End, *Bladen uit mijn levensboek*, pp. 174–75.

[11] Derk Hendrik Willem Weenink van Loon is born on 25 April 1870 at Ambt Almelo as son of Hendrik Willem Weenink van Loon, bookkeeper, and Johanna Berendina Wolbert. On 20 October 1897 he marries Louise Cornelie Obdam (1877–1944). Derk is a head teacher, he dies 16 July 1944 at Bandung in camp Tjihapit and is buried on the Dutch burial ground in honour of the war dead at Pandu at Bandung. https://www.genealogieonline.nl/genealogie-opdam-obdam/19763.php.

[12] Frederik Mari Baron van Asbeck, lawyer, leaves in 1919 for the Dutch Indies to work for the General Secretary in Buitenzorg. In 1924 he becomes professor of international public and comparative colonial law at the University of Law in Batavia. In 1934 he returns to Holland and becomes professor of comparative colonial law at Leiden. From 1959 until 1964 he is judge in the European Court of Human Rights. Already before his departure to Java Van Asbeck had some contact with the Dutch Pentecostal Movement.

Friday, fifteen of them are baptized in a river by Thiessen and Groesbeek.[13] That evening, while Thiessen administers the Lord Supper, a young man receives the baptism with the Holy Spirit. He speaks in tongues and has visions. More follow on Saturday and Easter Sunday. Weenink van Loon is present and writes an enthusiastic report for *Vredebode*. The article is published, without Hoekendijk being able to read it.[14] It announces a new Pentecost for Java. Hoekendijk has to act. Following his proposal, the annual meeting of the Union, in May 1923, resolves to remove all members sympathetic to the Pentecostal Movement. Weenink van Loon and Baron van Asbeck resign from the Committee.[15] Several judgmental articles from Hoekendijk follow in *Vredebode*.[16] Thiessen's attempt to integrate the Pentecost message into existing evangelical circles fails. He and Van Loon will become important leaders in the emerging Pentecostal Movement, which will now develop as a separate movement. Looking back, Hoekendijk writes: 'Thank God, the storm broke again, even though it destroyed a lot'.[17]

The events in Tjepu in March 1923 are seen as the beginning of the Pentecostal Movement in the Dutch Indies. According to Weenink van Loon, this was a major breakthrough: 'Neither on Bandung nor elsewhere in Java, so far, had one human child received the Baptism of the Holy Spirit (after Joel 2). This happened for the first time in these days in Tjepu'.[18] His report mentions a Menadonese girl, a servant of Van Gessel, who, in tongues, sings a heavenly song, singing 'Glory to Jesus' in correct English. The sequel when the girl lays hands upon Van Gessel is particularly moving:

> Even more it touched us, when she shortly after kneeled beside her master. While he was heartily pleading for the Holy Baptism of the Spirit, she prayed to her Saviour and blessed him laying her

---

[13] *Dit is Het* 1.1 (July 1923), p. 8.
[14] Weenink van Loon, 'Doorbraak te Tjepoe naar Joël 2 en Hand. 2 en10', *Spade Regen* 16.3 (June 1923), pp. 38–41. Reprinted from *Vredebode* and dated 4 April 1923.
[15] 'Bond voor Evangelisatie in Ned. O.-Indië', *Ons Orgaan* 18.280 (August 1923), pp. 268–69. Weenink van Loon, 'Korte uiteenzetting van mijn uittreden uit den Bond van Evangelisatie', *Dit is Het* 1.1 (July 1923), pp. 12–13.
[16] 'De Pinksterbeweging', *Ons Orgaan* 18.282 (October 1923), pp. 282–83; 18.283 (November 1923), pp. 290–91; 19.285 (January 1924), pp. 308–309; 19.286 (February 1924), pp. 315–16.
[17] Van den End, *Bladen uit mijn levensboek*, p. 176.
[18] Van Loon, 'Doorbraak te Tjepoe', p. 38.

hands on his back. Truly, with God there is no respect of the person, and with Him every difference of colour, race and status is absent from His holy sight! Hallelujah! Glory to Jesus! Ten souls received the baptism of the Holy Spirit.[19]

These are remarkable words in a colonial context. No wonder this article in *Vredebode* caused quite a stir. Thiessen enthusiastically writes to Polman:

> Finally, the first flames of fire fell over the Dutch Indies. Another era has come, also here for these islands. The first ten children of God were baptized with water and the Holy Spirit, according to God's Word, accompanied with tongues and visions and revelations, as if God has begun throughout the whole world to prepare His Bridal Church for the coming Christ ...] What has never happened in the [Dutch] Indies, happened at Easter 1923.[20]

A few days later several believers in Surabaya receive their Spirit baptism and then some in Bandung. No longer under the umbrella of the Union, it is necessary for the new grouping to obtain recognition from the government. On 19 June 1923, Thiessen and Weenink van Loon in Bandung found the Pinkstergemeente in Nederlandsch-Indië (PGNI – Pentecostal Church in the Dutch Indies).[21] The current Gereja Pantekosta di Indonesia (Pentecostal Church in Indonesia), the largest Pentecostal church in the country, is a direct continuation of the PGNI. From 18–22 May 1923, the first Pentecost Conference is held at Bandung. Van Klaveren, Groesbeek, Bernard, and Gnirrep are present and also Baron van Asbeck.[22] On Sunday morning, forty-two people are baptized in water by Thiessen and Bernard.[23] The same month the first issue of the monthly periodical *Dit is Het (This is That)* appears with Thiessen as editor. The paper explains that it has nothing to do with the Union of Evangelization or with *Vredebode*. On 4 June 1924, the PGNI is recognized by the government as

[19] Van Loon, 'Doorbraak te Tjepoe', p. 41.
[20] 'Letter from J. Thiessen', (June 1923), pp. 33–45.
[21] *Spade Regen* 16.4 (July 1923), p. 63. J. Thiessen, 'Dit is het' *Dit is Het* 1.1 (July 1923), p. 69.
[22] Letter from Wm. Bernard in *Things Old and New* 3.3 (August 1923), p. 7.
[23] Letter from Wm. Bernard in *Spade Regen* 16.4 (July 1923), p. 63.

a legal institution.[24] Thiessen and Weenink van Loon are licensed to evangelize in the regency of Preanger (Bandung etc.) among Europeans and Chinese. Thiessen does not obey the geographical restriction and therefore collides with the established order. The relationship between Thiessen and Weenink van Loon is becoming difficult, possibly because the latter represents a different attitude towards the government. Weenink van Loon informs the press in July 1924 that the PGNI no longer associates itself with Thiessen.[25] Thiessen sets up a new group: De Pinksterbeweging (The Pentecostal Movement). While Thiessen continues the periodical *Dit is Het*, the PGNI, in October 1924, starts to issue *De Pinksterbode* (*The Pentecostal Messenger*), edited by Marie Bernard-Blekkink. In 1925, when the Bernard family has to leave the mission field due to illness, the *Pinksterbode* will be replaced by *Pinksterkracht* (*Pentecostal Power*), edited by Feodoor van Abkoude.[26]

Through the years 1923–1926, Thiessen is frequently mentioned in the newspapers. Originally, it is because he evangelizes without permission and is fined for it.[27] In the course of 1924, the reports become more hostile. Thiessen is called a fanatic who, during his 'séances', victimizes children and mentally defenseless women. The descriptions are full of contempt and bias: 'When the show really gets going, women writhe on the floor, screaming epileptically; girls are shouting and crying, until a kind of fit associated with religious mania

[24] N.A.C. Slotemaker de Bruine (zendingsconsul) to the Directeur van Onderwijs en Eeredienst, Weltevreden, 30 August 1924. Cf. 'De Pinkster-beweging', *Bataviaasch Nieuwsblad* (6 June 1924). Besluit gouverneur-generaal 4 April 1925 no. 28.

[25] 'De Pinkstergemeente te Bandoeng', *Indische Courant* (22 July 1924). Thiessen announces his meetings in Weltevreden in advertisements. The last time that he uses the name Pinkstergemeente is on 5 July 1924 (in *Het Nieuws van den dag voor N.I.*). One week later he uses the name Pinksterbeweging.

[26] In April 1924, Bernard was in England by himself for a short period. In December 1924, their eight-year-old daughter, Dorothy Mary, died of an illness in Temanggung. In January 1925, the Bernard family had to leave the mission field due to Bernard's illness. *Spade Regen* 17.2 (May 1924), p. 28; 17.11 (February 1925), p. 176; 17.12 (March 1925), p. 192. In the Summer of 1927, Bernard visits Java again and spends a few day in Gambang Waluh. In his report of this visit, published in 1928, he writes about having been a missionary there for about three years, which would fit 1922–1925, but then adds: 'coming home last September on account of broken health'. This would imply a missionary service during 1925–1927, which contradicts the many reports in *Spade Regen* and, therefore, seems to be in error. Wm. Bernard, 'Pentecost in Java', *The Latter Rain* 20.6 (March 1928), pp. 22–23.

[27] 'Voortgaande propaganda', *Bataviaasch Nieuwsblad* (15 June 1923).

follows'.[28] According to the same author, while the 'devil is being banished', the patient is laying on the floor and is bumped about and stepped upon until the devil is out! Another author warns that it could easily arouse the Javanese audience to cause accidents, because the 'light-receptive and fanatical Oriental' could, out of pure excitement, start to make stabbing movements.[29] Weenink van Loon informs the readers that the PGNI has no business with the 'famous Thiessen' and has nothing to do 'with his despicable jokes'.[30] The psychiatrist, Dr. E.A.G. Van Loon, accuses Thiessen of being dangerous to people's health. The police start an investigation, but eventually the matter is hushed up, and Thiessen gets his desired freedom to evangelize.[31] This venomous press campaign probably explains why it takes Moes a few years before joining the Pentecostal Movement, and why, in her autobiography, the role of Thiessen is so minimal.

Contact with the Pentecostal Movement

Her diary reveals that already in 1911 Moes is searching for a baptism with the Holy Spirit. Having read the periodical *Spade Regen* in June 1912, she longs for the 'full Pentecostal blessing … with unknown languages, healing, prophecy – but above all – the love'.[32] She has already internalized many of the ideas of the Pentecostal Movement:

> I have learned that a healthy Christian life consists of three parts. First is justification, which is rebirth. Second is sanctification, what is what the Salvation Army calls having a clean heart. This means that you have given yourself into death with Christ in order to rise in a new life with Him. Finally, third is the baptism with the Spirit, revealed in gifts and powers.[33]

---

[28] 'De z.g. Pinkster-gemeente en hare gevaren', *Nieuws van den Dag voor Nederlandsch-Indië* (13 December 1924).

[29] 'De geestdrijver Thiessen', *Sumatra Post* (5 June 1924).

[30] 'Pinksterbeweging', *Nieuws van den Dag voor Nederlandsch-Indië* (22 December 1924), on the front page.

[31] H. Patoir, *De waarheid omtrent de Pinksterbeweging in Nederlands-Indië* (Bandung: De Pinksterbeweging, [1926]), gives a summary of the letters of protest from the Board of the Pinksterbeweging to the Parliament and the People's Council.

[32] M.A. Alt, 'Dagboek 1910–1919', 18 June 1912.

[33] Alt, 'Dagboek 1910-1919', 18 June 1912.

Moes positions herself somewhere halfway through the second step and sees sanctification as a condition of receiving the Spirit baptism: 'It is perfectly clear to me that I have to obey in everything to be able to receive the blessing'.[34] She writes to Gerrit Polman of the Pentecostal church in Amsterdam and receives a reply: 'I received a wonderful letter from Brother Polman, which comforted and delighted me'.[35] Marie Jansz, too, is searching for the Spirit baptism. Jansz reads the Pentecostal periodical *Cloud of Witnesses to Pentecost in India*, which she receives from a missionary in India. Since 1907, the periodical has been issued by Max Wood Moorhead at Bombay. Jansz writes to the editor how much she and Moes pray for the Spirit: 'Sister Alt is sorry that she cannot read English, but I have told her everything that I read in your paper. She is a very sweet girl that with all her heart longs to receive the baptism with the Holy Spirit.'[36]

William Bernard and Marie Bernard-Blekkink
in Amsterdam (1921)

---

[34] Alt, 'Dagboek 1910-1919', 18 June 1912.

[35] Alt, 'Dagboek 1910-1919', 5 September 1912.

[36] Max Wood Moorhead, 'Clouds of Latter Rain Gathering Over Island of Java', *The Bridegroom's Messenger* (1 February 1913), p. 4. In the report an extended letter from M. Jansz dated 25 October 1912.

The subject keeps Moes occupied for some time, but then it seems to move into the background. Possibly she has become frightened by the warnings against the movement.

In 1918, her co-worker, Vizjak, gives her several issues of the German Pentecostal periodical *Pfingstgrüsse*. Moes is cautious, but Vizjak speaks with enthusiasm of a Conference of the Pentecostal Church he attended at Zurich.[37] Curious, Moes starts to read deep in the night. A new world opens up to her. She subscribes to the Swiss Pentecostal periodical *Verheissung des Vaters* and reads books by Jonathan Paul, the German Pentecostal leader. She prays for the fullness of the Holy Spirit. A brochure by Jonathan Paul about the true Sabbath, Moes writes, 'shakes the foundations of my legalistic building'. Although it takes a few more years before she receives the Spirit baptism, she would later write that it was through the writings of Jonathan Paul that she came to Pentecost.[38]

In February 1922, she receives definitive new light on the Sabbath. In a dream, she sees an empty cross on a hill. Where once 'It is finished' has been spoken, she now sees 'The Seventh-Day', written in large letters.[39] She breaks with the Seventh-Day Baptists. Immediately, she calls the church members together, and they decide to follow her. From that moment they have their meetings on Sunday.[40] The earlier splitting up of the work in late 1921, leaving Moes at Gambang Waluh by herself, will have made her choice a lot easier. The rupture causes her much pain, as she had a strong tie with the SDB-church:

> My letting go of the Sabbath necessarily caused a rupture with this lovely assembly in Holland, but I could not but follow my principles. The Holy Spirit forced me to act. A storm of reproach broke out around my head, especially when it became clear that the whole assembly followed me.[41]

Moes now stands alone with her Javanese assembly. She understands that it is important to adhere to an existing denomination for the future of the congregation: 'So I prayed earnestly to God to show me a church that shared my principles and with whom I would feel

---

[37] Alt, 'Hoe Gods Geest op Gambang Waloeh viel 1', *GS* 17.5 (May 1948), p. 4.

[38] M.A. Alt to E. van der Molen, Surabaya, 11 July 1950.

[39] M.A. Alt, 'Gedachten over de Sabbat', *GS* 9.3 (February 1936), p. 4.

[40] M.A. Alt, *Herinneringen uit mijn leven* (Velp: Pinksterzending, 1963), pp. 56–58.

[41] Alt, 'Autobiografie 1943', p. 55.

one'.[42] Nonetheless, it takes a few years before Moes joins the Pentecostal movement. While Moes has more than forty orphans to care for, the financial support for the missionary work ended with her departure. There is no money for djagung (corn) and rice, so they live from the marrow of the sago-tree and from ketela (cassava).[43]

At the home of the aforementioned Rev. R.J. Horstman in Temanggung, Moes in 1920 has met the Pentecostal missionary, Elise Scharten, who was giving lectures on Java on her way from China to the Netherlands. For the first time in her life, Moes hears someone speaking in tongues. Horstman is Committee member of the Mission Enterprise that oversees Gambang Waluh and is a friend of Graafstal. His son, Henri E. Horstman (1899–1988), his daughter, Regien (1896–1988), and her husband, Feodoor N.M. van Abkoude (1895–1988) will later all become leaders in the Pentecostal movement, together with Moes. In 1922, the Bernards and Mina Hansen move to Temanggung to work there together with the elderly Rev. Horstman.

In September 1922, Thiessen and Gnirrep come to visit Moes. Thiessen afterwards describes Moes as someone 'who had tired herself in legalism, but now throws herself with everything she is and has into the full Pentecostal stream ... The veils of unnecessary martyrdom fell from her eyes'.[44] One month later, Thiessen is again in Gambang Waluh. Together with Bernard, he baptizes thirty-seven people on Sunday morning. All the baptized receive a new self-chosen name. In the evening they celebrate the Lord's Supper and pray for the baptism with the Holy Spirit. According to Thiessen, nobody is as happy as Moes: 'Repeatedly she went on her knees and thanked God with tears of joy for the blessing received. The Spirit of liberty broke through. And, they all began to pray aloud and praise and thank God, which had never happened before'.[45] In the report, it is as if Thiessen was instrumental in her break with the Sabbath, but we have already seen that this happened half a year before. Thiessen further mentions that Moes received letters from a friend with warnings about the Pentecostal movement copied from the periodical *Het*

[42] Alt, 'Autobiografie 1943', p. 55.
[43] M.A. Alt, 'Hoe Gods Geest op Gambang Waloeh viel 1', pp. 4–5.
[44] 'Letter from J. Thiessen', *Spade Regen* 15.9 (December 1922), p. 143. Letter dated 30 September 1922.
[45] 'Letter from J. Thiessen', *Spade Regen* (January 1923), pp. 159–60. Letter dated 1 November 1922.

Zoeklicht (*The Searchlight*). In the report made by Bernard, mention is made of the thirty-seven baptized, but we do not read how Moes responds to the visit.[46]

It is striking that, in her publications, Moes does not mention Thiessen's visits, while Thiessen makes so much of them. Her unpublished autobiography of 1943 reveals that Thiessen left a completely different impression on Moes:

> When I told him I longed for the Spirit baptism, he laid hands upon me. But his busy and passionate prayer, while shaking my head to and fro, frightened me in such a way that I said to myself, 'The Spirit baptism can never come in this manner. God is a God of order and the Holy Spirit a dove of peace'. After that, I decidedly turned away from the Pentecostal movement. But the Lord led me peacefully to His will, and, yes, in the direction of Pentecost.[47]

This unfavourable experience with Thiessen, the negative messages in various publications, and the warnings of friends make Moes careful. Meanwhile, she talks to the church about the baptism with the Holy Spirit. In 1926, George van Gessel (1893–1958) visits Gambang Waluh. He has resigned from his job at the BPM and is now the pastor of the Pentecostal church in Surabaya.[48] He preaches in the church and invites Moes to the forthcoming conference in Surabaya. On the last day of the three-day conference, 31 July 1926, everyone in the room is praying. Kneeling in front of her chair, Moes pleads for the Pentecostal blessing. Nobody lays hands on her or talks to her. She feels urged to praise God, first softly and then louder. All

---

[46] Wm. Bernard, 'Java never had revival', *Things Old and New* 3.1 (April 1923), pp. 8–9.

[47] Alt, 'Autobiografie 1943', p. 59. Perhaps her turning away from the Pentecostal Movement here refers to the 'Pinksterbeweging' that Thiessen would found in 1923. In one of the few other occasions that Thiessen is mentioned by Moes, she writes in answer to a question of a reader: 'Brother Thiessen was not present at my water baptism, nor at my Spirit baptsm. My spiritual father in Pentecost was not Brother Thiessen, but Pastor Paul'. M.A. Alt, 'Correspondentie', *GS* 11.21 (November 1938), p. 17. Remarkably Thiessen writes in the same month that a woman is not permitted to stand on the platform or to lead the assembly or to act as as an evangelist. J. Thiessen, 'Verklaren van moeilijke teksten', *Dit is Het* 15.11 (November 1938), p. 9. In an earlier article Thiessen had been more positive about the role of women allowing them to act as evangelists: J. Thiessen, 'De Dienst der Vrouw', *Dit is Het* 15.11 (November 1938), pp. 324–26.

[48] Cf. *Biografie F.G. van Gessel* (Amsterdam: Bride Tidings International, n.d.).

fear of men disappears: 'The glory of God flooded me'.[49] Her whole body is trembling, and she hears herself singing and talking in strange sounds.[50] Then it is as if she hears the singing of angels, 'tender, tuneful and high pitched with the plucking of harps'.[51] Soon she sings a wonderful song in tongues. Until two o'clock at night, she continues to prophesy, and she has glorious visions: 'Everything was shown to me in images and visions, along with many things concerning the future'.[52] This experience marks her transition to the Pentecostal movement.[53]

The little ones with the great ones

> After I had been baptized with the Holy Spirit, I longed to return quickly to my assembly in the mountains. The Lord had answered my prayer, and I felt happy in my soul. During my trip, I saw in a vision a mountain with streams of water descending from the top downwards.[54]

Back in Gambang Waluh, Moes calls together her family of forty-six children and three helpers and tells them what has happened to her. The same evening a number of them receive the Spirit baptism, including fifteen-year-old Dorcas. She is the first among the Javanese to receive this blessing. In a vision, Moes sees a bubbling waterfall next to Dorcas and feels that this contains a promise of streams of living water for the entire Javanese people.[55] That night Moes sees in a dream sweet angels floating over the children's house and hears the voice of the Lord: 'I will bless them, the little ones with the great ones'.[56] The next day the whole assembly is called together. Full of surprise because it's an ordinary working day, they come from the

---

[49] M.A. Alt, 'De doop met de Heilige Geest', *GS* 21.3 (March 1952), p. 5.

[50] Alt, *Herinneringen, p.* 63. Cf. M.A. Alt, 'Java', *Spade Regen* 20.4 (July 1927), pp. 63–64.

[51] Alt, 'Hoe Gods Geest op Gamabang Waloeh viel 1', p. 6.

[52] Alt, 'Autobiografie 1943', p. 61.

[53] In this book the term 'Pentecostal Movement' is generally used in the broader sense. Whenever the term refers to the group led by Thiessen, it will be indicated or the Dutch term 'Pinksterbeweging' will be used.

[54] Alt, 'Autobiografie 1943', p. 63.

[55] M.A. Alt, 'Gambang Waloh', *Pinksterkracht* 3.2 (February 1927), pp. 15–16. Also in *Spade Regen* 20.2 (May 1927), pp. 31–31.

[56] Alt, 'Gambang Waloh', (February 1927), p. 15.

field. With silent awe, they listen to the testimony of their spiritual mother. One of the brothers asks permission to speak:

> He began to speak, but could not continue. Overcome by emotion, he stuttered and began to tremble – and in the same moment God's Spirit fell on him and he praised God in foreign languages. That stirred the assembly. The people began to cry and to confess their sins. One after another was baptized with the wonderful Spirit – about sixty were baptized in succession. The Spirit of the Lord also fell on the little ones. We heard children, aged from three to four, praising God in tongues. They later formed small prayer groups, entirely on their own initiative.[57]

A revival now starts among the mountain people. Five months later, Moes writes that every day seeking souls come to her house. Every evening, Christians gather in their own homes to read God's Word, 'Their singing sounds sweet in the silence of the evening'.[58] And four months later she: 'My church, formerly so stiff and predictable, has changed completely. Five young men regularly go out to evangelize in the surrounding villages, voluntarily without payment. In a short time, seven villages are reached with the Gospel.'[59] These five 'workers' or 'evangelists' watch over the congregation when Moes is away and anoint the sick with oil.[60]

During the prayer sessions there are striking visions and prophecies among the children also. Moes writes them down in a book. A little boy sees heaven opened and the angels of God descending. A little girl sees the Lord Jesus nailed to the cross and kneels down before Him. The same girl sees in a vision a well filled with water, to which many sheep come to drink. Martha, a nine-year-old girl, sees a white dove besides a flame of fire. The ten-year-old Jakobah finds herself in a flower filled courtyard where the Saviour is surrounded by children who offer him flowers. A nine-year-old boy sees the Saviour with a lamb in his arms.[61] An old brother, a former dukun (traditional healer), moves his hand as if drinking from a cup. Moes touches him and asks what he is doing. 'Well', he said with a radiant

---

[57] Alt, 'Autobiografie 1943', p. 65.
[58] Alt, 'Gambang Waloh', (February 1927), p. 16.
[59] Alt, 'Java', p. 64.
[60] Alt, 'Gambang Waloh', *Pinksterkracht* 3.8 (August 1927), p. 15.
[61] Alt, *Herinneringen*, pp. 66–68; M.A. Alt, 'Hoe Gods Geest op Gambang Waloeh viel 2', *GS* 17.6 (June 1948), p. 4.

face, 'the Lord Jesus stands here in front of me. He is giving me water from a jar and He says, "Drink, Paq (father), drink!" Will I then not drink?'[62] Under inspiration of the Holy Spirit, new songs come up spontaneously. There are also visions and prophetic dreams about the coming war. Moes sees a male figure with the appearance of a beast, hairy and frightening. His mantle is striped and spotted like a panther. He opens his robe, and on his chest is a large, jet-black swastika. He points to it with a stretched out finger and a proud gesture.[63] Hitler is still a rising star in this year (1926). In a dream (1927), a church member finds himself in a port city where there is a great stir and noise from explosives. Everyone is anxious and people are fleeing. A gentleman who is busy loading a car, says that our fleet is at war and that the city will be destroyed. Moes adds later that this city is likely to be Surabaya and that the prophecy was fulfilled in 1942.[64]

Pupils of the Christian Dutch-Chinese School from Temanggung journey up the hill with their teachers. Some keep on praying for half the night until they receive the blessing. Aaf Graafstal is also teaching in Temanggung. She comes with thirty-three children from her Sunday school to stay the weekend. Eight children receive their Spirit baptism.[65] Frequently people are healed after prayer. The son of a village chief head is cured after the evangelists pray for him. They now receive many invitations to bring the gospel into the Islamic desas. From the beginning, Moes has a kind of a clinic for sick Javanese. Since her Spirit baptism, she and her housemates have decided not to use any medicine. She leaves the church members completely free, but gradually the members refuse medicine and trust God for healing. Moes still keeps the clinic open for the sick from outside the church. When the doctor at Ambarawa writes that he is no longer able to provide medication, she decides to close the clinic.[66] From now on she prays with those who come to her from the surrounding kampongs; some are healed, but many are not.[67]

---

[62] M.A. Alt, 'Hoe Gods Geest op Gambang Waloeh viel 4', *GS* 17.8 (August 1948), p. 3.

[63] Alt, *Herinneringen*, p. 69; M.A. Alt, 'Hoe Gods Geest op Gambang Waloeh viel 3', *GS* 17.7 (July 1948), p. 4.

[64] Alt, *Herinneringen*, p. 69. Alt, 'Hoe Gods Geest op Gambang Waloeh viel 3', p. 4.

[65] Alt, 'Hoe Gods Geest op Gambang Waloeh viel 4', p. 4.

[66] Alt, 'Gambang Waloh', *Pinksterkracht* 3.8 (August 1927), pp. 15–16.

[67] Alt, 'Hoe Gods Geest op Gambang Waloeh viel 3', pp. 4–5.

Convent Evangelists in 1930 in Bandung
Standing: H. Horstman, F. van Abkoude, couple Van Klaveren
Sitting: F.G. van Gessel, M.A. Alt, D. Weenink van Loon.

There are also confrontations with evil powers. Moes is reluctant to write about this herself, but a witness tells the following story. A dukun from a neighbouring village sees his customers decreasing in number. He visits the meetings and tries to silence Moes with his powers. When this fails, he stands up and challenges Moes to a power test. The loser must leave the area. Before the eyes of all the people of the church, he lies on the ground, and after some moments, he becomes stiff. His body slowly rises and glides at knee height above the ground. The people are getting excited. Moes pushes him to the ground and shouts: 'Down, in Jesus' Name'. She commands the evil spirits to leave. The dukun shakes violently and vomits. In the end, he stands up, delivered, and says: 'Something has happened! My strength is gone, but I feel joy in my heart'. He repents and receives the Holy Spirit through the laying on of hands.[68]

In spite of the miracles, Moes is tortured by malaria day and night, with head and back pain, dizziness, and pressure on the brain. Since her baptism in the Holy Spirit, she uses no medication. Her prayers for healing are not answered; instead, she hears, 'My grace is sufficient'. The special time of revival passes and Moes comments in a down-to-earth manner: 'All revivals are of a temporary nature and then we are led in quiet paths again'.[69] In her autobiography she writes:

> What were the results of this revival? In most Christians, the life of faith was deepened, and many who still had secretly held to pagan habits now turned to the Lord entirely. The glory of the awakening slowly passed – but the fruits have remained.[70]

As an example of lasting fruit, Moes also describes the great freedom of expression. Moes writes that the Javanese are extremely sensitive to mocking or criticism. Therefore, it is very difficult to get someone in the congregation to testify. However, since the baptism with the Holy Spirit, there is boldness to testify. When Moes begins to pray, the congregation responds with, 'Hallelujah!' 'Glory!' or 'Amen!' There is singing in the Spirit, crying and rejoicing.[71]

---

[68] Lester Sumrall, *Adventuring with Christ* (London: Marshall, Morgan & Scott, 1938. Reprint South Bend, Indiana: LeSea, 1988), pp. 41–43. During the visit of Sumrall to Gambang Waluh in 1935 the former dukun shared his testimony. Cf. Lester J. Sumrall, 'How the Sorcerer's Power was Broken', *Pentecostal Evangel* (17 February 1940), p. 4.

[69] Alt, *Herinneringen,* p. 75.

[70] Alt, 'Autobiografie 1943', p. 71.

[71] M.A. Alt, 'Bruiloft in de desa', *GS* 8.13 (July 1932), p. 17.

9

NATIONAL MINISTRY

The prophecies in the Pentecostal churches almost always refer to great blessing: golden sheave of wheats, open doors, sparkling waterfalls, rustling rice fields, labourers sent out to the surrounding islands and to faraway lands – in short, abundance of fertility and blessing.[1]

After her Spirit baptism, Moes gets many invitations to preach in existing Pentecostal circles. More and more she becomes involved in a national ministry. It is as if the Lord is releasing her from Gambang Waluh. She experiences a commission from God to edit a periodical. In a vision, the Lord also shows her a large songbook with staves. From this she understands that she must publish a songbook. This motivates her to compile *Glo1ieklokken* (*Bells of Glory*) some years later. Her writing talents and musical gift are much in demand in the growing Pentecostal Movement.

Pinkstergemeente in Nederlandsch-Indië

Moes is recognized as an evangelist in the Pinkstergemeente in Nederlandsch-Indië (PGNI – Pentecostal Assembly in the Dutch Indies). The four-day Conference at Pentecost in Surabaya in April 1927 reveals a strong longing for unity. Reference is made to Psalm 133.1 'How good and how pleasant it is for brethren to dwell together

---

[1] M.A. Alt, 'En 't was avond geweest – en 't was morgen geweest – een nieuwen dag', *GS* 6.1 (January 1930), p. 16.

in unity'.[2] To advance the unity and take care of the spiritual affairs, a council is formed in September 1927 called a 'Convent of Evangelists'.[3] The Convent is seen as a concentration of power geared towards unity amongst the leaders. Van Abkoude agrees with the assessment made by Moes: 'The breadth and the depth of the greatness of the revival that is coming will depend upon the spiritual power of the leaders'.[4] Moes is the first secretary of the Convent. In the photos, she is now clothed in a white dress with a black tie, just like all the other female PGNI evangelists. The tie will later disappear, but a white dress will remain her standard outfit when she is leading meetings.

During the turbulent growth of the PGNI in this period, Moes plays an important role in binding people together. She writes articles for the periodical *Pinksterkracht (Pentecostal Power)*. From January 1928, she succeeds Feodoor van Abkoude as editor of *Pinksterkracht*. The periodical appears in Dutch, but for the Malay and Javanese readers, a separate magazine is anticipated. In September 1928, Moes changes the name of the periodical to *Gouden Schooven (Golden Sheaves* after Charles Price's *Golden Grain)*.[5] Moes writes: 'Our Pentecostal paper in a new robe and with a new name! … We are in the days of open doors, mature cornfields, golden sheaves: the wonderful days of the church.'[6]

The magazine becomes a lot more attractive. It gains illustrations, new columns for the youth, as well as correspondence with readers and extra pages. More attention is given to news from the member churches and evangelists. Readers are invited to submit family advertisements at low cost, as this strengthens the mutual love bond. Moes is clearly visible as editor, giving the magazine a face. Each issue begins with a poem or song, usually from Moes herself, followed by an article from her hand. She answers letters from readers, publishes her travel reports, and translates articles and songs from German and English Pentecostal periodicals. She also copies them from other

---

[2] F. van Abkoude, 'Uit den Arbeid', *Pinksterkracht* 3.10 (October 1927), p. 11
[3] M.A. Alt, 'De Pinkstergemeente', *GS* 6.2 (February 1930), pp. 19–20.
[4] Van Abkoude, 'Uit den Arbeid', p. 11.
[5] M.A. Alt, 'Wat verwacht de Gemeente Gods voor 1960?', *GS* 33.1 (1960), p. 4.
[6] Alt, 'Aan de lezers en lezeressen van ons blad', *GS* 4.9 (September 1928), p. 2.

Dutch magazines like *Pniël* and *Het Zoeklicht*. The translation work is time-consuming and will increasingly be taken over by others.

7e. JAARGNAG.   1931   No. 1

GOUDEN SCHOOVEN

Want de oogst is rijp geworden
Joël 3:13.

Aanschouwt de landen

Zij zijn reeds wit om te oogsten Joh. 4:35.

Typ. Theag Tjoen Gwan Magelang.

Gouden Schooven *cover (January 1931)*

The goal of reinforcing the bond between existing circles of believers on Java is soon expanded to all of the Dutch Indies. Each issue lists the addresses and hours of all the church meetings. The paper preaches the fourfold gospel: 1) Jesus the Saviour and Deliverer; 2) Jesus the Physician; 3) Jesus the Baptizer with the Holy Spirit; 4) Jesus the coming Bridegroom, Lord and King of Kings. Before the year 1929, Moes publishes a 'Pentecostal Daily-book,' *Het Volle Licht* (*The Full Light*), containing a morning and evening text for each day. It is the forerunner of the more extensive book of daily readings that appears in 1940 and will see many reprints.

Moes makes several round trips to the churches spread throughout Java. On a monthly basis, she visits the women's prison, Bulu, in Semarang with Mina Hansen. In April 1929, she looks back on her transition to Pentecostalism. Her former labour, she writes, was powerless; her Christian life a constant stumbling. She was advised to accept her sickness. In the Pentecostal assembly she learned freedom from sin, to pray for healing and for the baptism with the Holy Spirit.[7]

Departure from Gambang Waluh 1929

Several times George van Gessel has asked Moes to assist him in the work of the Pentecostal church in Surabaya. When he permits her to bring all the Javanese children who are under her care, she finally agrees. On 30 May 1929, she leaves Gambang Waluh, after almost fifteen years:

> In His great mercy, the Lord has given me many souls. He has been willing to glorify Himself in these few plain farmers in the midst of dark, pagan desas. When I hear them in the evening after their work in the field, singing our lovely Pentecostal songs in their own language,so beautifully and slowly as is their nature, I thank God that He has proved me worthy to sow His Holy Word here. I have no regrets, having spent nearly fifteen of the best years of my life here in the mountains.[8]

When she arrived in 1914, there were no converted Javanese in the area. At her departure, there is a village with only Christians and a

---

[7] M.A. Alt, 'Waarom ik mij bij de Pinkstergemeente heb aangesloten', *GS* 5.4 (April 1929), pp. 3–6.
[8] M.A. Alt, 'Gambang Waloeh', *GS* 5.6 (June 1929), pp. 18–19.

church with over 300 baptized members. She leaves Joenoes, from nearby Porot, for years her right hand man, in charge of the assembly, together with Elias, Jakoboes, Stefanoes, and Iskaq.[9] Those who predicted that the assembly would fall apart after her departure are proved wrong. The assembly remains stable and even grows when, in 1931, Joenoes receives his baptism with the Spirit. Every day seeking souls come to his home, and many sick are healed.[10]

Moes remains in touch with the church. Every two months she visits the village. Every time it is a feast and everyone participates. Parents want their babies dedicated to God, and couples want to wed, because they like having their 'mother' perform the ceremony. Before Christmas, Moes always comes with presents for the orphans and the children that are still being taken care of. The land is poor, and if the harvest fails, the residents cannot pay the rent. Due to the intervention of Moes and Piet Graafstal, in 1930 the rent is greatly reduced. In 1935, ownership is even entirely given over to the Pinksterzending (Pentecostal Mission).

Surabaya and Waru 1929–1932

With thirty Javanese children, Moes moves to Surabaya in 1929. It is an important city-port in East Java, and next to Batavia, by far the largest city in the Dutch Indies. In the census of 1930, the city has 342,000 inhabitants, including 26,000 Europeans and 39,000 Chinese.[11] At 57 Embong Malang, Van Gessel has rented a large house, including a meeting hall large enough for 250 seats. Moes, with her children, stays temporarily with Van Gessel. The beginning is difficult. The children get sick, and the two youngest die.[12] On an earlier visit a few months before her arrival, Moes had prophesied in a meeting about a new church building and where to build it. The

---

[9] Moes speaks of five leaders without naming them. It is certain that Joenoes was one of them, the identities of the other four names are deduced from other references. Elias and Stefanoes are young evangelists who also intinerate. Elias and Jakoboes are mentioned together with Joenoes as performing a baptismal ceremony. Iskaq is called by Moes 'the scribe'.

[10] M.A. Alt, 'Nieuwe opwekking te Gambang Waloeh', GS 7.7 (April 1931), pp. 11–12.

[11] Volkstelling 1930 Deel VIII (Batavia: Landsdrukkerij, 1936), p.79.

[12] M.A. Alt, 'Onze Vader in den hemel, Die de gebeden, verhoort …', GS 7.1 (January 1931), p. 18.

construction of this church building will be an important project in the coming years.

GOUDEN SCHOOVEN
WEEKBLAD, TOT VERHEERLIJKING VAN JEZUS.
Officieel orgaan van de Pinkstergemeente, in Nederlandsch - Indië.
(Als rechtspersoon erkend bij Gouvernements Besluit No. 29 4 Juni 1924)

ABONNEMENTSPRIJS F 6.— PER JAAR.
LOSSE NUMMERS 20 Ct.

Redactie				Halte Waroe.
Administratie	}	Zr. M. A. Alt.	{	S. S. O. L.

Evangelisten - Convent:

F. G. van Gessel	Embong Malang 57 Soerabaia.
D. Weenink van Loon	Julianalaan Bandoeng.
Br. D. en Zr. C. L. van Klaveren	Sluisbrugstraat 48 Weltevreden.
H. E. Horstman	Temanggoeng,
F. van Abkoude	Djocja. Ngoepasan 37.
Zr. M. A. Alt	Halte Waroe. S. S. O. L.

Evangelisten en Hulp - Evangelisten.

Br. en Zr. Abell-Hansen. Evangelisten.	) Mritjan 7. Semarang.
Br. W. Mamahit. Evangelist. Mal. Gemeente. Soerabaia.	) Embong Malang 57. Soerabaia.
Br. C. J. H. Theys. Evangelist.	) Djember.
Zr. M. v. Gessel Evangeliste.	) Embong Malang 57. Soerabaia.
Zr. R. van Abkoude Evangeliste	) Ngoepasan.
Br. Ong Tjhay Bo. Evangelist.	) Gang Hotel Baroe Madioen.
Br. P. Lumoindong. Evangelist.	) Ngoepasan 7. Djokja.
Br. W. Hornung. Evangelist.	) Tjepoe Kapoeanweg.
Br. Lesnoussa. Evangelist.	) Hatifoestraat Amboina.
Br. J. Repi. Br. A. Tamboewoen. } Hulp - Evangelisten.	) Langoan Menado.
Br. N. Runkat. Hulp - Evangelist.	) Pasoeroean.
Zr. A. Pati Radjawané. Hulp-Evangeliste.	) Pohon Poelihstraat Amboina.
Br. Ong Ngo Tjhwan. Hulp-Evangelist.	) Kasri bij Lawang.
Br. Keasberry. Hulp-Evangelist.	) Sitoebondo.
Br. Th. den Daas. Hulp-Evangelist.	) Mr. Cornelis.
Zr. Determyer-Vorst. Hulp-Evangeliste.	) Karanganjar Salatiga.
Br. Ogi. Hulp-Evangelist.	) Poerwodadi Semarang.
Br. J. Oenen. Hulp-Evangelist.	) Djati straat 235. Probolinggo.
Zr. A. Leeflang. Hulp-Evangeliste.	) Bandoeng. Tjitjendo 7.

Gouden Schooven *list of Convent of Evangelists and other evangelists in (March 1930)*

Along with *Gouden Schooven*, Moes begins to publish a weekly magazine in July 1929: *De Pinkster Evangelie Courant 'Komt tot de wateren'* (*The Pentecost Gospel Courant 'Come to the Waters'*), subtitled: A weekly magazine to spread the fourfold gospel, namely full redemption through the blood of Jesus.[13] At the same time, P. Lumoindong, PGNI auxiliary evangelist, begins the publication of a Malay Pentecostal periodical, *Nafiri Pentekosta*.[14] In January 1930, the *Pentecostal Gospel Courant* is included in *Gouden Schooven*, now appearing weekly. Resources to publish weekly are inadequate. From April 1930, *Gouden Schooven* will be published twice a month until the war makes further publication impossible. After the war, it becomes a monthly magazine.

On 1 February 1930, Moes and her now thirty-four children move to a more spacious home in Waru, just outside of Surabaya. The house is being refurbished and is called 'Elim'. This becomes the standard name for the houses where Moes and her housemates are to live. A joyful opening ceremony takes place with a choir from Surabaya.[15] From her office she writes:

> We now live in Waru in a lovely old house and we all feel 'krasan' [at home]. The Javanese children are delighted with all the fruit trees … , a whole orchard and there are a hundred ideas for planting corn and cassava. The court is about 1.5 bau large – so an Eldorado for the rural children.[16]

At the same time, Moes is appointed by the Convent as an itinerating evangelist for all of the Dutch Indies with a supervisory task over the small congregations. In the three years and three months that Moes operates from Surabaya (including Waru), she regularly visits the dozens of churches in East and Middle Java and occasionally the

---

[13] The first four issues of the paper are located in the Koninklijke Bibliotheek at The Hague. The last part of the title 'Komt tot de wateren' is continued by *Gouden Schooven*. As from no. 16, April 1930, *Gouden Schooven* appears twice a month.

[14] *Nafiri Pentekosta* is the replacement of the Malay-Javanese paper *Maranatha* that from September 1928 until March 1929 appeared as a supplement to *Gouden Schooven*. No copies have been found. Lumoindong was first an auxiliary evangelist in Tjepu and now in Djokjakarta. M.A. Alt, 'Kennisgeving', *GS* 5.4 (April 1929), pp. 37–38. In May 1931 *Gouden Schooven* reports that *Nafiri Pentekosta* has stopped due to lack of finances. In January 1931 Ong Tjhay Bo from Madiun, also auxiliary evangelist of the PGNI, starts publication of the Malay Pentecostal paper *Terang Doenia*. Of this paper only the cover of the second issue has been found.

[15] M.A. Alt, 'De inwijding van ons huis', *GS* 6.15 (April 1930), p. 17.

[16] M.A. Alt, 'Onze verhuizing', *GS* 6.10 (March 1930), 17. A bau is about 0.7 hectare.

churches in West Java. On a trip to Gambang Waluh, she also visits the churches in Semarang, Ambarawa, Salatiga, and Temanggung. In East Java, a number of pioneer posts in and around Kediri develop under her supervision.

In addition to the leading evangelists in the Convent, there are ten other evangelists mentioned who are not part of the Convent. Another ten helpers lead home cells and small churches under the supervision of an evangelist. At the opening of a church or at baptismal services, one or more evangelists come to lead the service. A baptismal service is always followed by a celebration of the Lord's Supper. Every month new assemblies are added. Other evangelists active in East Java in this time include the Van Gessels, W. Mamahit, N. Runkat, C.J.H. Theijs, Ong Tjhay Bo, and W. Sick. Several couples are operating in Middle Java: the Horstmans, the Abell-Hansens, the Van Abkoudes, the Groesbeeks, as well as P. Lumoindong, Ong Ngo Tjwan, and Sister Determeijer-Vorst. In West Java: Weenink van Loon, H. Hornung, Th. den Daas, Sister Leeflang, along with the Van Klaverens.

Soon there are also churches in the outer areas: Ambon (1929), Borneo (1929), Celebes (1930), and Sumatra (1930). Often these churches are started by church members who, because of their jobs, have moved to a remote area and begin prayer meetings in their new homes. Often this is followed up by an auxiliary evangelist who receives a calling for that area. For instance, G.F. Boum Bletterman from Magelang is transferred by his employer to Bandjermasin, South Borneo. Through his testimony, some people come to repentance, and a home cell is launched.

In November 1929, Moes, together with evangelists H. Horstman and Ong Tjhay Bo, travels to Bandjermasin for ten days. Daily meetings are held in the 'Harmonie' club and in the 'De Eendracht' cinema. Inlanders, Arabs and Chinese are affected, along with a few Europeans. At the end of the eighth evening, Moes invites people to come forward to repent. Forty people respond. The next day, thirty are baptized by immersion. Horstman and Moes appoint Boum Bletterman as leader and two other brothers as deputy assistants. Missionaries of the Basler Mission submit a complaint to the government because the Pentecostals are evangelizing among the Dajakkers without permission.[17] Six months later, Moes returns to Bandjermas in in company of her interpreter, Choa. Her licence to evangelize in all of the Indies has not yet been issued.[18] Therefore no public gatherings are held. This time, seven people are baptized.[19]

In October 1931, Moes travels with Weenink van Loon to Makassar, South Celebes, where a church has been founded by the Pattiradjawanés. Gifts from readers of *Gouden Schooven* have enabled Moes to purchase a new, portable organ for her travels, as the old one 'suffered from asthma'.[20] During this week, Van Loon and Pattiradjawané baptize the first twenty-nine converts. There are friendly contacts with representatives of other churches. On Sunday morning, Weenink van Loon and Moes visit the service in the Protestant Church and afterwards drink coffee with Rev. P.S. Binsbergen and the elders. Moes is invited to present a Bible Lecture at a meeting of the Christian Women's Association. Rev. Binsbergen and his wife, in turn, attend an evening meeting of the Pentecostal church. Moes regrets that few Europeans want to sit next to the Javanese:

> It is a pity that so few Europeans can decide to visit a gathering where they have to take a seat among the simple people, and we once ask ourselves: How will it be in heaven? There we will stand in line with converted Africans, Chinese, Javanese, Arabs, etcetera, and belong to the crowd 'from all nations and tongues'. How will these Christians feel at home there when they have not already learned on earth to be one with all children of God? Looking down at the lower classes of society! Oh, we must never forget that Jesus first preached the gospel to 'the poor' and left the treasures of heaven to live among us as a simple carpenter's son. And the Bible teaches us to follow 'His footsteps' (1 Pet 2:21).[21]

---

[17] M.A. Alt, 'Opwekkingsdiensten te Bandjermasin, Zuid-Borneo', *GS* 5.12 (December 1929), pp. 30–37.

[18] In 1927 Moes obtains permission as evangelist of the PGNI based on article 177 to evangelize among Europeans and Chinese in Middle-Java. In 1932 the permission is extended for all of Java also including the rural members of the church. In 1934 the permission covers the whole population, also in the outer areas, except certain areas and groups. In 1936 Moes obtains a similar license on behalf of the Pinksterzending. Cf. *Indische Courant*: 25 April 1927; 25 February 1932; 10 August 1934; 23 December 1936.

[19] M.A. Alt, 'Bandjermasin', *GS* 6.19 (June 1930), pp. 15–17.

[20] M.A. Alt, 'Tegal', *GS* 7.12 (June 1931), p. 10.

[21] M.A. Alt, ' Onze reis naar Makasser', *GS* 7.22 (November 1931), p. 10.

In her years in Taju (1910–1914) and in Gambang Waluh (1914–1929, Moes has worked in isolated places where only Javanese is spoken. Now she works in cities where life is very different. The services are mostly in Dutch and Malay and much less in Javanese. Although Moes can converse in Malay, she does not master it sufficiently to preach in Malay. Among the licensed evangelists, Moes is the only European who, in addition to Dutch, also preaches in Javanese, while the others preach in Dutch or Malay. Although in the beginning the PGNI has no permission to work among Javanese, but only among Europeans and Chinese, there are always Javanese in the audience.[22] Once, a representative of the government urges Moes not to preach to the Javanese for fear of trouble. Moes replies that her belief prohibits her from withholding this message from any creature.[23] In her article, 'Our Cosmopolitan Pentecostal Circles', she writes in 1935 that Javanese, Chinese, Ambonese, Menadonese, and Europeans visit the mixed services. To those who scorn the Pentecostals for this reason, Moes refers to Rev. 7.9: 'When we are ashamed to sit next to a Chinese or inlander, how can we ever belong to that cosmopolitan crowd?'[24]

In addition to her travels, she spends a lot of time editing *Gouden Schooven* and the songbook. Since many of the converts have a Roman Catholic background (according to some as many as three-quarters), Moes, in *Gouden Schooven,* answers questions about praying to Mary, praying to the saints, and doing good works.[25] Although Moes is firm in her rejection of Roman Catholic teaching on these points, she endorses the appreciation of contemporary Roman martyrs of J.H. Gunning in his paper *Pniël.*[26] Regularly, Moes publishes works by mystics like Teresa of Avila, John of the Cross, Gerhard Tersteegen, and Madame Guyon. 'These mystics, men and women, stood above all church-form and religion – above all they loved their master with unspeakable love and lived through Him and for Him alone.'[27]

---

[22] M.A. Alt, 'Soemobito', *GS* 7.4 (1931), pp. 11–12.

[23] M.A. Alt, 'Ngoro', *GS* 7.11 (1931), p. 12.

[24] M.A. Alt, 'Onze cosmopolitische Pinksterkringen', *GS* 11.23 (1935), p. 11.

[25] M.A. Alt, 'Aan onze Roomsch-Katholieke broeders en zusters', *GS* 6.17 (1930), pp. 7–8. Moes does not name her source, but writes that it agrees with her own observation.

[26] 'Roomsche martelaren uit onze dagen', *GS* 6.22 (1930), p. 13.

[27] M.A. Alt, 'De heilige Theresia', *GS* 6.14 (1930), pp. 14–16.

Baptismal Service in Surabaya with Moes Watching (1930)

Moes finds it important to agree on the main points of the faith and to connect to the global Pentecostal movement. From March 1930, she has a standard page in *Gouden Schooven* with 'What the Pentecostal Assembly believes and teaches' in twelve articles. She explains: 'The teaching of the Assemblies of God has, through the years, found acceptance in sound Pentecostal assemblies. Also, the

Pentecostal Assembly in Dutch Indies adopted it, because it is entirely in accordance to the Holy Scriptures.'[28]

At the end of 1930, the first edition of *Glorieklokken* (*Bells of Glory*) appears, with 200 songs and thirty choruses. These are 'solely our own Pentecostal songs'. The music is in numerical notation. The first printing of 1,000 is sold out within six months. Moes urges the assemblies to start a choir and an orchestra that can play Pentecostal songs. Pentecostal meetings without music are impossible for Moes.[29] More editions of the songbook will follow, and they will also find their way to the Netherlands. On her journeys, Moes observes a shortage of young workers. In 1931, she pleads for a fund for young workers in *Gouden Schooven*, because 'financial difficulties have a paralyzing effect on the energy of the young people'.[30]

As a national leader, Moes supervises a number of assemblies in East Java. She accepts the appeal of one of these assemblies (in Kediri) to become their pastor. She must leave behind the lovely, old home with its large garden, right now when the manga trees are in full blossom. The small ones regret missing the main harvest, but the trip with the truck is also attractive. In August 1932, everything is packed, and, of course all the children go along. Moes feels called to:

> give an open door to all that are poor, rejected, or fallen and a warm place in our hearts. God's pleasure apparently continues to rest upon this labour. For twenty-five years, I always had enough clothing and food for everyone. I am determined also to open my house in Kediri to all who God wants to send me. His Name be praised. Many have told me: 'Look at the meager results! See how little thankfulness or love is offered in return!'– But I am convinced that no one can die unconverted, to whom we, by the grace of God and led by Him, have been allowed to preach the Word, even if it takes years! That is impossible.[31]

---

[28] M.A. Alt, 'Wat de Pinkstergemeente (over de gehele wereld) gelooft en leert', *GS* 10.15 (Aug. 1934), p. 4. Moes has taken the twelve articles from the Swiss periodical *Verheissung des Vaters*, which in turn had taken them from *Redemption Tidings* of the British Assemblies of God.

[29] M.A. Alt, 'Aanvragen om opwekkingsdiensten', *GS* 7.10 (1931), p. 24.

[30] M.A. Alt, 'Onze jonge werkers', *GS* 7.12 (1931), pp. 19–20. It seems that the 'Maaiersbond', founded early 1929 to support young workers, was short lived. M.A. Alt, 'Uit de correspondentie', *GS* 5.4 (April 1929), pp. 23–24.

[31] M.A. Alt, 'De bevolking van Elim', *GS* 8.16 (August 1932), pp. 16–17.

There is a warm farewell from the assembly in Surabaya. A poem from a church member reveals that Moes has won all hearts by her love, and that she is loved by white and brown.[32]

Kediri 1932–1936

In that place [Kediri] I was allowed to work four successive years with many blessings – several hundred were baptized in those glorious times. We lived in a beautiful and large Chinese house that we fitted out as a hall for Pentecostal worhip. About twenty or thirty young people resided with us, who helped me with everything. It was a happy time, although malaria kept troubling me and undermining my strength.[33]

By 1932 , there has already been a relationship with the Pentecostal assembly in Kediri for two years. On 28 April 1930, the assembly is constituted by Moes as supervisor, on which occasion, J.C. Gabriel is appointed as pastor and two others as elders. Moes preaches there once a month. In August 1930, Moes is leading revival meetings in a cinema. On the third day, thirty-eight converts are baptized, the first Pentecostal baptismal service in Kediri.[34] The miraculous healing of a lame man in November draws many to the meetings.[35] In May 1931, the second baptismal service is held with forty-two being baptized, followed by a third baptismal service in June.[36] Moes now regards Kediri as the main centre of this area. When Gabriel has to move because of his job, Moes accepts the request to become pastor of the assembly.

Kediri, capital of the residentship of Kediri, is situated in a fertile valley on both sides of the river Brantas, 130 kilometers southwest of Surabaya. In the area, coffee, cocoa, tobacco, rice, and sugar are grown. The city has a lively trade, a train station, a city council, and its own mayor from 1929. At the census in 1930, the residentship of

---

[32] Een Pinksterbroeder (A Pentecostal brother), 'Scheiden', *GS* 8.19 (October 1932), p. 16.

[33] Alt, *Herinneringen*, p. 77.

[34] J.C. Gabriël., 'Opwekkingsdiensten in Kediri en omstreken', *GS* 6.24 (1930), pp. 10–11.

[35] 'Opwekkingsdienst te Paree', *GS* 6.28 (1930), pp. 10–11.

[36] 'Doopdienst te Kediri', *GS* 7.11 (June 1931), p. 11; *GS* 7.13 (July 1931), pp. 12–13.

Kediri has 2.4 million inhabitants.[37] The city of Kediri has a population of nearly 49,000 in 1930, including 1,000 Europeans and 3,700 Chinese (7.6%).[38]

From 1860, the Captain of the Chinese in Kediri has been from the ancient family Djie.[39] From 1920 it is Djie Ting Hian. He owns some large plantations and a weaving plant.[40] He becomes a Christian in one of Moes's meetings and is the first Christian in his family. In May 1931, he, his wife, and children are baptized in water. This is for Moes: 'Like opening a door to the conversion of the Chinese people'.[41] Djie makes one of his houses available for Pentecostal meetings. Earlier, as a Buddhist, Djie donated a lot of money for the construction of the Chinese temple (klenteng) in the city. Moes wants to get into the life of the Chinese and asks Djie to show her the inside of the temple. She writes about this: 'One feels as if placed in a devil's den'.[42] More of Djie's family members repent and join the Pentecostal assembly, as well as many other Chinese people. One of Djie's children, Theo, will later go to a Pentecostal Bible School in England and then study Theology in The Netherlands.

On 1 September 1932, Moes and her thirty housemates move to a house at 117 Klenteng Street. One large room is fitted out for Pentecostal meetings. The opening service, on 3 September, is attended by 120 people, the maximum capacity of the room. Half a year later, Moes, housemates and assembly move to a larger residence at 95 Djagalan Lor with a meeting room for 200 people. In the spacious yard, they build a baptismal tank, which is first used on 16 April 1933. For baptismal services, they often go to the springs of Sumberbulus outside of Kediri. There are many activities in the church. During the

---

[37] Widjojo Nitisastra, *Population Trends in Indonesia* (Jakarta: Equinox, 2006), pp. 5, 78.

[38] *Volkstelling 1930 Deel VIII* (Batavia: Landsdrukkerij, 1936), p. 79. The residentship Kediri is divided into five regencies, including the regency of Kediri. In 1934 the regency of Kediri has 350,000 inhabitants among whom are 2800 Europeans and 9,100 Chinese. G.F.E. Gonggryp (ed.), *Geïllustreerde Encyclopaedie van Nederlands-Indië* (Leiden: Leidsche Uitgeversmaatschappij, 1934), p. 642.

[39] Cf. Stuart Pearson, *Bittersweet: The Memoir of a Chinese-Indonesian Family in the Twentieth Century* (Singapore: National University of Singapore), pp. xv; 25–26.

[40] Francesca Djie Chen Chu and Westa Kwee Oen Hwie, "Hian Ting Djie: Our Beloved Opa," in *To Tjhoe Khee Pok: Djie Family Reunion* (Kediri: private publication, 2014), pp. 41–45.

[41] Doopdienst te Kediri', *GS* 7.11 (June 1931), p. 11.

[42] M.A. Alt, 'Teekenen des Tijds', *GS* 7.14 (July 1931), pp. 16–18.

week, there are separate meetings in Dutch and Malay. Beginning in 1933, there is Sunday school on Sunday morning, followed by Bible study. Sunday evening there is a mixed meeting. Services in Malay are led by the Chinese evangelist, Liem Hong Bo. In the four years (1932–1936) that Moes is pastoring, more than 400 converts are baptized.

Elim Home in Kediri (January 1933)

Moes also opens churches in the nearby cites of Agung, Kertosono, and Ngandjuk and visits them monthly. In 1934, a church is started in Madiun where Hendrika Jansz (granddaughter of Pieter Jansz) is in charge. Pastoring a local assembly leaves Moes less time to travel. Nevertheless, she continues her regular visits to Gambang Waluh. On the way she visits the churches in Temanggung, Ambarawa, and Salatiga. In September 1933 Moes begins the publication of a monthly periodical in Malay, *Gandoem Mas*. Her staff translate articles from *Gouden Schooven*.

In order to reach out to the surrounding villages more effectively, Moes starts a one-year training school for auxiliary evangelists in May 1934. It is announced as a 'Bible School for Javanese boys'.[43] Students must have completed fifth grade of the Javanese school and be resident at the Bible school. Each student must pay five guilders a month

---

[43] M.A. Alt, 'Bijbelschool voor Javaansche jongens', *GS* 10.9 (May 1934), p. 23.

for living expenses and accommodation. There is no tuition fee. Donations that are received for the school are accounted for in *Gouden Schooven*. Each day opens with an hour's prayer and then teaching (in Javanese) from Moes. In the afternoon, the students write about what they learnt in the morning, and in the evening, they go by bicycle with other evangelists to the surrounding villages to put what they have learnt into practice. Soemardi Stefanus (1916–1990) belongs to the first group of four students. Stefanus marries Lydia, one of Alt's children from the Gambang Waluh area.[44] He will be a great support in the work.

Liem Hong Bo and Family in Kediri (1940)

---

[44] S. Stefanus, 'Bezoek aan Gambang Waloeh', *GS* 26.11 (November 1957), pp. 18–19. The other three students are: Zacheus, Johannes, and Zénas.

The economic recession of the 1930s is also felt in the Dutch Indies. Trade is hit severely, causing most Chinese to suffer. Moes notices that many Chinese children no longer go to school because the parents cannot pay the school fees. She decides to set up a 'wild school' (a non-official school). With old school desks and discarded text books, the 'Elim Pentecostal School' starts. Two church members, Eveline Ferdinandus and Corry Dijkstra, are the teachers. Children who can afford it pay twenty-five cents a month, and for the others it is free. Soon there are fifty pupils who are taught every morning of the week. There is a Javanese class, and for the Chinese children, there is a class in Dutch. On Sundays, they visit Sunday school in the church.[45]

With the founding of the school, caring for thirty orphans in her house, and looking after the needy in Gambang Waluh, Moes demonstrates that the gospel is good news for the poor. She uses the Christmas celebrations to draw outsiders. The venues for these occasions are a cinema. There are announcements in the press and the meetings attract 500 to 600 visitors.[46] From 1935, Moes will have a major responsibility for the national work, which means less time for pastoring the church in Kediri.[47] In addition to the above-mentioned evangelist, Liem Hong Bo, Moes receives help from the husband and wife team of evangelists, the Schotborghs.

In the course of 1936, some circumstances come together that cause Moes to move again. Unexpectedly, the option of renting the large house in Kediri is withdrawn. The home owner wants to live there himself.[48] From Lawang comes the request to start a church. The cool climate there would be welcome. The most important thing is, however, that Moes experiences the call of the Lord. She knows that, like Abraham, she dwells in tents and can never drive in the tentpegs too deeply! On 1 June 1936, Moes moves with her thirty-eight housemates to Lawang. She hands over the leadership in Kediri

---

[45] M.A. Alt, 'Onze Pinksterzending-school', *GS* 9.3 (February 1936), p. 14.

[46] 'Kerstfeest Pinkstergemeente', *Soerabaiasch Handelsblad* (19 December 1934).

[47] From November 1935 Moes cancels the Dutch meetings on Sunday morning. The mixed service on Wednesday evening led by Moes will become the main meeting. The Bible Study she used to give on Monday evening transfers to Sunday morning. *GS* 11.21 (November 1935), p. 9.

[48] M.A. Alt, 'Onze verhuizing', *GS* 9.10 (May 1936), 20. Moes writes that the owner has bought an oil factory in Kediri and for that reason wants to live in the neighbourhood. Apparently it is not about Djie.

to Liem Hong Bo. In her farewell word, she reminds the people how she has served the congregation and what constraints were associated with it: 'All that the Lord has taught me, I have passed on to you and have always tried to bring your souls to Jesus. With many failings, though, that Word has been brought, but I trust that the Blood of Jesus will cover all my mistakes in preaching'.[49] Afterwards she writes: 'I will never have such a sweet congregation again ... we have never suffered here from arguing and loveless criticism'.[50] Moes keeps on visiting Kediri twice a month. On 17 June, she is present when the new hall at 38 Hoofdstraat is dedicated.

On a local level, the years in Kediri have been a period of progress for Moes and the assembly. On the national level, however, there is a hidden conflict among the leadership of the PGNI. At the end of 1933, Moes laments that a difficult year lies behind her, but that probably an even heavier year is in front of her.[51] 1934 will bring a rupture with the PGNI, and in the beginning of 1935, Moes will start the Pinksterzending (Pentecostal Mission).

[49] M.A. Alt, 'Afscheidssamenkomst te Kediri', *GS* 9.12 (June 1936), p. 19.
[50] Alt, 'Afscheidssamenkomst te Kediri', p. 19.
[51] M.A. Alt, 'Aan het einde van 't jaar', *GS* 9.24 (December 1933), pp. 23–24.

Tahoen ka 3   No.   12

GANDOEM MAS

Di kloearkan saben boelan oentoek kaoem Kristen,
dalam bahasa Melajoe rendah.

Pengatoer : kaoem pengerdja dari **Pinkster Zending** LAWANG.	Harga langganan setahoen f 1.50, harga sadjilid f 0.12⁵ fr.	Administratie : **Zr. M. A. ALT.** LAWANG.

Maka orang jang potong itoe mendapat oepah.

Joh. 4 : 63.

Orang - orang jang menaboer bidji - bidjian
dengan berlinang - linang aer matanja, jaitoe
akan memotong dia sambil bersoerak - soerak.

Mazm. 126 : 5.

Kediri Snelpers — 21723

Gandoem Mas (1936)

10

THE PINKSTERZENDING

After earnest prayer in which we laid open our grief to our heavenly Father who is not inattentive and does not overlook the needs of His children, we decided to found the Association 'De Pinksterzending' [The Pentecostal Mission] in the Dutch Indies.[1]

From 1927 to 1934, the PGNI expands every year. Based upon the number of meeting places mentioned in *Pinksterkracht* and in *Gouden Schooven*, we can see the following development: 10 assemblies in 1927, 24 in 1928, 33 in 1929, 45 in 1930, 50 in 1931, 67 in 1932, and 103 in 1933. By the middle of 1934 the number reaches 120. But then it suddenly falls back to 38. What has happened? The reasons for the break up that caused the foundation of 'De Pinksterzending' are presented below. More details of the background are found in the appendices.

Reasons for the Rupture

In historical accounts the rupture between Moes and the PGNI is usually dated in 1931.[2] However, the reports in *Gouden Schooven* as well

---

[1] M.A. Alt, *GS* 11.4 'De Pinksterzending', (February 1935), p. 19.

[2] Gani Wiyono, *Gereja Sidang-Sidang Jemaat Allah dalam lintasan sejarah: Sebua Sketsa* (Malang: Penerbit Gandum Mas, 2007), p. 34. Gani Wiyono, *A Sketch of the History of the Assemblies of God of Indonesia (Gereja Sidang-sidang Jemaat Allah)* (MTh Thesis, Asia Pacific Theological Seminary, March 2004), p. 39, citing Fridolin Ukur and Frank L. Cooley, *Jerih dan Juang: Laporan Nasional Survai Menyeluruh Gereja di Indonesia* (Jakarta: Lembaga Penelitan dan Studi-DGI, 1979), p. 111. Karunia Djaja, *Sejarah Gereja Pantekosta di Indonesia* (Semarang: GPdI, 1993), pp. 16–17. Paulus

as the announcements in the secular newspapers from those years, indicate that the break up took place in 1934.[3] This agrees with the letters that Van Abkoude wrote in 1933 to the British Assemblies of God. According to these letters the rupture had not yet taken place, but was anticipated soon.[4]

Howard Carter (middle up front) and Lester Sumrall (2nd left behind) visiting Feodoor and Regina van Abkoude (left front and left behind) (1935)

Wiratno, 'The beginning of Assemblies of God in Indonesia' (Term paper, Baguio City, Asian Pentecostal Theological Seminary, 1993), p. 5. Nicky J. Sumual, *Pantekosta Indonesia Suatu Sejarah* (Menado, 1981), pp. 67, 78. Mesakh Tapilatu, *Gereja-Gereja Pentakosta di Indonesia: Suatu Studie Tentang Sejarah, Organisasi, Anggota, Ibadah, Kegiatan, Ajaran dan Sikap Terhadap Gereja-Gereja Lain* (Th.M. Thesis, Sekolah Tinggi Theologia, Jakarta, 1982), pp. 35–36. H.L. Senduk, *Sejarah GBI. Suata Gereja Nasional Yang Termuda* (Jakarta: n.d.), p. 13.

[3] A permit to evangelize that was granted to Moes in August 1934 was still requested by the PGNI. 'De Pinkstergemeente', *Indische Courant* (10 August 1934). The same newspaper reported on 4 February 1935, the foundation of 'De Pinksterzending' by Moes.

[4] F. van Abkoude to the Home Missionary Reference Council att. of G.J. Tilling, Magelang, 19 September 1933. Present in the Donald Gee Centre.

At the start of 1933, Moes signals there is a 'crying need for more love and unity, cooperation and mutual sympathy'.[5] Nevertheless, the strong growth of the PGNI in 1933 suggests that the problem can still be solved. After much delay the huge new church building in Surabaya finally opens its doors to thousands of people. Evangelists from all over Java and also from Borneo, Makassar, and the Moluccas are present. The particular spot in the port area had been designated by Moes through a prophecy in 1929. At the opening, everyone is explicitly reminded that Moes put great effort into the fundraising through her magazine. Moes preaches about 'The Promises of God for Our Church'. It is a day of joy. In *Gouden Schooven* Moes is very positive about Van Gessel.

It is only after the conflict has become public in 1934 that Moes expresses her opinion of the causes. She complains about quarrels, enmities, envy, and ambition. A new doctrine, which according to Moes is non-Biblical on many points, has replaced the old one. Knowledge has displaced love.[6] Moes strongly opposes the idea that a baptismal formula is valid only when the names of the Trinity are followed by the formula, 'who is the Lord Jesus Christ,' which led to the rebaptism of believers.[7] Also, she opposes the emerging emphasis on giving tithes:

> The superstition about 'the tithes' begins to take root. One says, 'If I have not yet paid my tithes, I will get sick'. If any kind of accident hits the family, you soon hear, 'Oh, that's because I have not given my tithes this month'. There are also those who give their tithes only in the hope of receiving more salary or to buy some kind of blessing.[8]

Moes see the imposition of tithes as a return to a life under the law. She just wants to teach the congregation to give wholeheartedly.[9] In addition, Moes constantly has to defend herself against criticism of her leadership based on her gender. According to her critics, a woman cannot have a leading position in the congregation. She may not

---

[5] M.A. Alt, 'Bij intrede 1933', *GS* 9.2 (January 1933), pp. 16–17.

[6] M.A. Alt, 'Wat de Pinkstergemeente (over de gehele wereld) gelooft en leert', *GS* 10.15 (August 1934), p. 4.

[7] M.A. Alt, 'De bediening van den Heiligen Doop', *GS* 10.17 (September 1934), pp. 4–7.

[8] M.A. Alt, 'De Tienden', *GS* 10.19 (October 1934), pp. 4–6.

[9] M.A. Alt, 'Vragenrubriek', *GS* 11.12 (June 1938), p. 6.

preach, anoint the sick, minister through laying on of hands, nor administer the Lord's Supper.[10]

In September 1934, Moes releases the brochure, *Van hart tot hart* (*From Heart to Heart*), explaining her reasons further. In 1947, an edited version is published. Moes points to deviations in doctrine, as well as the lack of solid organization. She further mentions issues of pride, envy, and fanaticism. She names the introduction of the tithing charge, rebaptism in the name of Jesus, several particular doctrinal perceptions of Offiler, and finally the teaching that only those who speak in tongues are included in the rapture of the church.[11] The brochure does not talk about the position of women.

These reasons are compatible to what we encounter in other historical accounts. Commonly the reasons given are: the teachings of Offiler, the rebaptism of believers, and the position of women.[12] Tapilatu adds that rivalry between Van Gessel and Moes is a further underlying reason. As both work in East Java, and together with Horstman, are the main evangelists in the area, an element of competition might have arisen between them. Van Gessel was very influential in the early 1930s, leading the largest congregation and an imposing construction project. Moes is also influential through *Gouden Schooven* and her many trips. Moes may have less authority, but she is perhaps more loved. Rivalry could be an underlying reason, but Tapilatu has only one source, an interview, to substantiate this claim.[13] If rivalry was a factor, it may also be that the rivalry was not mutual. There are no indications of its existence in the publications of Moes.

[10] M.A. Alt, 'Het spreken van de vrouw in de gemeente', *GS* 11.5 (March 1935), pp. 4–6.

[11] M.A. Alt, 'Van hart tot hart' (Surabaya: 1947), 17 pages. The original edition of 1934 has not been found. The particular perceptions of Offiler deal about the sun as God's dwelling, the angel Gabriël as the Holy Spirit, the angel Michael as Jesus Christ, the tabernacle, the millennium, and the book Revelation. Offiler is the leader of the Bethel Temple Church the mission base of the American missionaries. For the meaning of the rapture see 17.2.

[12] Sumual, *Pantekosta Indonesia*, pp. 78, 82; *Tapilatu, Gereja-Gereja Pentakosta* (1982), pp. 35–36; Wiyono *Gereja Sidang-Sidang* (2007), p. 34; Wiyono, 'A Sketch' (2004), pp. 38–39. Th. van den End and J. Weitjens, *Ragi Carita 2: Sejarah Gereja Di Indonesia 1860-an-Sekarang* (Jakarta: BPK. Gunung Mulia, 1999), p. 272.

[13] Tapilatu in *Gereja-Gereja Pentakosta*, pp. 47–48, refers to an interview with Pdt. Akip of the Gereja Bethel Tabernacle and further to Sumual (82), but I could not find this reason for the rupture in Sumual's book. According to Febe, daughter of Van Gessel, the reason for the rupture was that her father did not allow women to preach. F.J. The-van Gessel, e-mail to author 22 August 2014.

She is always positive about Van Gessel, and she fully supports him in his construction project until the opening of the new building in 1933.

Elim Home in Lawang (1939)

In her published autobiography, Moes is very brief about this time: 'Difficulties, which I do not want to describe in detail, with the church I had connected to, became too big in those days'.[14] In her handwritten autobiography of 1943, not meant for publication, Moes is more open and critical about the events. It appears that the relationship with the assembly in Surabaya, and thus with Van Gessel, was already problematic in 1932: 'In Surabaya, every door was closed to me. I was no longer asked to speak in any meetings without any reason being given, when the request came from Kediri to come and live there and to form a congregation.'[15]

At Kediri, Moes also experiences opposition from Surabaya. At a conference of the PGNI, it is decided that young evangelists can settle anywhere, even in the territory of another evangelist. A young worker from Surabaya settles in Kediri and starts to hold meetings, 'which understandably produced difficulties'.[16] The assemblies in the Blitar-Kediri-Kertosono area, where Moes has been the leader for

[14] M.A. Alt, *Herinneringen uit mijn leven* (Velp: Pinksterzending, 1963), p. 77.
[15] M.A. Alt, 'Autobiografie 1943', p. 75.
[16] Alt, 'Autobiografie 1943', p. 76.

many years, are now placed under the supervision of Horstman from Malang. Furthermore, Moes writes that the decision to terminate *Gouden Schooven* as official periodical of the PGNI has been made because Surabaya wants to publish its own periodical.[17]

Nevertheless, when Moes is elected to the General Committee in November 1934, she is still willing to accept the position. But when she wants to address the assembly during the meeting, she is silenced. She returns to Kediri with great sadness. A little later, the General Committee informs her that, in a petition, eight to ten evangelists have asked for her resignation. 'Then,' Moes writes, 'it began to dawn on me that my time had come to withdraw'.[18] As she is used to doing, she pours out her heart to the Lord. In a vision she sees a beautiful road overshadowed by trees and lined with flowering bushes. She sees no one on that path which leads upwards. She hears the voice of the Lord: 'This is the way that is "excellent" (1 Cor. 12:31) – the way of love, but nobody wants to take it'.[19]

Shortly thereafter, Moes gets an invitation to a meeting on 22 January 1935, from a number of members of the PGNI who disagree with the state of affairs. At that meeting in Malang, they decide to separate from the PGNI and to continue as De Pinksterzending (The Pentecostal Mission). It is clear that when Van Gessel and others turned against women preachers, it would have consequences for Moes. Since she is convinced that God has called her to this ministry, she feels compelled to remain faithful to his call, with the result that she eventually moves outside of the PGNI. Although in the autobiography of 1943, the teachings of Offiler are also named, the lack of love receives the most emphasis as a cause of the break. While the PGNI will experience other splits, it will remain the largest Pentecostal body. The name will later be changed to Gereja Pantekosta di Indonesia (GPdI). During the Japanese occupation, Weenink van Loon

---

[17] Alt, 'Autobiografie 1943', p. 76. Moes does not mention a year, so it may refer to both 1932 as to 1934. The first seems more likely. She also writes that many subscribers transferred to the Surabayan periodical that did not survive a long time. No details about this periodical have been found. As from 1935 the periodical *Het Volle Evangelie* is published from Malang. Two copies have been found that date from February and March 1936. under editorship of C.J.H. Theijs. It is the official organ of the PGNI. In the list of meeting places 106 addresses are mentioned.

[18] Alt, 'Autobiografie 1943', p. 77. Moes erroneously mentions 1935.

[19] Alt, 'Autobiografie 1943', p. 77.

dies in an internment camp.[20] Horstman survives the camp and, after the war, moves to America, where he becomes a preacher in the Presbyterian Church.[21] Van Gessel leaves the GPdI and in 1952, together with H.L. Senduk, founds the Gereja Bethel Injil Sepenuh (now: Gereja Bethel Indonesia).[22] In 1954 Van Gessel moves to Hollandia, New Guinea, where he founds the Bethel Pentecostal Church. He dies in 1958. The close relation of the GPdI with the Bethel Church of Offiler will disappear and make way for a connection with the American Church of the Foursquare Gospel, established by Aimee Semple McPherson herself a woman ...

Foundation of De Pinksterzending

The participants at the meeting of 22 January 1935 in Malang, choose to 'return to the old paths, to the first love – the first works'. It marks the establishment of the Vereeniging De Pinksterzending in Nederlandsch-Indië (The Pentecostal Mission in the Dutch Indies), located in Kediri and with *Gouden Schooven* as its organ. The Executive Committee consists of: M.A. Alt, Kediri (Chairman), F.A. Abell, Semarang (Secretary), F. Boum Bletterman, Malang (Treasurer), W.J. De Graaff, Wonosobo (Commissioner), and Lammeree, Malang (Commissioner).[23] The new association is based on the 'ancient Pentecostal faith,' namely that of the fourfold gospel and the twelve articles of faith in *Gouden Schooven*. The newspaper *Soerabaiasch Handelsblad* writes in a sympathetic report that Moes wants to lead the many scattered Pentecostal groups. According to this report, there are around 20,000 baptized Pentecostal believers throughout the whole of the Dutch Indies.[24] On 19 September 1935, the Pinksterzending is recognized by the government as a legal entity and can operate anywhere in the Dutch Indies.

Nine days after its foundation, the Pinksterzending opens a Malay-speaking assembly in Malang, with Ong Ting Swie as pastor. The

---

[20] Sumual, *Pantekosta Indonesia*, p. 66.

[21] E-mail 24 June 2014 from Pierre Dupuy, grandson of H. Horstman to author.

[22] H.L. Senduk, interview by the author, Vlaardingen, 18 January 1981. Sumual, pp. 81, 83, gives as reason for Van Gessel's departure that he was not re-elected as chairman of the GPdI.

[23] 'De Pinksterzending', *GS* 11.4 (February 1935), pp. 18–19.

[24] 'De Pinksterzending', *Soerabaiasch Handelsblad*, (4 February 1935).

opening service is led by Moes. Present are the Executive Committee, the evangelists Liem Hong Bo, Ong Ngo Tjwan, Schotborgh, and Pello, along with 200 members. At the first annual General Council in January 1936, there are twenty-six member departments. A department being an independent assembly with an evangelist and often with outposts. A city can only have a single department, while other assemblies in the same place are called suburb assemblies.

Glased Hall Pinksterzending Lawang (August 1938)

Each issue of *Gouden Schooven* lists the meeting places, giving an indication of the number of assemblies that are involved. As we have already seen, at the time of the rupture in July 1934 the number of meeting places has fallen dramatically from 120 to 38. September 1934 sees the number fall to 28, the lowest point, after which it slowly rises. By the end of 1935 it has grown to 52. By January 1942, just before the Japanese occupation, the number of assemblies reaches 60.

The *Nederlandsch Zendingsjaarboek* (*Dutch Mission Year Book*) provides the following information for the Pinksterzending in 1937: sixty-two congregations on Java, with approximately 4,000 baptized members; 15 European, 10 Chinese and 12 Javanese evangelists, in addition to many preachers and young workers.[25] The work on Java

---

[25] *Nederlandsch Zendingsjaarboek voor 1937–1939* (Zeist: Zendingsstudie-Raad, 1938), p. 65.

is among Europeans, Javanese, Chinese, Menadonese, and Ambonese. According to the same yearbook, the PGNI has 115 congregations and the Pinksterbeweging of Thiessen thirty-eight congregations. It seems that about a third of the PGNI joined the Pinksterzending during the rupture.

In 1937, Japanese preacher Susho Miyahira, with his Japanese assembly in Surabaya, becomes a member of the Pinksterzending.[26] Miyahira also becomes friends with the Reformed missionary, Herman Hilderig. In 1939, Miyahira is expelled by the authorities on suspicion of espionage. In 1942, he returns as an officer of the Japanese Navy. During the war years, he is important for the protection of Christians in South and Central Celebes.[27]

In the new organization, Moes's leadership is no longer contested. Does the new organizational form differ from the old one? By comparison, the new organization seems more transparent and democratic. The articles of association state that there is an annual General Council of members. The Executive Committee is elected for only one year and therefore has to be re-elected each year at the annual members meetings in January. *Gouden Schooven* publishes extensive reports of these meetings, in which critical voices are not ignored. Around Moes's birthday in August, multi-day conferences are held. The conferences begin with a meeting of evangelists, followed by two conference days for congregational members and evangelists, and conclude with a day of fasting and prayer.

Whether the mutual relationships in the new format are more loving is difficult to judge. There are still conflicts. Sometimes there are members who need to be suspended, while others leave on their own accord.[28] The departure of the Abells in January 1939 is very painful, they having been faithful co-workers for many years. Abell is opposed

---

[26] M.A. Alt, 'Onze Japansche evangelist', *GS* 10.18 (September 1937), p. 17. M.A. Alt, 'Br. S. Miyahira', *GS* 11.16 (August 1939), p. 6. On 31 January 1939 he returns to Japan. *GS* 12.4 (February 1939), p. 20.

[27] See the introduction by Th. van den End to the private archive H.A.C. Hildering present in the Archive of the Council for Mission, entrance 1102–2, in the Utrecht Archive.

[28] In 1938 one evangelist is dismissed 'because of intolerable acts'. Abell, 'Verslag', p. 11. In February 1941 *Gouden Schooven* reports that one evangelist is suspended because of an unreconciling attitude in a year long conflict with a fellow evangelist. In the same meetings a Committee member is dismissed because of opposing the leadership of the Pinksterzending on the basis of its legal structure. *GS* 14.4 (February 1941), pp. 12–13.

to a national organizational form with an Executive Committee that regulates matters for the assemblies. During this time, the Committee urges the assemblies to develop membership records, which would be necessary for obtaining permission to perform marriage ceremonies. When Abell's proposal to abolish the legal status of the Pinksterzending is rejected, he leaves with his Danish wife, Mina Abell-Hansen.[29] Possibly the influence of the Scandinavian Pentecostal movement, which is usually against any form of national organization, has played a part.[30]

The new format shows similarities to a family, as Alt is increasingly addressed as Moes. *Gouden Schooven* continues to publish family ads (birth, marriage, and death), correspondence, question and answers, testimonies, field reports, baptismal services, comprehensive reports of the Christmas services and reports of the annual conferences in August. Regularly, there are articles of a pedagogical nature.

Moes intensifies the contacts with Europe. From late March to early May 1935, Howard Carter, Chairman of the British Assemblies of God, visits the assemblies on Java together with the American evangelist Lester Sumrall. Carter comes through the invitation of Feodoor van Abkoude, who had recently founded the Gemeenten Gods in Nederlandsch-Indië (Assemblies of God in the Dutch Indies), but he also speaks in the assemblies of the Pinksterzending and even in the assembly of Van Gessel in Surabaya.[31]

Moes is happy with the visit: 'How long had I looked forward to Brother Carter's arrival, in order to ask him advice about many difficult problems, and how wonderful his answers were! Truly this brother is a man full of the Spirit of Wisdom and certainly sent by God to Java to give us counsel.'[32]

Carter twice visits Moes in Kediri. At the farewell on 8 May the cinema is filled with 500 to 600 people. Then Carter and Sumrall accompany Moes to Gambang Waluh. It becomes an unforgettable visit

---

[29] Ch. Schotborgh, 'Verslag', *GS* 12.4 (February 1939), pp. 22–24.
[30] From May 1936 until September 1937, the couple is visiting family in Denmark and Ferdinand Abell extensively makes acquaintance with the Danish Pentecostal Movement.
[31] See appendix 1 for more information about the foundation of the Ge-meenten Gods.
[32] M.A. Alt, 'Bezoek van de Brs. Howard Carter en Sumrall', *GS* 11.9 (May 1935), pp. 14–15.

for them, to which they often refer.[33] After their departure, Moes writes: 'Our [request for] affiliation with the 'Assemblies of God' was done by airmail last month. We hope to publish the reply soon.'[34] It is not known why this affiliation did not pass.[35] In January 1936, Moes writes that the Pinksterzending 'is not definitively affiliated' with any association, 'whether in Europe, or here'.[36]

From June to August 1935, Elise Scharten, Pentecostal missionary in China, visits Java. She conducts a series of meetings in the assemblies of the Pinksterzending. At an earlier visit of Scharten, in 1920, she was the first Pentecostal believer whom Moes had ever met. From 1932, her circular letters appear regularly in *Gouden Schooven*. In a crowded room in Kediri, Scharten speaks to the Chinese in Mandarin. Contacts with the Pentecostal assemblies in the Netherlands expand, especially with pastors Piet Klaver (Amsterdam), Pieter van der Woude (Rotterdam), G. van Polen (Scheveningen), and Johan Rietdijk in Flanders. The *Gouden Schooven* magazine is highly appreciated in the Netherlands as are the songs from *Gloriekklokken*.

Since Moes is Chairman of the Pinksterzending, she has to travel more often. Most assemblies are located in East and Middle Java, but some are also in West Java (Batavia and Bandung) and in the outskirts of Borneo. In June 1935, Moes visits two assemblies in Madura. From August 1935, *Gouden Schooven* lists all her speaking engagements each month. In this period she preaches on average eighteen times a month spread over fifteen days, in twelve places – a considerable undertaking when we bear in mind that travelling in those days was very time-consuming. She fills most of the content of *Gouden Schooven* that appears twice a month. She keeps up a considerable correspondence, along with leading a local assembly, the national work, and a home community. A full agenda!

---

[33] Howard Carter, *New York ... Tokyo ... Moscow ... When Time Flew By* (London: Hampstead Publications, 1936), pp. 31–33. Lester Sumrall, 'A Visit to a Javanese Kampong', *Redemption Tidings* 11.14 (15 July 1935), p. 7. Lester Sumrall, 'How the Gospel Triumphed in Java', *Redemption Tidings* (28 July 1939), pp. 7–8.

[34] M.A. Alt, 'Afscheidsmeeting van de Brs. Carter en Sumrall', *GS* 11.11 (June 1935), p. 11.

[35] In the incomplete archive of the British Assemblies of God, no traces of this application have been found.

[36] M.A. Alt, 'De Pinksterzending in Belgie', *GS* 9.2 (January 1936), p. 8.

Contacts with Others

In November 1935, Moes addresses a four-day conference in Malang, for the 'Union of Evangelization'. It establishes a good relationship between Moes and Daniel Gutter, evangelist of the Union in Malang. Gutter is to speak several times in the Pinksterzending at Kediri. Also through Elise Scharten, Moes is able to broaden her contacts. Elise comes from a Lutheran preacher's family with special love for mission. Her sister, Jenneke, and her brother-in-law, Johannes Pik, are missionaries on Java, as well as two sons of her sister, Jacoba: Karl and Berthold Gramberg. Karl Gramberg is the medical director of the Mennonite leper colony, Dono Rodjo, in Japara, where Moes visits him once.[37] His brother, Berthold Gramberg, is a missionary of the NZG in Malang. Johannes Pik, married to Jenneke Scharten, also lives in Malang and is Chairman of the 'Conference of Missionaries of East Java'. The Conference of Missionaries is a meeting of the missionaries of the NZG, but missionaries of the Java Committee also join. Twice a year they meet for a few days. It is most likely Moes will have met the missionaries Pik and Gramberg in Malang. Possibly these contacts have encouraged Moes to join the Missionary Study Council.

In 1937, the Pinksterzending joins the Interconfessional Zendingsstudie Raad (ZSR – Missionary Study Council). Moes writes: 'We remain completely free in all respects, but feel solidarity with all workers in the Lord's vineyard, preaching the cross of Christ in fullness and proclaiming the gospel in heathen lands'.[38] The ZSR is founded in Amsterdam in 1909 to promote interest in missionary work. This is done, for instance, by publications such as the Dutch Missionary Yearbook (1910–1939) and by organizing conferences.[39]

The previously noted growth of the Pentecostal movement (1927–1934) also resulted in problems with existing churches and missionaries. Those who join the Pentecostals are not only new converts. When members of the Javanese Protestant Church transfer to the Pentecostal assemblies, they are baptized there by immersion. That naturally causes tensions. Occasionally, these problems arise at

---

[37] M.A. Alt, 'De melaatschen-kolonie Dana Radja', *GS* 8.8 (April 1932), pp. 4–6. Karl Gramberg is Lutheran, his wife Mennonite.
[38] 'Aansluiting bij den Zendingsstudieraad', *GS* 10.20 (1937), p. 18.
[39] H.D.J. Boissevain, *De zending in oost en west 2* (Zeist: ZSR, 1945), pp. 298–315,

the Conferences of Missionaries. In February 1934, H.W. Van den Berg, missionary on behalf of the Java Committee at Modjowarno, gives a lecture on the Pentecostal Church at the Conference of Missionaries in East Java. Van den Berg has studied the subject deeply and shows an open attitude. He only sees one way to prevent people from moving to the Pentecostal assemblies, and that is 'becoming more spiritual, more faithful in prayer, giving more love'.[40]

An incident of such a transition in East Java, described in detail by Chairman Johannes Pik, illustrates the conflict. The occasion involves Mas Soewaka, a Javanese nurse in charge of the missionary clinic in Sitiardjo (Swaru-South district). Early in 1934, he suddenly hears the sound of a gong being struck with force and then a voice saying: 'Jesus Christ is not a person from the past, but He is the Living One'. He decides to read the whole Bible anew. In a dream Christ appears to him. He then asks the pastor of the Javanese church to join him and two teachers to study the Bible. When the pastor does not comply with the request, the three start their own circle. Soon after, Soewaka comes in contact with the Pentecostal church and is baptized by immersion. He begins to hold meetings in Sitiardjo. According to the *Nederlandsch Zendingsblad* (*Dutch Mission Paper*), in the meetings 'the usual shouting and crying prayers are being uttered'.[41] Due to the commotion that this causes in the village, Soewaka is transferred to Malang, where the mission hospital is located. When more and more members of the Javanese hospital staff show interest in his message, there is a 'Pentecostal Turmoil'.

A missionary doctor, A. Nortier, investigates the matter and is convinced of the sincerity of Mas Soewaka. Nortier causes disturbances among the missionaries by visiting meetings of the Pentecostal Church, and he even attends a baptismal service. In addition to the unrest among the Javanese staff, there is now also friction among the European missionaries. At the 1936 Conference, Nortier pleads for tolerance. Berthold Gramberg, conversely, calls for a firm intervention. When the headquarters of the NZG in Oegstgeest gets wind of it, they react in shock. They accuse the Conference, and especially Chairman Pik, of a slack and wavering attitude and call the

---

[40] H.W. van den Berg, 'De Pinkstergemeente', *De Opwekker* 79 (1934), p. 152.
[41] 'Een bezoek aan Sitiardjo', *Nederlandsch Zendingsblad* 19 (1936), p. 57. Soewaka came in contact with the Pentecostal evangelist Daniel from Modjo-warno.

missionary doctor to order.[42] The example shows how sensitive the issue is. The neutral position Chairman Pik has taken in his reports does not seem to be appreciated. Pik will later be succeeded by Herman Hildering.

Lawang 1936–1943

What a rush at Kediri Station, the morning of our departure! Nearly the whole congregation had come up to say goodbye, and everywhere, you saw emotional faces and tear- filled eyes … Some lovely Chinese sisters brought me by car to Lawang, where we arrived much earlier than the train passengers. Packed with suitcases and parcels, we looked like a group of migrants on their way to the Congo.[43]

Beginning in June 1935, Moes preaches once a month in Lawang. There is a small circle led by Ong Ting Swie from Malang. Repeatedly, Moes has been warned not to go and live there, as three previous attempts to set up a congregation failed.[44] Moes, however, knows she has been guided by God as she makes her entrance on 7 June 1936, as pastor of the Pinksterzending in Lawang. The town lies in a mountain area, eighteen kilometers north of Malang, the city to which it belongs.[45] It is located on the railway from Malang to Surabaya. Moes has many memories of this place. Thirty years earlier, she started her training as a nurse right here. The cooler climate suits her well. From

[42] Executive Committee NZG to the Conference of Missionaries on East-Java, Oegstgeest, 21 July 1936; Dr. B.M. Schuurman to the Executive Committee NZG, Denpasar, 10 September 1936; Executive Committee NZG to Dr. B.M. Schuurman, Oegstgeest, 26 September 1936; Executive Committee NZG to Dr. A. Nortier, Oegstgeest, 1 December 1936; Dr. A. Nortier to the Executive Committee NZG, Heemstede, 2 December 1936; J. Pik to the Executive Committee NZG, Malang, December 1936. With thanks to Johan Luttik. The NZG-archive is present in the Utrecht Archive. On the Conference the two opposite positions were taken by Dr. Nortier on the one side and by Rev. Berthold Gramberg on the other side. Chairman Pik who took a position in between, was an uncle of Gramberg.

[43] M.A. Alt, 'Onze verhuizing', *GS* 9.13 (July 1936), p. 16.

[44] M.A. Alt, 'Berichten van het arbeidsveld', *GS* 10.15 (August 1937), p. 17.

[45] In 1934 the residentship Malang numbers 1.8 million inhabitants, among whom are 13,500 Europeans and 21,500 Chinese. The city of Malang, where Lawang is located, has 1.1 million inhabitants, among whom are 10,000 Europeans and 14,000 Chinese. Because of the favourable climate, Malang is attractive for retired Europeans. G.F.E. Gonggryp (ed.), *Geïllustreerde Encyclopaedie van Nederlands-Indië* (Leiden: Leidsche Uitgeversmaatschappij, 1934), p. 795.

this place she will lead all the work until 1943. The meetings are held in the 'glass hall,' a rented glass-walled room on the Talun Road. In Lawang, live many totok-Chinese (immigrants from China). Only a few of them speak Malay, and most like to speak Dutch. Many of this group come to the (bilingual) mixed services where Europeans and Javanese also attend. In October 1936, the first converts are baptized. An orchestra and a choir are formed. As usual, the celebration of the Lord's Supper follows the baptism and this time also a meal organized by members of the congregation.[46] After one year there is a thriving assembly in Lawang with 150 members (100 Javanese and Chinese and fifty Europeans).[47] The totok-Chinese, who make up most of the congregation, call Moes their 'mujien' (mother).[48]

For the first ten months, Moes and her thirty-eight housemates enjoy hospitality in the home of a church member. As the assembly can now afford to pay rent, the Elim residential community moves to a larger house next to the meeting hall. Moes still has contact with the psychiatric institution of Sumber Porong, where she had worked before. Occasionally, a child of a patient is entrusted to the care of Moes.[49] The older housemates participate in the work, for instance, by selling the *Gouden Schooven* magazine. The evangelist, Soemardi Stefanus, trained by Moes, has also become a co-worker.

Through contacts made by going door-to-door with the magazines, people are brought to the church. Often, a sickness in a family causes people to come, because in the Pinksterzending, they pray for the sick. Once, Moes is asked to pray for the De Vrij family, whose daughter, Tine, is sick. Her healing leads to the conversion of the whole family.[50] Another time two sisters of the Pinksterzending knock at the door of the Andes family, where the son Piet appears to be ill. They pray for the son, and, here too, the healing results in the

---

[46] M.A. Alt, 'Inwijding nieuwe zaal in Lawang', *GS* 9.21 (November 1936), pp. 9–10.

[47] Van onzen correspondent, 'Zuster M.A. Alt', *Indische Courant* (24 August 1937).

[48] M.A. Alt, 'Drieënvijftig jaren', *GS* 9.18 (September 1936), pp. 14-15.

[49] In 1936 Dr. Van der Made of Sumber-Porong brings a sweet 2-year old boy, whose the mother being insane and whose father is unknown. Moes asks the readers for a cot. *GS* 9.13 (July 1936), p. 19.

[50] Bart Sigmond-de Vrij, interview by author, Arnhem, 4 January 2007. Bart is the oldest daughter in this family and the first to come to conversion. Later she becomes an evangelist in the Pinksterzending. Cf. Bartje de Vrij, 'Getuigenissen', *GS* 13.13 (July 1940), pp. 19–20.

conversion of the family.[51] During 1936–1942 dozens of church members testify in *Gouden Schooven* of their conversion or baptism with the Holy Spirit, but they testify even more of their healing. Often it is a healing through prayer without the use of medicines. Some of these testimonies refer to the visit of John Sung.

In 1939, Chinese Revivalist John Sung (1901–1944) visits Java. Sung achieved a doctorate in chemistry in America, but subsequently he became an evangelist in the Methodist Church.[52] During 1927–1940, he makes many trips inside and outside China including to Java with remarkable results. Cornelie Baarbé, evangelist of the Reformed Churches in Middle Java, designates his visit as bringing 'a revival on Java'.[53] His first stay in January-March 1939 begins in Surabaya and ends in Batavia. Three times a day he holds meetings. His audience is mainly Chinese, some Javanese, but hardly any Europeans. In Batavia, the Chinese Protestant Buitenkerk is too small and so the meetings are held in the Portuguese church. The last day there is prayer for the sick. Attendance is huge. Under the heading, 'Portuguese Church bombarded. Dr. Sung's miraculous healings,' the *Bataviaasch Nieuwsblad* reports: 'Blind people left the Church building seeing, crippled walking normally according to eyewitnesses – reports which we have not been able to verify as yet'.[54]

A second visit in August-September 1939 ends with a 10-day Bible course in Surabaya. A large bamboo tent is set up that seats up to 5,000 people. In the morning and afternoon, Sung teaches the 2,000 participants who want to devote themselves to evangelism with evangelistic meetings in the evenings drawing a full house. Regrettably for Moes, she had missed the previous campaign, but now she visits many meetings in Surabaya. Extensive reports in *Gouden Schooven* follow. Moes is very pleased with the message, the presentation, and the results. Next to repentance, rebirth, and sanctification, Sung also

---

[51] Dave Andes, interview by author, Veenendaal, 6 March 2014. Dave is the son of Piet Andes who was healed upon prayer. Cf. P. Andes, 'Getuigenissen', *GS* 13.9 (May 1940), p. 20. F. Andes, 'Getuigenissen', *GS* 13.13 (July 1940), p. 20.

[52] Leslie T. Lyall, *A Biography of John Sung: Flame for God in the Far East* (London: China Inland Mission, 4th edn, 1961). Sung's father was also a Methodist preacher.

[53] C. Baarbé, *Dr. Sung: Een réveil op Java. Lichtstralen op de akker der wereld* 50.3 (The Hague: Voorhoeve, [1949]). Cf. A.K. de Groot, 'Een Chineesch Opwekking-sprediker te Batavia', *Nederlands Zendingsblad* 22 (1939), pp. 123–25. H.A.C. Hildering, 'John Sung', *Nederlandsch Zendingsblad* 23 (1940), pp. 16–18.

[54] 'Portugeesche Kerk bestormd', *Bataviaasch Nieuwsblad* (2 March 1939).

preaches about the baptism with the Holy Spirit. Moes writes that his preaching is breathing freedom. The fact that Sung, as a Methodist, favours infant baptism, becomes less important to Moes, because his whole being radiates love.[55] Baarbé writes that public opinion in the Chinese community has been reversed by the campaign and is now in favour of Christianity. Ten years later, the Chinese churches on Java still draw life from the blessings of Sung's revival.[56] In the Pentecostal assemblies also, Sung's visit has a favourable impact. Although not a spectacular increase, the growth of the Pinksterzending in Lawang, too, seems a bit stronger this year. In the period from October to December 1939, there are two baptismal services in which thirty-five people are baptized.

Last Photo of Moesje in Gambang Waluh (1941)

The youth work is developing. In June 1940, the youth department, Kleine Kracht (Little Power), is established. The same month the capacity of the glass hall is increased from 200 to 300 seats. At the same time, a suburb assembly is opened under the leadership of evangelist Papilajah in a Javanese kampong. In January 1941, 'the

---

[55] M.A. Alt, 'John Sung en zijn boodschap VI', *GS* 13.1 (January 1940), pp. 9–10.

[56] Baarbé, *Dr. Sung*, p. 40.

young brother' Sahelangi is introduced to Lawang as an evangelist and assistant of Moes.

On 13 February 1940, Moes is on a road trip to Modjokerto in stormy weather. Suddenly, the driver is forced to turn aside to avoid an oncoming car and loses control of the wheel. The car slides and comes to a stop against a thick tree along the road. The driver and Moes suffer serious injuries. The three girls in the back remain un-harmed. Semi-conscious, Moes is brought home by an unknown cou-ple. She has a lot of pain on the left side of her chest. The couple wants to call a doctor, because Moes has suffered internal injuries. Moes does not want a doctor, because she wants to rely entirely on God for healing. The pain increases in intensity. Two elders come to anoint her with oil in the name of the Lord. At night, church mem-bers watch at her bedside. The third night the pain is unbearable. Crying to God, she suddenly sees Elijah praying on Mount Carmel and hears the words: 'The prayer of the righteous has great power'.[57] The next morning she can rise without help, and she resumes her work a few days later.

Reports in the press indicate that Moes has a good reputation in Lawang. In August 1937 'the widely-known' Moes is esteemed for her Christian social work. Reference is made to the mountain colony in Gambang Waluh but also to the home community in Lawang with forty persons entrusted to the care of Moes.[58] Eight months later we read: 'Even in the circles of those who do not belong to the Pink-sterzending, you always hear good reports about the work and aspi-rations of Sister Alt and her followers'.[59] Once, Moes participates in a public debate. When the newspaper, *De Indische Courant,* cites an article from a Protestant church magazine stating that the woman has to keep silent in the church, Moes responds with a letter to the editor. She believes that, in a time when the world is on fire, there are more important issues. The church needs all available powers, male and fe-male, for the salvation of humanity.[60] From March 1941, Moes

---

[57] M.A. Alt, 'Ons auto-ongeval', *GS* 13.6 (March 1940), pp. 7–8. This indicates bruised ribs.

[58] Van onzen correspondent, 'Zuster M.A. Alt', *Indische Courant* (24 August 1937).

[59] Van onzen correspondent, 'Zuster Alt en de Pinksterzending', *Indische Courant* (21 April 1938).

[60] M.A. Alt, 'Vrouw en de Kerk', *Indische Courant* (9 October 1941), referring to 'Vrouw en kerk' in *Indische Courant* (3 October 1941).

delivers monthly talks on the radio for Java; and then 'after six months, twice a month'.[61]

As before, Moes is very busy preaching and giving Bible studies. In Kediri, this averaged eighteen times a month; in Lawang (including radio speeches) this averages twenty-one times a month, or five times a week.[62] In a 'sermon book' she keeps track of the sermons she has preached. Assemblies where Moes speaks once or more every month are next to Lawang: Malang, Surabaya, Probolinggo, and Kediri. Other assemblies in East Java where Moes regularly speaks include: Djember, Blitar, Modjokerto, Sitoebondo, and Glenmore. In Middle Java she ministers at Semarang, Ambarawa, Salatiga, Temanggung, Solo, Djokja, and Madonna. Three times a year she travels to Gambang Waluh and once a year to West Java (Batavia, Meester Cornelis, Weltevreden, Bandung, and Cheribon). In November 1937, she visits Sumatra again (Palembang, Pladju). Furthermore, Moes devotes a lot of time to *Gouden Schooven*, which appears twice a month until March 1942. In 1940 she publishes a new editon of *Het Volle Licht* (*The Full Light*), a daily devotional book for the family, with a Bible verse and prayer for every morning and evening.

The special bond with Gambang Waluh remains strong. Every month, Moes sends money for the care of the widows, orphans, and poor of the colony. In August 1937, after years of prayer, the property is formally assigned to the Pinksterzending.[63] It is a great relief, because of fears that the government would reclaim the land. Now, the land that Moes had already assigned to the residents becomes their property. It's always a spiritual feast for the residents when she comes to visit, and it is the same for Moes: 'In no assembly is there as much glory as at Gambang Waluh. What excited singing and fervent prayer!'[64]

---

[61] Since March 1941 Moes gives monthly Radio-sermons for the broadcast ARVO and as from September also for NICRO. *GS* 14.4 (February 1941), p. 6; *GS* 14.17 (September 1941), p. 22.

[62] Every month *Gouden Schooven* publishes the monthly speaking arrangements of Moes. The average is calculated from July 1936 until December 1941. Due to the war, the periodical stops early 1942.

[63] M.A. Alt, 'Een wonderbaar resultaat', *GS* 10.20 (October 1937), pp. 15–16. Moes had a judicial advisory agency at Salatiga to deal with the complicated procedure.

[64] M.A. Alt, 'Gambang Waloeh', *GS* 11.12 (June 1938), p. 11.

*Gambang Waluh, 3 Bridal Couples, Behind Them the
Elders Jakoboes, Elias, Stefanoes en Joenoes (1939)*

In 1939, three couples marry at the same time. Moes knows nearly
all of them from their childhood. The Pinksterzending has been
granted permission to solemnize legal marriages in the colony and to
report births and deaths[65] One picture shows the three couples together with the elders: Jakoboes, Elias, Stefanoes, and Joenoes. Elias
is one of the travelling evangelists who also speaks at the Pentecostal
conferences. In that year, the old barn, which serves as a church hall,
is refurbished and has new benches and chairs. During Christmas
1939, Moes looks back on twenty-five years of labour at Gambang
Waluh. The mortality rate has fallen considerably in those years. At
least 400 Javanese have been baptized. Some have left, but most have
remained faithful. One of the older women recalls the first Christmas, when she was fourteen years old: 'You (Moes) were still young,
your hair was still dark and you had red cheeks'.[66] In 1941, there are
plans for renovating the buildings. Evangelist D. Sahelangi settles
there in order to lead this work. Because of the war, it is not until
1947 that we receive messages about the colony again. From a report

    [65] M.A. Alt, 'Bruiloft te Gambang Waloeh', *GS* 12.20 (October 1939), pp. 18–
19.
    [66] M.A. Alt, 'Onze Kerstvieringen', *GS* 13.2 (January 1940), p. 7.

in 1951, it appears that a visit by Moes to Gambang Waluh in 1942 had been her last to that beloved place.[67]

In the vicinity of Plampangan near Blitar, there is a second full Javanese assembly. Since 1931, Moes is active in Blitar, where an assembly is formed with mainly Javanese and Chinese members. From Blitar, Tan Tjwan Ling begins to hold meetings in a desa near Plampangan in 1941. Marto Goenoeng, a converted dukun in whose house the meetings are held, appears to have a gift of healing. Several remarkable healings take place. From all the surroundering areas, people come to the meetings, sometimes walking five hours.[68] In the years that follow, hundreds of Javanese are baptized.

From the beginning of 1935, the Pinksterzending has grown into a national church with sixty assemblies, a magazine and song-book, bookshop, annual conferences, and affiliation with the Missionary Study Council. The outbreak of the Second World War has major consequences. From May 1940, contacts with the Netherlands are largely blocked. In January 1941, the mobilization of the army begins. Pastors and workers of the Pinksterzending are also mobilized. With the invasion of the Japanese, everything changes.

---

[67] M.A. Alt, 'Berichten arbeidsveld', (April 1951), 20. Further details are lacking.

[68] M.A. Alt, 'Opwekking onder Javanen', *GS* 20.4 (June 1941), pp. 5–6; Liem Hong Bo, 'Kan God niet wonderen van genezing doen?', pp. 15–16. Late 1949 the assembly counts 300 baptized members. In 1950 the parents of Stefanus settle here to assist Marto.

11

CAMP YEARS

How great and precious Christ was to me in the days when I was locked up in prison awaiting my death by beheading.[1]

In her publication, *Ons Kampleven gedurende de Japansche en Republikeinsche bezetting* (*Our Camp Life during the Japanese and Republican Occupation*), Moes shares her experiences in the camps from 1943 to 1947. It first appears in 1947 as a series of articles in *Gouden Schooven*. In 1948, the articles are published in book form.[2] In this chapter we follow her through these camps, starting with how she, as a Pentecostal leader, viewed the pre-war developments and with a sketch of the historical context.

The Threat of War

During the 1930s, there are five, Dutch Pentecostal periodicals. In the Netherlands these are: *Spade Regen* (*Latter Rain*) first published in 1933 and edited by Pieter van der Woude at Rotterdam, *Het Middernachtelijk Geroep* (*The Midnight Cry*) from 1937 and edited by Nico Vetter at Haarlem and *Kracht van Omhoog* (*Power from on High*) from 1937 and edited by Piet Klaver at Amsterdam. In the Dutch Indies they are: *Dit is Het* (*This is That*) from 1923 and edited by Johan Thiessen at

---

[1] M.A. Alt, *Herinneringen uit mijnleven* (Velp: Pinksterzending, 1963), p. 78.

[2] M.A. Alt, *Ons Kampleven gedurende de Japansche en Rupublikeinsche bezetting* (Surabaya: De Pinksterzending – Assemblies of God in Indonesië, [1948]). It first appeared as a series of articles from January 1947 until January 1948 in *Gouden Schooven*.

Bandung and *Gouden Schooven* (*Golden Sheaves*) from 1928 edited by Moesje Alt.

Moes is by a long way, the first among these editors to discern the dangers of impending national-socialism in Germany. In this connection the vision she receives in August 1926 of the crucified Messiah is important. Not far from the cross, she perceives a figure rising up with the appearance of a beast. The figure opens his clothes, he has the skin of a panther, and on his breast a big jet-black swastika becomes visible. He points to it with a proud gesture. A voice says: 'This is the mark of the Beast!'[3] In 1931, when Moes reads of the introduction of the swastika as the mark of the Nazis in Germany, she returns to her diary where the vision is written down and publishes it in *Gouden Schooven*.[4] Several times she repeats her warning (1931, 1932, 1938, and 1940).

In 1932, she speaks of the appalling persecution of the Jews and warns that the Nazis who wear the mark of the Beast in particular hate the Jews.[5] At the same time, Moes discerns God's plan in the suffering of the Jewish people: 'We may assume that the present persecution of the Jews is the means of the people returning soon to Palestine by the hand of God. Only then, according to Scripture, will the Jewish people come to conversion.'[6] Regularly, she writes about the increasing hatred against the Jews and about the Jewish refugees travelling to Palestine. She disapproves of the placidity of the so-called 'German Christians' in the face of the Nazi government. In contrast, she supports the opposition of the 'Confessional Church' and imprisoned preachers like Martin Niemöller. She keeps informed about the situation in the Netherlands. With pleasure, she reports a protest meeting of the Freedom Union in Amsterdam against the growing antisemitism: 'How wonderful it would be if *all* the Christian churches were to have such a protest meeting. Why are the Christians silent, when they are so indebted to Israel?'[7] In November 1939, Moes commences public Bible Studies in Surabaya on the book of Revelation for believers of every church affiliation.

---

[3] M.A. Alt, 'Het swastica-kruis', *GS* 8.18 (September 1932), p. 4.

[4] M.A. Alt, 'Het merkteeken van het Beest', pp. 16–17. The diary concerned has not been found.

[5] M.A. Alt, 'De Joden-vervolgingen', *GS* 8.21 (November 1932), pp. 9–10.

[6] Alt, 'De Joden-vervolgingen', pp. 9–10.

[7] M.A. Alt, 'Een echt-Hollandsche protestmeeting', *GS* 9.11 (June 1936), pp. 14–15.

The German occupation comes unexpectedly: 'As a thunder from clear sky, we received the message of the crushing battle that happened in our precious homeland ... God who never fails has allowed this terrible visitation on our people, so that we would return to the old rugged cross.'[8] Moes views the acts of war from a dispensational understanding of the Bible. God has divided humanity into three groups: the Church, Israel, and the Gentiles (the nations). In the end times, Israel will become an independent state. The Church will be raptured (taken up in the sky). A time of 'Great Tribulation' will plague the world, leading to a major battle at Armageddon, followed by the 'Millennium', a thousand years of peace.[9]

At a so-called 'time lecture' in the Loge Building in Surabaya, Moes talks about two crosses that are diametrically opposed: the cross of Christ and the cross of the Antichrist. Referring to Daniel 7 and Revelation 13 and 17, Moes expects the creation of a German-Roman empire.[10] In 1941, Moes begins a series of articles about the book of Revelation which will be published as a brochure. This topic is also discussed in her radio addresses. The above shows how Moes, in her own way, follows the major developments in world politics. She tries to interpret the changes for her readers. Political events are mostly explained spiritually, by giving them a place in the end-times scenario. In this way, she offers believers the prospect of a better future in the purpose of God.

War and Revolution

One day after the Japanese attack on Pearl Harbor on 7 December 1941, the Dutch government in exile declares war against Japan. One month later, the Japanese armies attack the Dutch Indies. On 8 March 1942, the Dutch troops on Java surrender. The victory of an Asian nation against the Dutch feeds Indonesian aspirations for independence. The Japanese aim is for one great Asian empire under their leadership. From now on, Western influences are regarded as hostile. Dutch schools are closed. People are prohibited from reading Dutch newspapers and magazines as well as listening to allied radio

---

[8] M.A. Alt, 'Rouw en droevenis', *GS* 13.11 (1 June 1940), p. 4.
[9] M.A. Alt, 'Het profetisch woord dat zeer vast is: Tijdspredeking', *GS* 13.12 (June 1940), pp. 4–5.
[10] M.A. Alt, 'De Wederkomst van Christus', *GS* 13.15 (August 1940), pp. 4–7.

messages. Malay is now the common language.[11] The Japanese era is introduced, and the year 1942 has become 2602. European men, later the women and children, are interned in camps, Moes included.[12] On Java, only a small number of Indo-Europeans are interned. Because of their Asian origin, they are initially left undisturbed, but, because of their pro-Dutch attitudes, their situation will become increasingly difficult. Vacant positions in government and business are filled by Indonesians. The Japanese promise the Indonesians future independence. About two million young people receive a semi-military training. After the war, they will play a crucial role in the struggle for independence. Sukarno and other political prisoners are released. They cooperate with the Japanese government because of the prospect of an independent state. During the Japanese occupation, they gain useful experience in political leadership, and with the military-trained youth, they quickly raise an armed force.[13]

On 15 August 1945, Japan surrenders to the Allies. Two days later, Nationalists led by Sukarno proclaim independence as the Indonesian Republic. The news of the proclamation spreads rapidly and is welcomed by most Indonesians, especially among young people. It is a confusing situation. The English, who will take over the authority on behalf of the Allies, have not yet arrived. The Japanese prefer an independent Indonesian Republic to a return of the Dutch. However, they must follow the command of the Allies to maintain order until the arrival of the British. Wherever possible, they try to avoid confrontation with Indonesians.[14] Indonesian youth groups (pemudas) manage to capture weapons without much opposition from the Japanese army.

The last three months of 1945 are very violent. This chaotic period is later called the Bersiap (Be Alert). Dutch, Indo-Europeans, Chinese, and others who have cooperated with the Dutch (Ambonese and Menadonese) are at risk. Their houses are plundered and an unknown number of people are killed. At the end of September, the first British soldiers arrive. They come to maintain order, take

---

[11] Mary C. van Delden, *De republikeinse kampen in Nederlands-Indië October 1945–May 1947: Orde in de chaos?* (Kockengen: by the author, 2007), pp. 15–18, 43–50.

[12] Of the 42,000 prisoners of war only a few remain on Java. In the Japanese camps for civilians on Java about 80,000 persons are interned. Van Delden, *Republikeinse kampen*, p. 26.

[13] Leslie Palmier, *Indonesia* (London: Thames and Hudson, 1965), pp. 105–106.

[14] Van Delden, *Republikeinse kampen*, pp. 71–81, 106.

responsibility for the internees, evacuate them where necessary, and remove the Japanese, but they do not want to get caught up in a colonial war. On Java, they operate from the urban centers of Batavia, Bandung, Semarang, and Surabaya without entering any deeper into the Republican areas. Former Japanese camps in allied territories are now refugee or shelter camps. In Surabaya and Bandung, the British fight a fierce battle against Indonesian forces. During this troubled period, Europeans and Indo-Europeans in Republican areas are again interned in camps for their own safety. These are called Republican camps or Bersiap camps. The internees often do not see themselves as under protection but as hostages. It is in the interest of the Republican government to prevent a massacre in order not to lose the support of the international community.[15] Those interned in these Republican camps are mostly Indo-Europeans. Only 4,500 out of the 46,000 interned in Republican camps on Java are totok.[16]

The international community exerts pressure on both the Dutch and the Nationalists to reach an agreement. The talks end in a deadlock. Meanwhile, the Dutch send in their troops. In July 1947, the first euphemistically called 'police action' begins. In December 1948, a second police action follows. The international community strongly rejects the violent interventions. Under pressure from the United States, the two parties reach an agreement. On 27 December 1949, the sovereignty of the Dutch Indies, except New Guinea, is formally transferred to Indonesia. Batavia is now officially renamed Jakarta.

This is the context of the years Moes spent in camps. The first three (in Malang, Solo, and Ambarawa) are Japanese camps, followed by a Republican camp (in Lawang) and finally, until June 1947, a shelter camp (in Surabaya) under British and later Dutch governance.

Japanese Camps 1943–1945 (Malang, Solo, Ambarawa)

A loud noise, screaming, the door opens,
A woman is carried in, her head bleeding.

---

[15] Van Delden, *Republikeinse kampen*, p. 147.
[16] Van Delden, *Republikeinse kampen*, p. 149.

She has committed a heavy crime
Too late she greeted the Nippon guard[17]

Almost immediately after the Japanese invasion the publication of *Gouden Schooven* is halted. The last issue appears in early March 1942. For the camp period, we mainly depend on *Ons Kampleven*, summarized below. From December 1945, Moes keeps a diary, and in December 1946, *Gouden Schooven* reappears in a slim volume. In the beginning of the Japanese occupation, Moes is still able to travel. She is equipped with a proof of registration, a travel pass, a red band around her right arm, and a silver cross in her button-hole. Soon she travels alone because it becomes dangerous for the young girls to join her. The trains are crowded, and she often has to stand. Sometimes, there are spies in the meetings. The humiliations and abuses by Japanese on the streets and in houses get more and more brutal.

On 24 August 1943, Moes is arrested in her house, together with her assistant Stefanus. The whole house is searched. The fact that she lists the birthdays of the Dutch Royal House and asks a blessing for the Queen and county in her publication, *Het Volle Licht*, is a subversive act in the eyes of the Japanese. For this 'crime' she is sentenced to death by decapitation. Stefanus is released after ten days while Moes waits in her cell for her execution. Then a message arrives. Because of her age (two days before her arrest she had turned sixty), the 'fair' verdict is changed to an internment in De Wijk a women's camp in Malang. Just in time, Stefanus has been able to submit her birth certificate. Her church members are allowed to come to say goodbye before she leaves. Tears are flowing while Moes prays for them in Javanese.

On 5 September 1943, Japanese officers bring her to De Wijk in the Bergen suburb of Northwest Malang. Among the 7,000 women and children behind the barbed wire are some housemates and church members. She also meets the mother and three daughters (Bartje, Manda, and Ella) of the De Vrij family. They will stay in all the camps with Moes. The residents themselves are responsible for their own food. There is a small market where they can buy nearly everything they need. A church member of the Pinksterzending in Lawang supplies milk to the camp and is sometimes able to smuggle

---

[17] M.A. Alt, 'In de Ziekenzaal van het Nipponsche interneeringskamp', *Ons Kampleven*, p. 40.

in money for Moes. Conditions during the three months in this camp are bearable. Frightened by her near beheading, Moes starts her first autobiography in September 1943 (in Japanese era 2603). The 82-page script survives the Japanese camps.

On 30 November 1943, Moes is transported with 400 other detainees. The windows and doors of the overcrowded train are covered. When the train slowly runs through Lawang, some windows open briefly. Many church members, including Stefanus, wave at her with raised arms. In a flash, Moes sees their smiling, loving faces as they pass. After a tiring 24-hour journey, the train arrives at Solo in the middle of the night. Many have fainted from the unbearable heat of a wagon without ventilation. At the station, standing in rows of five, they are repeatedly counted. Eventually, they go to the camp called Mangku Bumen, also called Bumicamp, by lorry and bus. It is a former hospital in the Western district of Solo where over 4,000 women and children are interned.[18] Moes is grouped together with the other elderly women to cut vegetables for three hours every morning. During the work, she testifies of her life with God. In the afternoon, some of them meet in small groups under a tree to discuss the Bible and pray. They must not be seen because meetings are forbidden. Church services for Protestants and Catholics are allowed on Sunday, although without preaching and singing. At Christmas and New Year, songs from *Johan de Heer* and *Glorieklokken* are sung softly in the barracks.

The food is very poor. The sick-wards are crowded with patients suffering from oedema. Doctors who come to tend the sick are abused by the guards. Many of the detainees die. Moes prays at several deathbeds. Giving Bible talks, teaching Sunday school, and speaking heart-to-heart bring her joy in the midst of misery. There is a lot of violence. For the slightest offense, detainees are beaten or have to stand in the burning sun for hours. While doing house searches, the Javanese auxiliary soldiers walk on the beds with their dirty boots and take everything they find useful. During a roll-call, Dr. Engels does not bow deep enough in the eyes of Japanese. She receives a blow to her face, but, to the surprise of everyone, she quickly strikes back. A shock goes through the rows of people

---

[18] Cf. the sites www.japanseburgerkampen.nl and www.bersiapkampen.nl, by Henk Beekhuis; D. van Velden, *De Japanse burgerkampen* (Franeker: Wever, 2nd edn, 1976).

present at the roll-call. She is severely mistreated and locked up for a month. Not long after that, she dies of her injuries. The whole camp attends her funeral. When ten young girls are summoned to work as 'bar girls', unrest breaks out. The camp leader, Mrs. Smidt, a former officer of the Salvation Army, refuses to cooperate. The camp committee files a petition with the Japanese Governor at Semarang while Christians unite in prayer. When the command is reversed, prayers of thanksgiving abound.

On 30 May 1945, Moes and others are transported to Ambarawa Camp 6. She is sick and has lost a lot of weight. On her feet are large, red burning spots. Ambarawa is forty-five kilometers South of Semarang. It is a former KNIL (Dutch army) camp. The food is as bad as in Solo, but it is a little less violent, and the atmosphere is more optimistic. After half-an-hour in the camp, Moes gets a pamphlet from a co-resident with the good news that the Netherlands has been liberated. Moes gets along well with Mrs. Reinders, who is in charge of the spiritual care of the Protestants. In the open air, Moes teaches catechism and Sunday school to a large crowd of children, and in the barracks, she prays for the sick. Rumors that the Japanese are on the verge of losing arouses hope of a speedy release.

On the evening of her 62th birthday (22 August 1945), the coverings over the lamps along the wall of Camp Ambarawa 6 are removed. Moes realizes: we are free! During the following days, air-crafts drop food packages and orange-coloured leaflets. Dutch flags appear on all sides. The gate opens and there is trade through barter with the local people who are well disposed towards the detainees at that moment. The Japanese guards look fearful. Co-workers of the Pinksterzending visit Moes. Five brothers from Gambang Waluh bring chickens and eggs. There are tears of joy because Moes is still alive. In the camps, her weight has dropped from sixty-seven to forty-two kilos.

Residents leave the camp in groups: first the Indo-Europeans and then the 'totok'. Moes leaves in the third vehicle. Many wear orange ornaments or the Dutch tricolour. The euphoria soon gives way to disappointment. When the train arrives in Magelang, the population reacts with hostility to the Dutch national decorations. On the advice of the Red Cross, these are wisely removed. In Djokja, the Red Cross brings them to a large hotel. Moes is not prepared for the changed, political relations and is bitterly disappointed: 'There was no sign of freedom; everywhere turmoil and enmity ruled. No Indonesian looked at us kindly in those days, the hatred shone out of their eyes.'[19] From there, they go via Surabaya to Lawang where they arrive on 9 September 1945. It is a happy reunion with loved ones. Stefanus has faithfully guarded the house and the books. With great wisdom and diplomacy, he has led the assemblies in Lawang, Surabaya, and Malang under difficult circumstances. Immediately, Moes resumes her work. The Indonesian authorities initially allow Dutch services to be held. At night, however, it is restless around the house. Javanese walk the streets armed with knives or bamboo spears and force Europeans to shout, 'Merdeka!' ('Freedom!'). After a month, Dutch and Indonesians are no longer allowed to live in the same house. Moes is forced to leave her home and moves in with a local church member. 'A true feeling of terror engulfed them. No European was allowed to speak or to cooperate with an Indonesian. A boycott was declared. No light, no water, no servants – and no one was allowed to buy food from Indonesians, including the Chinese and other Oriental people.'[20] Eventually all Europeans are interned in Lawang.

Republican Camp Tawangsari 1945–1946

There is no greater enemy of the soul, except sin, than fear. The fear of death that sprung upon me multiple times over the past two years, like wolves attacking their prey, made my soul almost insusceptible to the comfort of fellowship with the Lord.[21]

On 4 December 1945, Moes arrives in the Republican camp at Tawangsari, in the Wilhelmina Park in Lawang. She stays here until 11 July 1946. The camp is guarded by the Indonesian police. Among the 1,100 residents is a small group of older men. The rest are women and children. Almost all inhabitants are Indo-Europeans with only twenty-five totok.[22] All Indo-European members of the Pinksterzending in Lawang are also in the camp. Shortly before the detention, Moes began to write some brief thoughts on paper. The first page

---

[19] Alt, *Ons Kampleven*, p. 25.
[20] Alt, *Ons Kampleven*, p. 26.
[21] M.A. Alt, 'Dagboek 1945–1961', November 1945, p. 15.
[22] Dr. Descoeudres, 'Camp d'Internement Tawangsari à Lawang', report of a visit on behalf of the International Red Cross dated 13 February 1946. With thanks to Mary C. van Delden.

gives the title: 'Meditations of a redeemed and Christ-connected soul'. She takes the script along and uses it as a diary that will continue until 1961.

The camp head, the police officer Soedarmo, knows Moes from Lawang and respects her. He gives her permission to hold meetings on Sunday and even has a piano brought in. There is no other minister or priest in the camp, so Moes takes the lead. The hall is always full, and of course, there is a choir. People come to repentance or deepen their faith. Eleven days after arrival, Moes has to lead a funeral; she writes, 'I am actually against graveside preaching – the Lord Jesus never liked it. His graveside preaching was: "Lazarus arise." But to those who are left behind, I speak a word of consolation, hoping that it may reach their soul.'[23] The Sunday School she soon starts is attended by 150 children from all religious persuasions. To celebrate Christmas, her third in exile, Moes gets the full co-operation of the police. There are 400 children and 200 adults. On New Year's Eve: 'A lovely full meeting, with choir and piano. God's Spirit was in our midst. Catholics and Protestants sang bravely together from *Glorieklokken*.'[24] Moes also gives Bible Studies and occasional lectures on particular subjects, such as marriage or the second coming of Christ. With all these activities, as well as home visits and choir practices, her time is completely filled. For years to come, she receives letters from people who remember the sacred moments in Tawangsari.

The rooms in the camp are crawling with vermin and the buildings have dreadful, leaking roofs. Mattresses lie on the ground and have to dry in the sun after the rain. Compared to the hunger and terror in the Japanese camps, life in Tawangsari is relatively good. The residents have to buy their own food. Because virtually no one has money, bartering with Javanese is done at the fence in whispered tones. Occasionally, they receive baskets of food. Stefanus brings the baskets to police officers who are sympathetic to Moes. Just behind the fence at the laundry is the house of a church member (Nelly van de Berg). Occasionally a choir made up members of the local congregation meets in the house and sings songs from *Glorieklokken*. The comforting songs are heard by Moes and her fellow believers and sound like a message from above.

---

[23] Alt, 'Dagboek 1945–1961', 15 December 1945, p. 24.
[24] Alt, 'Dagboek 1945-1961', Nieuwjaar 1946, p. 31.

In February 1946, Swiss medical doctor Descoeudres visits the camp on behalf of the International Red Cross. His overall impression is favourable. However, he reports that many residents have no money to buy food. Therefore he calls on the camp authorities to provide residents with some basic food for free, as is done in some other camps.[25]

In July, by order of the British, any Dutch who have suffered in the Japanese camps (the APWIs: Allied Prisoners of War and Internees) may leave the camp. Before she leaves, Moes is given permission to say goodbye first to the church in Lawang. The choir sings her a moving parting song, and Moes transfers the work to Stefanus.

On 11 July 1946, Moes is transported to Solo Airport by train. She feels unwell. With stops in Malang and Blitar, the journey takes fourteen hours. At Solo, Moes is taken to the airport infirmary with a high fever. The other camp residents fly to Semarang the next day and from there leave for Batavia by boat. The sick Moes stays behind and later flies by plane straight to Batavia, where she stays in the hospital for eleven days. Moes, who has not used any medicine for twenty years, is given a compulsory quinine cure against her will. She is too sick to resist.[26] Discharged from the hospital, she stays in the camp at Tjideng, reunited with the De Vrij family until 7 August. Many around her ask her to stay in Batavia, but she feels led to go to Surabaya.

---

[25] Descoeudres, 'Camp d'Internement Tawangsari à Lawang'.
[26] Alt, 'Dagboek 1945–1961', 17 July 1946, p. 68.

12

SURABAYA 1946–1951

After my release from the last camp, it was my plan to settle in Surabaya. Together with our evangelist, Stefanus, I took up my work again in the assembly.[1]

The next five years in Surabaya are the last for Moes on Java. The war years had brought changes in the Pentecostal assemblies. When the Europeans and some of the Indo-Europeans were interned in camps, a large section of the leadership was suddenly gone. Out of sheer necessity the Indonesian Christians were put through a course in independence.[2] Organizations took Indonesian names to replace the Dutch ones. The PGNI continued as Gereja Pantekosta di Indonesia (Pentecostal Church in Indonesia, abbreviated as GPdI). When the former leaders were released from the camps in 1945, the situation in the churches had changed irreversibly. In the new Indonesian Republic, there was only room for Indonesian leadership. This is also true in the churches. From 1945–1949, the country is divided into the Republican territory and the territory controlled by the Allies or Dutch.

In 1946, Moes does not return to her assembly and home in Lawang. In the Republican area there is an unfriendly climate for Dutch people. She moves to Surabaya in Allied territory, where many other Dutch and Indo-Europeans go. The camp years have affected

---

[1] M.A. Alt, *Herinneringen uit mijn leven* (Velp: Pinksterzending, 1963), p. 79.

[2] J.S. Aritonang and K. Steenbrink (eds.), *A History of Christianity in Indonesia* (Leiden: Brill, 2008), p. 186.

her nervous system and, also the heat of Surabaya oppresses her.[3] Nevertheless she begins to rebuild the assembly. Meetings can be held in Dutch without objection and Dutch-language literature can be published. In the first years, there is hardly any contact with the assemblies that are in the Republican territory. Travelling is dangerous, especially for Dutch citizens.

De Pinksterzending in Surabaya

On 9 August 1946, Moes arrives in Surabaya by boat. The city has been in the hands of the British since December 1945 after a violent battle, and since the end of 1946, it is under the Dutch government. The population is reduced but will now grow steadily. In December 1946, there are 189,000 inhabitants; by February 1949 this increases to 462,000 and in September 1950 to 656,000.[4] Until June 1947, Moes, along with seven housemates, has a room in the Metropole shelter camp. In the hall of the former hotel, she can conduct meetings almost immediately. Surabaya is familiar to Moes. From 1936, she travelled from Lawang to Surabaya twice a month to conduct services. From October 1939 to her arrest, she held weekly services in a hall at 130 Plampitan. The old church members soon find their way to the meetings in Metropole. The assembly begins to blossom again. A choir, Sunday School, and Bible Studies follow. In December 1946, Moes, to her great joy, can publish *Gouden Schooven* again. For the time being, the magazine can only be distributed 'in all cities occupied by our Government'.[5] The 500 monthly copies will gradually increase to 2,600 in 1951. After many years, Moes can once again correspond with her loved ones in the homeland. From her sister-in-law Tine, she learns that her brother Bram had already died in 1940.[6]

---

[3] In her diary Moes writes several times about the consequences of the camp years on her body and spirit. She mentions fear, fright, sleeplessness, and fainting. M.A., 'Dagboek 1945-1861', pp. 84, 122–23, 140–41.

[4] 'Soerabaja's Bevolking' in *Het Dagblad* (28 December 1947); *De Vrije Pers Ochtendbulletin* (4 April 1949 and 7 October 1950).

[5] M.A. Alt, 'Kerstviering in vrijheid', *GS* 19.1 (December 1946), p. 2.

[6] Alt, 'Dagboek 1945–1961', 19 November 1946, p. 101. Earlier Moes already had a feeling that her brother had died: 29 October 1946, p. 96. Also her aunt Sophie (the last remaining sister of her mother) died during the war. Only nephews and nieces are still alive from her family.

Pinksterzending Assembly Surabaya (16 May 1948)

Moes pays a visit to Rev. Herman Hildering (1898–1986) as he provides free Bibles. Hildering has been a missionary since 1930.[7] From 1932, he works in cooperation with the NZG among the Chinese in East Java. In 1939, he becomes Chairman of the Conference of Missionaries, and he then joins the NZG. Hildering is befriended by the Japanese pastor, Susho Miyahira, a member of the Pinksterzending. In 1939, he enthusiastically supports the campaign with John Sung. At Sung's first visit to Surabaya, Hildering was still an observer. However, on the second visit, 'when I decided to attentively follow a full evening from the beginning to the end, it became different and I automatically became a participant, pulled into the stream. I have spent five nights there and enjoyed it.'[8] He invites Moes for an ecumenical service on Christmas Day 1946 in the Bubutan Church.[9] Moes preaches in Javanese, and her choir sings a song. All the Protestant churches are represented. When a sun beam shines through one of the coloured windows, it is like a revelation to her: 'This is the beginning of the great global revival promised by God to prepare the bridal Church for the Rapture'.[10]

---

[7] Hildering first was a missionary of the Gereformeerde Kerken in Hersteld Verband, a secession from the Netherlands Reformed Church.

[8] H.A.C. Hildering, 'Dr. John Sung', *Nederlandsch Zendingsblad* 23 (1940), p. 17.

[9] Alt, 'Dagboek 1945–1961', 2 November 1946, p. 97; cf. 14 October 1946, pp. 91–92.

[10] M.A. Alt, 'Opdat zij allen een zijn', *GS* 16.2 (February 1947), p. 1.

Moes has now been a missionary for thirty-six years, twenty of which are in the Pentecostal movement. She has become more open to believers from other churches: 'The more I grow in spiritual experience, the more things I leave behind on my faith journey: rules, dogmas, and legal regulations. The Holy Spirit makes me *free*. No more hobby-horses. I become more *evangelical*, softer in my judgment towards those who think differently.'[11] Every Christmas, ecumenical services are held with participation by the Protestant Church, Reformed Church, Salvation Army, Pinksterzending, and the Union of Evangelization. Occasionally, joint services are held with D. Kuijken of the Union of Evangelization. There is, however, no contact with the Pentecostal church where Van Gessel is pastoring. The pain of the rupture is too deep.[12]

In June 1947, the camp period ends when the residents of the Metropole are asked to move out. Moes makes a great effort to regain the old location at 130 Plampitan, but without success. The number of housemates is much smaller than before the war. A beautiful house with marble floors and a suitable meeting-hall is rented at 24 Sumatra Street. To their disappointment, they have to leave after one month without having any alternative to go to: 'After all those years of wanderings, we feel as sheep before the slaughter, hunted, and scattered'.[13]

A church member (Sister Van Middelkoop) owns a heavily damaged property in the city centre, in the district of Krembangan: 55 Westerkade. The house without doors and windows is made habitable with the help of church members. There are only a few rooms, and they are small. Moes uses her single room for both an office and a bedroom. The hall has a capacity of 200. From 13 July 1947, meetings are held here. The Dutch-speaking assembly is led by Moes and the Malay-speaking assembly by evangelist Oen. Once a month there

---

[11] Alt, 'Dagboek 1945–1961', undated, p. 18. Cf. M.A. Alt, *Het Innerlijk Licht* (Surabaya: Assemblies of God), p. 53.

[12] *Gouden Schooven* does not mention it, but from the diary it is obvious that the relation with Van Gessel is broken. According to Moes, there is even opposition (such as slander) from the side of the Pentecostal church. However, from the view of the Pentecostal church, the reprint in 1947 of the brochure 'Van hart tot hart' ('From Heart to Heart', originally published in 1934) in which Moes explains why she left the PGNI, could also be seen as an act of opposition. My attempts to check this with the GPdI were fruitless.

[13] Alt, 'Dagboek 1945–1961', 27 June 1947, p. 114.

are joint services. The youth department, Kleine Kracht (Little Power), brings together the young people from both assemblies. In August, thirty-seven believers are baptized. On the fourth Sunday in August 1947, for the first time in four years, Moes's birthday is celebrated again in the assembly. 'It was again today a really old-fashioned, cozy gathering, like we Pentecostal people who are one big family are so familiar with.'[14] The hall is decorated and a lovely program prepared. Three choirs sing songs in Dutch, Malay, and Javanese. The assemblies from Bandung, Cheribon, and Makassar send their congratulations. A photo of the Surabayan assembly taken in November 1947, pictures more than hundred people.

Moesje Alt Behind Her Desk, Surabaya (1951)

Gradually messages arrive from the assemblies in the Republican area. In Lawang, the Elim Home has been plundered. Stefanus and his workers fear for their lives. Wim Sleebos is a church member and officer in the army. Along with five armed soldiers, he manages to evacuate Stefanus, his family, and the assistants, Delle and Mowilos,

---

[14] M.A. Alt, 'Onze Feestdag', *GS* 16.10 (October 1947), p. 5.

by truck to Surabaya.[15] The old volumes of *Gouden Schooven* and the remaining book stock are also rescued. Stefanus says that the Chinese brothers and sisters especially suffer a lot. Later on, it will be possible to resume meetings in Lawang under the guidance of Liem Swie Hoo from Malang. From Surabaya, Stefanus will regularly visit the assemblies in East Java.

There is close cooperation with the missionaries of the American Assemblies of God who are active on the field from 1946, especially with Ralph and Edna Devin and Raymond and Beryl Busby. The Devins are working in Ambon and the Busbys in Batavia, where Raymond leads the assembly started by Van Klaveren. In December 1947, *Gouden Schooven* reports that the Pinksterzending has joined the Assemblies of God and publishes a list of fifteen addresses of 'our evangelists as currently available'. Three of the listed addresses are of the Assemblies of God and twelve of the Pinksterzending.[16] This is a lot fewer than the sixty addresses which the Pinksterzending had before the war. The books and brochures that Moes publishes in the coming years name her as 'Evangelist of the Assemblies of God'.

Gradually, more messages from the other assemblies reach Moes (including Kediri, Madiun, Ponorogo, Solo, Kutuardjo, Pasuruan, Probolinggo, and Plampangan). The growth of both the Dutch assembly under Moes and the Malay assembly now under Stefanus in Surabaya continues. There are regular baptismal services, and many receive the baptism with the Holy Spirit. There is revival among the youth. They, themselves, organize prayer sessions and go to the city to evangelize.[17] The hall is too small, but they fail to find a larger one. From the end of 1948, Dutch services will be held twice each Sunday to handle the numbers. During Christmas, Easter, and Pentecost, services are held either in a spacious hall in the Juliana Camp or elsewhere.

Because of the dangerous situation, Moes can travel much less often than before. However, whenever possible, she visits the assemblies in Lawang, Malang, and Batu. During the second police action,

---

[15] M.A. Alt, 'Berichten arbeidsveld', *GS* 16.11 (November 1947), p. 2. Stefanus was at the point of being kidnapped and murdered.

[16] Assemblies of God at Batavia, Ambon, and Makassar. Pinksterzending at Bandung, Cheribon, Malang, Lawang, Batu, Djember, Surabaya, and outside of Java: Borneo, Celebes (4x). See Appendix 2.

[17] M.A. Alt, 'Berichten arbeidsveld', *GS* 17.5 (May 1948), p. 9.

Moes leads a Christmas celebration in the Chinese church of Liem Swie Hoo in Malang, while bombs are exploding outside. Once a year she travels (now by plane) to Batavia for meetings in the Assemblies of God church, led by Raymond Busby. Evangelists from many of the assemblies where Moes cannot go, visit Moes in Surabaya or correspond with her. From 1949, Moes, once again, has radio talks and gives lectures in the Loge Building about the Second Coming of Christ.

Now that the periodical only appears once a month, and she is travelling less, Moes finds more time for other publications. These are productive years. From her hand appear: *Bergopwaarts: Vijf Christelijke Indische novellen* [1948] (*Uphill: Five Christian Dutch Indian Novels*); *Ons Kampleven* [1948] (*Our Camp Life*); *Overvloeiend leven* (1948 – *Overflowing Life*); *Mag de vrouw spreken in de gemeente?* (1948 – *May a Woman Speak in the Assembly?*); *Handleiding en wegwijzer voor Evangelisten* [1948] *(Manual and Guide for Evangelists)*; *Het innerlijk licht* [1949] (*The Inner Light*), and, (just before leaving Surabaya in 1951): *Bijbelstudie voor zelfonderricht (Bible Study for Self-education)*, which will see several reprints.

New Political Realities

In Surabaya, Moes has access to Dutch newspapers. She also writes little items in her diary about the political changes and a few in *Gouden Schooven*. Wherever this happens, she describes events mostly from a Dutch perspective. In July 1946, she notes that the outer areas, except Sumatra, sided with the Netherlands and that they will have full freedom (self-government) under Dutch authority.[18] In September she reports: 'A general strike broke out in Amsterdam, aimed at preventing the troops (30,000 men) from leaving for the Dutch Indies,' to which she adds: 'A communist action'.[19] And after the second police action (December 1948), she writes: 'On the 31st, all cities in the Republican territory were occupied. Many among our young boys fell. Almost all powers are against the Netherlands, but the Lord will help us … The poor Chinese have to suffer everywhere. They are

---

[18] Alt, 'Dagboek 1945–1961', July 1946, pp. 68–69.
[19] Alt, 'Dagboek 1945–1961', 26 September 1946, p. 87.

abducted, slaughtered, robbed; it is terrible'.[20] On 11 March 1949: 'There is a fierce battle between the Netherlands and the Republic. Who will win? The coming Round Table Conference will decide the matter. The guerrillas murder and rob throughout the interior. Hundreds of our boys are falling for the sake of the fatherland. If they were not here, all Europeans would already have been slaughtered.'[21] In the following months, it becomes clear that the Netherlands must give up its claims on the colony. Moes has to adjust to a post-colonial era. In August 1949, Moes not only accepts, but also justifies, the new realities and even sees a future for herself:

> The great Round Table Conference will take place this month. Then, the Dutch Indies will cease to exist, and we will become strangers in this good country. It is not difficult for me, as Dutch, to submit to the Indonesian Government. The people have the right to want to control their own country. If it is advantageous to preaching the Gospel, I am perfectly prepared to become Warga-Negara [a citizen]. May God grant that there will be no persecution because of the faith and that we may continue to publish our magazines and books in the Dutch language.[22]

The years of bloodshed, terror, and wearisome negotiations have soured the relations between the Netherlands and Indonesia. In coming years, the contested authority over New Guinea will stand in the way of repairing the bad relationship. Dutch people and Indo-Europeans do not feel safe, let alone welcome in the new republic. Already, before the transfer, a number of church families leave for the Netherlands or elsewhere. In Surabaya, there is a 'New Guinea Fever' among Indo-Europeans. New Guinea is seen as 'the Promised Land'.[23] On 26 October 1949, Moes notes in her diary: 'We strongly think about New Guinea (Manokwari). I pray for guidance and wisdom.' A month later, Moes seems to have decided in her heart:

---

[20] Alt, 'Dagboek 1945–1961', 8 January 1949, p. 135. Referring to the radio speech of Queen Juliana, Moes writes that the plan is to bring the Dutch Indies under Indonesian government with only one High Representative of the Dutch Crown.

[21] Alt, 'Dagboek 1945–1961', 11 March 1949, p. 138.

[22] Alt, 'Dagboek 1945–1961', 13 August 1949, p. 141.

[23] Hans Meijer, *In Indië geworteld: De twintigste eeuw* (Amsterdam: Bert Bakker, 2004), pp. 292–93.

Thousands move to New Guinea. Terrible pamphlets are scattered, threatening to kill all Dutchmen and rape their women. There is mass hysteria – everyone wants to leave. I have already started packing. I received ten boxes free of charge. God is good.[24]

Immediately after the transfer, Moes writes in *Gouden Schooven*:

We sincerely congratulate the Indonesian people on their sovereignty. No nation would like to be dominated by another nation, and the Dutch people have never desired this ... For those rooted here and the Indo-Europeans, the future looks less hopeful, especially from the economic perspective, and it is therefore understandable that many people will make a future in another country ... A large number has already left for the Netherlands or abroad, and an even bigger number is ready to choose New Guinea as its new homeland.[25]

Under the circumstances, Moes prepares herself for a departure, but she refuses to be repatriated to the Netherlands. Since August 1948, the church has a building fund, but all attempts to buy a larger meeting hall fail. Would the Lord perhaps have another purpose for the fund? On 10 December 1949, she writes in her devotional book, *Voor iederen morgen* (*Morning by Morning*): 'Great blessing and faith strengthening after prayer for guidance for New Guinea'.[26] In March 1950, Moes reveals in *Gouden Schooven* that in recent months God has directed her eyes to New Guinea: 'Many European Brothers and Sisters have already gone there and the faithful Guide showed me in several ways that He wants me to open a new field of labour in Manokwari ... The church will thus be built in Manokwari.'[27] During this period, Moes presents three young evangelists who are prepared to go to

---

[24] Alt, 'Dagboek 1945–1961', 29 November 1949, p. 145.

[25] M.A. Alt, 'Jaarwisseling', *GS* 19.1 (January 1950), p. 3.

[26] Since 1921, Moes, in her prayer time, also makes use of C.H. Spurgeon, *Voor Iederen Morgen* (*Morning by Morning*) with a Scripture verse and a meditation for every morning. In the margins she makes hundreds of notes, especially in the period between 1950–1954.

[27] M.A. Alt, 'Kennisgeving', *GS* 19.3 (March 1950), p. 15. As the collected *f*12,500 is considered sufficient, the building fund closes. In March 1950, the money devalues 50% due to currency devaluation. In her Bible (Utrecht Translation) she writes 'currency devaluation' next to Heb. 13.5 'Be content with what you have'.

New Guinea in the future: Bartje de Vrij, Hans Sigmond, and Dick Groeneveld.

Farewell to Evangelists in Surabaya 1951
Standing: Groeneveld, Sigmond, Stefanus, Switsma, Liem Hong Bo,
Liem Swie Hoo. Up front: Soeprodjo couple, Moes, Petrus Oei couple,
Liem Sik Hian, Sahelangi, Ie Sing Gwan

In April 1950, Moes quotes from a journal that 'New Guinea is perhaps the largest open Mission area in the whole world, and there are wonderful opportunities to preach the Lord Jesus and bring souls to His feet'.[28] The same issue has an enthusiastic letter from Gerrit Koetsier who went ahead to explore the situation there and make preparations for building a church and a home for the workers. There is enough work, the land is fertile, and the climate is good. Outside the city, at a bay, a strip of land is assigned to them where they can begin contruction.[29] Building materials, purchased with money from the building fund, are already on their way.

The date of departure is still indefinite. The expectation is that many more from the assembly will move to Manokwari. Later it will become much harder to obtain permission from the government. In the end, most of the Dutch church members go to the Netherlands. Moes keeps in contact with many of them. In August 1950, the

---

[28] Quote from *Kracht van Omhoog* in Alt, 'Nieuw-Guinea', *GS* 19.4 (April 1950), p. 15.
[29] Gerrit Koetsier, 'Goede tijding uit een ver land', *GS* 19.4 (April 1950), p. 20.

Salvation Army, Pinksterzending, Protestant Church, and the Reformed Church all work together in an evangelization campaign of the Union of Evangelization in Surabaya. Moes gets acquainted with Wim Hoekendijk (1899–1986), Chairman and evangelist of the Union.[30] In September 1950, Moes makes a round trip to West and Middle Java, once again, to visit the assemblies in Batavia, Bandung, Bogor, Solo, Madiun, and Tulung Agung. In October, she visits the assemblies in Malang and Batu and in November on the island of Madura. After more than a year of waiting for a permit, Moes and her co-workers finally leave on 30 April 1951. The assembly in Surabaya is left in the hands of Soemardi Stefanus, with the help of Dick Groeneveld, who for some time will take care of the Dutch-speaking congregation. One group of assemblies of the Pinksterzending joins the Assemblies of God, and another continues as Utusan Pantekosta. This is explained further in the appendices.

Gambang Waluh

It is a considerable time before news arrives from Gambang Waluh. During the Japanese period, Joseph Ranoedihardjo, father of Stefanus, is pastoring the church. He is imprisoned and barely escapes death. Others are forced into labour. Many flee or perish. During the Bersiap (1945–1946), the church building and house are destroyed. The demarcation line between the Dutch and Republican territories runs right across the area. Church members on one side of the line are not allowed to communicate with those on the other side. In May 1948, Moes starts a series of articles in *Gouden Schooven* entitled, 'How God's Spirit fell on Gambang Waluh'. Shortly afterwards, contact with the Dutch side is possible and Moes can send parcels of clothes. In the Dutch part, house meetings in Gambang Waluh are led by

---

[30] M.A. Alt, 'Een vijfdaagse Evangelisatie-Conferentie', *GS* 19.10 (October 1950), pp. 17–18. Speakers were: Major Jansen, Rev. Visser, Rev. Meynen, Rev. Popma, Rev. Hildering, Rev. Van Veen, Peek, Hoekendijk and Kuijken, and Moesje Alt. Wim Hoekendijk is the son of J.A. Hoekendijk (brother of C.J. Hoekendijk from Chapter 8). In September Moes will meet Wim Hoekendijk again on her visit to Batavia. Two sons of C.J. Hoekendijk, Hans and Karel, are also in the Dutch Indies during this period. Karel Hoekendijk would later become the founder of the Pentecostal Stromen van Kracht (Streams of Power). Hans (J.C.) was in Batavia during 1945–1946 as missonary consul and would later become a famous missiologist.

Barnabas and Markus. At the end of 1948, there is a baptismal service in Gambang Waluh for the first time since the war. Dutch soldiers guarding the demarcation line take photos.[31]

The desa Porot lies in the Republican part. After many years as a teacher at the desa school, Zacheus is chosen as lurah (village head). Moes has known him since his birth. He is a faithful Christian and helper in the church. He allows *Gandum Mas* and Javanese literature to be spread in the surrounding desas.[32] With the ceasefire on 3 August 1949, communication with the Republican area is getting better. In a letter, Zacheus informs Moes that soon he and Barnabas will baptize twenty-five converts.[33] In 1953, Zacheus is killed in his home by gang members.

Moesje with Raymond Busby in Jakarta (July 1948)

In 1950, Barnabas travels to Surabaya to meet Moes. There are only 190 baptized members left, but the work begins to grow again. The members have remained faithful to the church's principles.[34]

---

[31] M.A. Alt, 'Berichten arbeidsveld', *GS* 16.3 (March 1947), p. 12; *GS* 17.9 (September 1948), p. 13; *GS* 17.11 (November 1948), p. 23; *GS* 18.1 (January 1949), p. 18. The photos have not been found.

[32] M.A. Alt, 'Heerlijke berichten van Gambang Waloeh', *GS* 17.10 (October 1948), p. 8.

[33] M.A. Alt, 'Goede tijding van Gambang Waloeh', *GS* 18.9 (September 1949), p. 16.

[34] M.A. Alt, 'Onze Indonesische gemeenten', *GS* 19.6 (June 1950), pp. 16–17.

Barnabas happily tells about the return of Iskaq. The thoughts of Moes go back to 1915. Iskaq is seriously ill and calls for Moes. She does not know him yet, but goes to his home. Upon her entry, he is much moved. He has sold his buffaloes to pay the dukuns, but to no avail. In a dream, he is told to call the Pendita of Telaga (the sister of Gambang Waluh). He repents and is baptized shortly thereafter. For a long time, he serves as an elder. However, in 1926 he could not agree with the transition to the Pentecostal movement. With his family, he transfers to the Reformed Church in Temanggung. Now, twenty-four years later, he is back in the old church of Gambang Waluh.[35]

The Indonesian government deprives the Pinksterzending of all rights to the Gambang Waluh property. Without any right of reply, the Christians have to accept that they are losing a lot of land. They cultivate the remaining pieces but find it difficult to survive.[36] Because it is dangerous for Moes to travel in the remote area, her visit in 1942 will remain her last, much to her regret. Occasionally local leaders come to Surabaya to discuss the work. Moes also arranges monthly support for the workers and the poor. After her departure to New Guinea, Stefanus will take care of the colony.

Co-workers

At the last Christmas in Surabaya, Moes thanks all her faithful workers: 'First, Brother Stefanus, who, like my own son, has shared more than fifteen years joy and grief with me and helped me bear all the burdens and worries of this hard work'.[37] Then she mentions Rosa Dekkers, who 'in spite of her weakness', has performed the administration of *Gouden Schooven*. Next she thanks Mies Kooken, Frieda Royot, Nelly Sahertian, and Nelly Mowilos who going from door to door 'daily perform their duties for the Master in the glowing sun'. Moes continues by referring to the choir, 'with their untiring leader, Brother Van Gestel, always ready for service and Sister Paula Delle, who still assists us with the correction of the Bible Study'. Finally,

---

[35] Alt, 'Onze Indonesische gemeenten', pp. 16–17.
[36] M.A. Alt, 'Kerstfeest te Gambang Waloeh', *GS* 28.6 (June 1959), p. 18.
[37] M.A. Alt, 'Berichten arbeidsveld', *GS* 20.2 (February 1951), p. 20.

she thanks the three young evangelists: Dick Groeneveld, Hans Sigmond, and Bartje Sigmond-de Vrij.

Soemardi Stefanus (1916–1990) is born in Temanggung.[38] His father, Joseph Ranoedihardjo, and mother, Marnianah, are both Muslim. When Stefanus is two years old, his parents are converted and are baptized by Rev. Merkelijn. They move to Kendal where his father becomes a police officer. At the age of six, Stefanus goes to the Dutch Indies School. He is the only Christian in his class. In these years, his parents transfer to the Pentecostal church. Stefanus also dedicates his life to God. The whole family is baptized in the river in Semarang. When Stefanus is in his last year of school, his father has a conversation with him about his future. What does he want to become? A teacher or a doctor? Or a pendita (preacher) maybe? Stefanus wants to tell people about Jesus. In *Gouden Schooven* (April 1934), he reads that a Javanese Bible School will start in Kediri under the leadership of Moes. From 1 May 1934, Stefanus lives in the Elim Home in Kediri and receives daily instructions from Moes. Of the four students, he is the only one who speaks Dutch. At the end of the program, Moes asks him to work with her. Together with an elder evangelist, he evangelizes in the surrounding villages. He marries Lydia, one of the girls in Elim raised by Moes. Lydia comes from the area of Gambang Waluh. Her mother died shortly after her birth. Because her father did not know what to do with the baby, he brought her to Moes.[39] In 1936, Stefanus and his wife move to Lawang together with Moes. Increasingly, he becomes Moes' right hand man. Between 1938 and 1942, he is doing the administration for *Gouden Schooven*. In 1941, he becomes Chairman of the youth association Kleine Kracht. When Moes is interned in a Japanese camp in 1943, she gives him responsibility for the Pinksterzending in Lawang. He leads the assemblies in Lawang, Malang, and Surabaya for those years. His leadership qualities come to the fore in this difficult time. Because of the unsafe situation in Lawang, he moves to Surabaya in 1947. He becomes responsible for the Malay-speaking assembly in Surabaya but also travels regularly to the surrounding assemblies. From May 1948, he edits *Gandum Mas*. When Moes departs for New Guinea in

---

[38] S. Stefanus, 'Uit het leven van Br. Stefanus', *GS* 49.4 (April 1978), pp. 8–10.

[39] M.A. Alt, 'Bezoek aan Gambang Waloeh', *GS* 26.11 (November 1957), pp. 18–21.

April 1951, Stefanus is able to continue the work. Nobody else stood for so long and served so faithfully beside Moes in her work.

Moes Saying Goodby to Evangelists Sahelangi and Stefanus (1951)

Bartje de Vrij (1922–2013) grows up in Balikpapan, Borneo, as the eldest of four daughters in the Protestant family of a pharmacist, Herman de Vrij.[40] In 1936, Bartje is the first in her family to be converted in the Pinksterzending in Lawang. Her sisters, Tine, Manda, and Ella, her mother, and later her father follow. Four years later, she is trained by Moes as an evangelist and regularly accompanies Moes on her travels. In 1946, she goes to the Netherlands. From there she goes to England to study at the International Bible Training Institute in Leamington Spa from 1947–1949. Upon returning to Java, she is ordained as an evangelist in the Pinksterzending. On 30 October 1949, she delivers her first sermon. Six months later she marries Hans Sigmond.

Hans Sigmond (1918–1985) is born in Probolinggo (East Java) in 1918. His father works on a sugar plantation.[41] His father is

---

[40] Bart Sigmond-de Vrij, interview by the author, Arnhem, 4 Janaury 2007.
[41] H.Ch. Sleebos, 'In Memoriam', *Parakleet* 17 (Winter 1985), pp. 27–28. D. Groeneveld, 'In Memoriam', *GS* 56.3 (March 1985), p. 4. J. Sigmond, 'Ingezonden Getuigenissen', *GS* 16.5 (May 1947), p. 12.

Protestant and his mother Roman Catholic. After high school, he has to join the army (KNIL). During the Japanese occupation, he is a prisoner of war for three and a half years. During this time, he learns to pray and trust in God. He is brought to Japan via Singapore. He has to work at the blast furnaces of a copper factory. He survives the heavy bombing when the American Air Force destroys the factories. After the war, he is baptized in a Pentecostal church in Makassar. His mother is already a member of the Pinksterzending in Surabaya. Hans receives Bible training from Moes and becomes an evangelist in the Pinksterzending in 1950. In June 1950, he marries Bartje de Vrij. The couple go to New Guinea with Moes.

Dick Groeneveld (1927–2010) is born in Rotterdam into a Reformed family. When he is ordered to go to Germany for work in 1944, he hides on a farm in Herxen.[42] In 1947, he is drafted for military service in the Dutch Indies. Since he does not want to use arms, he is assigned to a medical unit after six weeks of training. During the first police action, he is stationed in Madura. Afterwards, stationed in Surabaya, he becomes acquainted with Moes and the Pinksterzending. During the second police action, his unit is sent to Malang. In the year and a half he is stationed there, he assists the army chaplain with evening devotions. With his friend and colleague, Siep Priester, he visits the house meetings in the home of the Sleebos family in Malang. Mother Corrie Sleebos has been converted under Moes and is now an evangelist in the Pinksterzending. On the same day that Dick is struggling over the issue of water baptism, he receives a letter from Moes:

> Dear Dicky, I will just tell you that we have a baptismal service in our hall here on the first day of Pentecost (Sunday, 5 June) at 10:00 o'clock. We now have a beautiful baptistry. Perhaps you feel called to devote your life to the Lord – yes, you already did it a long time ago, but I mean to also follow him in baptism? I know that it will be a very serious step for you, but obedience to God's command can never disappoint you. You are seriously reading Romans 6, right? That chapter contains the whole secret of baptism. It will be so wonderful to say to the Lord when He comes: 'I've done what I could'. Now, dear boy, make baptism a matter of prayer.[43]

---

[42] Personal data taken from: D. Groeneveld, … *Naar onbeperkte ruimte: Memoires van D. Groeneveld* (Duiven: GMI Music, 2007).

[43] Groeneveld, *Naar onbeperkte ruimte*, p. 106.

Assembly Surabaya at Farewell Moes in April (1951)

On that Sunday, Dick is baptized in Surabaya. A few days later, his resistance to the Dutch Indies, the land he so disliked, is completely taken away. He feels called to this people. After the demobilization, he stays as a citizen. On 26 February 1950, he is ordained by Moes as an evangelist and delivers his first sermon. In November 1951, he marries Manda de Vrij (1926–1984). After some years of serving in the Pinksterzending in Surabaya, they move to New Guinea in June 1954 to assist Moes in the work over there.

At the end of April 1951, Moes leaves Java after forty-eight years. At the farewell of the assembly in Surabaya, 22 April 1951, Moes sings the testimonial song she wrote, 'The friend of my heart':

> *Yes, like a candle that consumes itself in the flame*
> *I want to sacrifice my life to Him.*
> *Until I will be united together with God's children*
> *In the New Jerusalem*

Moes is sixty-seven years old, weakened by malaria and by the dreadful years in the camps; yet, she is full of confidence she is on her way to a new field of work:

> It is with a heavy heart that we have to leave the city of Surabaya where the Lord, in His mercy, gave us many souls and dear friends. Only the thought that the Lord calls us with great certainty to start a new work for Him in Manokwari keeps us standing firm.[44]

---

[44] M.A. Alt, 'Paas-Opwekkingsdienst te Soerabaja', *GS* 20.6 (June 1951), p. 14.

13

MANOKWARI 1951–1961

The Lord began to awaken in me a longing to go to New Guinea to bring full salvation by Jesus' blood to brown and white. The longing grew stronger until it became certain to me that God still had a task for me in my old age.[1]

On 30 April 1951, the motor vessel, Van Riebeek, leaves the port of Surabaya on a voyage to Sorong, the oil city of New Guinea. From there, the journey continues by coastal boat to Manokwari. On 11 May 1951, Moes and her company arrive at their destination. They will stay there for more than ten years.

Manokwari

Manokwari is located on the North East coast of the Vogelkop peninsula. The Doreh Bay makes it very suitable as port and capital. In the 1930s, many Indo-Europeans come here as 'colonists' to cultivate the land.[2] Due to the difficult circumstances, most return disappointed. The bombings during the war years leave Manokwari in ruins. After the Japanese capitulation, Hollandia (Yayapura) becomes the new capital for the re-installed Dutch government.[3] Slowly,

---

[1] M.A. Alt, *Herinneringen uit mijn leven* (Velp: Pinksterzending, 1963), p. 79.

[2] Hans Meijer, *In Indië geworteld: De twintigste eeuw* (Amsterdam: Bert Bakker, 2004), pp. 128–37.

[3] F.C. Kamma, `Dit wonderlijke werk': Het probleem van de communicatie tussen Oost en West gebaseerd op de ervaringen in het zendingswerk op Nieuw-Guinea (Irian Jaya) 1855–1972. Een socio-missiologische benadering* (Oegstgeest: Raad voor de Zending der Ned. Hervormde Kerk, 1976), p. 743.

Manokwari is rebuilt. The independence of Indonesia results in a new flow of Indo-Europeans to New Guinea, where they settle as colonists, especially around Manokwari.[4]

The population of New Guinea is estimated at one million in the early 1950s, of which 400,000 are registered.[5] The interior is largely an unknown area. At that time, Manokwari has about 4000 inhabitants. Because of developments like the construction of a shipyard, sawmill, power plant and airport, the city will grow to 25,000 inhabitants by 1960. The total population of New Guinea is estimated at 737,000 in 1960, including 16,000 Europeans.[6] Missionaries have been active in this area for a century. Initially there was only the Utrecht Mission, which merged in 1951 with the Reformed Church Mission, and after that the Roman Catholic Mission started. The Evangelical Faith Missions first arrive in the 1950s.[7] The Papuans on the coast have, in large number, become Christians, but those in the interior have not yet been reached. There is often distrust between the tribes because of a long history of kidnapping and slave trading.[8] In Manokwari, Moes encounters the Reformed Mission and its partner, the Evangelical Christian Church (ECK, independent in 1956 and called Gereja Kristen Injili).

In the next few years, tensions between Indonesia and the Netherlands will escalate further. Indonesia claims New Guinea, while the Netherlands does not want to give it up.[9] For the leadership of the Netherlands Reformed Church (NHK), who have missionary interests in both Indonesia and New Guinea, this is a worrying development. The NHK questions the sustainability of the Dutch position. In June 1956, the Synod of the NHK addresses Dutch society with a 'call for reflection'. A storm of protest breaks out in the

---

[4] Meijer, *In Indië geworteld*, pp. 310–12.

[5] F.C. Kamma (ed.), *Kruis en korwar: Een honderdjarig vraagstuk op Nieuw-Guinea* (The Hague: Voorhoeve, 1953), p. 7.

[6] Ministerie van Binnenlandse Zaken, *Rapport inzake Nederlands-Nieuw-Guinea over het jaar 1960* (The Hague: MBZ, n.d.), appendix IVA.

[7] Kamma, *Dit wonderlijke werk*, p. 786. The CAMA arrives already in 1938, and others like TEAM, begin from 1950. In 1962, the evangelical faith missions unite in The Mission Fellowship.

[8] Jelle Miedema, *De Kebar 1850–1980: Sociale structuur en religie in de Vogelkop van West-Nieuw-Guinea* (Dordrecht: ICG Printing, 1984), pp. 157–58.

[9] C. Smit, *De liquidatie van een imperium: Nederland en Indonesië 1945–1962* (Amsterdam: Arbeiderspers, 1962).

Netherlands as well as among the missionaries in New Guinea and in the partner church.[10]

*Manokwari Baptismal Service with TEAM Missionaries
Erikson and Tritt (24 August 1952)*

At the end of 1957, Indonesia imposes economic sanctions against the Netherlands. Dutch companies are nationalized, Dutch-language publications are prohibited, and groups of Dutch are expelled. The lowest point is reached when Indonesia breaks diplomatic relations with the Netherlands in August 1960. Meanwhile, the Netherlands is accelerating the process of self-government for New Guinea, including the installation of a New Guinea Council. War is looming. Under strong pressure from the international community, the Netherlands and Indonesia reach an agreement in August 1962. New Guinea is temporarily transferred to the United Nations, after which the area is ceded to Indonesia on 1 May 1963. The planned peoples consultation, by which the Papuans can decide on their own future in 1969, will be steered by Indonesia in such a way that only one outcome is possible.

---

[10] Hans van de Wal, *Een aanvechtbare en onzekere situatie: De Nederlandse Hervormde Kerk en Nieuw-Guinea 1949–1962* (Hilversum: Verloren, 2006), pp. 323–24. Van de Wal concludes that the authors of the call may have been right, but that the call lacked political support (p. 324).

Mission Post

Moes and her team settle five kilometers outside Manokwari (towards
Wosi). A year and a half earlier, Gerrit Koetsier had gone ahead to
prepare for their arrival. The house, built for Moes and her housemates, is nearly ready. It is a simple, wooden building with bamboo
walls, large enough to host church meetings as well for the time being.
The roof made of palm leaves is not waterproof, which will be very
inconvenient as well as unhealthy. Water comes from the well behind
the house. Electricity will only be installed in 1959.

From the first Sunday, church meetings are held in the house. The
heat is almost the same as in Surabaya, but the nights are cooler. The
furniture came along from Java because there is none for sale in
Manokwari. Moesje's first impressions are: 'of a barely civilized country, with poorly built houses; half a wilderness full of hardworking
people, many of whom are disheartened and grumbling'.[11] The coun-
tryside is beautiful with its majestic mountains and dense forests.
From behind her writing desk, Moes looks through a small hatch
onto the forest. There are large rose bushes in front of the window.
In *Gouden Schoven,* monthly reports of the missionary work appear
under the heading, 'Letters from New Guinea'.[12] Shortly after arriving, Moes gets acquainted with the assistant governor, who gives his
full cooperation to the Pinksterzending. Throughout the years, there
will be a good understanding with the local government. Moes also
gets along well with Mauritz Kokkelink (1913–1995), a resistance
hero during the Japanese rule and recipient of the Military Order of
William.[13]

Soon the house is too small to host the meetings. Across the road,
a new church building rises. The wooden building has walls of plaited
bamboo, a zinc roof, and windows that are always wide open due to
the tropical heat. In September 1953, the local newspaper, *Nieuws van*

---

[11] M.A. Alt, 'Reisbrieven', *GS* 20.9 (July 1951), p. 23.

[12] From this chapter I follow the spelling *Gouden Schoven* that was introduced
mid-1956.

[13] M.A. Alt, 'Brieven uit Manokwari', *GS* 26.1 (January 1957), pp. 20–21; 28.1
(January 1959), pp. 22–23. Kokkelink is born on Java and in 1933 went to
Manokwari as a colonist. In 1940, he was drafted as a soldier in the army. During
the occupation, he and his men fought a guerrilla war against the Japanese.
http://www.nederlandsekrijgsmacht.nl/index.php/kl/269-officieren-van-het-ne-
derlandse-leger/infanterie/1034–kokkelink-mauritz-christiaan.

de Week (*News of the Week*), reports the initiation of the 'Church of Sister Alt': 'There is joy, for here the community in Christ is visible, uniting all: white, brown and black, rich and poor, people with and without a fixed basic salary. Before God, all are equal.'[14] That the work of the Pinksterzending is appreciated is also seen on 29 April 1955. Moes receives the gold medal of Orange Nassau from Manokwari's governor 'because of her forty-five years of hard missionary work , which she continuously carried out out of love to God and her neighbour'.[15] In particular, her work among the handicapped, mentally ill, needy, and orphans is highlighted.

Co-workers Nelly Sahertian, Mies Kooken, and Rosa Dekkers spread Christian literature in the hospital, prison, and among the colonists (distributing papers like *Gouden Schoven, Gandum Mas, Zoeklicht, Heilsfontein, De Oogst, Open Deur* and *Joodse Hope*). Hans and Bartje Sigmond are both involved in the church work, but when Hans accepts a job with an oil company, they move to Sorong. Later, when they again reside at the mission post (1956–1958), Bartje preaches occasionally and Hans assists with the *Gouden Schoven* magazine. In 1958, Hans, now working for the government, is transferred to Hollandia (Jayapura). At home, they lead house meetings while Hans continues to work for the magazine. In 1960, they pass through a deep valley when their six-year-old son Jopie dies of leukemia in the hospital.

Originally, members of Pinksterzending planned to emigrate to Manokwari, either directly or from the Netherlands. However, this plan comes to nothing. Restricted admission regulations and the ever-worsening relationship between the Netherlands and Indonesia allow only a few families to succeed. After two years of waiting for an entry visa, Dick and Manda Groeneveld arrive on 28 June 1954 with their two children. For Moes, it is a relief to have Dick at her side. Now that she is in the seventies, it is hard for her to travel. Moreover, malaria constantly lies in wait. Unlike in her time in Java when she made many trips, her preaching ministry is limited to Manokwari and its immediate surroundings.

Regularly, people from the city or villages are converted. On Sundays, separate meetings are held in Dutch and Malay. On all church feast days and at the celebration of the Lord's Supper, the services

[14] M.A. Alt, 'Brieven uit Nieuw-Guinea', *GS* 22.13 (December 1953), pp. 17–19.
[15] M.A. Alt, 'Brieven uit Manokwari', *GS* 24.7 (July 1955), pp. 21–22.

are mixed. In addition, Sunday School and weekly prayer sessions are held in different places. Moes takes care of the Bible Study for adults, the catechization of young people, preaching, and doing home and sick visitation. In addition, she edits the *Gouden Schoven* magazine, keeps up an extensive correspondence, and prepares new editions of *Glorieklokken* and the daily devotional book, *Het Volle Licht* (*The Full Light*). Of course, there are several choirs. The Papuans have a gift for music and soon form a flute orchestra.

Baptized Papua Youngsters from Wandammen (1952)

The housing of Moes and her housemates urgently needs to be replaced. Groeneveld is not only a gifted evangelist, but he also develops skills as a home builder. In October 1957, the new home for Moes and her housemates is ready. It is much more pleasant and is right next to the church. On that side of the road, the soil is better, and more flowers can grow at the house. Flowers are always to be found on Moes's writing desk and on the stage in the church. A truck is being converted to serve as a church bus, picking up visitors from surrounding villages for services. Previously, they had used borrowed lorries. On the Sunday closest to 22 August, there is always a big party for Moes's birthday. She receives hundreds of letters each year from the Netherlands and Indonesia. At the celebration there are presentations from the different departments of the church, with Papuans always included.

Outreach to the Papuans

In the distance, on the other side of the bay, lie the Arfak Mountains. Many Papuan tribes live there, each with its own language and tribal chief. They wear hardly any clothes. Although Protestants and Catholics have already done a great deal of missionary work, few of the Papuans in the mountains and in the jungles are Christians. Regularly small groups (especially of the Hatam and Manicion tribes) come down the mountains, about a seven-day walk, to Manokwari and the surroundings. After a few months, they return home and other groups come. For convenience, they are all called Arfaks. The short duration of their stay makes it difficult to teach them. Connections are made with some of those who speak Malay. After seven years, the first Arfaks come to faith, and after that many follow.

The Papuans living on the coast (Biak-Numforese) are, at least in name, mostly Christian and have adapted more to the European lifestyle. They have steady jobs and are well dressed. Much to the regret of Moes, they copy the cursing and drinking alcohol of the settlers and the gambling and fighting of the Japanese. The Pinksterzending will win few converts from this group. In the first years, a number of the Papuans from the islands come to repentance. They, too, come to find temporary work. Nelly Sahertian leads the work among the Papuans until 1957. In 1952, twenty-two Papuans are baptized. They mainly come from the Waprak isles (three days away by boat) and the Wandammen isles (seven days away) and return home over time.

Moes, in her monthly reports, shows interest in the culture and religion of the Papuans. In particular, she follows the missionary activities of the Christian and Missionary Alliance (CAMA) in the interior. She refers to the CAMA magazine, *Pionier*, as well as the mission journal of the Netherlands Reformed, and, to other magazines like *Oost en West* and *Nigi Magazine*. She sees a glimpse of truth in the Papuan legend, Mansar Mangundi, praying that the Papuans would recognize their Mansren (= Lord) in Christ.[16]

---

[16] M.A. Alt, 'Brieven uit Nieuw-Guinea', *GS* 23.7 (July 1954), p. 21.

Moes has interesting talks with a Papuan leader Johan Ariks (1897–1967). Ariks is the son of a slave who was freed from the Kebar tribe by missionaries. He is educated by the missionaries as a guru (teacher). In 1949, he participates in the Round Table Conference. Now, he is the leader of a political party that is striving for an independent New Guinea. In 1965, he ends up in jail because of his opposition to Indonesian domination and dies in prison.[17]

Moes trains some of the Papuan converts to become gurus, and they begin to lead meetings on the islands of Wasior (Wandammen) and Waprak. Daniel Sawiki and Dorotheus Moesieri remain and become elders in the Malay-speaking assembly of Manokwari. In later years (from 1957), Henk Lit leads this work. From that point on, the mountain tribes come to repentance.

A poster of the broad and narrow roads in Jesus' little parable that Moes has pinned up attracts much attention. The Arfaks come specially to see the picture, which proves to be a powerful means of explaining the gospel. The poster has such an appeal because it has drawings of evil spirits (suings) on it. Full of fear, the Papuans stare at those figures and rub their fingers over them. The fact that the picture needs some explanation is evident when Groeneveld asks which way they would choose, the broad or the narrow road? The broad path, of course, because at the end there is fire. For the Arfak, fire stands not for hell but for life, warmth, food, and defense against insects and vermin.[18] The poster is brought to the mountains and to the islands of Waprak and Wasior (Wandammen). Also the magic lamp with biblical pictures is helpful. Bibles and other literature in Malay (like *Gandum Mas*) are spread among the people.

In 1957, a kampong for the Hatam arises in the immediate vicinity of the mission post. It facilitates contacts with the population. Occasionally, Moes is asked to pray for a sick person. A Hatam woman nearly dies at child birth. Somewhat later, when Moes asks the husband about the child, he answers that the child is dead and buried. A little later she meets the neighbour, a Christian, with a baby. It turns out that the neighbour took the child when the mother wanted to bury it alive. If a mother dies at child birth, or almost dies, the child is cursed.[19]

---

[17] Miedema, *De Kebar 1850–1980*, 37, pp. 239–40.
[18] Groeneveld, *Naar onbeperkte ruimte*, p. 215.
[19] M.A. Alt, 'Brieven uit Nieuw-Guinea', (November 1958), p. 20.

Besides some condescending generalisations of the Papuans as 'lazy, stupid, slow learning and half-wild', Moes makes many comments that are neutral or complimentary. She sees the Papuans, in general, as religiously inclined but filled with a fear of spirits. They sing well and willingly accept the gospel. In comparison with the Javanese people, Moes finds that the Papuans lack an innate politeness and hospitality. They are outspoken and rather direct in their communcation, yet 'difficult for Westerners to understand'.[20]

The Hatam regularly walk past Groeneveld's house to their kampong. They drink water from the big vessel that Groeneveld has specially provided for them.[21] When they return to their mountains loaded with pigs and chickens, they are occasionally transported by the church bus to the edge of the mountains, where the road stops. Henk Lit gives reading and writing lessons to young and old. Partly through these acts of kindness, they open their hearts to the gospel. During the last four years in Manokwari, more than hundred Papuans are baptized. They are mainly from the Hatam and Manicion tribes. In 1961, Moes writes about the mountain tribes: '[They] are most sympathetic to us; they are also the most open to the gospel'.[22]

At Manokwari in 1952, two American missionaries are preparing to go to the interior. Walter Erikson and Edward Tritt are Baptist missionaries from The Evangelical Alliance Mission (TEAM). Erikson has already met with Moes in Surabaya at the end of 1950. Now they meet again. Erikson and Tritt attend the meetings, and, if there is a baptism service, Moes asks Erikson to participate. They baptize, Moes writes, 'just like us by immersion and agree with all our principles, including those of the baptism of the Spirit'.[23] Frederik Franson, the founder of the missionary organization, is a supporter of women in the ministry.[24]

---

[20] M.A. Alt, 'Brieven uit Nieuw-Guinea', GS 27.9 (September 1958), p. 22.

[21] D. Groeneveld, ...Naar onbeperkte ruimte: Memoires van D. Groeneveld (Duiven: GMI Music, 2007), p. 217.

[22] M.A. Alt, 'Brieven uit Nieuw-Guinea', GS 32.5 (May 1961), p. 22.

[23] M.A. Alt, 'Brieven uit Nieuw-Guinea', GS 21.10 (October 1952), p. 20. The baptismal service was 24 August 1952.

[24] Frederik Franson is a son of Swedish immigrants in the United States. In 1890 he founds the Scandinavian Alliance Mission (in 1949 renamed as TEAM). Letha Dawson Scanzoni and Susan Setta, 'Women in Evangelical, Holiness and Pentecostal Traditions', in Rosemary Radford Ruether and Rosemary Skinner Keller (eds.), Women & Religion in America 3 1900–1968 (San Francisco: Harper and Row, 1986), p. 224.

184 Margaretha A. Alt

In September, the two missionaries leave for the interior, where they are murdered by their carriers at the end of September 1952. When the tragic death of the two is reported to the Bible School where they were trained, twenty students declare themselves willing to take their place.[25] In the following years, new missionaries arrive, among them Tritt's fiancée. They will work with much fruit among the tribes in the interior, beyond the Arfak mountains. Manokwari serves as their base which creates a cordial connection with the Pinksterzending. In 1959, the Erikson-Tritt Theological College is founded in Manokwari. Eventually, the work of the Pinksterzending will be transferred to TEAM in October 1962.

Pentecostals in relation to other churches

According to research by Freerk Kamma, the Pentecostal Movement enters New Guinea only after the Second World War.[26] The first Pentecostal church originated in the village of Tabiti (Humboldt Bay) after a resident had returned from Surabaya, where he was in contact with the movement. The research also speaks of Pentecostal activities in Sorong (led by Itar among Indo-European colonists), Hollandia (from 1954 under Van Gessel), Waropen, Waren, and in the Wandam Bay. The movement is portrayed as sectarian and mixed with pagan elements. In particular, members of the tribes in the interior who feel disadvantaged compared to the coastal population join. In the Pentecostal movement, they are treated as equals and can be trained as pastors without many demands. Moes has no contact with all these Pentecostal communities. The rupture in her relationship with Van Gessel of Bethel Pentecostal Church continues in New Guinea.[27]

---

[25] Nancy Kennedy, 'The Story of Walter Erikson and Edward Tritt', *CIU Connection* (Spring 2010), pp. 16–20. Herbert Marcus (1915–2000), Mennonite missionary, assisted Harold Lovestrand in finding the graves of the two deceased missionaries. After reading the diaries of the two, Marcus is of the opinion that their death in part was due to a lack of understanding of the culture of the guide and carriers. R.E.H. Marcus, *Van eeuwigheid tot Amen* (1996), pp. 175–76 [http://www.papuaerfgoed.org/files/Marcus_nd_eeuwigheid%202.pdf].

[26] F.C. Kamma, 'Pinksterbeweging en heidendom (De Beweging op Nieuw-Guinea)', [1959], on behalf of the Evangelical Christian Church in New Guinea.

[27] In a letter to Hans and Bartje Sigmond dated 13 August 1955, Moes makes clear that contact with this group is out of the question. Moes writes that she had sent a letter to Van Gessel and had admonished him, 'in great love', to abandon the

"On my 71st birthday", in Front of the New
Church Building (August 1954)

In 1957, the Pentecostal movement also settles on the island of
Japen, in the villages of Ambai (led by Frits Karubaba) and Man-
tembu. Within the Evangelical Christian Church (ECK), this leads to
so many problems that the Synod of the Japen-Waropen province
discusses the issue in 1958. Second Secretary, N. Semboari, issues a
report 'about the deceit of the sect of Pentecost'.[28] His report shows
an even worse image of the Pentecostal movement than Kamma's
research reveals.

Freerk Kamma (1906–1989) has been a missionary in the area
since 1931. In 1954, he receives a doctorate for his research into the
Messianic Koreri Movements in the Biak-Numforese cultural area.
From 1955, he is the field leader of the NHK Mission and also general secretary of the ECK. Kamma is deeply concerned about the
Pentecostal movement and sees all kinds of similarities with pagan-
ism. He mentions, among other things, ecstasy, fainting, gibberish
(later explained as glossolalia), Messianic expectation, the compulsive

---

teachings of Offiler. Van Gessel replied that he would remain faithful to this teaching until his death.
[28] The report of N. Semboari is incorporated in full in the cited introduction
of F.C. Kamma, pp. 4–7. Another example of an unfavourable report within the
ECK is from Rev. Drost, 'De Pinksterbeweging en wij' in *Kerkbode van de ECK te
Hollandia*, 2.9 (1 October 1957).

practice of healing, and the binding of spiritual powers.[29] In April 1959, Kamma, on leave in the Netherlands, presents an introduction of his experiences to the Commission for the Study of Sects of the NHK. In 1960, this Commission publishes the Shepherding Letter, *The Church and Pentecostal Groups*. Although Kamma describes the dangers sharply, he speaks positively about Moesje Alt at Manokwari, who does 'no church destroying work'.[30]

In 1976, when Kamma reflects on his missionary work in New Guinea in his *Dit Wonderlijke Werk* (*This Wonderful Work*), the Pentecostal churches are only mentioned in the margin. However, what he says about the contacts with the faith missionaries is likely to also apply to the Pentecostal movement. In personal contacts, there is a good atmosphere between the Reformed and Faith missionaries in the field, but they work completely separate from one another. Kamma takes it poorly that the Faith missionaries do not seem to recognize the ECK as a church and is completely ignored in their publications. At the same time, he is impressed with their devotion and willingness to sacrifice. He also believes they are better adapted to the indigenous culture.[31]

From the beginning, Moes builds up relationships with the Reformed missionaries and tries to remove prejudices against the Pentecostals. At the end of March 1952, she invites the choir of the Protestant Church in Manokwari, led by missionary doctor A.H. Dekker, to sing in the Pinksterzending. Missionary Otto Ewoldt (1913–1972) is also present. 'This first attempt at cooperation has energized us. Do not we all serve one Lord, and do not we all belong to the Church under the Cross that will soon meet the Lord in the air?'[32] On Easter Monday of 1953, Moes is one of the speakers in a revival service of the Protestant church in Manokwari. She notes that there is great interest 'also from our Pentecostals'.[33]

Six months later, Reformed ministers Rev. A.H. Smits and Rev. Ewoldt, along with the choir led by Dr. Dekker, participate in the initiation of the new church building of the Pinksterzending. A few

---

[29] Kamma, 'Pinksterbeweging', [1959].

[30] J. Swijnenburg (scribe), 'Notulen van de zesde bijeenkomst van de Commissie voor het Sektewezen', in the New Church in Amsterdam, 24 April 1959, p. 4.

[31] Kamma, *Dit wonderlijke werk*, pp. 787–88.

[32] M.A. Alt, 'Brieven uit Nieuw-Guinea', *GS* 21.6 (June 1952), p. 22.

[33] M.A. Alt., 'Brieven uit Nieuw-Guinea', *GS* 22.6 (June 1953), p. 20.

months later, Moes is present at the inauguration of the new missionary church in Kwawi (Manokwari) under the direction of Rev. Ewoldt. In 1954, Rev. Smits and Dr. Dekker depart. Moes writes: 'Dr. Dekker was also in sympathy with our work, ecumenical as he is, and has visited us several times'.[34] On Pentecost Monday in 1956 and 1957, Moes is invited by Rev. Roeland G. ten Kate to a large missionary gathering in Kwawi with hundreds of Papuans and various choirs. Moes is pleased to see that Pentecostal songs from *Glorieklokken* are sung in Malay.

However, there is nothing about the 'call for reflection' of the NHK in 1956 in *Gouden Schoven*. The contacts with the Reformed missionaries are admittedly friendly, but probably, like those of all the Faith missionaries, do not have profound repercussions.

Contacts with Indonesia and the Netherlands

Moes remains in close contact with Stefanus. Through the periodical and correspondence, she maintains close ties with the assemblies in Indonesia as well. Every month, the text for *Gouden Schoven* goes to Surabaya to be printed there. Stefanus takes care of the administration within Indonesia. He forwards gifts from the assemblies in Indonesia. Every year donations are requested for the poor of Gambang Waluh and Plampangan. At least once a year, Stefanus visits these assemblies and reports extensively in *Gouden Schoven*.

The church in Gambang Waluh is still led by Barnabas. Of the old generation, Joenoes is still alive, living in Porot as a patriarch in the midst of his children. At the Christmas celebration in 1958, Stefanus brings a letter from Moes and has Joenoes read it. With emotion in his voice, the old man reads the letter of his 'spiritual mother'. The church is deeply affected by the call to remain faithful to the Lord Jesus. Joenoes turns to the congregation: 'Brothers and sisters, let us do what our ibu [mother] says: We must follow the Lord and serve Him faithfully until death'.[35] After the service, all the old members come to Stefanus, asking him to pass their greetings to Moes.

In December 1957, it becomes clear that the periodical can no longer be printed or distributed in Indonesia because of the imposed

---

[34] M.A. Alt, 'Brieven uit Nieuw-Guinea', *GS* 23.6 (June 1954), p. 21.
[35] M.A. Alt, 'Kerstfeest te Gambang Waloeh', *GS* 28.6 (June 1959), pp. 18–21.

restrictions. From January 1958, the periodical is printed in the Netherlands. The paper quality improves, and songs are no longer in number notation but on staves drawn by Hans Sigmond. The loss of subscribers in Indonesia is compensated by the increase of readers in the Netherlands. In 1952, the administration of *Gouden Schoven* in the Netherlands is passed from Piet Klaver to Dirk Koppelle. Between 1954 and 1959, a new edition of the song-book, *Glorieklokken,* appears in ten parts. It is an immediate success in the Dutch Pentecostal movement. The new edition is also used even outside the movement. Some of the songs are recorded on gramophone. From 1957, Moes is occasionally heard on the IBRA radio station.[36]

In *Gouden Schoven,* Moes reports developments within church life in the Netherlands. Frequently, she quotes messages from the Netherlands Reformed Church Press Office. She also quotes from magazines like *De Oogst, Elisabethbode, Timotheüs, Zoeklicht,* and the Pentecostal periodicals, *Kracht van Omhoog* and *Volle Evangelie Koerier.* Likewise, Moes gives a great deal of attention to the Jewish people, especially by quoting from *De Joodse Hope (The Jewish Hope)* edited by Daniel Gutter, whom Moes knows from Java.

These are exciting times for the Pentecostal movement in the Netherlands. After years of stunted growth, the movement begins to advance quickly. The traditional churches show great interest in the messages of divine healing and the gifts of the Spirit. Moes is pleased with the positive tone of the Shepherding Letter of the NHK, *The Church and the Pentecostal Groups* (1960). She also appreciates the corrections given: 'The friendly and well-meaning critique of the mistakes that we made, we accept with gratitude and humiliation, recognizing as Paul that we only know "in part"' (1 Cor. 13.12).[37] Moes also realizes the importance of a training institution and is therefore pleased with the establishment of the Pentecostal Bible School in Groningen. She fully endorses the ambition of David du Plessis to enter into dialogue with the historical churches.[38]

---

[36] IBRA is a radio broadcast of the Swedish Pentecostal movement that works from Tangier. It is the time of pirate broadcasts. The Dutch Pentecostal movement is also assigned some hours. In Manokwari some sound recordings are made that are transmitted through IBRA to the Netherlands.

[37] M.A. Alt, 'De Kerk en de Pinkstergroepen', *GS* 32.3 (March 1961), pp. 6–8.

[38] M.A. Alt, 'De wereld van heden', *GS* 30.10 (October 1960), pp. 10–11.

The 1950s are the heyday of American faith healers William Branham, Tommy Hicks, Tommy Osborn, and Oral Roberts. *Gouden Schoven* reports, in detail, the remarkable conversions and healings that occur in many places in the world. In 1954, Osborn visits Jakarta and Surabaya where, there too, many witness of miracles that have taken place. At a later visit to Jakarta in 1959, Osborn is only allowed to speak to Christians in a church. Shortly after his visit to the Netherlands (1958), Osborn contacts Moes about a campaign in New Guinea. The Pinksterzending is too small to organize such an event. Her attempt to get support from pastors of other churches fails.[39] In 1961, evangelist Morris Cerullo informs Moes of his plan to visit New Guinea. In spite of giving repeated assurances, Cerullo changes his plans. It does not stop Moes's prayers for a revival.

In the meetings of the Pinksterzending, no offerings are taken. There is an offering box on a table at the door where members can leave their gifts.[40] Besides the donations of the members in New Guinea, gifts come from the Netherlands, and until 1957, they also come from Indonesia. All gifts are accounted for in *Gouden Schoven*. In addition to general gifts 'For the work of the Lord', there are projects such as 'building' and 'the church bus'. Former church members who live in Holland faithfully send gifts as do a number of Pentecostal churches and the new readers of the periodical.

The Dutch begin to leave New Guinea because of the uncertain future from 1959. In April 1960, Moes writes that the assembly is preparing for an exodus, but she does not personally believe there will be a rapid change in the political situation. One month later, she notes that, since the Papuans have been promised self-determination, developments are progressing at a rapid pace. 'Their isolation has really lasted long enough, and we truly want to see them advance.'[41] As the Dutch-speaking assembly begins to shrink, the Papuan assembly is expanding. In March 1961, fifty Papuans are baptized, and two more baptismal services follow in August.

---

[39] M.A. Alt, 'Brieven uit Nieuw-Guinea', *GS* 27.12 (December 1958), p. 23.
[40] Information from Henk Lit Jr. in e-mail to author, 21 September 2015.
[41] M.A. Alt, 'Brieven uit Nieuw-Guinea', *GS* 30.5 (May 1960), p. 23.

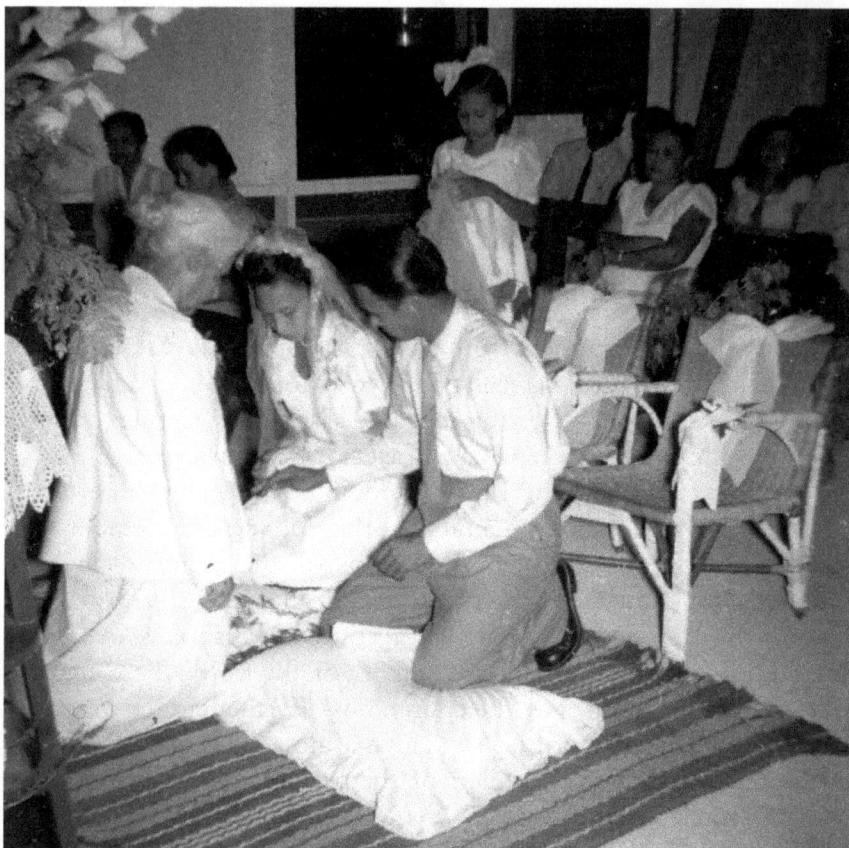

Marriage Ceremony Led by Moes (1958)

On 11 May 1961, exactly ten years after her arrival, Moes hears these words during the morning prayer: 'Prepare yourself for a journey. The time has now come.'[42] At first, she really wants to stay. That afternoon, however, she receives a letter from a former church member in the Netherlands with similar words. She understands that the Lord is calling her back to the Netherlands. The departure is set for 22 September 1961. Not everything she had hoped for has been achieved : 'The great revival for this heathen land has not yet fully come, but we are looking forward, waiting and praying, for the time when the cripple will jump like a deer, the deaf hear, and the blind see. God also has His appointed time for revival.'[43] For many years,

---

[42] M.A. Alt, *Herinneringen*, p. 86.
[43] M.A. Alt, 'Brieven uit Manokwari', *GS* 32.6 (June 1961), p. 22.

Moes has fasted and prayed for an awakening and battled against the satanic powers she felt pressing in on the land and people. In the Netherlands, she will continue to conduct this prayer struggle. At the same time, she highlights the fear of the Papuans that the Dutch government will soon succumb to political pressure to transfer New Guinea to Indonesia. 'We grant this people the right of self-determination and hope and pray that it may develop into a healthy and powerful society, especially in the spiritual sense.'[44]

With her return to the Netherlands in view, Moes appears well aware of developments in the Dutch Pentecostal movement. For years she has been reading the Pentecostal periodicals and has corresponded with many leaders along with readers of *Gouden Schoven*. In a letter to Henk Sleebos, she writes that she would like to join the good Pentecostal circles that seek unity, but 'never circles where unsanctified leaders rule despotically and where no love is'.[45] On 17 September, the farewell service closes with the celebration of the Lord's Supper. The whole congregation is present as well as TEAM missionaries and some members of the Protestant Church. The Papuan assembly is temporarily left in the care of evangelist Henk Lit and his assistant Tom Timmermans. Lit will remain for some time because of his job at the electricity company. It is agreed that the assembly will in time be transferred to the TEAM missionaries.

On the day of departure, the Papuan assembly gathers in front of the house and sings in Malay: 'Now then, until we meet again. Be it here or by God's River.' Moes and her co-workers Mies Kooken, Rosa Dekkers, the Groeneveld family, as well as a number of members of the congregation, board the motor vessel Zuiderkruis. The Sigmond family leaves from Hollandia and will join them in the Netherlands. Because of the threat of war, the vessel does not stop over in Indonesia. The journey goes via Singapore, Port Said, Naples, and Southampton before reaching Amsterdam. The trip takes a month. In the restaurant, there is a piano on which Moes plays her songs. She is asked to play gospels songs, which she describes as 'religious practices without preaching'.[46]

---

[44] M.A. Alt, 'Brieven uit Manokwari', *GS* 32.7 (July 1961), p. 23.

[45] M.A. Alt to H. Sleebos, 15 February 1960.

[46] M.A. Alt, 'Onze reis met M.S. Zuiderkruis', *GS* 32.12 (December 1961), p. 20.

14

BACK IN THE NETHERLANDS 1961–1962

So we arrived ... at Amsterdam. What a joy to see all the happy faces, down at the quay. The weather was icy cold and raining. For those of us used to the tropical sun, it is a whole new experience.[1]

After more than fifty-eight years, Moes arrives back in the Netherlands on 23 October 1961. Through *Gouden Schoven* and *Glorieklokken,* she has become a celebrity in the Dutch Pentecostal movement. It is a happy reunion with many friends. In Arnhem, the Pinksterzending assembly is established. But on 22 March 1962, just before it really gets going, Moes dies without having spent a day in bed sick.

Pinksterzending in the Netherlands

The dock is full of people. The press is present to interview the 300 repatriates from New Guinea. Old acquaintances from Java and New Guinea, friends, and family welcome Moes and her companions. They sing to her: 'I walk in the light with Jesus'. In the afternoon, the company travels to Lunteren, where they are housed in a boarding-house. Although Moes herself does not complain about it, many years later Groeneveld is still angry about the cold reception they received from the government: 'In a manner unworthy of our country, the old missionary and her two co-workers were accommodated in a small room. They slept on a mattress on the floor. Ice extended for

---

[1] M.A. Alt, 'Onze reis met Zuiderkruis', *GS* 32.12 (December 1961), p. 22.

threequarters of a meter up the walls of their little room.'[2] After two weeks, the three ladies are transferred to a guest house in Velp, where they have a small, cold room, mattresses on the floor, only one chair, and a wardrobe. Fortunately, a solution is quickly found. From 1 December, they are offered a well-heated apartment which belongs to a female friend at 2 Betuwestraat in Arnhem. Moes now has a writing desk. A busy time is ahead.

Moes receives invitations to preach from churches all over the country. She begins to travel in November. Everywhere she speaks, the meeting halls are crowded. Groeneveld accompanies her as her driver and assistant, and often they come home after midnight. Moes preaches about sanctification and dedication to the Lord. Sound recordings have been preserved from a number of the meetings. Listening to these recordings, you hear her compelling way of preaching: fast, driven, with a slight Indonesian accent, using many illustrations, and always ending with a strong appeal to the congregation.

After each meeting, old acquaintances gather to talk with her or invite her to their homes. She meets the Pentecostal leaders, with some she has been in correspondence for many years. Also people who only know her through the *Gouden Schoven* or *Glorieklokken* want to speak to her. Moes is touched by the warm love she receives in the assemblies. Some leaders are abroad, such as Piet Klaver and Karel Hoekendijk. In January, Moes visits the 93-year-old Marie Graafstal in Haarlem: 'I have rarely met someone in my life as full of love and patience as Mother Graafstal'.[3] She mainly preaches in Pentecostal churches, but she also speaks in other interdenominational or Baptist groups in Amsterdam and Zwolle.

In December, she attends a meeting with David du Plessis: 'How gloriously he spoke of the Holy Spirit and His gifts – how carefully he touched upon the mistakes we made, and he spoke with a serious admonition, mixed with humor, about the questions he is often asked'.[4] In comparison with the past, much has changed. Moes writes about a meeting of the Full Gospel Businessmen led by Peter van den Dries: 'For the first time in my life, I saw Reformed brothers (there were many guests present) lifting their hands whilst singing the

---

[2] D. Groeneveld, *Naar onbeperkte ruimte: Memoires van D. Groeneveld* (Duiven: GMI Music, 2007), p. 245.

[3] M.A. Alt, 'In Memoriam Moe Graafstal, *GS* 33.3 (March 1962), p. 23.

[4] M.A. Alt, 'Ons maandelijks verslag', *GS* 33.2 (February 1962), p. 16.

happy songs of praise and I heard fervent hallelujahs rise from their midst'.[5] The meeting with Stroethoff in a crowded 'Hospice Wallon' in Amsterdam causes her to remark: 'For one who has lived in the tropics for fifty-eight years in a row, it was a new experience to notice how boldly the believing Dutchmen today are in confessing the truth compared to the reticence in my youth!'[6]

While still in New Guinea, Moes has been asked by Johan Maasbach to take over the responsibility of a small group of believers in Arnhem. Since many of her former church members are also living in or around Arnhem, Moes feels led to bring them all together and establish a Pinksterzending assembly in Arnhem. There is a good understanding with the existing Pentecostal assembly Philadelphia led by the Swedish missionary, Göte Johansson. On Sundays, Moes travels all over the country and often preaches two, or even three times. On the 'free' Sundays, she preaches in Arnhem. She leads a weekly evening service in Arnhem, together with Groeneveld, and on another evening the Bible Study in her home. Often there is another meeting elsewhere. From May she plans to travel less and lead the weekly meetings in Arnhem every Sunday morning, but she will not live to do that.

Death

On Sunday, 18 March, she preaches her last sermon in Arnhem. During the dedication of six children, she makes a mistake with one of their names. It is quite possibly a sign of fatigue. Arriving home, she feels her strength decreasing. The next day, however, she is again at her desk, keeping up her correspondence. To a housemate, she says: 'If the Lord wants to take me home, then, hallelujah! But I still have so much to do.'[7] She prays a lot for the Papuans, the church in Manokwari, and the threatening situation in the distant country. Several times during prayer, she sees an angel of death. She writes: 'A battle between the followers of Sukarno and those who want to hold to the right of self-determination will be inevitable in the future'.[8] On

---

[5] Alt, 'Ons maandelijks verslag', (February 1962), p. 17.
[6] M.A. Alt, 'Ons maandelijks verslag', *GS* 33.4 (April 1962), pp. 16–17.
[7] 'De levensloop van Zuster Alt', *GS* 33.4 (April 1962), pp. 6–7.
[8] M.A. Alt, 'Berichten uit Indonesië en Nieuw-Guinea', *GS* 33.4 (April 1962), p. 19.

Wednesday, 21 March, she listens to the news about New Guinea in the evening. Then she goes to her room and tells her housemates, Dekkers and Kooken: 'There is an impending danger. God has again shown me the angel of death stretching out his sword.'[9] At that moment, she sits on her bed and falls unconscious.

Funeral in Arnhem (26 March 1962)

Groeneveld is called to come quickly to the Betuwestraat. 'Arriving there, I saw our beloved missionary lying on the bed in a coma with her sad co-workers, Aunt Mies and Aunt Rosa in the room with her. The attending physician could not do anything but ascertain that she would not survive until the next day.'[10] Many in the country are called and asked to pray. That evening and through the night she is no longer conscious. The following morning, Thursday, 22 March 1962, at 6.45 a.m., she calmly and peacefully slips away. Groeneveld writes:

> A heart attack, we say, but from God's throne the command had come to cut the silver cord (the fragile chain of life) and break the jar (the heart) at the source (Eccl. 12:5–6). God had taken his

---

[9] D. Groeneveld, 'Hoe het gebeurde', *GS* 33.5 (May 1962), pp. 17–18.
[10] Groeneveld, *Naar onbeperkte ruimte*, p. 253.

brave child home after a life full of toil, struggle, and wrestling with Satan but also a life full of great blessing.[11]

The weather is cold and raw on Monday, 26 March. Hundreds have come to attend the funeral service of Moesje Alt. The auditorium on the Renssenstraat cannot contain all the people. Several pastors speak with great respect about her life. Ernst Graf compares her to Deborah, the female judge of Israel. He prays that God will ignite many young people with the same fire that was burning in her. A little while later, a long row of cars and buses follows the mourning procession to the Moscowa cemetery. Eight of her spiritual children bear the coffin to the grave.

Many wreaths and flower arrangements decorate the open grave at the final ceremony. Groeneveld recalls that Moes died wearing her armor. The Lord took her away in the midst of her labour. This was the death she always wanted.[12] He recalls that Moes had calluses on her knees from praying so much and that her only wish was not to miss any of her children in the heavenly wedding hall.[13] Johan Maasbach remarks how her death has united friend and foe: 'We believe that this fact would have pleased her if she had known it because love among all the true children of God has always been her prayer and desire'.[14] Pastor Robert has known Moes for more than thirty years. To those who believe that God does not want to use women in a leading role, he claims, Moes proves the opposite in her fruitful life as an evangelist. Jo van den Brink agrees with this: 'Has the centuries long silence of women not caused the church of God a great deal of harm? Whoever sees the life of Sister Alt knows that even the most dogmatic Pentecostal never questioned the calling of this evangelist.'[15] Finally Wout van Beek speaks: 'Moesje has meant much to me. I was baptized in her assembly in Surabaya, and she was the one who identified that I had the gift of an evangelist.'[16]

---

[11] Groeneveld, 'Hoe het gebeurde', p. 18.

[12] 'De teraardebestelling van Zr. M.A. Alt', *GS* 33.4 (April 1962), p. 10.

[13] W.A. van Beek, 'In memoriam Zr. M.A. Alt', *Pinksterboodschap* 3.4 (April 1962), pp. 4–5.

[14] 'De teraardebestelling', p. 10.

[15] J.E. van den Brink, 'Bij het heengaan van Zuster Alt', *Kracht van Omhoog* 25.19 (6 April 1962), p. 10.

[16] Van Beek, 'In memoriam', p. 5.

Reactions

The October issue of *Gouden Schoven* carries reactions from many readers to the death of Moes. Annie, her first foster child, is deeply upset. As a two-year-old girl, she came to Moes in 1912, in Taju. She now lives in the Netherlands, and writes: 'Moes has been so good to me … I am so grateful to her.' Others have corresponded with Moes for many years:

> Already while I was in Indonesia, I corresponded with Moesje. Her letters were my moral support. She always answered my letters faithfully and wrote words full of comfort and counsel, even here in the Netherlands, despite being so busy … She meant more to me than my own mother.

An orphan writes:

> To me, her letters were often like a sunbeam in a dark night and now that is over … She has been like a mother for me in those twenty years that I have known her. A mother, no, more than a mother, because she always had such an understanding of me. How grateful I am for all the wise lessons she has given me. I still have our correspondence from the first to the last letter, and I keep them carefully. I feel that Moesje was the only person who loved me. If one goes through life as an orphan, there is such a great lack of love and understanding.

Evert van der Molen has been stimulated by Moes to become a writer: 'So she was to me an inspiration to write … I intend to continue with God's help, thanks to the encouragement I received from Sister Alt years ago.'[17]

A letter from Stefanus comes from Indonesia. As a thunderclap in a clear sky, the message has reached him. At the end of his sermon on Sunday, 25 March, his daughter, Naomi, comes with the telegram. He reads it, and the whole congregation bursts out in sobs. A few days later, he goes to his parents in Plampangan. His parents are weeping like children. They and other workers of the Plampangan church cannot stop talking about their spiritual mother's love and

---

[17] D. Groeneveld, 'Wat lezers schreven over Zuster Alt', *GS* 33.10 (October 1962), pp. 21–23.

goodness. On 6 April, Stefanus receives a letter from the Netherlands. It appears to be from Moes, dated 18 March 1962:

Dear Stefanus,

I received your letter and thank you for your messages. I was glad
to hear from you, no matter how dark the situation is. My heart
goes out to our poor people in Gambang Waluh, and I would like
to help them if I only knew how. Who knows but that the Lord
will still work it that an agreement may be found between the two
countries, so that the breach can be reconciled. That would be
nice, Stefanus. And I would meet you once again in my life. That
would be an answer to prayer. I am meeting so many former members during my 'walk around' in the country, and many ask about
you. I travel throughout the country from South to North. What
a pity I cannot send you *Gouden Schoven* now. When will the Lord
give relief? Here is there is nothing but snow, ice, and cold wind,
but spring is happily coming. We are doing very well. The Lord
blesses me with crowded halls everywhere I am invited to speak.
It is beyond all we ask and think that the Lord still wants to use
such an old woman like me.

Also, here in Arnhem the church begins to flourish. May God
comfort and encourage you, my dear boy. We will not forget you.
Maybe we will see you one day showing up here. The Lord is powerful. Many kind sweet regards and blessings from your loving
MOES.[18]

Continuation in the Netherlands

Although Moes continued to perform her daily work, she seems to
have felt that her time was nearing an end. To be sure some of the
preparations she made indicate that. In January, she transfers the
leadership of the assembly in Arnhem to Groeneveld.[19] At that time,
she speaks to her co-workers about her funeral. On her grave, she
just wants the inscription, 'Jesus alone'.[20] Her autobiography is made
ready for publication. One week before her death, she writes the

[18] S. Stefanus, 'Indonesië: Een brief van br. S. Stefanus', *GS* 33.7 (July 1962),
pp. 19–20.
[19] M.A. Alt, 'Ons maandelijks verslag', *GS* 33.2 (February 1962), p. 17.
[20] Groeneveld, 'Hoe het gebeurde', p. 18.

preface for the long-cherished edition of all her songs in one volume of *Glorieklokken*. It is her heartfelt-wish that her co-workers, Groeneveld and Sigmond, would continue the work on the same footing. The desire is mutual, so Sigmond takes responsibility for the magazine and Groeneveld for the church. The song-book, *Glorieklokken,* is published by Kracht van Omhoog, while the copyright of the remaining literature stays with the Pinksterzending.

Her books are in demand for many years, especially *Herinneringen uit mijn leven* (her autobiography), *Bijbelstudie voor zelfonderricht, In het volle licht,* and *Glorieklokken.* After the death of Hans Sigmond in 1985, the periodical, *Gouden Schoven,* is taken over by the Broederschap van Pinkstergemeenten (Assemblies of God in the Netherlands, now called VPE). In 1988, it is renamed *Oogsttijd Magazine* (*Harvest Time Magazine*) and, in 1993, it changes into a newsletter of the Home Mission department.

Regularly, *Gouden Schoven* brought reports from Stefanus, especially about the progress in Gambang Waluh and surrounding areas. Readers donated clothing and money to the poor in Indonesia annually. They also contributed to the construction of church buildings or for the support of pastors. For many years, these contacts are maintained through the Sinar Anugerah Foundation (originally founded in 1965 as the Salem Aleikum Foundation). Missionaries Karel and Thalia Schubert in Salatiga act as the contact persons in Indonesia. Today the Pinksterzending has two assemblies in Arnhem. Both are affiliated with the Verenigde Pinksteren Evangeliegemeenten (VPE). The VPE is affiliated with the Assemblies of God World Fellowship.

Continuation in Indonesia

Manokwari

The Dutch-speaking assembly in Manokwari closes in mid-1962. However, the Papuan assembly continues to grow. Henk Lit baptizes fifty-eight Papuans before he is evacuated around September 1962. As agreed, the congregation, with 200 baptized Papuans, transfers to the missionaries of TEAM. The church building and Moes's house are donated to TEAM. At the end of 1966, missionary Doug Miller writes to Henk Lit. He states that since the transfer in 1962, 1,300

Papuans, especially Hatam, have been baptized.[21] After that, the announcements in *Gouden Schoven* stop for several years. In June 1982, Netty van Heek, Committee member of Salem Aleikum, visits Manokwari. A new church building is now erected on the site of the house where Moes lived. Because the coastal residents and the mountain tribes do not get on well with each other, TEAM has decided to separate the groups. The new church building in Sanggeng is for the coastal inhabitants (Namemforese and Wandamese). Further toward Wosi is the church for the Hatam. The old church building of the Pinksterzending is torn down in December 1981. Anything of use after the demolition of the old church was taken by the Hatam to the forests for the construction of a prayer house there. Netty is able to find the half-finished prayer house. Noah, an evangelist from the time of Moes, leads a small group who prefer to gather in the woods. The elderly still remember Moes and Lit. The pulpit and benches have been brought from the old church. The group lives isolated and, apparently, is not connected to any Mission organization. During the farewell, they repeat with tears: 'Do not forget us'.[22] In the Netherlands, Salem Aleikum Foundation starts collecting gifts for the completion of the prayer house. Nevertheless, the connection with Manokwari does not seem to continue. The contacts remain limited to occasional visits by former members of the congregation and their children. In 2003, Groeneveld returns to Manokwari after forty-two years, together with his two sons Hans and Bram.

Gambang Waluh
In the 1950s, Stefanus travels annually to Gambang Waluh. Others also visit the area. From 1959, Stefanus is Chairman of the GSJA. In the mid-sixties there is a revival, partly due to some visits by the Evangelist Agus Manuhutu from Ambon.[23] Hundreds of people are converted. Young converts go to the GSJA Bible School and become pastors. Some feel called to go to other islands. In different villages near Gambang Waluh, churches emerge, such as as in Porot (1967)

---

[21] 'Bericht uit Nieuw-Guinea', *GS* 38.1 (January 1967), pp. 19–20.

[22] A.J.C. van Heek-de Graaf, 'Vergeet ons niet', *GS* 53.11 (November 1982), pp. 14–16.

[23] Andi Winarko, *Gereja Pinkster Zending Gambang Waluh Sebagai Cikal Bakal GSJA di Jawa Tengah* (BTh Thesis, Satyabhakti Advanced School of Theology, Malang, Indonesië, 2001), p. 54. S. Stefanus, 'Doopdienst te Gambangwaluh', *GS* 36.10 (October 1975), pp. 21–22. S. Stefanus, 'Opwekking in de dessa', *GS* 38.8 (August 1967), pp. 17–18.

and Sumowono (1968). In 1978, ten assemblies are established, and in 1983 fourteen. With help from the Netherlands, church buildings are erected in of all these villages. In Ngadiroso, the village head wants to have a big banyan tree taken down. For fear of the evil spirits, nobody wants to take the job, so he asks the Christians. After prayer, the tree is taken down.[24] Today there is a church in that place.

In 1983, Stefanus is in Gambang Waluh to dedicate the new church building, which replaced an old shed. He brings two paintings from Surabaya. The first painting, Jesus praying in the garden of Gethsemane, is hung above the platform. The second painting, a portrait of Moesje Alt, is placed above the exit, so it is only noticed when leaving the church. Stefanus has previously seen portraits of former ministers hanging in the Protestant church in Surabaya:

> Thinking back on this, I decided to hang a portrait of Sister Alt in the first assembly she founded and that – as she would have wished – in a modest place. She was a servant of God who served not only her four years, but throughout her life she served the Lord in the land He had directed her to … she fulfilled her mission without the help of a sponsor or a sending assembly on which she could fall back. She lived trusting exclusively in God. She did not care about comfort or valuable possessions. She lived among the Javanese people that she loved and ate the same food they ate.[25]

Stefanus enjoins the young generation not to forget this extraordinary history and to reach out to be filled with the Holy Spirit. In 1988 Stefanus visits Gambang Waluh and Sumowono for the last time.

The traces of Moes's work are still clearly visible. Gambang Waluh is a fully Christian village. From this small place twenty-five assemblies are founded in the surrounding villages by 2015. Elsewhere on Java, and on Kalimantan (Borneo), Sumatra and Papua Barat (New Guinea), dozens of assemblies are founded by pioneers from Gambang Waluh. Among the leaders are many grandchildren of converts from the time of Moes. The assemblies belong to the GSJA (Assemblies of God). In 1950, a section of the Pinksterzending joined the GSJA. In 2013, the GSJA numbers 2,200 assemblies with almost

---

[24] S. Stefanus, 'Brief van Br. Stefanus', *GS* 53.11 (November 1982), p. 18.
[25] S. Stefanus, 'Over de kerkinwijding in Gambangwaluh', *GS* 54.11 (1983), pp. 24–25.

200,000 members. Another part of the Pinksterzending continues as Gereja Utusan Pantekosta and numbers seventy-three assemblies with over 23,000 members.[26]

In July 2016, Gambang Waluh celebrates its hundred years of existence as a village. The church building is enlarged. On the site next to the church, where Moes used to live, a new building is erected: the Moesje Alt Museum. Hundreds attend the opening of the museum. This author is privileged to present the first copy of his biography of Moesje Alt in the Indonesian language to the representative of the district authorities.

Gambang Waluh and, on the right, Museum Moes M.A. Alt (2016)

Christians in the post-colonial era

With the declaration of independence in 1945 the new born Indonesian Republic under Sukarno formulated Five Principles or Five Pillars (*Pancasila*) as the foundation of the state: Belief in the one Supreme God, Humanitarianism, National Unity, People's Sovereignty,

---

[26] E-mail Gani Wiyono to author, 14 April 2015. *Direktori Gereja-Gereja, Yayasan, Pendidikan Agama dan Keagamaan Kristen di Indonesia 2013* (Jakarta: Kementerian Agama Republik Indonesia, Direktorat Jenderal Bimbingan Masyarakat Kristen, 2013), p. 352.

and Social Justice. While religious freedom is hereby granted by constitution, Muslim nationalists continue to advocate an Islamic state. Efforts to implement this puts adherents of other religions under pressure.[27] During the presidency of Suharto (1965–1985), also called the 'New Order', the tension between Muslims and Christians intensifies, leading to many conflicts and violence. The government issues restrictive regulations controlling the activities of Christians.[28] As official permits to construct new church buildings are very hard to obtain, some Pentecostal-Charismatic churches build large multi-purpose buildings and use them for worship. Many Pentecostal congregations across Indonesia assemble in restaurants, hotels, or conference halls, often without permits.[29] When meeting places do not have the appearance of a church they provoke less resistance.

Ecumenical relations between the churches have improved in recent decades. Officially the government only acknowledges two kinds of Christians: Protestants and Catholics. Whereas the Catholics are represented by the Indonesian Bishops's Conference (*Konferensi Waligereja Indonesia* – KWI), Protestant Christianity is very diverse. The three most important national representations of Protestant church bodies are the Ecumenicals, the Evangelicals, and the Pentecostals. In 1950 the first formed the Indonesian Council of Churches, which in 1984 changed its name to the Communion of Churches (*Persekutuan Gereja-gereja di Indonesia* – PGI). For the government the PGI is the main mouthpiece of Protestantism. The second category is represented by the Indonesia Evangelical Fellowship (*Persekutuan Injili Indonesia* – PII) established in 1971. The third and the fastest

---

[27] Only six religions are officially recognized: Islam, Christianity (read Protestantism), Catholicism, Hinduism, Buddhism, and Confucianism.

[28] Chang-Yau Hoon refers to several controversial laws, like the Joint Decree No. 1/1969, issued by the Minister of Religion and Minister of Home Affairs to control religious activities and erecting places of worship (later replaced by the Joint Ministerial Regulation on Places of Worship, 2006), and the Marriage Law No. 1/1974, which recognizes only marriages registered with the Civil Registration Offices. The Joint Decree of 1979 prohibits religious propagation, and restricts foreign aid to religious institutions. The Education Law No. 2/1989 (replaced by Education Law No. 20/2003) requires religious education teachers to be from the same religion as the students. Chang-Yau Hoon, 'Between evangelism and multi-culturalism: The dynamics of Protestant Christianity in Indonesia', *Social Compass international review of sociology of religion* 60.4 (December 2013), pp. 457–70 [http://journals.sagepub.com/doi/abs/10.1177/0037768613502758]   20–11–2017.

[29] Hoon, 'Between evangelism', p. 462.

growing one is the Pentecostal-Charismatic movement. The Pente-costal Council of Indonesia, founded in 1979, later changed its name to the Communion of Pentecostal Churches in Indonesia (*Perseku-tuan Gereja-gereja Pentakosta Indonesia* (PGPI). The two largest Pente-costal churches, the GPdI and the Indonesian Bethel Church, are members of the PGPI. Although the GSJA is a Pentecostal church it is member of the PGI and of the PII, but not of the PGPI. A large number of Pentecostal and Neo-Charismatic churches are independ-ent. The Pentecostal–Charismatic churches and some of the Evan-gelical churches are less active in interfaith dialogues and have often been accused of using aggressive methods to win converts while showing a lack of cultural sensitivity.[30]

The years 1996–1998 were especially full of violence towards Christians. Because of their more confrontational missionary meth-ods and their noisy worship style, Pentecostal churches are extra vul-nerable to the attacks of hardline Islamic groups. Out of the 275 churches that were closed, vandalized, destroyed, or burnt down 121 (44%) were Pentecostal churches.[31] The situation remains delicate in most areas with a Muslim majority.

---

[30] Hoon, 'Between evangelism', p. 465.
[31] Gani Wiyono, 'Pentecostals in Indonesia', in Allan Anderson and Edmond Tang (eds.), *Asian and Pentecostal: The Charismatic Face of Christianity in Asia* (Baguio City: Regnum Books, 2005), p. 320.

15

GLORIEKLOKKEN

I have a new song, a wonderful song
I have a new song in my heart,
And now happyily I sing: The old has gone long!
I have a new song in my heart.
(Glorieklokken no. 6)[1]

Music is interwoven into the life of Moesje Alt. As a child, she is moved by organ music and singing in the church. She recognizes the importance of singing as a carrier of the message of the gospel. Raised with the singing of psalms and hymns, she later learns the songs of the Salvation Army, Seventh-day Baptists, and the popular songbook, *Johan de Heer.* The last of these is also used in the Pentecostal churches. Through a vision, Moes experiences the call to publish a songbook. Combined with her aptitude for music and language, this call results in the writing, translating, and editing of songs for the assembly.

Around 1920, she translates a number of well-known Dutch spiritual songs into Javanese. It is probable that this edition is similar to the songbook she issues in December 1928: *Kidoeng Panggoegah,* which is subtitled: *Revival songs for the Javanese people with familiar tunes.* It contains 200 songs and thirty choruses. A reprint appears in 1931. Unfortunately, no copies of these Javanese songbooks have been found. Moes called it a Pentecostal songbook. Possibly some songs that

---

[1] 'Ik zing een nieuw lied' ('I sing a new song') in M.A. Alt, *Glorieklokken: Liederen voor solo en samenzang* (Gorinchem: Kracht van Omhoog, 1963) no. 6.

spontaneously came up during the revival have been included. In her autobiography, Moes quotes from a song 'that the Lord had given us in words and music':

> Doeh Jeruzalem! Doeh Jeruzalem! (Oh Jerusalem! Oh Jerusalem!)
> Panggénanné Penganten Poetri. (Dwelling of the heavenly Bride)[2]

From the moment that Moes assumes the editorship of the periodical *Pinksterkracht* (later renamed *Gouden Schooven*), she publishes a song in nearly every issue and often one or more poems. In the meantime, she prepares her own song-book, *Glorieklokken*.

Publication in the Dutch Indies

In November 1930, the first edition of *Glorieklokken*, subtitled 'Pentecostal Songbook' appears with 200 songs and thirty choruses. The tune is written in numbered musical notation. In the preface, Moes calls it a precursor of a future, larger songbook with staves. The songs are listed by theme. The seven most common themes are: Faith and Devotion (54), Salvation (24), Invitation (21), Second Coming (19), Mission (17), Heaven (17), and Baptism with the Holy Spirit (11). Within four months, the first printing of 1,000 copies is sold out. Some songs are translated in Malay by a brother, Siwi, while Moes prepares a translation in Javanese. In 1931, Siwi releases the Malay songbook, *Lontjeng Soerga,* in which most songs come from *Glorieklokken*. From 1934, Javanese-translations of songs from *Glorieklokken* appear in *Gouden Schooven* and *Gandoem Mas*. In May 1936, an edition with the first hundred songs of *Glorieklokken* in Malay and Javanese appears without staves.

In February 1932, the first part of *Glorieklokken* appears with staves. The subtitle reads: 'Christian songbook for use in meetings and in homes in particular for the Dutch Indies'. Part One has forty-four songs, and 3,000 copies are printed. The cover states that over 400 songs and thirty choruses are anticipated. Moes publishes the songs without mentioning her name.[3] In April 1935, there are five

---

[2] M.A. Alt, *Herinneringen uit mijnleven* (Velp: Pinksterzending, 1963), p. 74.

[3] The earlier Javanese song-book was also published anonymously: 'I was rather taken up with my work, but when the Lord revealed this to me, I decided to publish the book without mentioning my name' (Alt, *Herinneringen*, 60). In the editon *Glorie-Klokken* of 1930 her name does not appear on the title page, but her initals do

parts issued with a total of 244 songs. In 1936, the first two parts receive a second unchanged printing.[4] Part Six only appears in March 1938, which increases the number to 305 published songs. The final two parts will never appear, although all the songs are delivered to the printer. Moes hopes to be able to publish the complete eight parts in the Netherlands.

In the preface of 1932, Moes speaks of a commission from God to collect and translate these songs. 'The Pentecostal assembly likes to sing', she writes. With the growth of the Pentecostal assemblies, the need for their own songbook is felt. But Moes has a broader goal in mind as well:

> We also hope that the songbook may find its way into other churches and religious circles. Next to the songbook, *Johan de Heer,* and other good song-books, *Glorieklokken* would like to take its own humble position. Our purpose is not to separate but to unite us as much as possible with groups that confess the same Name, which is dear to us.[5]

The six parts are classified by theme: Salvation (1–34), Invitation (35–67), The Baptism of the Holy Spirit (68–96), Healing (97–107), The Second Coming of the Lord (108–31), Faith and devotion (132–214), Sanctification (215–44) and, finally, Praise and Faith (245–305). This format suggests that already in 1932 Moes has the intended 400 songs more or less ready. The internal problems leading to the establishment of the Pinksterzending in 1935, delays the release of the further parts. After the war, a large number of the songs have been

---

appear with the songs, where applicable, as translator or composer. In the six volumes of 1932–1938, her name does not appear at all, except in the mailing address. Only the preface of volume 1 has her initials. When others copied and published her songs without asking permission, she felt obliged to mention her name in the publication of *Glorieklokken* in the 1950s.

[4] In the second printing in 1936, the preface of the first printing of volume 1 is a little shortened but now includes place and year: Waru, 1930, which should read: Waru, 1932. As this preface introduces the book as the first publication with staves, it cannot refer to the edition of 1930 which was without staves. The announcements in *Gouden Schooven* show that volume I first appeared in 1932. The earlier edition of *Glorie-Klokken* in 1930 was still with number notation. The preface of the second printing mentions: Lawang, September 1936. As far as is known, only the first two volumes of the 1932–1938 Series have been reprinted. The addition of 'in 't bijzonder voor Nederlandsch-Indië' ('especially for the Dutch Indies') in the title disappears from this moment forward.

[5] M.A. Alt, 'Voorwoord', *Glorieklokken* I [Waru, 1932].

translated in Malay by Stefanus and others. Among the repatriates from the Dutch Indies who arrive in the Netherlands during the 1950s are many Pentecostals who are familiar with *Glorieklokken.*

Publication in the Netherlands

In the mid-thirties, *Glorieklokken* also becomes popular in the Pentecostal churches in the Netherlands, especially with choirs. In the years 1954–1959, the publisher at Gorinchem, Kracht van Omhoog (Power From on High), publishes the songbook, *Glorieklokken,* in ten parts with staves. In these years, Moes is in New Guinea and chooses a publisher in the Netherlands. The songs are given completely new numbers. For the first time, the name M.A. Alt appears on the title page. Given the long period taken for all ten volumes to appear, each volume now has an assortment of themes. The well-known themes of the previous edition are continued, along with songs for the annual church feasts (Christmas, Good Friday, Easter, Ascension, Pentecost, New Year Eve, and New Year), for special services (Baptism, The Lord's Supper, Marriage, and Funeral), and special themes (Suffering of the Lord, Heaven, and Youth songs). In 1959, a text edition of all songs in one volume appears as well as a 10-volume edition of all songs in a music edition for piano. Even gramophone records (series of *Glorieklanken*) with songs from *Glorieklokken* are released. Eventually in 1962, the year of her death, her long-awaited edition of 553 songs appears in one volume. A few songs have been replaced and some new ones added. The words of 90% of the songs are by Moes, mostly free translations of existing songs. Of the few songs for which she wrote text and music, only one was included.[6] With a few exceptions, the themes are no longer mentioned next to the songs. Around 1960, the songbook is used in almost all Pentecostal assemblies, but the songs are also in demand in other circles. Because *Glorieklokken* is often used together with the songbook, *Johan de Heer,* Kracht van Omhoog publishes a combination songbook (1965) with the texts from both works. This will increase familiarity of the

---

[6] 'Loflied van genezing na krankheid', *Glorieklokken* no. 32. In the edition of 1930 there were five songs for which Alt wrote the text and music: 'Voor Java' (no. 73), 'Het lied van de bruid' (no. 99), 'Jezus en ik' (no. 119), 'Jezus alleen' (no. 208), and 'Alles in Hem' (no. 209).

songbook outside the Pentecostal assemblies. In 1971, a nearly un-changed reprint of *Glorieklokken* appears with three additional songs.

A thematic analysis of the most popular songs was done by Nathalie Zeijl-Versluis. She shows that the majority of the texts are about Christian life and salvation, with great attention given to the feelings and experiences of the believer.[7] In another study of the songs, Miranda Klaver distinguishes five strong themes: Repentance, Cross, Sanctification, Second Coming, and the Pentecostal experi-ence.[8] Songs with the theme of repentance show a clear difference between the old life without God and the new life with God. Singing the songs confirms the identity of the believer. They also serve to proclaim the Gospel to hearers. The second theme, the cross, em-phasizes the decisive meaning of the suffering and death of Jesus. Participation by the believer is the characteristic element in these songs. In the text the singer finds himself, as it were, at the foot of the cross. In the third theme of sanctification, the separation between old and new life is further elaborated. The believer is separated (sanc-tified) and is now is walking in the light with Jesus. Klaver notes that the sanctification motif leaves little room for the brokenness of ex-istence or for doubt in the life of the believer.[9] As a fourth theme, the imminent return of Jesus is expressed in figurative language. The fifth theme is specifically about the Pentecostal experience: the bap-tism with the Holy Spirit, speaking in tongues, and healing. Apart from the last theme, which accounts for fewer than 10% of the songs, there is a high degree of consensus with the music of the broader evangelical world.[10]

---

[7] Nathalie Zeijl-Versluis, *Zing voor de Heer. Onderzoek naar de hoofdthema's in liederen van de honderdjarige pinksterbeweging in Nederland* (Bachelor thesis, Azusa theologische hogeschool, Amsterdam, 2007), pp. 34–52. First it was researched which songs from *Glorieklokken* were most popular in the Dutch Pentecostal churches. The 209 songs that were nominated were analysed. The most important themes were Chris-tian Life and Salvation. Next in order of frequency came: Christ, End times, Wor-ship, and Holy Spirit.

[8] Miranda Klaver, 'Glorieklokken: Spiegel van geleefd geloof', *Parakleet* 33.125 (2013), pp. 13–15.

[9] Klaver, 'Glorieklokken', p. 14.

[10] Klaver, 'Glorieklokken', p. 15.

Glorieklokken and *Johan de Heer*

The songbook, *Johan de Heer*, first appearing in 1905, appears in several editions. Along with psalms and hymns, it contains a large number of songs from the Salvation Army and Ira D. Sankey. In addition, there are Adventist songs, Sunday School songs, and other choruses. These sources have also been used by Moes. There are some striking similarities between the lives of Moes and Johan de Heer (1866–1961). Both are raised in the Reformed Church. For several years, both observe the Sabbath and are baptized by immersion during those years, although Johan de Heer remains a member of the Reformed Church. Both receive a calling through a vision. The first book each one publishes is a songbook, consisting of selected songs and songs translated from foreign texts. They are both involved in writing music to a much lesser degree. Both edit a periodical and publish various books. In their messages, they both have a strong emphasis on evangelism, end times, and a life dedicated to God. In comparison, *Glorieklokken* is less influenced by the Dutch and Reformation heritage. Although Johan de Heer makes use of the Anglo-Saxon Evangelical song culture, Moes draws from more works and also uses books from the Pentecostal movement, such as: *Assembly Songs, Elim Evangel, Four Square Melodies, Full Gospel Songs, Harvest Hymns, Pfingstjubel, Songs of Praise, and Spiritual Songs*.[11] Moes writes repeatedly with great appreciation for Johan de Heer.[12] Unfortunately, the letters that the two have exchanged are untraceable, but certainly both have understood the binding value of music.

In her book, *De kracht van een lied (The Power of a Song)*, Helen Colijn describes how women in Japanese camps are empowered by the formation of a 'vocal orchestra' to survive in the dreadful circumstances.[13] During these years of oppression, the songs of *Glorieklokken* are also a blessing to many. Besides the Bible, some

---

[11] Cf. Robert A. Johnson, 'A Bibliography of Hymnals Published by American Pentecostal Denominations', *The Hymn* 38.1 (1987), pp. 29–30.

[12] M.A. Alt, 'Broeder Johannes de Heer: In Memoriam', *GS* 32.5 (May 1961), p. 24.

[13] Helen Colijn, *De kracht van een lied: Overleven in een vrouwenkamp* (Franeker: Van Wijnen, 1989).

believers carry *Glorieklokken* with them in the Japanese camps. In the secret gatherings, the songs are hummed with tears or softly sung.[14]

Alt as translator

In the preface of the 1932 edition, Moes indicates that she has changed the text of the songs: 'They are not specifically American, English or German but, as much as possible, translated to fit the characteristics of the churches here'. On closer inspection, it shows that Moes deals freely with the original text. With her excellent mastery of the Dutch language and a strong sense of rhythm, she regularly writes her own text. It is important to her that a song is easy to sing and has good content.

The famous song, 'Lichtstad met uw paarlen poorten' (*Glorieklokken* 52), from 'He the pearly gates will open', is an example of how Moes translates. The original Swedish text was written in 1917 by Fredrick A. Blom (1867-1927).[15] Nathaniel Carlson translated the song into English, after which it was published in *Favorites II*. Except for the words 'pearly gates', Alt wrote a whole new text.

The original song is about the love of Jesus who purchased our redemption by his blood and who will (in the future) open the pearly gates of heaven for us. The believer is situated waiting before the door. The translation by Moes is much more about what is behind the door. Moes brings the words 'city' and 'New Jerusalem' to the song. Behind the door, we find a city of light, a holy resort, a golden city of God, and a home for weary pilgrims, where the Tree of Life blossoms and the stream of Living Water flows.

The song 'Toen de kracht Gods op mij viel' (*Glorieklokken* 7) from 'When the power of God fell on me' goes even further. The music is written in 1934 by P.P. Bilhorn of the Church of the Nazarene, a church belonging to the Holiness Movement. The original song has been published by the Assemblies of God in the songbook, *Assembly Songs* (no. 71). The song is about Pentecost, but Moes incorporates specific characteristics of Pentecostal teaching. To the text she adds the term 'baptized with God's Spirit' and the idea of speaking in new tongues. The original song contains three verses. Moes adds a fourth about the return of Jesus, because to her, the baptism in the Holy

---

[14] M.A. Alt, 'Gevraagd: Hartelijke voorbede voor Glorieklokken', *GS* 22.5 (May 1953), p. 22.
[15] The music is from the Norwegian Alfred O. Duhlin.

Spirit and the 'second coming' belong together. The Spirit baptism is about filling the lamp and preparing your bridal gown.

Her chosen words always align closely with the music. Choir director, Willem Harold Boog, describes the strong connection between text and music in the song, 'Ik wandel in het licht met Jezus' ('I walk in the light with Jesus'), as follows:

> When you look at the connection between text and melody with a critical eye, you will hear the walking characteristic in the rhythm, the cheerfulness of the progression in the melody and the determination of the refrain and the conclusion … The song 'Walk in the Light' repeatedly tells me that Jesus walks beside me and goes with me like a Loving Friend. The text and the melody reinforce that trust in me. At the same time, I underline, with the words of the chorus, that nothing ever separates me from Jesus when I walk in the Light with Him. The power of this song is therefore mainly in the combination of text and melody, which affects the hearts of many. Mine too.[16]

Glorieklokken Today

Until the eighties, *Glorieklokken* is the most widely used songbook in the Dutch Pentecostal churches. Gradually its place is taken by the collection *Opwekkingsliederen (Revival Songs)*. When the latter gradually evolves into an independent songbook, some well-known songs from *Glorieklokken* are included. The 1991 edition of the songbook, *Johan de Heer*, also contains a number of songs from *Glorieklokken*. Similarly some songs are found in the Evangelical Song Book and in the songbook of the Baptist Union. 'Lichtstad met uw paarlen poorten' is one of the most popular hymns played on the radio, and on YouTube the song has scored millions of hits. Eric and Tanja Lagerström prove that *Glorieklokken* appeals not just to the older generation. They bring out songs of *Glorieklokken* in a contemporary form, as was seen in the television program 'Glorieklokken in Lapland' (Zendtijd voor Kerken, 2010). Remco Hakkert on his cds *Dan Zingt mijn ziel* (2011) and *Stromen van zegen* (2013) has also revived some songs from *Glorieklokken*. In this way, the songs of Moes have found a way to the heart of many, many Dutch people.

---

[16] http://www.willemharoldboog.nl/wandel.html [25 February 2013]. *Glorieklokken* 63 comes from *Gospel Songs*, but no further details are known.

16

LIFE AS THEOLOGY

It is not the Bible alone, with little of God's Spirit!
It is not the Holy Spirit alone, with little of God's Word!
But the Bible and the leading of the Spirit together, is what keeps us from
one-sidedness: Rigidity on the one side or over-spirituality on the other side.[1]

The last chapters deal with the theological thinking of Moesje Alt. These chapters assume some knowledge of the Bible and its terminology on the part of the reader. For Moes, theology is not an academic activity. Doctrine and life are completely intertwined for her. Doctrine takes root in life and so becomes a lived reality. Life is influenced by doctrine, but this also works the other way around. Points of doctrine that remain detached from normal life disappear into the background or are modified. Time, so essential to life, plays an important role. Each era comes with new questions and challenges to which doctrine responds.

Moes uses her own biography to help the reader's life of faith. Whether it is in a sermon or article, she regularly uses events from her own life or that of others as illustrations for her teaching. For *Gouden Schoven,* she writes many short stories about daily life and some especially for young people. With these dramatized real life stories, she knows how to bring home a spiritual lesson. Similarly, her songs and poems are examples of a living faith. The stories, songs, and poems open the window to new beginnings and stimulate change.

---

[1] M.A. Alt, 'Dagboek 1945–1961', December 1945, p. 18.

In her personal life, Moes wrestles intensely with the interaction between doctrine and life. Sometimes she revises a previously obtained insight after having received more light on the issue. Modestly, she writes: 'I am a lay-person, just a simple woman, without theological knowledge'.[2] Through an intense life of prayer and Bible reading, she gains a deep knowledge of the Bible. She lives through each text. In addition she studies faith building books as well as theological works. She passes on whatever she learns and experiences. Through her magazine, she tries to help readers who are struggling with questions.

This chapter and the next one, try to capture her theological development. The starting point for the doctrine is always the Bible, the Word of God. The guidance of the Holy Spirit is necessary in order to understand and apply the Bible correctly. But how do you know you are led by the Holy Spirit and not by your own mind? The closing chapter also looks at the way in which she deals with this last question. Does she realize this distinction between the Holy Spirit and her own mind, and if so, how does she make that distinction? Let us start by looking at the theological influences on her religious life and then discuss the points of faith that she emphasizes.

Theological influences

In the development of her theology, her religious background plays a role. Moes grows up in the Reformed Church and is confirmed around her eighteenth year. By her own admission, that belief was very superficial. Nevertheless she is formed by it. She has become familiar with the Apostolic Confession and with the Heidelberg Catechism.[3] After a dramatic conversion and joining the Seventh-Day Baptist (SDB), she feels called to missionary work. Without theological education she takes her first step as a missionary nurse. Under the guidance of Marie Jansz, she learns to lead a colony for the poor and to conduct meetings. Marie is the daughter of a Mennonite missionary but has joined the Salvation Army and the SDB. She is a pioneer who baptizes and administers the Lord's Supper. Together with Marie, Moes is looking for more of the Holy Spirit. She is

---

[2] M.A. Alt, 'Waarom ik mij bij de Pinkstergemeente heb aangesloten', *GS* 5.4 (April 1929), p. 5.

[3] M.A. Alt, 'De twaalf geloofs-artikelen', *GS* 23.11 (November 1954), p. 6.

captivated by books by Hannah Whitall Smith, Andrew Murray, and Charles Spurgeon. The themes of sanctification and healing by prayer will continue to fascinate her, perhaps because of her personal battle with malaria. Together with Marie Jansz, she edits the paper, *Sanctification,* for a short while.

From 1914 to 1929, she leads her own colony in Gambang Waluh, during the first eight years as a missionary with the SDB. In 1922, Moes breaks with the doctrine of Sabbath observance. The baptism with the Holy Spirit, four years later, marks her transition to Pentecostalism. In this isolated post, a large Javanese church develops under her ministry. With almost no help from outside, she has to find her way. She shares both love and sorrow with this poor community, which fosters a bond that remains even when she lives elsewhere. From 1928, she becomes more and more involved in the national work of the Pentecostal Church in the Dutch Indies (PGNI). She preaches in churches all over the country. She is responsible for the periodical, *Gouden Schoven.* In preaching, articles, songs, poems, and her life, she elucidates the faith. She begins a Javanese Bible School. She sees the Pentecostal movement as a work of the Holy Spirit, but also knows about people and churches coming off the rails. She writes that it is because of disagreements about doctrine and life that she breaks with PGNI in 1934. As founder and prime leader of the Pinksterzending, she has to show leadership even more than before, including in the area of doctrine. She develops a correspondence course for Bible Study. The lesson material she wrote is published in 1951 in her *Bible Study for Self-education.*

Through its literature and her correspondence, she is well-informed about the Pentecostal Movement elsewhere in the world. In doctrine, she follows mainstream Pentecostalism, the Assemblies of God in particular. She also draws on the Holiness Movement, the Salvation Army, and Pietism. She shows a lot of interest in mystics, dedicated men and women who sought to be Christ-like. Their overall devotion to God and ecstatic experiences attract her. In *Gouden Schoven,* she gives a great deal of attention to the practical application of communion with God in prayer and Bible reading. She also covers the education of children and more general and ethical subjects. For instance, she warns against birth control, takes up the cause of animal welfare, and makes her case against hunting. Compared to other Pentecostal periodicals from those years, it is striking that Moes is not afraid to use psychological insights for understanding the inner life. It is possible to discern the influence of her education as a psychiatric nurse in this context.[4]

Articles of Faith

The periodical, *Pinksterkracht*, predecessor of *Gouden Schoven*, has on the cover: 'Jesus Christ is the same yesterday, today and forever' (Heb. 13.8). In addition, it reads: 'Our Gospel is: Jesus, the only Deliverer and Saviour; Jesus, the greatest Physician; Jesus, the Baptizer with the Holy Spirit; Jesus, the coming Bridegroom, Lord and King of the Kings'. These four points of faith are called the 'Fourfold Gospel' or the 'Full Gospel'. In all pre-war issues of *Gouden Schoven*, the text of this Fourfold Gospel is a fixture on the first page. From March 1930 to March 1942 we also find twelve articles of faith on the second page under the heading: 'What the Pentecostal assembly believes and teaches'. It is the first time that a Dutch-speaking Pentecostal periodical adopts such a statement of faith. The other Pentecostal periodicals follow: *Spade Regen* (P. van der Woude, Rotterdam, 1933) and *Het Middernachtelijk Geroep* (N. Vetter, Haarlem, 1937). In short, the twelve articles deal with:

1. Inspiration of the Bible
2. One God in Three Persons
3. Fall and hereditary depravity
4. Incarnation, reconciling death, and resurrection of Christ
5. Salvation for all people through faith in Jesus Christ
6. Repentance and rebirth by the Holy Spirit and sanctification
7. Water Baptism for believers and the Lord's Supper
8. Baptism with the Holy Spirit with signs following
9. Divine healing through the finished work on Calvary
10. Gifts of the Holy Spirit and the Biblical ministries

---

[4] Several times, Moes refers to D. Weatherhead, *Psychologie en leven* (Utrecht: Erven Bijleveld, 1936) [Psychology and Life]. Cf. M.A. Alt, 'Voor het dagelijksch leven: Zenuwachtigheid', *GS* 9.18 (September 1936), pp. 12–13. M.A. Alt, 'Waarom heb ik geen contact meer met God?', *GS* 11.7 (April 1938), pp. 4–5. In 1938, the list with recommended books to order includes T.W. Pym, *Moderne psychologie en het leven van de christen* (Amsterdam: Paris, 1926) [Psychology and the Christian Life]. In 'Ons ziele-leven' *GS* 10.23 (December 1937), pp. 4–5, Alt discusses the four temperaments (choleric, sanguine, phlegmatic, and melancholic) to explain that people often misunderstand one another, but that the bond of love unites all character types.

11. Imminent return of Christ and the premillennial
    rapture of believers
12. Last judgment

In 1934, four years after its introduction, Moes explains the reason
for the publication of this 'so-called confession of faith' in every issue
'is that it fully complies with the Scriptures'.[5] Her source is the Swiss
Pentecostal periodical, *Verheissung des Vaters*, which had taken it over
from *Redemption Tidings*, the magazine of the British Assemblies of
God.[6] All these points of faith are regularly discussed in articles in
Gouden Schoven. Her translation of the statement of faith shows that
Moes considers connection to a wider, well supported body of teach-
ing important. Already in 1930, when she still belongs to the PGNI,
she follows the teaching of the Assemblies of God, while all the
American missionaries working with the PGNI belong to another
Pentecostal church. Did she perhaps anticipate a problem in the area
of doctrine?

Bible Study by Self Education

The book, *Bijbelstudie voor zelfonderricht (Bible Study for Self-Education)*, is
the most important doctrinal work that Moes publishes and therefore
deserves special attention. Since later editions (1968 and 1976) appear
years after her death and are revised to some extent, we will use the
original edition of 1951. The whole Bible is discussed. Of its 544
pages, the first 192 deal with the Old Testament, and the rest concern
the New Testament. There is no introduction or conclusion to the
book and no chapter divisions, but there is a list of subjects. It is a
collection of thirty-four issues, each containing one or more lessons
which are concluded with questions. The issues had first appeared
separately as a correspondence course for church workers.

---

[5] M.A. Alt, 'Wat de Pinkstergemeente (over de geheele wereld) gelooft en leert',
GS 10.15 (August 1934), p. 4.

[6] Some differences are noticable. Following *Verheissung des Vaters* and different
from the British version, *Gouden Schooven* includes 'the inherited depravity of the
whole of humanity'. Perhaps her Calvinistic background has played a role here.
Remarkable is that *Gouden Schooven*, again following *Verheissung des Vaters*, omits immersion with water baptism (article 7) and speaking in tongues with Spirit baptism
(article 8). Maybe Moes was unaware that these characteristics, which she endorsed,
were included in *Redemption Tidings*.

The first lesson begins with the 'Divine Trinity' and comes to the conclusion that God is love. The application is that love is the new life principle of the born-again human being. By the power of God, humanity can maintain the highest commandment: love God above all and your neighbour as yourself. In this way, Moes sets the tone for the rest of the book. In the revised editions of 1968 and 1971, the order of the first two sections (Trinity and Bible) has been reversed. It is an unfortunate oversight by the editors because the choice of Moes to start with the Trinity is theologically very interesting and her emphasis on love as the life principle is characteristic of her theology.

Then follows a section about the Bible. It speaks of an organic inspiration: 'The Bible was written by humans, inspired by the Holy Spirit. They were organs of God and spoke and wrote what the Spirit was giving to them (2 Pet. 1.21).' Moes rejects a mechanical word by word dictated inspiration of the Bible. The Biblical writers were not passive. The Divine Spirit worked together with the human spirit in writing the Scriptures.[7] The Biblical writers interpreted the thoughts of God in human language and in a form fitting to the time of the contemporary peoples.[8] In order to understand the Bible properly, knowledge of past cultures is needed. Thus, Moes regards head-covering for women and foot washing for believers as culturally determined and not as a universal rule or principle.

The Old Testament (OT) is the foundation of the New Testament (NT), like the foundation on which a house is built. At the same time, the Old is called the shadow of the New, which becomes visible in an often typographical use of the texts. Eve, for instance, is a type of the Church and Adam a type of Jesus. An unexpected explanation is that the four rivers in the Garden of Eden (Gen. 2.10) are a type of the fourfold gospel preached in the Pentecostal churches! The next lessons cover parts of the Bible books. The second lesson deals with creation, the fall, and paradise. The third lesson covers the Sabbath and Cain and Abel. The fourth lesson teaches about Enoch, the Flood, Noah's ark etc.

About half the Old Testament books and all of the New Testament books are treated in succession. The narrative parts of the Bible get the most attention. There is also information about the background

---

[7] M.A. Alt, 'Inspiratie', *GS* 8.16 (August 1932), p. 5.
[8] Alt, 'Inspiratie', p. 6.

of the Bible as well as the period between the Old and New Testaments.[9]

In addition to the traditional *Statenvertaling* (comparable to the *King James Version*), Moes makes extensive use of the modern Utrecht Translation by professors H.Th. Obbink (OT, 1924) and A.M. Brouwer (NT, 1927). For the New Testament, she also looks at the German translation by the Pentecostal leader Jonathan Paul and at that of Ludwig Albrecht.[10] She often uses the new translation of the Dutch Bible Society (NBG), which produced the NewTestament translation in 1939 and the Old Testament in 1951. Her use of these modern Bible translations and her rejection of a mechanical inspiration certainly are progressive in the context of the Pentecostal Movement in those years. Although Moes uses many sources for her teaching and seeks to connect to a broader body, she does not just repeat traditional orthodoxies. Sometimes she makes choices that are beyond those accepted by the majority of Pentecostals. With her good command of German, she often uses German and Swiss Pentecostal sources, especially in the early years.

The Christian's Journey

Typically, Pentecostal believers tend to read the Bible in a subjective way. In particular, this reflects the viewpoint that God dealings with

---

[9] Among the authors that are consulted by Moes, a number are Dispensationalists, such as: A.C. Gaebelein, C.I. Scofield, H.C. Voorhoeve, J.N. Voorhoeve, and Johan de Heer. Besides them, Moes also consults F. Delitzsch, F. Bettex, H.Th. Obbink, O. Stockmayer, E. Modersohn, A.B. Simpson, and the Pentecostal teachers J. Paul, E. Edel, C. Price, G. Jeffreys, and Smith Wigglesworth. Not mentioned by her here, but also very influential in her life are: Andrew Murray, Charles H. Spurgeon, Hannah Whitall Smith (also known as Mrs. Pearsall Smith), Sadhu Sundar Singh, Barones M. von Brasch, and Donald Gee.

[10] Ludwig Albrecht, *Das Neue Testament* (Gotha: Evangelische Buchhandlung von Paul Ott), first appeared in 1920 and had many revised reprints. [J. Paul], *Das Neue Testament in der Sprache der Gegenwart* (Mülheim-Ruhr: Missions Gesellschaft), first appeared in 1914 and is also called the *Mülheimer Neue Testament*. Moes used the third strongly revised edition of 1924. As from 1929 regular references to this translation are made in *Gouden Schooven*. Moes also translated parts of this NT from German to Dutch for *Gouden Schooven*. Jonathan Paul directed a team of translators, but their names are not mentioned. It is assumed that Paul translated the larger part himself. The third edition contains more explanatory footnotes than the first editon and also has a concordance. Cf. Carl A. Simpson, *A Critical Evaluation of the Contribution of Jonathan Paul to the Development of the German Pentecostal Movement* (PhD Thesis, Glyndŵr University, Wrexham, 2011), pp. 267–75.

humanity in Scripture are directly applicable to the reader. In this way, they stand in a long line of Mystics, Pietists, Methodists, and the Holiness Movement. Following many from these traditions, Moes sees the journey of the Israelites out of Egypt to the Promised Land as an image of the Christian journey. First, they leave Egypt, which represents repentance. Then they crosse the Red Sea, which represents water baptism. At the same time, they come under the cloud of God's glory, the baptism with the Holy Spirit. Next, the journey leads through the wilderness of testing, where they eat the manna (God's Word) and drink the water (Holy Spirit) from the rock (Christ).[11]

According to Moes, we begin our Christian life with repentance, water baptism, and Spirit baptism. Then comes the temptation in the wilderness. Many Christians prefer to stay in the wilderness instead of entering Canaan, which is complete salvation or 'full deliverance' in Christ. The wilderness is a life of falling and rising, of doubt and sin, and of a carnal and miserable Christian life. To come from the wilderness to a life of victory, the believer must cross the Jordan river signifying spiritual death. The old selfish 'I' must die. Many Christians complain about their daily, recurrent sins but fail to take the step of laying down the old sinful nature. They continue to fight against the old Adamic nature without overcoming. They see Canaan from afar, but they do not enter because they have insufficient faith. 'You can be converted, born again, be baptized with water and Spirit, and yet be a wilderness-Christian.'[12] The remedy is to refrain from struggling in your own power in order to surrender the whole direction of your life to the Holy Spirit. Entering in Canaan means entering into the completed work on Calvary and then abiding in Him. Then, you say with Paul: 'I live, but no longer I, but Christ lives in me' (Gal. 2.20).

Moes divides the Christian journey into periods, which she also calls phases or even rungs on a spiritual ladder. Often there are four of these: Repentance, Rebirth, Baptism with the Holy Spirit, and Sanctification. Sometimes the first three are understood to constitute one phase. Another time, the number is extended with one or more of the following refinements: Water baptism, Filling, Sealing, Fruits, and Gifts. Under the heading of Salvation, the next section discusses conversion or repentance together with rebirth.

---

[11] M.A. Alt, *Bijbel-Studie voor zelf-onderricht* (Surabaya: Pinksterzending, [1951]), p. 38.

[12] Alt, *Bijbel-Studie*, p. 39.

Salvation

I serve a faithful Saviour, Who died at the cross for me.
Who paid for all my sins, bought me from Satan free.
He's from the grave arisen, and challenged death and shame
To clear the way before us, to heaven's lane.[13]

From Rom. 3.23–24, Moes quotes that no human being (Jew and Gentile) is righteous. All have sinned.[14] The gospel (the good news) is that we receive forgiveness of sins through the redemptive death of Jesus. The call is: repent and believe the gospel. It is the Holy Spirit that convinces of sin, but repentance demands human action. It is turning away from the sinful way of living and turning to God. It involves a sincere, deeply-felt confession of guilt and repentance. A sincere conversion always results in rebirth.[15]

Rebirth is an act of the Holy Spirit. It is not moral improvement of the old nature but an overall renewal.[16] The sinner is no more a sinner. The mind cannot comprehend this; it has to be experienced.[17] This rebirth brings joy because of the certainty of the experience: I am a child of God. The old has passed; the new has come (2 Cor. 5.17).[18] For Moes, a true child of God cannot be lost anymore. He can sin or wander, but even the lost sheep remains the sheep of the Good Shepherd.[19] At rebirth the believer receives the Holy Spirit. To describe this, she uses the terms 'indwelling' or 'sealing' but sometimes also 'baptism with the Holy Spirit'. According to her, the disciples in the upper room, waiting for the outpouring of the Holy Spirit, were converted but not yet born again. For them, the rebirth and the baptism of the Spirit occurred together. Yet, rebirth and Spirit baptism are not identical.

---

[13] 'Hij leeft', *Glorieklokken,* no. 140, Words M.A. Alt, source: A.H. Ackley. Known as 'He lives'.

[14] Alt, *Bijbel-Studie,* p. 481.

[15] M.A. Alt, 'Bekeert U!', *GS* 11.5 (March 1938), p. 20.

[16] M.A. Alt, *Het innerlijk licht* (Surabaya: Assemblies of God, [1949]), p. 37.

[17] Alt, *Bijbel-Studie,* p. 429.

[18] Alt, *Bijbel-Studie,* p. 462.

[19] M.A. Alt, 'Kan een kind Gods verloren gaan?', *GS* 11.20 (October 1938), pp. 16–17.

Water Baptism

Baptism is to be administered to adults, or older children, who know themselves to belong to Christ and are prepared to follow Him.[20]

With the Seventh-Day Baptists, Moes was baptized upon confession of faith and by immersion. She no longer regarded her infant baptism in the Reformed Church as a Biblical baptism. For her, baptism does not replace circumcision. The new dispensation has a spiritual circumcision, that of the heart, aimed at repentance and rebirth. Small children, who do not know the distinction between good and evil, cannot be lost although they are not born again. It is enough to dedicate them to God prayerfully in the assembly. When they reach the age of being able to distinguish between good and evil, and they repent, they can be baptized.[21] Water baptism is a funeral that follows the experience of having died with Christ (Rom. 6.3–11). First is death and afterwards the funeral; first is conversion and afterwards baptism.[22] The old life is buried, and the believer rises like a new human being. Water baptism and Spirit baptism belong together.

Among other things, Moes breaks from the PGNI in 1934 because of the new baptismal formula that comes from America. This practice stated that a baptism in the name of the Father, Son, and Holy Spirit is not valid unless it is followed by: 'In the name of the Lord Jesus Christ'.[23] Moes strongly rejects the practice that people who are already baptized upon confession of faith should be baptized again with the new formula. She finds the addition superfluous and the rebaptism a mistake. The use of 'baptism in the name of Jesus' in Acts is, to her, merely a shortened form of the Trinitarian

---

[20] M.A. Alt, 'De Waterdoop', *GS* 13.18 (September 1940), p. 7.

[21] M.A. Alt, 'De Waterdoop', *GS* 11.13 (July 1938), pp. 6–8; M.A. Alt, 'Nogmaals de Waterdoop', *GS* 11.17 (September 1938), pp. 19–21. Elsewhere Moes speaks of children from ten to twelve years. In 'De Waterdoop' she quotes Rev. Adema van Scheltema as supportive of water baptism upon confession and Luther as acknowledging that infant baptism could not be proven from Scripture. In 'Nogmaals de Waterdoop' Moes reacts to an article of Rev. K. about infant baptism in *De Zaaier,* periodical of the Gereformeerde Kerken in Dutch Indies, and she quotes from the baptismal formulary of the Gereformeerde Kerken.

[22] Alt, *Bijbel-Studie*, p. 224.

[23] Offiler taught that a water baptism without this formula was not acceptable to God. A church or assembly that rejects this will never be part of His Bride. W.H. Offiler, *God and His Bible* (Seattle: Bethel Temple, 1946), pp. 94, 97.

baptismal formula.[24] Because baptism symbolizes a funeral, Moes finds bending the body forward during the baptism rite or squatting in the water as inappropriate. You put a dead person backwards in the grave.[25] Performing the ritual of baptism itself is something she will always leave to the brothers.

Baptism with the Holy Spirit

Lord grant us Your victory,
Pentecostal power and glory,
Fill us with blessing,
With streams of forbearing.[26]

Moes defines the baptism with the Holy Spirit as follows: 'That Baptism is not rebirth, not sanctification, but that Baptism is a separate outpouring of divine power for service'.[27] The baptism of the Holy Spirit makes it possible to live as a Christian, gives strength to witness, and opens the way to the gifts of the Spirit. The born again need not pray to receive the Holy Spirit. They may pray for a deeper and further filling of the Holy Spirit, a Spirit baptism with gifts and powers.[28] The difference between receiving the Holy Spirit at rebirth (the indwelling or sealing) and the baptism with the Holy Spirit sometimes

---

[24] M.A. Alt, 'De bediening Heiligen Doop', *GS* 10.17 (September 1934), pp. 4–7. Cf. *Van hart tot hart Open brief aan de leden van alle Pinksterkringen in Ned.-Indië* (Surabaya, 1947), pp. 3–6, revised edition of the original from 1934.

[25] Alt, *Bijbel-Studie*, p. 225.

[26] 'Pinksterkracht en glorie', *Glorieklokken,* no. 398. Words M.A. Alt, source: *Victory Songs* no. 4.

[27] M.A. Alt, 'Het bewijs van den Geestesdoop', *GS* 11.8 (April 1938), p. 11.

[28] M.A. Alt, 'Moet de gelovige bidden om de Heilige Geest?', *GS* 19.7 (July 1950), pp. 3–4. Sometimes the terminology seems to shift. With approval, Moes quotes an article by Johan de Heer about Spirit baptism. The baptism that initiates believers into the Body of Christ (1 Cor. 12.13) is not water baptism, but Spirit baptism. An invisible body can only have invisible features. Spirit baptism is here 'only' the initiation into the Body of Christ. Next there is the filling of the Spirit that fills the individual believer with His Spirit to enable him to walk after His will. This way Spirit baptism seems identical to the rebirth, and the surplus is called the filling with the Holy Spirit. M.A. Alt, 'Eén doop', *GS* 10.5 (March 1934), pp. 12–13. Of the difference between the Spirit baptism and the Filling, she writes in 1947: 'The Baptism with the Holy Spirit is received only once as a sign of the indwelling of the Spirit in the heart, thus at conversion. The filling refers to an absolute holy and blameless life … In the life of those fully dedicated to Him, there are regular new anointings of God's Spirit.' M.A. Alt, 'Vragen-rubriek', *GS* 16.10 (October 1947), p. 9.

seems more gradual, than foundational in her writings. At the time of rebirth, we do not fully understand what we have received in the Holy Spirit. We possess the Holy Spirit, but He does not yet possess us completely.[29]

Spirit baptism should actually follow the rebirth immediately, as in the early church. Subsequently, she writes, Spirit baptism has fallen into the background. Because of lack of teaching or lack of faith, many born again Christians do not receive the experience even though it is ready for them. Moes calls this a 'gap in our spiritual education'. It is the purpose of the Pentecostal movement to return this lost truth to the church.[30] From her own life she gives the following example of this gap in education:

> Years ago, for instance, this writer came to repentance and rebirth, was baptized by immersion, and then was initiated by the Holy Spirit into the crucifixion of Christ (read carefully Romans 6) to learn to die to self and only after a long time was I to experience the Spirit baptism. The reason for this long waiting was, in fact that I had never heard of such a Baptism.[31]

Following the teaching of John Wesley, others such as Charles Finney, Dwight Moody, and Ruben Torrey have pleaded for a second experience of power from on high. The rise of the Pentecostal Movement at the beginning of the twentieth century is taken by Pentecostals as the fulfilment of this longing. It is the outbreak of the 'Latter Rain'. Throughout the world, the spiritual gifts emerge again, especially that of glossolalia. Moes finds little of this in the traditional churches, so she prays for a return to the experiences of apostolic times.[32]

Having received the Spirit's baptism, Moes understood physical reactions differently. In the past, she saw speaking in tongues as a result of suggestion and hysteria. In her search for the baptism with

[29] M.A. Alt, 'Kom Heilige Geest!', *GS* 16.3 (March 1947), pp. 1–3. Elsewhere Moes calls the sealing with the Holy Spirit at rebirth the first touch. The second touch is a new anointing. The first had been complete, but due to ignorance, lack of guidance, or unbelief, we did not fully understand what we had received in Christ. M.A. Alt, 'De eerste en de tweede zalving', *GS* 16.1 (January 1947), pp. 2–3.

[30] M.A. Alt, 'Vragenrubriek', *GS* 16.10 (October 1947), (October 1947), pp. 9–10; *GS* 16.12 (December 1947), p. 12. Alt, *Het innerlijk licht*, p. 31.

[31] Alt, 'Het bewijs van den Geestesdoop', p. 11.

[32] Alt, *Bijbel-Studie*, p. 474.

the Holy Spirit, she sometimes felt that as she prayed she was being lifted up from the earth. Her hands and body began to tremble.[33] She blamed herself for being nervous while praying. Later she understood that these vibrations of the body during prayer were a consequence of the workings of God's Spirit.

In accordance with the PGNI, Moes sees speaking in tongues as the scriptural sign of baptism with the Holy Spirit. Without that sign, Spirit baptism is incomplete.[34] However, she opposes the novel teaching in PGNI circles that speaking in tongues is a prerequisite for the rapture.[35] Moes is certain that all those reborn in Christ will be included in the rapture. Speaking in tongues may be the outward sign, but the inner sign is love.[36] She realizes that many Christians show the fruit of the Holy Spirit but do not speak in tongues. 'The Holy Spirit never works in a dogmatic way. Therefore, let us not condemn them.'[37] Avoiding an argumentative attitude, she writes, 'Is this not the actual baptism with the Holy Spirit: that we love God above all and bear each other's burdens?'[38]

She makes a distinction between the sign of tongues, which can be limited to a single occasion, and the gift of tongues that is lasting. These languages are understood by the angels around us (1 Cor. 13.1). Screaming and yelling in tongues, which apparently also occurred in her era, is not of the Spirit.[39] Against the assertion that speaking in tongues is harmful, she answers that she daily speaks in tongues without having suffered any damage. In the meetings usually incomprehensible sounds (glossolalia) are heard, but the miracle of known languages also occurs. Moes has once heard a little Javanese girl, from a mountain village, speaking in pure Dutch about the Second Coming after the girl's Spirit baptism.[40]

---

[33] M.A. Alt, 'Correspondentie', *Pinksterkracht* 4.1 (January 1928), pp. 8–9.

[34] M.A. Alt, 'Wat is het teeken van den Geestesdoop?', *GS* 11.24 (December 1935), pp. 14–16.

[35] Alt, *Van hart tot hart* (1947), p. 15.

[36] M.A. Alt, 'Hebt gij den Heiligen Geest ontvangen als gij geloofd hebt?', *GS* 13.9 (May 1940), pp. 4–5.

[37] M.A. Alt, 'De vervulling met den Heiligen Geest', *GS* 14.2 (January 1941, pp. 4–5.

[38] Alt, *In het volle licht: Dagboekje voor het huisgezin* (Manokwari: 3rd edn, 1960), Morning, 27 October.

[39] M.A. Alt, 'Vragen-rubriek', *GS* 16.10 (October 1947), p. 9.

[40] M.A. Alt, 'De lofzang des Geestes', *GS* 10.23 (December 1934), pp. 4–6.

In the functioning of the gifts of the Spirit, she sees a connection with our natural dispositions. In her diary, she writes that persons who are sensitive and poetic are more receptive to the gift of prophecy than cool and sober persons. The latter tend to receive the gifts of healing, discernment of spirits, and miracles.[41] In her diary, she repeatedly writes about not having received the gift of healing, even though she longs for it. The gift of prophecy, however, is clearly present in her. In an early article about spiritual gifts and our personality, she speaks in connection with prophecy and revelation of quiet, devoted persons who naturally tend to be mystical.[42]

The tendency to be mystical also has its pitfalls. Speaking of her experiences in Gambang Waluh, she writes that the Javanese people are mystically inclined and therefore receptive to superstition. When the Spirit baptism fell, she had a lot of trouble explaining that not every dream or revelation was from God.[43] Of the 'charism of ecstasy', she writes that Sadhu Sundar Singh had this gift to a great extent. She also names other great mystics with this charism, such as Bernard of Clairvaux, Catharine of Genoa, Teresa of Avila, and Francis of Assisi. The state of ecstasy is not understood by most Christians. It is not a hypnosis or trance. It's a conscious state, not a dream state. The believer is drawn to God.[44] Spirit baptism extends our spiritual awareness, but it does not change our character. Spirit-baptized believers can still be subject to gross errors of character. Therefore, the path of sanctification is necessary. Spirit baptism refers more to the gifts, while sanctification refers to the fruit, of the Holy Spirit.

Sanctification

For in me sounds and sours the human 'I,'
The longing for happiness and earthly pleasure!
But I know that only in doing Your will

---

[41] Alt, 'Dagboek 1945–1961', p. 13.

[42] M.A. Alt, 'Geestelijke gaven in verband met onze persoonlijkheid, *GS* 7.16 (August 1931), pp. 4–5. The article mentions three types. Moes found confirmation of this thought in a brochure by Jonathan Paul, *Die Göttlichen Gaben* (Mülheim: Emil Humburg, 1908).

[43] M.A. Alt, 'Bruiloft in de desa', *GS* 8.13 (July 1932), p. 15.

[44] M.A. Alt, 'Het charisma der extase', *GS* 9.24 (December 1936), pp. 11–13. Free translation after Friedrich Heller.

My soul finds rest and peace, oh my God!
You know the dark depths of my heart
The tears of despair cried in the night.
But when in obedience I broke my own will
The light of eternal bliss surrounded me![45]

Sanctification is a great theme in the works of Moes. 'A conversion not followed by sanctification is worthless.'[46] Sanctification in the Old Testament, she teaches, is being set apart for the service to God. In the NewTestament, sanctification means that Jesus has sanctified himself for us, that we may be sanctified in Him.[47] The Father sees us in Christ as sanctified (our position). Besides this positional sanctification, Moes also speaks of sanctification as an ongoing process, that is, the sanctification of our character:

> Again and again I discover sins and flaws in me that I did not see before. The more I strive for a holy, impeccable life, the deeper the Holy Spirit digs into my soul and reveals to me the caves and caverns of my dark self.[48]

Gradually, she has learned that you do not achieve victory over sins by fighting in your own power but by abiding in Christ. The 'in Christ' union seen in the letters of the apostle Paul, speaks of a hidden relationship with Him. It comes down to a daily encounter with Christ and being influenced by his love, holding fast to the faith that Jesus has redeemed you from the power of sin.[49] Our old human being is crucified with Christ and is therefore dead (Rom. 6.6). We are called to consider the old man dead; to let him hang on the cross by abiding in Christ. Unlike Jonathan Paul, she does not believe that the 'old man' is really dead: 'I feel all too well that he is still alive. The Bible, by the way, states that we are liberated from his *power* through Christ in us, but nowhere does it say that he is no longer active.'[50]

Moes discusses the inner struggle that Paul describes in Romans 7, which is about the believer who tries to keep the law of God. It is

---

[45] M.A. Alt, 'Overgave', *GS* 17.9 (September 1948), p. 2. In the original only the last line is in italics.

[46] M.A. Alt, 'Bekeert U!', *GS* 11.5 (March 1938), p. 21.

[47] Alt, *Bijbel-Studie*, p. 463.

[48] Alt, *Het innerlijk licht*, p. 41.

[49] Alt, *Het innerlijk licht*, p. 40.

[50] M.A. Alt in a typed, pasted-in sheet in *Das Neue Testament* (Mulheim, 1924).

the converted person who, through tears and prayer, wrestles against sin but does not notice that they are fighting in their own power.[51] They do not see that the Lord has not only forgiven their sins but also has delivered them from sins. Forgiveness and salvation are two different things. By being filled with the Holy Spirit, we are saved from our greatest enemy, the 'self'. At the time of rebirth the Holy Spirit has replaced the old, Adamic nature. We are delivered from the 'self' and we remain free from sin, as long as we continue to look to Jesus by faith. Romans 8 shows us the victorious life. Those who are in Christ Jesus walk after the Spirit.[52] In this connection, Moes speaks of a 'full deliverance' of mind, soul, and body. She believes that a full deliverance of sins is attainable. That is, we no longer *have to* sin, but it is not that we *can*not sin.[53] 'We are still living in an "enemy land" and are always exposed to temptations.'[54]

In 1937, she feels compelled to publish a series of brochures about sanctification, written by 'Fathers in Christ'. The first three volumes are by Jonathan Paul.[55] In the preface, Moes speaks of three stages in the life of faith: childhood in the Saviour, youth in Jesus, and fatherhood in Christ (after 1 Jn 2.12–14). From her diaries, it appears that in her own life she struggles against certain traits of character, especially irritability and temper. Her conscience is quickly stirred, which she takes as a warning. She sets the bar higher for herself than for others.[56]

Sanctification has consequences for how you relate to other people and to the 'world'. Although nothing is obligatory and everything is allowed, since the believer is not under law but under grace, yet there are rules to go by 'out of free will'. Everything that keeps the

51 Alt, *Bijbel-Studie*, p. 484.
52 Alt, *Bijbel-Studie*, p. 485.
53 M.A. Alt, 'Hebben wij de overwinning over de zonde?', *GS* 18.5 (May 1949), p. 10. Alt follows Hannah Whitall Smith, *The Christian's Secret* that repeatedly is referred to in *Gouden Schoven*.
54 M.A. Alt, *Raadgevingen en Persoonlijke ervaringen* published in *Herinneringen*, p. 111.
55 1. [J. Paul] *Geeft den Heiligen Geest plaats*. Lawang: Pinksterzending, [1937]; 2. [J. Paul], *Pinkstervuur*. Lawang: Pinksterzending, [1938]; 3. J. Paul, *Hoe kan ik heilig leven*. Lawang: Pinksterzending, [1939]; in a second series: 1. G. Steinberger, *Het geheim van overwinning over de zonde*. Surabaya: PZ/AG [1948].
56 Alt, *Het innerlijk licht*, p. 42. In her diary, Moes writes that she does not allow herself to read Christian novels, no matter how innocent. At the same time, the diary shows her struggle on this issue.

believer from God has an evil origin. This includes a lot of 'worldly entertainment':

> We Pentecostal people, meaning those who are truly converted, and all Christians, do not smoke and drink, do not visit the cinema or theatre – we do not use makeup and also do not, by preference, dine in the evening in restaurants with music – we do not wear showy clothes and do not display jewels and all of this, not from a legalistic point of view, but from our own free choice, because we intuitively feel that such things hinder our communion with God.[57]

The rejection of alcohol is based on texts from the OT (like Prov. 23.29–32). Moes believes the wine that Jesus made at the wedding in Cana did not contain alcohol, but was, in fact, grape juice.[58] Smoking does not occur in the Bible, but it hinders the devotion to God because it is addictive and unhealthy. Dancing cannot be accepted: 'No young man or young girl comes back spiritually unharmed from dancing or cinema'.[59] Moes also objects to religious films or enhancing biblical stories with dance. A simple hairstyle is difficult for the sisters of the assembly to maintain. In 1958, Moes writes with disapproval in her diary that everyone has their hair styled. 'The church seems like a hairdressing salon.'[60] By maintaining restrictive rules for clothing and entertainment, Moes seems to lose connection with a changing society. Moreover, these rules can also conceal and undermine what is really at stake. Such rules risk reducing sanctification to external behaviour, while neglecting the inner life.

Healing

Oh, call upon Him, your Saviour,
He makes you from fetters free.
Bring Him your burdens and worries,

---

[57] M.A. Alt, 'Hoe Jezus te volgen?', *GS* 19.8 (August 1950), pp. 22–23.

[58] M.A. Alt, 'Mogen christenen wijn drinken?', *GS* 25.6 (June 1956), pp. 13–14. 'New wine' according to Moes is the freshly pressed, unfermented must. The saying about not having new wine in old skins (Lk. 5.37) means the new wine would be fermented by the residue of the old wine and the old skin would burst.

[59] M.A. Alt, 'Muziek', *GS* 6.27 (October 1930), pp. 4–5.

[60] Alt, 'Dagboek 1945–1961', 18 August 1958.

Jesus is passing today.[61]

The full deliverance of mind, soul, and body includes healing. Moes wants to trust in God alone for her healing, without the use of medicine. She follows the teachings of Andrew Murray, *Jezus, de Geneesheer der kranken* (1884–also published as *Divine Healing*) and A.B. Simpson, *The Gospel of Healing* (1888).[62] Murray and Simpson explain that healing is included in the atonement (Isa. 53.4–5).[63] If we believe Jesus for the forgiveness of our sins, why don't we believe him for the healing of our bodies? In case of illness, the believer may pray in faith that God will heal (Jas 5.14–15). At the prayer of faith, healing is expected without medical aid. Healing is in the will of God, so there should be no reservation expressed in prayer, such as: 'If it is your will'. God works according to our faith. On the basis of God's word, the sick must assume that the prayer for healing has been heard and thank God for the healing, even if he does not feel it in his body yet. Medical help is not forbidden, but it is a sign of weak faith. Murray notes that, when using medical care, we are focused on our body, while the prayer of faith focuses us on sanctification and dedication to God. The doctrine of divine healing is closely linked to a sanctified life. Simpson sometimes expresses himself a bit more radically than Murray. We should not ask for healing but claim it (!); not wish for it but seize it. Faith must be turned into action by acting like someone who is already healed. Symptoms of illness must be ignored.

This view of Divine healing or prayer healing becomes commonplace in early Pentecostalism. In 1911, under Marie Jansz in Taju, Moes comes into contact with this teaching by reading Murray. Perhaps she had already internally accepted it, but it will take up to 1926 before she will apply it in her own life. For her it is a very weighty

---

[61] 'Jezus gaat heden voorbij', *Glorieklokken*, no. 24. Words M.A. Alt, source: *Greatest Hymns*.

[62] Regularly *Gouden Schoven* publishes articles of Andrew Murray and A.B. Simpson. In 1936 Simpson's book about healing is translated in a series of articles. In 1940 both books are available in Dutch and can be ordered through the periodical: Andrew Murray, *Jezus, De Geneesheer der Kranken* en A.B. Simpson, *Een blijde boodschap van Genezing*, n.p., nd. Simpson's translation is based on the new edition of 1915.

[63] Matthew 8.16–17 tells of Jesus delivering the oppressed and healing the sick, 'that it might be fulfilled which was spoken by Isaiah the prophet, saying, Himself took our infirmities and bare our sicknesses'. This use of the text from Isaiah by Matthew serves as a proof text for faith healing. Jesus at the cross bore not only our sins, but also our sicknesses.

subject. Since her arrival in the Dutch Indies in 1903, she has to battle against malaria. In 1951, she writes:

> This writer suffered chronic malaria-tertiana for many years. Nothing she tried could help her. Her blood was poisoned; her heart was weak due to the continuous use of quinine; her skin was yellow. Regularly, every other day, the fever returned and wore her out, so much so, that she became almost unfit for the Lord's service.
>
> Being at her wits' end, she decided to set aside all medications and to fix her hope only on the miraculous power of JESUS. She accepted in faith that, at the cross, He had not only borne her sins but also her sicknesses (Isa. 53.4–5; Ps. 103.3). As a result, she could be free from both indwelling sin and sickness.
>
> Simply, she began to thank the Lord for freedom from every satanic sickness. He had accomplished it for her on Calvary, and he had accomplished a full deliverance for all who believe in Him.
>
> The healing did not come immediately. But as her faith grew, she experienced new power coming upon her and strengthening her. At every attack of the disease, she praised the Lord, her Saviour. He completely rescued her from this aggressive illness and renewed her youth like an eagle, so that she can, now in her old age, do a great deal of work for her Master.[64]

At her baptism with the Holy Spirit in 1926, she stops taking medication. After twenty-three years of intensive use of medicines with little result and many damaging side effects, she comes to this decision when she is at her 'wits' end'. Because of her chronic condition the medicines only provide some relief during the attacks. However, Moes applies this practice to all forms of medical care. In 1940, when she suffers internal injuries as a result of a car accident, she does not want to consult a doctor. Likewise, when in the Japanese camp, Ambarawa 6, her thumb is dislocated while cutting vegetables. She only wants to receive healing from God and that is what happens.[65]

---

[64] Alt, *Bijbel-Studie*, p. 385.

[65] M.A. Alt, *Ons Kampleven* (Surabaya: Pinksterzending/Assemblies of God, [1948]), p. 21.

In *Gouden Schoven*, the message of divine healing, as taught by Murray and Simpson, gets a lot of attention. At a conference in 1928, Weenink van Loon says that in the New Testament healing does not come from medicine and doctors but only from the name of Jesus.[66] The strong emphasis on divine healing is reflected in testimonies from readers. Many testify of healing without medical help, sometimes after struggling to decide whether or not to seek medical assistance. Others bear witness to prayer in combination with medical care. Once, Moes cannot fail to point out a better way: 'We warmly rejoice in the healing of our young sister, and the answered prayers, but would not the Lord have been powerful enough to cure without hospital and medical help?'[67]

Yet, the strong emphasis on divine healing is occasionally downplayed. A series about 'Brother Frits' (1931) shows that there are also exceptions. Frits is severely disabled physically, but the Lord lets him know that His mercy is enough. In an afterword, Moes writes that in particular cases, like Frits, God is glorified in weakness, but it does not annul the doctrine of divine healing.[68] Sometimes God allows sickness to educate or discipline us. When we come to repentance, then healing usually occurs.[69] On the one hand, Moes wants to hold on to the principle that the prayer of faith will heal the sick, but on the other hand, she leaves room for the words of Job: 'The Lord has taken, the name of the Lord be praised'. Pentecostals are not 'prayer healers' or 'prayer mills' but only weak tools in the hand of a strong God. 'When it pleases God to use us to heal a sick person, that is His free grace – and if the healing does not occur, that too is God's business.'[70] With this Moes tries to find an answer to the fact that many do not get healed. She also warns against putting the blame on the sick person in the absence of a healing. Nevertheless, the message to trust God for healing, without any other means, remains dominant in all her years of ministry.

In 1952, she appears to adjust her position. In an article against legalistic Christianity, she is grateful for the many healings that come

[66] M.A. Alt, 'Onze Conferentie', *Pinksterkracht* 4.6 (June 1928), p. 6.

[67] M.A. Alt, 'Naschrift Redactie', *GS* 11.11 (June 1938), p. 10.

[68] M.A. Alt, 'Broeder Frits IV', *GS* 7.6 (March 1931), pp. 10–12. Biography of Frits Oetsbach (1850–1909), after H. von Redern, *Ein Lebensbild*.

[69] M.A. Alt, 'Genezing door het geloof', *GS* 10.0 (May 1937), pp. 5–7; 'Vragen-Rubriek', *GS* 11.11 (June 1938), pp. 13–14.

[70] M.A. Alt, 'Gedachten over gebedsgenezing', *GS* 10.2 (January 1937), p. 5.

by prayer. But, at the same time, she observes that many believers are healed by the use of medicinal herbs, 'which the Lord has allowed to grow for our healing'. She continues that we do not have the right to condemn other believers, 'because they do not receive Spirit baptism according to *our* teaching or method, or who accept medication as a means of healing from God's hand'.[71] A testimony of healing through an operation accompanied by prayer is now given a sympathetic response. Moes sees it as an example that the Lord does not heal along legalistic paths. 'In heaven, our Lord will truly not ask: "Have you used medicine or not?" But: "Did you truly love God and your neighbour?"'[72] One month later, she writes that tens of thousands of praying people were rescued from death by surgical intervention or other medical aid. Abstaining from medication is now the exception: 'In certain cases, God can tell us (usually in the case of incurable diseases): "Get up, renounce all medicine go – Jesus Christ will heal you", but usually we see that He accomplishes healing through natural means'.[73] Healing is still understood as included in the atonement, but the overall deliverance of our body will only take place at the rapture. Her diary shows that she modifies her position, after much struggle, during a period where she again uses medicines against malaria. Later, she sees this temporary use of medicine as a relapse and returns to the old position of healing by faith without other means. Use of medicine is not a sin, but it does show a lack of confidence.[74] It is a pity that she does not elaborate on the previously expressed thought that full deliverance is in the future. This topic will return in the last chapter in references to her diary.

[71] M.A. Alt, 'Wettisch Christendom', *GS* 21.4 (April 1952), p. 13.
[72] M.A. Alt, 'Noot van de redactie', *GS* 21.11 (November 1952), pp. 20–21.
[73] M.A. Alt, 'De zalving met olie volgens Jakobus', *GS* 21.12 (December 1952), pp. 17–18.
[74] M.A. Alt, 'Hoe kan ik gezond worden?', *GS* 33.1 (January 1962), pp. 7–8.

17

THE LATTER RAIN

And it shall come to pass in the last days, says God, I will pour out my Spirit upon all flesh: and your sons and daughters shall prophesy, and your young men shall see visions, and your old men shall dream dreams. And on my servants and on my handmaidens I will pour out in those days of my Spirit; and they shall prophesy Acts 2.17–18 (KJV).

When the Holy Spirit is poured out on the day of Pentecost, the bystanders ask the meaning of what is going on. Peter explains: 'This is what has been spoken by the prophet Joel', and he then quotes Joel 2.28–32. In the last days, God's Spirit will fall on all people: young and old, men and women. Pentecostal believers saw the outpouring of the Spirit at the beginning of the twentieth century as a repetition of Pentecost. Soon they associated this with the early and latter rains of Joel 2.23. It is an image borrowed from the agricultural setting of ancient Israel. The early rain is required for sowing and the latter rain shortly before harvest. James 5.7 connects the latter rain with the second coming of Jesus. Pentecostals interpret the outpouring on Pentecost as the early rain and the outpouring of the Spirit in their own days as the latter rain.[1] This means that the time is short: the Lord is coming soon. But it also implies that the fields are white and ready to harvest. This explains the strong missionary urge that characterizes the movement. Holy Spirit baptism with the gifts of the

---

[1] Cornelis van der Laan, *Sectarian Against His Will:Gerrit Roelof Polman and the Birth of Pentecostalism in the Netherlands* (Studies in Evangelicalism 11; Metuchen, NJ: Scarecrow Press, 1991), p. 93.

Spirit form the necessary equipment for harvesting. We can see it reflected in the names of the Pentecostal periodicals. Polman calls his paper, *Spade Regen* (*Latter Rain*) and Thiessen calls his, *Dit is Het* (*This is That*). Moes uses *Gouden Schoven* (*Golden Sheaves*) to emphasize the harvest.

Initially, Polman identifies the Pentecostal movement with the 'Latter Rain'. Later he modifies this high expectation to the 'drops prior to the Latter Rain'. Moes follows him: 'The first, the early rain, was poured out on the day of Pentecost – of the last, the Latter Rain, we see the first drops falling. God has promised us greater things.'[2] And five years later: 'A fresh wind is beginning to blow in the church of God, and our ear already hears the noise of the Latter Rain, which will soon overflow the world. We are now living in the last days preceding the Lord's return.'[3] This chapter looks at the consequences of the Latter Rain framework for the understanding of the church, for the expectation of the future, and for the role of women in ministry.

Church

> There is only one Church or Assembly – consisting of all true born-again children of God, which is the Church of Jesus Christ. This is formed of all churches, circles, Christian fellowships and associations – including Protestants, Reformed, Adventists, Pentecostals, etc.[4]

To Moes, the one, holy, catholic, Christian Church is an organic unity: the mystical Body of Christ. She sees existing churches, circles and sects of all sorts and colours as visible expressions of this mystical body. In her view these differences in expresson are because our mind, education, and personality all play a part when we read the Scriptures.[5] If we have received blessing and salvation in a particular church, then we should stay there. It is our task to build up and strengthen that church. Moes also sees a mission for the Pentecostal church towards the larger body:

---

[2] M.A. Alt, 'En zij werden allen vervuld met de Heilige Geest," *GS* 23.6 (June 1954), pp. 3–4.

[3] M.A. Alt, 'Jaarwisseling', *GS* 28.1 (January 1959), pp. 3–4.

[4] M.A. Alt, 'Ik geloof in één heilige algemeene kerk', *GS* 10.23 (December 1934), pp. 7-8 (7).

[5] Alt, 'Ik geloof in één heilige algemeene kerk', p. 8.

As far as I am concerned, I stand above every kind of religious form, sectarian spirit, or commandment of men, but in my heart I feel one with every child of God, from whatever background he or she may be. That is the true church, that is the church of the first-born, that is the Bride of Jesus Christ, this great multitude of all nations and ... churches, that make up the body of Christ ... *To build up this Church and to bring it to the ancient apostolic maturity is the purpose of the Pentecostal church* – not to establish their own church or sect.[6]

Gerrit Polman, the Pentecostal Pioneer in the Netherlands, saw the same goal: 'To further the unity among the different denominations, and to lose ourselves as the Pentecostal movement into the larger body of Christianity'.[7] Restoring the Church to the ancient apostolic maturity, signifies a restoration of the gifts and powers of apostolic times. As soon as the churches return to the ancient apostolic teaching (baptism upon confession, recognition of the gifts, and separation from the world), the Pinksterzending is ready to join them. 'May God grant that before the inauguration of the Millennium it may become: one flock and one Shepherd.'[8] At the same time, Moes warns against liberal theology: 'Never visit a church denying Christ's deity, or where the redeeming Blood of the cross is denied its honour. *There is no other way by which one may be saved.*'[9]

Moes is happy to notice the increasing interest in Pentecostalism among churches during the 1950s and 1960s. She supports David du Plessis, who wants to build a bridge to the historic churches. Du Plessis refers to the open attitude towards Pentecostalism of Henry Pitney van Dusen and Lesslie Newbigin. This brings Moes to express her hope for the fulfilment of her long-cherished expectation, the realization of one flock under one Shepherd, the bridal Church made up all churches and sects.[10] A lecture from Feitse Boerwinkel about the appeal of the Pentecostal groups to the churches fills her with

---

[6] M.A. Alt, 'Groote overgang', *GS* 6.19 (June 1930), p. 4.

[7] G.R. Polman, 'Uit den Arbeid', *Spade Regen* 18.1 (April 1925), p. 14.

[8] M.A. Alt, 'In welk opzicht verschilt de Pinksterzending van de Protestantsche Kerk?', *GS* 14.3 (February 1941), p. 13. Alt writes this in the question and answer column.

[9] M.A. Alt, *Bijbel-Studie voor zelf-onderricht* (Surabaya: Pinksterzending, [1951]), p. 480.

[10] M.A. Alt, 'Pinksterzegen als in de dagen der Apostelen', *GS* 25.5 (May 1956), pp. 3–4.

gratitude: 'After all the opposition, contempt, criticism, and mockery, we see how our Lord, who loves us, is beginning to steer things in a new direction'.[11]

The church is the God-appointed educational institute for believers.[12] She teaches the congregation to look after the orphans and the poor and not to make distinctions between persons. Continuously, she emphasizes the primacy of love. At the time of the rupture in 1934, her great complaint was that knowledge had replaced love.[13] Moes writes, 'Is this not the actual baptism with the Holy Spirit that we love God above all and bear each other's burdens?'[14]

Restoration of the apostolic church also includes the ministry offices. These include not only those of shepherd, teacher, and evangelist but also the apostle and prophet. Nevertheless, in the Pinksterzending nobody will assume the title of apostle or prophet because of the danger of pride. In an article about the office of apostle in *Gouden Schoven*, Donald Gee defends the teaching that there may also be contemporary apostles, but it is better not to use the title. 'The true apostle does not care about names and titles ... He avoids whatever smells of flattery and human worship.'[15]

Second Coming

> *He comes, yes He comes, – In majesty and power.*
> *No worries and sadness will be there – gone is the gloomy night.*
> *He comes, yes He comes – put on the bridal gown.*
> *Awake, oh soul as Jesus comes – oh, have your lamp prepared.*[16]

Latter Rain is the specific, pentecostal component in an end-time teaching, which otherwise closely corresponds to that of Dispensationalism, developed in the nineteenth century by J.N. Darby.

---

[11] M.A. Alt, 'Predikantenvergadering Nederlands Hervormde Kerk', *GS* 28.6 (June 1959), pp. 22–23.

[12] Alt, *In het volle licht*, p. 264.

[13] M.A. Alt, 'Wat de Pinkstergemeente (over de geheele wereld) gelooft en leert', *GS* 10.15 (August 1934), p. 4.

[14] M.A. Alt, *In het volle licht*, p. 315.

[15] Donald Gee, 'Het Apostel-ambt: Heeft het opgehouden te bestaan?', translation M.A. Alt, *GS* 13.11 (June 1940), p. 16, Cf. M.A. Alt, 'Worden in de Pinksterzending ook de ambten gehandhaafd?', *GS* 11.19 (October 1938), p. 10.

[16] 'O, morgen van eeuwige glorie', *Glorieklokken*, no. 252. Words M.A. Alt, source: *Glad Gospel Songs*.

Internationally, it is disseminated by C.I. Scofield and in the Netherlands by Johan de Heer. Moes writes that she first received light on
the Second Coming from Johan de Heer's periodical, *Het Zoeklicht*.[17]
In particular, she refers to the Second Coming in two stages. In outline form, the end time teaching is as follows.

The first stage of the return of Christ is just for believers. This is
the Rapture of the believers which introduces a period of Great Tribulation on earth. The state of Israel gets a king who is worshiped as
Messiah, and the temple is rebuilt. A united Europe works together
with a false religious power. There is war and violence everywhere.
The beast or the Antichrist emerges. As emperor of the restored Roman Empire, he signs a covenant with the king of Israel. Many from
Israel and other nations will repent and die as martyrs. At the height
of the tribulation, the second stage of the return of Christ brings
relief. Jesus now comes as king with his saints. The Millennium,
which is a thousand year reign of peace, begins. At the end of that
time, a last uprising takes place. The devil is finally thrown into the
lake of fire. The final judgment occurs. A new heaven and a new
earth are established.[18]

Whereas Johan de Heer places a global revival in the millennial
empire, Moes expects it as the Latter Rain before the first stage of
Christ's return.[19] They also differ in their thinking about who is included in this revival. De Heer includes all those who belong to
Christ. Moes speaks only of a small flock, those who walk the narrow
path of sanctification.[20] They are the true born-again believers who
come from all churches. Worldly, carnal Christians go through the
Great Tribulation. The letters to the seven churches in Asia Minor in
Revelation 2–3 are read as a prophetic picture of church history in
its entirety. We are currently living in the era of the churches of Philadelphia and Laodicea. Philadelphia stands for the true believers

---

[17] M.A. Alt, 'Wat verwacht de Gemeente Gemeente Gods voor 1960?', *GS* 30.1
(January 1960), p. 4.

[18] Alt, *Bijbel-Studie*, pp. 543–44.

[19] M.A. Alt, 'Verwachten wij de groote opwekking of eerst het Duizendjarig
Rijk?', *GS* 7.16 (August 1931), pp. 11–12. Other writers to whom she refers in
connection with the end times are: Otto Stockmayer, Cyrus Scofield, and Arno
Gaebelein; and from the Pentecostal side: Eugen Edel, Jonathan Paul, and Charles
Price.

[20] M.A. Alt, 'Worden alle geloovigen opgenomen?', *GS* 10.22 (November 1937),
pp. 12–13.

from various churches who are being raptured. They are the wise virgins from Matthew 25. Laodicea stands for the half-converted or 'half' Christians who are left behind at the rapture. They are the foolish virgins from Matthew 25. However, Jesus continues to knock at their door so that, even in the days of the Great Tribulation, people will come to repentance, including 144,000 from the Jewish people.[21]

There is a lot of attention in *Gouden Schoven* given to the Second Coming of Jesus. During the period of the rupture, it serves to distinguish it from other views that emerged in the PGNI. In the run-up to World War II, all kinds of political and social developments are interpreted as 'signs of the times'. There is an intensification of the expectation of the Second Coming. Visions and prophecies emphasize the urgency. The rise of Benito Mussolini is soon seen as the restoration of the Roman Empire. When he appears to be superseded by Hitler, Moes acknowledges: 'Perhaps we had our eyes too much on Mussolini'.[22] In January 1941, she writes that the end of this dispensation approaches rapidly: 'Only the ten toes (the 10 kings who will rule with the beast) are still lacking'.[23] At the same time, she realizes her knowledge is limited: 'On the subject of interpreting Biblical prophecies, everyone can err in part. After all, we are human.'[24]

After the war, the Second Coming remains a strong theme. However, there is greater reticence in terms of interpreting political events, except in the case of Israel. There is also more space given to signaling positive developments in society and the church. This is also evident in the name change of the section called 'Signs of Time' in 1948 to 'From here and there' and, in 1950, to 'The world of today'. The establishment of the state of Israel in 1948 is seen as fulfilling Biblical prophecies. Later developments are also closely monitored. Moes has contacts with Messianic Jews, such as Daniel Gutter, whom she knows from Malang. Gutter publishes the periodical, *De Joodse Hope*, the Dutch edition of *The Jewish Hope* by Arthur Michelson. Michelson has established a Hebrew-Christian synagogue in Los Angeles and carries out missionary work among the Jews.[25]

---

[21] Alt, *Bijbel-Studie*, pp. 510–11, 517. Moes sees the 144,000 not as a concrete number but symbolic of a great part of the Jewish people from the twelve tribes.

[22] M.A. Alt, 'De Wederkomst van Christus', *GS* 13.15 (August 1940), p. 5.

[23] M.A. Alt, 'Teekenen der Tijden', *GS* 14.2 (January 1941), p. 11.

[24] M.A. Alt, 'De Openbaring van Johannes XIV', *GS* 14.15 (August 1941), p. 16.

[25] M.A. Alt, ''Israël het Wondervolk', *GS* 26.4 (April 1957), pp. 12–13.

Role of women

There are many examples of the fact that God also uses women as preachers of truth. We do not believe that the pulpit ministry is the personal privilege of the man, yet a truly spiritually minded female messenger of the Gospel will surely remain modestly in the background if the occasion requires it and give the brothers priority as far as possible, without neglecting her assigned duty. [26]

Gouden Schoven gives ample space to women. Many of the letters to the editor are from women, but also a remarkably high number of articles are written by women. Along with the large contribution of Moes as editor, most of the text of each issue is often written by a woman. Until the war, the pictures on the cover of the magazine more often show women than men bringing in the harvest. These pictures also include children who are harvesting. Over the years, it appears that Moes develops her position on the role of women and what was formerly a cautious position becomes a bold one.

Already as a child, Moes is impressed by the preaching of women in the Salvation Army. On the missionary field, Marie Jansz, who preaches and ministers the sacraments, serves as her first example. Jansz thus violates the rules within the SDB, which do not allow women to lead in the assemblies.[27] In March 1920, Moes as a member of the SDB congregation, writes a letter to her pastor, Velthuijsen, about the place of the woman. Very carefully, she defends the position that Paul's counsel about the silence of women cannot apply to the mission field where there is a lack of men.[28]

She reads books and articles by Catherine Booth, Hannah Whitall Smith, La Maréchale, Maria Woodworth-Etter, Carrie Judd Montgomery, and Aimee Semple McPherson, among others. All are strong women who are also leaders. In *Gouden Schoven*, Moes responds to a question from a reader in 1930, confirming that a woman is allowed to preach in the congregation, but she sees this as an exception.[29] In 1931, she writes: 'The woman is not *lower* than the man, but she is

---

[26] M.A. Alt, *Mag de vrouw spreken in de Gemeente?* (Manokwari, 1956), p. 11.

[27] G. Velthuijsen Jr., 'Vragenbus: Mogen vrouwen in de gemeente voorgaan?', *De Boodschapper* (February 1916), pp. 62–63.

[28] M.A. Alt, 'Een brief van Zuster Alt over de plaats der vrouw in de gemeente', *De Boodschapper* (June 1920), pp. 156–57.

[29] M.A. Alt, 'Voor nadenkende geloovigen', *GS* 6.18 (June 1930), pp. 12–13.

different.[30] In an article about how God uses women for His service (1932), she writes that the Salvation Army understood this well and that the Pentecostal Church takes the same broad position.[31] That broad position is, however, being challenged around this time.

In March 1933, it is even 'a burning issue', and Moes comes with an extensive defense. Opposition comes from those who use the well-known 'silence texts' (1 Cor. 14.34 and 1 Tim. 2.12). According to Moes, these texts are about married women, but even then, there are exceptions to the rule, like Mrs. Booth. She assumes that female co-workers, such as Phoebe (Rom. 16.1), were unmarried. Then she gives her own testimony, that after her conversion she made a covenant with the Lord to break all natural ties, referring to her engagement. The unmarried state exacts a high price but provides opportunity for ministry:

> In every healthy young woman or man lives the urge to create. The young girl dreams of the man whom she will love and of a happy motherhood. However, those who, according to God's order, must remain unmarried, can sublimate their creative desire by performing labour in the service of the Lord or in the life of society.[32]

Due to circumstances beyond her control, she writes, she was left alone at the head of a church. She feels that God Himself had entrusted her with leadership and believes that the Lord gives the same gifts to men and women. Are not the twenty-four elders in Revelation the representation of the whole raptured church (men and women)? Will they not both be kings and priests?[33]

Several times, Moes has to address the issue. It is very painful, because her person and her ministry are at stake: 'This question always comes back and affects our freedom in the Holy Spirit. When women get discouraged and lay down their duties, Satan has achieved his purpose.'[34] The following objections are raised: (1) women must

---

[30] M.A. Alt, 'De ontplooiing vrouwelijk kunnen', *GS* 7.13 (July 1931), p. 20.

[31] M.A. Alt, 'Hoe God de vrouwen gebruikt voor Zijn dienst', *GS* 8.9 (May 1932), p. 16.

[32] Alt, *Het innerlijk licht*, p. 19.

[33] M.A. Alt, 'Mag de vrouw spreken in de gemeente?', *GS* 9.6 (March 1933), pp. 4–7.

[34] M.A. Alt, 'Het spreken van de vrouw in de gemeente', *GS* 11.5, (March 1935), pp. 4–6.

be silent in the congregation, (2) women may not lay hands upon believers, (3) women may not administer the Lord's Supper, and (4) women may not have a leading position in the assembly. Moes deals with points 1 and 4 since the other objections are not based on the Scriptures. In her reply, she quotes an article by W.F.P. Burton. The one 'silence-text' (1 Tim. 2.11–12) concerns the situation at home and does not refer to the church gathering , while the other (1 Cor. 14.34) concerns the making of disruptive comments and not preaching. In addition, she refers to her own struggle: on the one hand being called for this task and on the other hand finding the brothers against you. She will always give priority to the older brothers and evangelists, 'but silence in the congregation, where God has called her to speak, no man may claim of her'.[35] In the following years, she feels little need to defend herself and confines herself to repeating the previous article. For the brothers, she still has this reminder: 'Do not you know that God has chosen the weak and that which is nothing?'[36]

After consulting other, foreign, translations, she concludes that the 'messengers who bring good tidings' in Ps. 68.12 refer to women and not to men, contrary to the Dutch *Statenvertaling* (Authorized Version).[37] The later translation (1951) by the Dutch Bible Society will prove her right. In 1941, she refers to her brochure, *Mag de vrouw spreken in de Gemeente? (May a Woman Speak in the Assembly?)*. She challenges women to do spiritual work: 'Instead of wasting her time on tea-parties or shopping and instead of spending hours in polishing furniture, to which her heart clings like idols, it would certainly be better to do something for Jesus'.[38]

A final edition of *Mag de vrouw spreken in de Gemeente?* appears in 1956. It is a repetition of the above-mentioned arguments. Phoebe is

---

[35] Alt, 'Het spreken van de vrouw in de gemeente', p. 6.

[36] M.A. Alt, 'Vragen-Beantwoording', *GS* 9.9 (May 1936), p. 13.

[37] M.A. Alt, 'Naschrift van de Redactie G.S.', *GS* 11.23 (December 1938), p. 10. Moes refers to German Bible translations (The Elberfelder and H. Menge), French (Louis Segond), and to English (Oxford – it is not clear which translation is meant here).

[38] M.A. Alt, 'Vragenrubriek: Mag de vrouw spreken in de Gemeente?', *GS* 15.22 (November 1941), p. 17. No copy of the brochure from 1941 has been found, it is only referenced in the article itself and not in the list of publcations that can be ordered. This may suggest that is was not in a printed format but a stencil, possibly the same as the stencil from 1948: Alt, *Mag de vrouw spreken in de Gemeente?*, with a text of W.F.P. Burton and a afterword of Moes. At the same time, another stencil appeared: M.A. Alt, *Wat gebeurt er met ongeboren kinderen?* (1948) against abortion.

now called an itinerating evangelist who would certainly not have been silent during her visit to the church. Humiliation came upon the woman as a result of the fall, but the redemptive work of Christ also includes her elevation.[39] In Christ, men and women are equal (Gal. 3.28). The criterion for ministry is the calling of God. The woman called for this task also receives the necessary gifts. The harvest is great, therefore all workers, both men and women, are needed.

The resistance to women preachers which Moes faced is exemplary of the ambivalent attitude on the subject in the broad, Pentecostal movement. What legitimizes a person to preach and administer the sacraments? Where the legitimacy depends on the gift of the Holy Spirit, there is plenty of room for women in the ministry. In the Scripture our attention goes to the passages where God's Spirit falls on both man and woman (Acts 2.17 and Gal. 3.28). If legitimacy is seen as a matter of order, tradition, or an 'office,' then the position of women is compromised. In the Scripture, the more limiting passages are emphasized. The influential *Scofield Reference Bible*, a Bible with explanatory comments from a dispensational point of view, is hostile to the leadership of women.[40] In Pentecostalism, the first approach usually has the upper hand in the initial phase, but as the movement becomes more established, the second approach receives more support. Following the sociologist, Max Weber, some speak of a prophetic phase (based on calling or gifts) versus a priestly phase (based on appointment or origin).[41] This shift is apparent within the PGNI around 1930, which resulted in limiting the possibility of leadership for women within the church.

Examples of women in leadership in early Pentecostalism include Marie Woodworth-Etter, Florence Crawford, Aimee Semple McPherson, Cary Judd Montgomery, and Wilhelmine Polman. Both Crawford and McPherson founded their own denomination. In the United States, half of the itinerating evangelists and two-thirds of

---

[39] M.A. Alt, *Mag de vrouw spreken in de Gemeente?* (Manokwari: Pinksterzending, 1956), p. 12.

[40] Letha Dawson Scanzoni and Susan Setta, 'Women in Evangelical, Holiness and Pentecostal Traditions', in Rosemary Radford Ruether and Rosemary Skinner Keller (eds.), *Women & Religion in America 3 1900–1968* (San Francisco: Harper & Row, 1986), pp. 223–65 (233).

[41] Cf. Charles H. Barfoot and Gerald T. Sheppard, 'Prophetic vs. Priestly Religion: The Changing Role of Women Clergy in Classical Pentecostal Churches', *Review of Religious Research* 22 (1980), pp. 2–17.

the missionaries in that first period of Pentecostalism are women.[42] The growing resistance to women who are permitted to preach and administer the sacraments is especially strong in their own country. For women on the mission field, these restrictions are usually not put in place. To an increasing degree, single women with a call to preach are drawn to the mission field.

---

[42] Grant Wacker, *Heaven Below: Early Pentecostals and American Culture* (Cambridge: Harvard University Press, 2001), p. 160. Cf. Allan Anderson, *Spreading Fires: The Missionary Nature of Early Pentecostalism* (London: SCM, 2007), pp. 271–76.

18

LOVE KNOWS NO SACRIFICE

God is my Witness, how the inner urge for service consumes me like a candle is consumed by the flame. My whole life is devoted to Him, and His service is precious to me. Voluntarily, I gave up all youthful dreams: marriage, having children of my own, in order to follow Jesus. In that there is no merit – oh no, I was very pleased to do it because the Holy Spirit urged me. There is no question of a sacrifice. Someone who loves does not think of sacrifice.[1]

This last chapter considers some recurring features in the life of Moesje Alt and attempts to describe the meaning of her life. Having studied her life and thought, it is appropiate to draw even closer to her as a person. This is made possible by the insights she allows us in her diaries and her handwritten autobiography written in 1943. There is no other leader in the Dutch Pentecostal movement from whom we have so many personal writings. During her lifetime, she gave permission to her direct co-workers to read her diaries after her death. Moes did not foresee this biography, but in consultation with a close co-worker (now deceased) and with children of other co-workers, this author feels at liberty to use these personal writings for this book.

Two Angels of Satan

Shortage of money and sickness were the two angels of Satan who without interruption assaulted me during my stay at Gambang Waluh. The malaria tertiana undermined my body. The

---

[1] Alt, *Het innerlijk licht*, p. 13.

climate at Gambang Waluh is humid and unhealthy. The land is located at the Oengaran runners at 2500 feet and is surrounded by a dense fog in the evening. The house in which I lived later had bamboo walls so that the moisture came through and the wind blew. I was almost always sick and could tolerate little more than mashed potatoes and liquid foods. Changing the climate would have done me good, but I dared not leave the place where God had sent me. Due to the constant use of quinine, my heart weakened so that the distant trips I took to the villages around me greatly weakened me. Often I got home soaking wet from the rain, and soon I was in bed shivering from fever.[2]

Emulating George Müller, founder of orphanages in England, Moes wants to trust only God for her finances. In *Herinneringen*, she gives examples of how the Lord specially provided money or food. In her unpublished writings, she is more open to the other side, namely that of shortages. From her observation that money shortage and illness constantly followed her at Gambang Waluh, it is obvious that this must have been very difficult. In the first period, there is some support from the SDB assembly, but when this falls away, she is entirely on her own. Her lifestyle is very simple. In 1957, the old Joenoes tells Stefanus:

> of the difficulties that ndoro had during her stay in their midst. She took care of dozens of orphans and poor and sometimes went to Temanggung, where the friends once gave her sixty guilders as a contribution to the work. Coming home she had a lot of djagung bought for the sick and for the children, but she herself ate ketela because she said, 'First the children, they must have good nutrition, and then myself' ... Christianity has come here because our ndoro has brought the Gospel to the poor, especially to the poor.[3]

Not a single day of good health

After 1926 Moes no longer uses medicine. In the diary she keeps from 1945 to 1961, she describes extensively her fight against

---

[2] M.A. Alt, 'Autobiografie 1943', pp. 43–44.
[3] S. Stefanus, 'Bezoek aan Gambang Waloeh', *GS* 26.11 (November 1957), p. 20.

sickness. It's a touching account. Her nervous system has suffered greatly during the camp years. She is in a constant state of anxiety and is suffering from depression. On 2 November 1946, she writes that since 1910 she has not had a single day of good health, a statement she will repeat several times. Nobody around her knows this. In January 1947, she is so desperate that she takes pills against malaria for the first time in twenty years, but it does not help. Then she again trusts in God for full deliverance, and 'immediately healing occurred' (7 January 1947).[4] In the months and first years afterwards, she relives the pangs of death from the Japanese prison.[5] She suffers from palpitations, anxiety, confusion, depressing thoughts, and a tendency to fainting. In March 1949, she has two teeth extracted. Due to a complication, she gets a jaw inflammation, but she refuses further treatment. During a sermon, she must hold onto the pulpit to avoid falling. Slowly, the inflammation heals. Other symptoms of disease remain. She is afraid of getting a stroke, like her father and brother because to her it would be terrible to become a burden to others (13 August 1949).

Shortly after arriving in Manokwari (April 1951), Moes and her co-workers suffer from heavy attacks of malaria. After months of struggle, with death at her heels, she desperately begs the Lord for help. By faith, she turns to a page in her Bible at random and reads: 'You shall not tempt the Lord your God' (Mt. 4.6–7). She takes this to mean that she may use herbs like quinine (18 February 1952). Almost a year later, she writes that the Lord blesses the paludrine so that she can stay on her feet and not be a burden to others (11 January 1953). From January 1954, she is again standing on healing by faith without means, 'because paludrine is no longer benefiting me' (30 January 1954). Despite the illness, she continues to fulfill her ministry in the congregation. In June, the pain is unbearable, and for several weeks, on and off, she takes medications prescribed by a doctor. It's a big disappointment for her. She wonders, 'Is the teaching of healing by faith *without medicine*, then a deception? And have I erred for forty years and taught the same to others? It would be terrible' (23 June

---

[4] Dates between brackets refer to M.A. Alt, 'Dagboek 1945–1961'.
[5] In the diary 1945–1961, Moes describes the symptoms of her illness in detail. Upon the request of the author, a tropical physician analysed the written symptoms. According to him, Moes suffered from chronic malaria, and in the years after the war, she seems to have suffered from a post-traumatic stress disorder (PTSD).

1954). The same day she reads in the Bible that all things that God has created are good and can be accepted in thanksgiving (1 Tim. 4.4). So the medicinal herbs that God has made to grow can be used with thanksgiving. The sickness still does not disappear, and she consults a doctor who prescribes a cure. An inner voice says: 'If I have received the healing, according to God's Word, why am I still taking pills? After all, I'm healed?' (9 July 1954). Thus she is tossed back and forth between her preference for healing by faith, her doubts about this, and the ongoing illness. From 1951 to 1955, this fight goes back and forth, and she sometimes uses medication. As of September 1955, she succeeds in abstaining from medication permanently.

Referring back to this period in *Herinneringen* (p. 81), it seems to describe a single relapse, but the diary shows that it has been a long battle. In her diary, she is very open about the difficulties she is experiencing. She reflects on her own actions and thoughts and dares to question whether or not she may have been wrong all those years. A few times she tends to adjust her insights, but then she returns to her previous position. Reports of mass healings in the campaigns of faith-healers in those years, as well as books by T.L. Osborn and, later, E.W. Kenyon, confirm her in that direction. She is determined to continue to believe for healing, but the illness does not leave. Regularly, she believes she has won the victory over the 'malaria devil', but a few days later the battle starts all over again. The Lord makes it clear to her that He wants to demonstrate His strength in her weakness (30 October 1955). Despite severe headaches, insomnia, and now also rheumatism, she continues with her home visits, sermons, and Bible studies. Her attitude is that of: 'Ignore completely, take up the work … hand on the plough, do not mind the pain' (4 December 1956). Saturday and Sunday nights are especially heavy-going with only a few hours of sleep, with Saturday being her day of fasting and prayer and Sunday the sermon. In August 1958, she repeatedly writes in her diary: 'Nobody has ever known that I was never healthy, not even for a single day'.[6] Sometimes she is wobbly behind the pulpit, scaring the assembly (28 March 1959). During the boat trip to the Netherlands she writes with crooked fingers, pain in arms and hands: 'Terrible, always those devilish temptations. Nobody knows what I'm

---

[6] Handwritten note from Alt dated 22 August 1958 on loose sheet in C.H. Spurgeon, *Voor Iederen Morgen* next to meditation August 22.

going through. Under everything, I keep to the faith that the Lord has fully delivered me' (11 October 1961).

From the diary emerges a woman with great willpower. Physically, she is often a wreck, suffering from chronic malaria and the effects of the camp years. Nevertheless, she gives the appearance of strength in her ministry. From her perspective, common in the Pentecostal Movement of that period, everything that obstructs the ministry is evil. Thus she speaks of a 'malaria devil' that has to be fought while it makes more sense to see her malaria as a natural consequence of her long stay in the tropics. This way, the devil is given great prominence. Her attitude of ignoring the pain and continuing to work is a result of her believing that God heals without means. Confessing in faith to have been healed and at the same time denying the present symptoms pressurizes the sick and God. Her diary reveals her inner struggle with this conflict. She does not want to point an accusing finger at the sick person who is not healed, and allows church members the freedom to use medicines. Yet her preaching on healing without medicine and her own example will have felt like a kind of pressure, not least by her co-workers. For a period of time, it seems she wants to adjust her theology, but she returns to her old position. Nevertheless, an adjustment in which part of the full deliverance will be in the future and which reckons more with the sovereignty of God would have brought her theology more in balance.[7]

Ancilla Domini

Ancilla Domini (the handmaiden of the Lord). That is what I want to be called: that is my title. The service of the Lord is my bliss, my greatest happiness. That service is like a flame that consumes me inwardly and yet always gives me new life[8]

For many years, Moesje Alt served in loneliness, in remote places among the poor and orphans. She does not experience the motherhood she craves so much in the biological sense as in a spiritual sense. She becomes foster mother to dozens of orphans and other children

---

[7] Cf. C. van der Kooi, 'Theologie in de gloria: Opmerkingen bij de Bijbelstudie voor zelfonderricht van Moesje Alt', *Parakleet* 32.124 (2012), pp. 12–14. Lecture presented to the Symposium 'Moesje Alt: Boodschapster van goede tijding'. Amsterdam: VU University, 14 September 2012.

[8] Alt, *Het innerlijk licht*, p. 19.

and a spiritual mother of hundreds of church members. From the land colony at Gambang Waluh, a village has emerged that is still entirely Christian, a century later. That the inhabitants own the remaining land, they owe to Moes. From this small place, twenty-five assemblies have been established in surrounding villages, which is a remarkable result. At a time when the results of the mission among the Javanese are very modest, Moes has been able to establish a thriving assembly in a very remote place. Even in the then-emerging Pentecostal Movement, relatively few Javanese were converted. At that time, Gambang Waluh is seen as a shining example. Moes' willingness to go to the poor and stay there for fifteen years has opened Javanese hearts to the Gospel. Caring for orphans and the sick, educating boys and girls, and translating Javanese songs, she brought the love of God near to the people.

At the same time, this period also shows that Moes was pleased with a place in the shadows. She even recalls the years in loneliness as the happiest of her life. After this follows a period of national recognition, but when the time of farewell comes, she is willing to start anew at Manokwari. Although not seeking the spotlight, interviews with eyewitnesses reveal that her appearance made a special impression on many, both young and old. Two examples make this clear. The first takes place in Kediri, 1936. Corrie Aenmeij is nine years old when she comes home from school and meets Moes, in conversation with her mother. She sees a nice, kind woman with beautiful white hair who calls to her: 'Come up here on my lap'. Moes caresses and kisses her and says: 'The Lord will bless you, my child'. Corrie's parents are Catholic. She will never see Moes again, but the memory of that lovely woman and the words 'The Lord will bless you' will never leave her the rest of her life. It is as if Jesus himself spoke to her. Many years later, she experiences a calling from God and becomes the pastor of a small, Pentecostal church in Haarlem.[9] Around 1950, Rob van Gestel is a teenager in the Pinksterzending in Surabaya and sings in the youth choir. At the prayer sessions of the choir, he recalls, Moes would come in and take her place at the piano. When she would start to sing and play in the Spirit, God's Spirit would fall upon everyone. God's presence was so strong that you would not dare sin. He remembers Moes as 'a very stately, handsome

---

[9] Corrie van Dussen-Aenmeij, interview by the author, Haarlem, 31 May 2013.

woman'. When she preached in her white clothes and with that white hair, it was 'unthinkable that nothing special would happen'.[10] Rob becomes pastor of a Pentecostal assembly in Huizen.

The way Moes shapes the magazine *Gouden Schoven* and the way she leads the assembly and the Pinksterzending reflects a definite view of the church and of leadership. The assembly is like a family, and leadership is like motherhood. To her both church and leadership are strongly focused on loving relationships in which love and sorrow are shared. Mother keeps the family together with letters, visits, and intercessions and provides education and counseling.

As a writer and publisher of devotional and doctrinal books, poems, songs, and periodicals, she also built up thousands of others outside her own Pinksterzending. She built them up in faith and gave them direction. Of all the Dutch Pentecostal leaders from her generation, she has by far the most publications.[11] Additionally, her writings are theologically more interesting because of her wide reading. Supplemented by her candid, unpublished writings, her publications provide an excellent model of how an early Pentecostal pioneer thought and acted.

As regards the important matter of seeking the guidance of the Holy Spirit, in practice, it is often about the feeling of being led by the Spirit. Besides prayer and Bible reading, Pentecostal believers use other ways for finding the leading of the Spirit, such as dreams, visions, prophecies, turning pages in the Bible at random for a text, and an inner voice. The Bible is always the basis: the leading of the Holy Spirit is not allowed to go against the Word. In addition, fellow believers judge whether what is being preached or prophesied is pure. Of course, the feeling of being led by the Spirit can be mistaken. Even after decades of experience, Moes is still able to err, as evidenced by the fact that she shifts from one view to another about the use of medication. It is remarkable that Moes is very aware of her own failings. She is convinced of the importance of holding on to the right teaching, but from her own experience, she knows that she can also go astray. In a shepherding letter to Karel Hoekendijk, Moes asks him to consider whether he may be in error in some of his teachings. She writes: 'I personally made so many mistakes and errors in

---

[10] Rob and Trui van Gestel, interview by the author, Huizen, 3 March 2012.
[11] Not counting Johannes Rietdijk who worked in Belgium.

my seventy-two years, from which the Lord had to save me every time. In the end, we are only clay, but He is the great Potter.'[12]

Her message of sanctification is also important today. With her emphasis on the process of sanctification, Moes pleads for a lifetime of following Jesus. Her theme is: Do not put your self-interest first, but serve God and your neighbour out of love. Especially in leadership, she highly values the importance of a sanctified life. Otherwise, ambition, power, envy, and fanaticism will have free reign, as happened at the time of the rupture.[13] Her emphasis on the imminent return of Jesus Christ exhorts believers to be prepared to meet Him. From this end-time perspective, she looks at the world around her. She astutely comprehends the dangers of rising national-socialism, also through visions, and warns against it. However she seems to have much more difficulty in recognizing major changes in Indonesian society and the struggle for an independent Indonesia, as was the case with most Dutch citizens in those days. By standing up for the equality of men and women in the ministry, she has helped many women find boldness to follow their vocation.

She made an indelible impression on countless people. She was on familiar terms with her co-workers and church members and kept in contact with many of them. Through her periodicals, books, songs, poems, devotional books, and the assemblies she founded, her influence is much larger than the geographical area of her travels. She lived her own message, which was marked by the strong emphasis on a sanctified life for Jesus. During her last five months in the Netherlands she is allowed to see some of the fruits of her investment invested in the lives of thousands of believers.

She is an example in her simple lifestyle, spiritual leadership, perseverance, dedication, loyalty in relationships, the quest for unity, and openness to correction. At her request, the headstone on her grave reads: 'Jesus alone', to which Groeneveld and Sigmond added her honorary title: *Ancilla Domini*. Her life shows what this means. After her conversion, she breaks up the engagement with Dirk. She experiences it as a sacrifice that the Lord demands of her. How much pain

---

[12] M.A. Alt to Karel Hoekendijk, Manokwari, 23 November 1955. Hoeken-dijk had written Moes a letter requesting permission to copy articles from *Gouden Schoven* in his own paper *Stromen van Kracht*. In her reply, Moes first wants to know whether what she has heard about his teaching is true or not.

[13] M.A. Alt, *Van hart tot hart* ((Surabaya: Pinksterzending, 1947), pp. 2–3.

this causes is shown in her diary from 1910–1919. Many hardships, disappointments, and a constant struggle against sickness ('not a single day of good health') follow. Nevertheless, she continues to serve out of love for her Lord and her neighbour – like a candle that is consumed. In contrast to the beginning, she no longer sees it as a sacrifice, because love does not know sacrifice.

Should shortly the rest time come
And darkness fall
Will the work be taken from me
That I hold so dear
Then it is the Lord of Lords
To Whom I look up
Him I will honour eternally:
Ancilla Domini.[14]

[14] Alt, 'Dagboek 1945–1961', p. 11. Poem from A.M. Swaanswijk after the German of Mother Eva.

APPENDIX 1:
RUPTURE WITH THE PGNI

The Pinkstergemeente in Nederlands-Indië (PGNI) is not highly structured when Moes joins in mid-1926. William and Marie Bernard have left the mission field, and the two couples, Dik and Christine van Klaveren and Cornelis and Mies Groesbeek are on a long furlough in America. In addition to the constitutional General Committee, which has more of a legal function, a 'Convent of Evangelists' is formed in September 1927.[1] This Convent guides the PGNI. Derk Weenink van Loon and George van Gessel are the most important leaders. Besides them, Henri Horstman, his brother-in-law Feodoor van Abkoude and the only woman, Moesje Alt complete the Convent. After returning from furlough, the Van Klaverens (late 1929) and Groesbeeks (late 1930) also participate in the Convent. At the end of 1930 and later, new missionaries arrive from the Bethel Temple Church in America. The North-American influence is getting stronger. This involves introducing new teachings and an increasing rejection of female leadership, which will put Moes's position under pressure.

One big issue is the baptismal formula. W.H. Offiler, founder of the Bethel Temple in Seattle, is convinced that the 'Lord Jesus Christ' is the actual name of 'Father, Son, and Holy Spirit'. Therefore, the correct baptismal formula must be: 'I baptize you in the name of the Father, Son, and the Holy Spirit, *which is the Lord Jesus Christ*'.[2]

---

[1] F. van Abkoude, 'Uit den arbeid', *Pinksterkracht* 3.10 (October 1927), p. 11. The Convent was formed during a special Conference for evangelists on 26–27 September 1927, at Djokja. The meeting of the apostles and elders in Acts 15.6 is taken as example of a Convent for Evangelists providing spiritual oversight over the assemblies.

[2] W.H. Offiler, *God and His Name: A Message for Today* (Bethel Fellowship Int., 2001, reprint of the 2nd edn of 1932. Cf. C.J.H. Theijs, 'Sitoebondo', *GS* 9.9 (May 1933), p. 16 Theijs writes that the immersion is 'in the Trinitarian Name of the Triune God: THE LORD JESUS CHRIST. Only the revelation of the Spirit is true!' Theijs quotes Offiler that this method of baptism is preceded or followed by a mighty baptism with the Holy Spirit. The use of this baptismal formula is not paired with a denial of the Trinity such as in the 'Jesus Only' groups.

According to Offiler, 'Lord' is the name of the Father, 'Jesus' the name of the Son, and 'Christ' the name of the Holy Spirit. Without this addition, according to Offiler, the baptism is 'nameless' and without power. Through the missionaries from the Bethel Temple Church, this teaching is introduced in the PGNI, where it leads to disagreement. Among the leaders, Moes and Van Abkoude reject this doctrine. Other disputes concern the doctrine of the end times and the payment of tithes.

In February 1932, the Convent of Evangelists is subdivided into West Java (led by Weenink van Loon and the Van Klaverens), Middle Java (Van Abkoude and Groesbeek) and East Java (Van Gessel, Horstman and Alt).[3] When a few months later missionary Johnson (Borneo) also becomes a member of the Convent, five out of ten members are missionaries from Bethel Temple. This is the year the conflict comes to the surface. It is rumoured that the continuation of *Gouden Schooven* is at stake and Moes receives many questions from readers about it. In response to these questions Moes reports in October 1932 that the Convent has been dissolved by mutual agreement in September. The PGNI however has not been dissolved. There is still the General Committee consisting of Weenink van Loon (chairman), Van Klaveren (secretary) and Groesbeek (treasurer). Each leading evangelist now works completely independently with the workers 'assigned to him by God'. *Gouden Schooven* remains, but is no longer the official organ of the PGNI. Moes finds the latter incomprehensible and adds that she feels free to serve others and does not wish to join an existing group. She hopes to continue with the ministry of the Word, in addition to the supervision of the five assemblies.[4] One month later *Gouden Schooven* announces that the decision to no longer acknowledge the magazine as official organ was taken by Van Gessel and Horstman, but was reversed by the General Committee.[5]

It is clear that this is a very sensitive issue for Moes. She sees the publication of the magazine as a commission from God. She is also worried that the loss of readers will endanger the aid to the poor in

---

[3] Inside cover *GS* 8.19 (October 1932). Cf. *GS* 8.17 (September 1932), p. 20.

[4] M.A. Alt, 'Correspondentie', *GS* 8.20 (October 1932), p. 18.

[5] M.A. Alt, 'Kennisgeving', GS 8.22 (November 1932), p. 19. Of this issue two copies have been found. In one copy the announcement was cut out and in the other copy it was neatly glued with a piece of paper contained the poem 'De hand aan de ploeg' ('The hand on the plow'). It was possible to read through the glued paper the original text. It is not known whether the whole edition was glued over.

Gambang Waluh. Possibly she had been too quick with her announcement in October 1932. In any case, the action reveals a
dormant conflict. In November 1932 *Gouden Schooven* again presents
itself as the official organ of the PGNI. In addition to the three
members of the General Committee mentioned, all other known
members of the Convent are now referred to as 'other Committee
members', including Moes. In 1933, the composition of the General
Committee is changed to: Van Gessel (Chairman), Horstman (Secretary) and W. Mamahit (Treasurer). The remaining members are now
called 'further chief evangelists'. In December 1933, Weenink van
Loon speaks against the rumors that there would be a rift among the
chief evangelists.[6]

In July 1934, Moes writes that she heard 'unofficially' that at the
General Council of 20 June, 'the Combination of Van Gessel and
Horstman' had decided to no longer recognize *Gouden Schooven* as the
organ of the PGNI. Moes wonders whether 'the Combination' is entitled to this, but she submits to it. For years, she has tried to promote
unity. Moes continues with *Gouden Schooven* as 'Pentecostal periodical
of the Dutch Indies', which will proceed 'separate from the Combination and her doctrine, but all the more strongly connected to all
true Pentecostals, who still hold to the ancient, tested and blessed
Pentecostal Gospel, and with us want to go the way of the cross'.[7]
The phrase 'official organ of the PGNI' has now finally disappeared
from the colophon. Instead, we now read: 'In the service of the
Church of Jesus Christ'.

The decision is controversial. In a meeting of evangelists in July
1934 at Bandung under the direction of Weenink van Loon, it is decided as a matter of need to divide the PGNI in Java into two regions:
West/Middle Java and East Java. Moes rejects the offer that *Gouden
Schooven* would become the organ for West/Middle Java and now prefers for it to stay a private magazine.[8] At the General Council in November 1934 in Surabaya, the entire General Committee steps down.
A newly elected General Committee is formed by: Weenink van Loon
(Chairman), R.C. Van Gessel (secretary treasurer), and Alt as Com-

---

[6] M.A. Alt, 'Berichten van het arbeidsveld', *GS* 10.1 (January 1934), p. 7. The
rumor was about a rupture with on the one side Weenink van Loon, Van Klaveren,
and Alt and on the other side Van Abkoude, Van Gessel, and Horstman.

[7] M.A. Alt, 'Kennisgeving', *GS* 10.14 (July 1934), p. 14 (emphasis original).

[8] M.A. Alt, 'Onze Broederbond', *GS* 10.16 (August 1934), pp. 7–8.

missioner.[9] This seems to be an emergency intervention, but it comes too late. When Moes wants to address the assembly during the meeting, she is silenced. A little later, the General Committee informs her that eight to ten evangelists have asked for her resignation in a petition. Then, Moes writes, 'it began to dawn on me that my time had come to withdraw'.[10] Three months later, Moes establishes her own group: De Pinksterzending (The Pentecostal Mission).

The announcements just referred to all come from *Gouden Schooven*, which up to June 1934 is the official organ of the PGNI except for a short interruption. As Moes herself is a party in the conflict, a bias in the reporting must be taken into account. From the magazine, however, it can be concluded that the conflict came out in the open in 1932, but it was not until 1934 that after a period of chaos it came down to a rupture. In the conflict Moes comes to stand against Van Gessel and Horstman. Weenink van Loon tries to bridge the gap, but eventually chooses Van Gessel and Horstman's side, while Moes and Van Abkoude leave the PGNI.

It is remarkable that the newspapers are silent about the rupture, since the Pentecostal church has the attention of the press whenever something negative happens.[11] It seems that the rupture develops without much public comment. Yet in 1932 Theo den Daas, evangelist in Meester Cornelis, resigns and establishes the Christelijke Vereeniging Pinkstervreugd (Christian Association Pentecostal Joy). In October 1933 he releases the periodical *Pinksterlicht* (*Pentecostal Light*).[12] In 1933 Feodoor van Abkoude anticipates a rupture. He disagrees with the new teachings which he believes are forced upon them from America. He has become acquainted with the English

---

[9] M.A. Alt, 'Kennisgeving', *GS* 10.22 (November 1934), p. 19.

[10] M.A. Alt, 'Autobiografie 1943', p. 77. Moes erroneously mentions 1935.

[11] In a number of negative cases the press minutely reports that the person involved belongs to the Pentecostal church. For instance a witness who lies before the court, someone suspected of fraud, a bicycle thief, a burglar, someone who spreads an occultistic circular (*Indische Courant en Soerabaiasch Handelsblad* 1931–1933).

[12] Theo C.E.J.M. den Daas was an evangelist with the PGNI at Meester Cornelis. Pinkstervreugd was recognized by the government on 28 September 1932, cf. *Bataviaasch Nieuwsblad*, 22 October 1932. Now and then the meetings are announced in the newspapers, for the last time in December 1940. Four issues of *Pinksterlicht* from 1938 have been found. All over Java there are twelve addresses of meetings at which four evangelists and three assistant minister. Moes accuse *Pinksterlicht* after its first issue of plagiarism, *GS* 9.20 (October 1933), p. 19.

Pentecostal periodical *Redemption Tidings* and with the writings of Donald Gee. That is why he is seeking to join the British Assemblies of God.[13] In March 1935 his Vereeniging De Gemeenten Gods in Nederlands-Indië (Association The Assemblies of God in the Dutch Indies) is recognized by the government.[14] As far as can be checked, both groups (Pinkstervreugd and the Gemeenten Gods) remained relatively small and generated little activity after 1941. Theo den Daas was tragically killed in 1951 when an assassin's bullet hit him in the heart while he was on his way to a sick member of the congregation.[15] In 1950, the Gemeente Gods at Makassar joined the Assemblies of God in Indonesia.[16]

---

[13] Cf. correspondence F. van Abkoude with the British Assemblies of God, present in the Donald Gee Centre, Mattersey, England.

[14] 'De Gemeenten van God', *Indische Courant* (16 March 1935). The rupture with the PGNI is extra painful because Van Abkoude and Horstman are brothers-in-law, moreover Mrs. Horstman is a niece of Van Abkoude. In 1935 Howard Carter, Chairman of the British Assemblies of God, together with Lester Sumrall of the American Assemblies of God visit the Dutch Indies. It is not clear whether there ever has been an official membership of the British Assemblies of God. From 1940 the announcements of the meetings in the newspapers have the addition 'vrije evangelische gemeente' ('free evangelical assembly'). During the war Van Abkoude is interned together with other ministers in Bandung. More and more he feels attracted to the reformed faith. After the war he studies theology in Zwolle and from 1948 until 1954 he is missionary of the Reformed Churches in the Netherlands on Sumba. Christine de Jongh-van Abkoude, interview by the author, Zevenaar, 10 March 2014.

[15] M.A. Alt, 'Br. Th. Den Daas', *GS* 20.2 (February 1951), p. 21.

[16] M.A. Alt, 'Makasser' [sic], *GS* 19.4 (April 1950), p. 16.

APPENDIX 2:
COOPERATION WITH THE ASSEMBLIES OF GOD

Before World War II several Pentecostal missionaries from North America went to the Dutch East Indies. They all went via the Pentecostal congregation, Bethel Temple Church, Seattle. On the field they worked with the Pinkstergemeente in Nederlandsch-Indië (PGNI). Due to differences in doctrine and practice some missionaries decided to work independently of the PGNI. This led to the foundation of the Indische Bethel Zending (Bethel Indies Mission) by Ralph Devin and Raymond Busby, which received government recognition in 1940.[1] During the war Devin and Busby stayed in the USA and joined the Assemblies of God. When after the War the Assemblies of God wanted to send missionaries to Indonesia, the government recognition of the Bethel Indies Mission was made use of. In 1946 ten missionaries of the Assemblies of God arrived in Indonesia. Officially they entered under the flag of the Bethel Indies Mission. Six of them had already been there before the war.[2] In 1951 the name Bethel Indies Mission was changed to Assemblies of God in Indonesia. One year later it received the Indonesian name: Gereja Sidang-sidang Jemaat Allah (GSJA). Previously it was assumed that it was not before 1952 that part of the Pinksterzending (Pentecostal Mission) joined the GSJA, but Moes reports having joined the Assemblies of God five years before this.

---

[1] Gani Wiyono, *A Sketch of the History of the Assemblies of God of Indonesia (Gereja Sidang-sidang Jemaat Allah* (Master Thesis, Baguio City, Philippines: Asia Pacific Theological Seminary, 2004), pp. 42–51.

[2] Six had been in Indonesia before the war: Kenneth and Gladys Short (1936–1940, Borneo), Ralph and Edna Devin (1938–1942, Ambon), Raymond and Beryl Busby (1939–1941, Sumatra). In 1946 they returned to Indonesia in the company of Margaret Brown, Harold and Jean Carlblom, and John Tinsman. See Carlblom, 'History of Pentecostal/Assemblies of God Missions in Indonesia' (1979), present in Assemblies of God World Missions Archive. Cf. Kenneth G. Short, 'Report of the Dutch East Indies', Missionary Conference held at Springfield, MO, 16–18 March, 1943.

By reading *Pentecostal Evangel* and other publications Moes has received a positive impression of the Assemblies of God. There is agreement in doctrine. A meeting between Moes and Devin in April 1947 leads to a cooperation that is confirmed in November 1947 when Devin and Busby both visit Moes in Surabaya.[3] Already in September 1947 *Gouden Schoven* mentions a non-official cooperation between the Pinksterzending and the Assemblies of God. In December 1947 *Gouden Schoven* reports that the Pinksterzending has definitely joined the Assemblies of God. The same issue starts a series about the origin and progress of the Assemblies of God. From now on the name Assemblies of God appears on the cover of *Gouden Schoven*. First between brackets after the name Pinksterzending and later in replacement of the Pinksterzending (November 1948). In these years (1948–1951) all of Alt's publications carry the signature: Sister M.A. Alt, Evangelist of the 'Assemblies of God in Indonesia'.

In May 1948 *Gandoem Mas* reappears after six year. It is a publication of the Pinksterzending, edited by Stefanus, in close cooperation with the Assemblies of God. This is a prime means of communication with the Indonesian assemblies. The leaders of both the Assemblies of God and the Pinksterzending write about the cooperation. In the introduction Chairman R.M. Devin speaks of *Gandoem Mas* as the official periodical of the Assemblies of God in Indonesia.[4] In two entries Alt speaks of an official joining and of a merger.[5] Moes understands from Devin that ten of the Pentecostal assemblies in The Netherlands have also joined the Assemblies of God. She welcomes the Dutch brethren in 'our Assemblies of God' and lists their

---

[3] Her diary 'Dagboek 1945–1961' reveals that Moes on 22 April 1947, two days before the visit of Devin, had already decided to join the Assemblies of God. The Pinksterzending at Bandung had given permission. Unfortunately, Moes had not yet been able to discuss it with Stefanus, so she writes: 'I have but to act according to God's leading'. On 12 May 1947 Moes writes that she had joined the Assemblies of God together with the Malay assembly in Surabaya under leadership of Oen. On 28 November 1947, after the visit of Devin and Busby, she writes: 'From yesterday we are affiliated with The Assemblies of God. I personally would rather quietly continue my work here, but by this affiliation I have made a choice for the benefit of our workers of the Pinksterzending. If I were to be taken away, they would be standing all by themselves. Now they have a strong help in the A.o.G.' Alt, 'Dagboek 1945–1961', pp. 111, 119.

[4] R.M. Devin, 'Pendahoeloean Kata', *Gandoem Mas*, 10.1 (May 1948), pp. 2–3.

[5] M.A. Alt, 'Pemberian Tahoe', *Gandoem Mas* 10.1 (May 1948), p. 16; Alt in preface to 'Asal moelanja dan riwajat berdirinja The Assemblies of God', *Gandoem Mas* 10.1 (May 1948), p. 9.

names and addresses.[6] In a survey of the Pentecostal work in Indo-nesia published in June 1949 in *Pentecost* Devin reports the merger of the Pinksterzending with the Assemblies of God.[7] From October 1950 *Gouden Schoven* is suddenly published by the Assemblies of God 'in Surabaya' instead of 'in Indonesia' and from May 1951 it is again published by De Pinksterzending, extended with: '(Utusan Pantekosta)'.

PEMBERIAN TAHOE.

Oentoek menghilangkan salah fa-ham, jang bertanda tangan dibawah ini menerangkan dengan *sesoenggoeh-soenggoehnja*, bahwa baik saja, maoe-poen sajapoenja Evangelisten tidak dapat gadjih atau sokongan oewang dari Geredja „The Assemblies of God", atau dari lain-lain Bidat atau Organi-satie. Sedari saja moelai bekerdja seba-gai Evangelist, saja selaloe hidoep da-lam pertjaja kepada Toehan, demikian-poen dengan pembantoe[2] saja tak pernah kekoerangan soeatoepoen apa.

Geredja Pinksterzending adalah sa-toe Djema'at jang hidoep dengan per-tjaja. Kita selaloe menolak subsidie atau gadjih jang ditawarkan.

Geredja kita telah menggaboengkan resmi dengan Geredja „The Assemblies of God" oleh karena kita mengharga-kan pengadjaran dan organisatienja.

M. A. ALT.

Voorzitster dari
Geredja „Pinksterzending
S'baja, Maart 1948.   di-Indonesia.

Gandum Mas (May 1948)

Since the archives of the Assemblies of God in Springfield, Mis-souri, as well as in Indonesia, contain scarcely any documents of this period, and *Gouden Schooven* does not give much information, a

---

[6] M.A. Alt, 'Gezegende samenwerking', *GS* 17.6 (June 1948), p. 12.

[7] R.M. Devin, 'Netherlands East Indies', *Pentecost* 8 (June 1949), p. 6. Although Alt speaks of an affilation of the Pentecostal assemblies in the Netherlands, it can-not have been a formal affilation, which came much later.

reconstruction is difficult. Perhaps the level of organization is such that one cannot speak of a formal membership before 1951, or it is the case that the membership is limited to the national field. It is certain that the Pinksterzending does not retract its recognition from the Dutch government. The Pinksterzending therefore retains its own governmental recognition, after joining the Assemblies of God in 1947. It is also important to realize that till the end of 1949 hardly any contact is possible between the assemblies of the Pinksterzending that are in Dutch territory and those in republican territory. This means that the latter group were not consulted about the union with the Assemblies of God. When full communication within the nation is restored in 1950, these assemblies are faced with the decision whether or not to join the Assemblies of God. Alt is in favour of joining, but believes that each assembly must decide for itself.[8] By the time Alt leaves for New Guinea clarity is needed.

Sometime before her departure a serious problem comes up. Devin has been on a long furlough since March 1949. It appears that Alt has a diagreement with Busby about compulsory tithing (Alt is against it) and about the question of authority over the periodicals *Gouden Schooven* and *Gandoem Mas*. This leads to a breach in the cooperation, which according to Alt is due to a 'intransigent attitude' on the part of Busby, but it does not last for long.[9] Probably the collision can be dated to the beginning of September 1950, during the visit of Alt and Stefanus to Busby in Jakarta, although the report in *Gouden Schoven* is silent on the matter.[10]

After a five-months voyage on board the missionary vessel 'Evangel' Devin arrives in Jakarta on 1 January 1951, the first day of the First General Conference of the Assemblies of God in Indonesia. On the second day the 'feasibility of receiving our Pinksterzending brethren into the Assemblies of God in Indonesia as an entire group' is discussed. The wording assumes there is no formal affiliation, but

---

[8] Cf. Wiyono, *A Sketch*, p. 69.
[9] M.A. Alt to E. van der Molen, Surabaya, 11 April 1951 and Manokwari, 14 September 1951.
[10] M.A. Alt, 'Onze Evangelisatie-reis door West- en Midden-Java', GS 19.11 (November 1950), pp. 3–5. As far as is known this is the last time Alt and Busby met. Mrs Devin was also in Jakarta, while her husband was on his way from America to Indonesia with his Evangelization vessel Evangel.

shows willingness to welcome the Pinksterzending under certain provisions, including the liquidation of the Pinksterzending.[11]

On the General Meeting of the Pinksterzending, 3–5 April, 1951, in Madiun, Alt resigns as Chairman. The new Executive Council consists of: S. Stefanus (Surabaya, Chairman), Oei Giok Siang (Solo), and Ie Sing Gwan (Batu). The Pinksterzending from now on is called 'Utusan Pantekosta'.[12] As from May 1951 *Gouden Schoven* is published by 'De Pinksterzending (Utusan Pantekosta)'.

A few months later the conflict is settled, with the approval of Alt who is in New-Guinea. At the Second General Conference of the Assemblies of God in July 1952 in Tomohon, Stefanus and six assemblies of the Pinksterzending with him formally join the Assemblies of God. At the same meeting the name is changed into Gereja-gereja Jemaat Allah (GSJA). Other assemblies of the Pinksterzending continue as Gereja Utusan Pantekosta (GUP). In both groups (GSJA and GUP) Alt is still remembered with much respect for her foundational work. In 1959 Stefanus becomes the first Indonesian President of GSJA.

As from December 1952 the covers of *Gouden Schoven* present Alt as 'Evangelist of the Assemblies of God in Manokwari'. In January 1953 Moes confirms that she and her co-workers, including the church in Surabaya and five other assemblies in Indonesia have definitely joined the Assemblies of God. She further emphasizes that the principles remain the same and that no financial support is received from the Assemblies of God.[13] Probably Alt is seen as a national worker by the Assemblies, which may explain why there is no file relating to her in Springfield. The Assemblies of God in these years have no permit for New Guinea. Moes secures a permit for the Pinksterzending in New Guinea (1955), but she remains an evangelist of the Assemblies of God. In September 1961 Moes leaves New Guinea and establishes a new work in the Netherlands. On the cover of *Gouden Schoven* after November 1961 she is no longer an Evangelist of the Assemblies of God, but of the Pinksterzending.

---

[11] 'Minutes of the First General Conference of the Assemblies of God in Indonesia (Bethel Indies Mission)', Jakarta, 1–5 January 1951, pp. 1–2. With thanks to Gani Wiyono.

[12] M.A. Alt, 'Kennisgeving', GS 20.5 (May 1951), p. 24.

[13] M.A. Alt, 'Kennisgeving', *GS* 22.1 (January 1953), 11. Gani Wiyono mentions the assemblies in Surabaya, Gambang Waluh, Plampangan, Batu, and Malang (pp. 70–71). Probably Pasuruan was also one of the six.

ANNOTATED BIBLIOGRAPHY OF M.A. ALT

Publications

Gouden Schooven (*Golden Sheaves*). The periodical edited by M.A. Alt. From January 1928 until August 1928 appearing under the name *Pinksterkracht*. From September 1928 to 1 March 1962 it appears as *Gouden Schooven*, with an interval from June 1942 until November 1946. After the war it appears once a month. In mid 1956 the name is spelled as *Gouden Schoven*. All 546 issues in 32 volumes have been located. The volume numbering on the covers is sometimes confusing. Until 1934 the periodical is part of the PGNI and from 1935 part of the Pinksterzending. A large collection is present in the library of the VU University, Amsterdam. This collection is digitally available on the Digital Library, University of Southern California site under Hollenweger Center. All missing issues have been traced in the National Library (Perpustakaan Nasional) in Jakarta, where the periodicals *Dit is Het* and *Gandoem Mas* are also located.

Pinkster Evangelie Courant 'Komt tot de wateren' (*Pentecostal Gospel Courant 'Come to the Waters'*), subtitled: 'Weekly magazine to spread the four-fold gospel, namely full redemption through the blood of Jesus'. A weekly periodical edited by M.A. Alt from July 1929 until December 1929. The first four issues are present in the Koninklijke Bibliotheek at The Hague. From January 1930 it is incorporated into *Gouden Schooven*. The latter part of the title 'Come to the Waters' appears from this time at the top of page one. After the merger in January 1930 *Gouden Schooven* appears weekly, but from April 1930 it reverts to being a twice monthly publication.

Gandoem Mas. A periodical published under the responsibility of M.A. Alt from May 1933 to 1942. Traced are the loose issues 1.2 (1933), 2.3 (1934), 3.12 (1936) and the complete volumes 4 to 8 (September 1936 until December 1941, present in the National Library in Jakarta). Originally published by the Pentecostal assembly at Kediri, then by the Pinksterzending at Kediri and as from 1936 at Lawang.

After the war it re-appears from 1948 edited by S. Stefanus at Surabaya. The following individual issues have been located: 1–3 and 7 from 1948.

Het Volle Licht. Tekstboekje voor het gehele jaar 1929 (*The Full Light: Booklet with texts for the whole year 1929*). Magelang: Pinkstergemeente in Ned.-Indië, 1929, 142 pp. Two texts from the Bible (morning and evening) for every day of the year. At the beginning of each month is a meditation.

Van hart tot hart (*From Heart to Heart*). Kediri: 1934. [Not found] see reprint in 1947.

Het volle Licht. Dagboekje voor het huisgezin. (*The Full Light: Book of daily readings for the Family*). Morning and evening text and prayer. Lawang: Kedirische Sneldrukkerij, 1940; second printing Surabaya, 1949 [Not found]; third printing Manokwari, 1960, 382 pp.; fourth printing Velp: Gouden Schoven, [1962] etc. 8th printing 1975; 9th printing 1979, 383 pp.; 11th printing 1994 The Hague: Gazon. 385pp.
The first printing contained the anniversaries of the Royal Family with a prayer. This led to Alt being imprisoned by the Japanese. For every day of the year a short morning and evening meditation with a Bible verse. Every month starts with a theme. From the fourth printing the title becomes *In het volle licht*.

Van hart tot hart (*From Heart to Heart*). Surabaya, 1947, stencil, 17 pp., revised edition of the original from 1934. Open letter to the members of all Pentecostal circles in the Dutch Indies. On request Alt describes the differences in teaching that caused the rupture with the PGNI. Discussion of water baptism in the name of the Lord Jesus Christ and of several points concerning the end times.

Wat geschiedt er met ongeboren kinderen? (*What Happens to Unborn Children?*) Surabaya: Pinksterzending/Assemblies of God, 1948, stencil, 14 pp. Argues against abortion, but God has mercy on the aborted children. The only permitted form of birth control is abstinence.

Mag de vrouw spreken in de gemeente? (*May a Woman Speak in the Assembly?*) Surabaya: Pinksterzending/Assemblies of God, [1948], stencil, 6 pp.

Contains a summary of an article by W.F.P. Burton in *Redemption Tidings* with an afterword by Alt.

Ons Kampleven gedurende de Japansche en Republikeinsche bezetting (*Our Camp Life during the Japanese and Republican Occupation*). Surabaya: De Pinksterzending/Assemblies of God in Indonesia [1948], 40 pp. This first appeared as a series in *Gouden Schoven* from January 1947 to January 1948. In 1972 it was included in the second edition of *Herinneringen uit mijn leven*.

Overvloeiend leven (*Overflowing Life*) Surabaya: De Pinksterzending/Assemblies of God in Indonesia, 1948, 44 pp. Circulation 1,000. Chapters about: conversion, rebirth, Spirit baptism, sanctification, walk with God, fullness of the Spirit, the overflowing life. Reprinted in *Christus in ons* (1964).

Het innerlijk licht. Gedachten en Meditatieën (*The Inner Light. Thoughts and Meditations*). Surabaya: Assemblies of God in Indonesia. Department Surabaya, [1949], 78 pp. Contains 'Meditations and thoughts of a redeemed soul abiding in Christ'. Thoughts about various spiritual subjects alternating with 19 poems. Alphabetic index on poems and subjects at the back. Reprinted in *Christus in ons* (1964) extended with 10 poems and 8 thoughts.

Bijbel-Studie voor zelfonderricht (*Bible-Study for Self-education*). Surabaya: De Pinksterzending in Indonesia, [1951], 544 pp. including appendix 'Short overview of the coming events' followed by 10 pp. with 'The Future: Gog and Magog' and index with subjects. Revised editions in 1968 and 1976.

Handleiding en wegwijzer voor Evangelisten (*Manual and Guide for Evangelists*). Surabaya: De Pinksterzending in Indonesia, [between 1947 and 1951], 31 pp. Reprinted as *Practische raadgevingen voor Evangelisten* (*Practical Counsel for Evangelists*) [1957]. Published at the request of co-workers. Short practical guidelines for evangelists about: Bible knowledge, sanctification, laying on of hands and anointing, clothing, manners, preaching, divorce, baptism, Lord's Supper, association with people who think differently, expelling of evil spirits and tithes. Then 55 questions and answers, especially about the Bible and doctrine.

Bergopwaarts. Vijf Christelijke Indische novellen in één band (*Uphill. Five Christian Novels in one volume*). Jakarta: Philadelphia, [1955], 158 pp. In the preface Alt speaks of 'simple tendenz-novels'. In *Herinneringen* (53) she writes that these are events from the years at Gambang Waluh which were then written down partly to pass the time in the Japanese camp at Solo. The 'dark powers' described in chapter 4 'are wholly historical and witnessed by the writer herself'. Also the extensive description of a spiritistic meeting in chapter 5 is historical fact.

Mag de vrouw spreken in de gemeente? (*May a Woman Speak in the Assembly?*) Manokwari: [Pinksterzending], 1956, 14 pp. About a woman's the freedom to preach if she has been called to do so and a discussion of the controversial texts.

Practische raadgevingen voor Evangelisten (*Practical Counsel for Evangelists*). Manokwari: Gouden Schoven, second printing, 32 pp., plento [1957]. Equal to *Handleiding en wegwijzer*. Reprinted in *Bijbelstudie voor zelfonderricht*, 1968 and 1976.

Posthumous Publications

De Openbaring van Johannes (*The Revelation of John*). No record of place or publisher, [1962], 63 pp. Reprinted 'upon many requests' from *Gouden Schoven* where it first appeared as a series from January 1961 until May 1962. Also included in the second edition of *Bijbelstudie voor zelfonderricht*. Two earlier series about Revelation from her hand appeared in *Gouden Schooven* January 1941 until March 1942 and from December 1946 until December 1948. The latter also appeared in the first edition of *Bijbelstudie voor zelfonderricht*.

Herinneringen uit mijn leven (*Memories from my Life*). Velp: Pinksterzending, 1963, 118 pp. Autobiography completed shortly before her death. Afterword by J. Sigmond. The appendix 'Raadgevingen en Persoonlijke ervaringen door M.A. Alt' (*Counsel and Personal experiences by M.A. Alt*) discusses theological issues that are approached in a practical manner. Written in the last months of her life. The second edition in 1971, 180 pp., is extended with 'M.A. Alt, Ons Kampleven' (*Our Camp Life*) and 'Zo is het verder gegaan' (*How It Has Continued*) by D. Groeneveld and J. Sigmond.

Christus in ons (*Christ in Us*). Velp: Gouden Schoven, 1964, 136 pp. Preface D. Groeneveld and J. Sigmond. Reprint in one volume of: *Overvloeiend leven* and *Het Innerlijk Licht*. The latter had been prepared for a reprint by Alt shortly before her death and extended with 18 small entries and poems.

Bijbelstudie voor zelfonderricht, een doelmatige gids tot gedegen bijbelkennis (*Bible Study for Self-education, An appropriate guide to solid Bible knowledge*). Velp: De Pinksterzending, 1968, 2ⁿᵈ revised edition, red cover, 722 pp.; third edition Velp: De Pinksterzending, 1976, yellow cover, 750 pp. Extended with preface by D. Groeneveld and J. Sigmond, table of contents, introduction, 'Praktische raadgevingen voor evangelisten and Beantwoording van vragen die vaak worden gesteld door M.A. Alt, zendingszuster en evangeliste van de Pinksterzending', appendix J. Sigmond, much enlarged index.

Songbooks

'Glorie-Klokken' Pinkster-Zangbundel (*Bells of Glory. Pentecostal Songbook*). Magelang: Magelangsche Drukkerij, [1930], 236 pp., 200 songs and thirty choruses with number notation, index, and themes.

Glorieklokken. Christelijk Zangboek ten dienste van samenkomsten en huisgezin in 't bijzonder voor Nederlandsch-Indië: 400 liederen en 30 koren.
First edition with staves. The first five volumes published between 1932–1935 by the De Pinkstergemeente in Ned.-Indië (PGNI) and printed by A.G. Nix at Bandung. In 1935 Alt has left the PGNI. In 1936 volumes 1 and 2 appear in a second printing without a named publisher and printed by Kolff at Malang. Finally in 1938 volume 6 appears also without a named publisher and printed by Kolff. The last two volumes (7 and 8) are with the printer, but will not be released. Of the planned 400 songs only 305 appeared in volumes 1–6. By mistake the numbering of the songs in volume 6 starts with 1 instead of 245.

Glorieklokken. Liederen voor solo en samenzang. Gorinchem: Kracht van Omhoog, 1954–1959, 533 songs with staves in 10 volumes. The songs are numbered 1–542, but number 346 is missing and 8 songs have mistakenly been included twice (nos. 385, 388, 402, 455, 494, 505, 538, 539).

Glorieklokken. Liederen voor solo en samenzang. Gorinchem: Kracht van Omhoog, 1962, 553 songs (nrs. 1–545 plus 8 unnumbered) with staves in one volume, blue cover. Nearly identical to the 10 volumes, 9 songs have been replaced (no. 50 plus the 8 included twice) and 12 songs are added (nos. 69a, 134a, 191a, 218a, 243a, 296a, 346, 390a, 431a, 543–545).

Glorieklokken. Liederen voor solo en samenzang. Gorinchem: Kracht van Omhoog, 1971, slightly revised edition with 556 songs (nos. 1–548 plus 8 unnumbered), 1 song replaced (45), 3 songs added (546–548), green cover.

Glorieklokken. Liederen voor solo en samenzang 50 jaar. Rotterdam: Continental Sound, 2013, unchanged reprint, green cover. Extended with prefaces by Leen Lariviere, Joop Gankema, Hans and Ina Groeneveld, Miranda Klaver, Peter Sleebos, Cees van der Laan.
Glorieklokken text editions:
[Arnhem]: Gouden Schoven, 1957, 295 songs from the first 5 volumes.
Laren: Gouden Schoven, 1959, 542 songs.
Gorinchem: Kracht van Omhoog, 1962, 545 songs. Also included in *Combi-bundel* together with *Johan de Heer* song-book.
Gorinchem: Kracht van Omhoog, 1965, 548 songs.
Gorinchem: Kracht van Omhoog, 1965, *Combi-bundel Glorieklokken* and *Joh. de Heer.*
Javanese song-book, 1920. [Not found]
Kidoeng Panggoegah. Opwekkingsliederen voor het Javaansche volk op bekende wijzen. 200 songs and 30 choruses in Javanese. December 1928. Reprint 1931. [Not found]
Lontjeng Soerga, Malay Pentecostal Song-book with songs from *Glorieklokken* with number notation translated by Siwi, 1931. Reprints in 1932, 1934 and 1935. [Not found]
Malay-Javanese *Glorieklokken,* with the first 100 songs, 1936. Translation started in 1934 by Siwi (Malay) and Alt (Javanese). [Not found]

Zestig nieuwe koren voor Gemeente en Huisgezin. Surabaya: Pinksterzending, 1948. Sixty new choruses with number notation and lyrics in Dutch and Malay. [Not found]

Koren ten dienste van zondagschool en Jeugdsamenkomsten. Manokwari: Assemblies of God, [1956], 113 choruses with number notation (34 pp.) in plento press.

Zangkoorliederen nrs 1–100, Dutch and Indonesian, 4-parts with number notation, stencil. Surabaya: Assemblies of God/Pinksterzending, 1950. 100 songs for choir, Dutch lyrics by M.A. Alt. Indonesian lyrics by S. Stefanus.

Zangkoorliederen nrs 101–200, Dutch and Indonesian, 4 parts with number notation, stencil. Surabaja: Gandum Mas, 1952. 100 songs for choir, Dutch lyrics by M.A. Alt. Indonesian lyrics by S. Stefanus.

Zangkoorliederen nrs 201–300, Dutch and Indonesian, 4 parts with number notation, stencil. Surabaja: Gandum Mas, 1955. 100 songs for choir, Dutch lyrics by M.A. Alt. Indonesian lyrics by S. Stefanus.

Unpublished and handwritten sources

'Gedichtenbundel 1899–1906' (Poem Book 1899–1906), 111 pp. Dedicated to D. de V.S. Handwritten poems with autobiographical elements from a period of which we otherwise have little knowledge. 'Dagboek 1910–1919' (Diary 1910–1919). On the cover: 'Dagboek van Margot Alt. Bethel-Taju,' 168 pp. Relating to the period at Taju and Gambang Waluh from 26 September 1910 until 17 March 1919. At the end 3 pages with short notes from Manokwari, dated 10 February 1952, ? October 1957 and 24 May 1961. Handwritten diary, started straight after arrival at Taju, at the beginning of her service as a missionary nurse. Open-hearted account with many details about her daily life and people she meets with self-reflections about her inner life.

'Autobiografie 1943', 82 pp. Handwritten autobiography written in 1943 after her death sentence was changed into confinement in a camp. She had looked death in the eye and apparently felt the urge to write down her life story. In the preface she writes: 'It is my intention to leave these pages behind after my decease for those that love me and follow in the steps of the great King'. Much from the autobiography is later used for *Herinneringen*. On some points this autobiography contains more details.

'Dagboek 1945–1961' (Diary 1945–1961), 298 pp. On the cover: 'Meditations and thoughts'. It starts with meditations, sometimes dated (27 November 1945 until 1 December 1945), 1–18. Pages 19–22 have been torn out because of fear of house searches during the time in the Republican camp. Pages 23–298 concern the period Lawang from 15 December 1945 until Manokwari 12 October 1961. [Alt SV Bijbel] *Bijbel, Staten Vertaling*. Amsterdam: NBG, 1928, 1172 pp. Bible with hundreds of handwritten notes in the margins and pasted in or loose sheets, often dated, mainly from 1948–1950. Many notes refer to sermons and mention where and when they were delivered. There are also many prayer topics or answers to prayers. The Bible was given by Moes to her co-worker Corrie Sleebos and is now in the possession of the latter's, son Henk Sleebos.

[Alt UV Bijbel] *Bijbel Utrechtse Vertaling* (Utrecht Translation, also known as Obbink-Brouwer Translation). Leiden: W. Sijthof, first printing OT 1924, first printing NT 1927. The Bible has been rebound. The NT is the third printing from 1934. Translation by H.Th. Obbink (OT) and A.M. Brouwer (NT), professors at Utrecht University.
This contains many handwritten notes in the margins and a small number of pasted in sheets with sermon notes, of which 255 notes have a date (1926–1962). The only date prior to October 1934 is from 1926 and may have been included later. The years 1926–1941 only have 14 notes; the years 1942–1943 (Japanese period) have 20 notes. The years 1950–1952 (around the transition to New Guinea) have the most, 150 notes. The OT has 205 notes of which 142 in Psalms. The NT has 50 notes. Alt has used the Bible intensely until January 1962. After her death it came in the possession of Dick Groeneveld who also made some notes and is now in the possession of his daughter Els Groeneveld.

[Alt NBG Bijbel] *Bijbel, NBG Vertaling*. Amsterdam: NBG, 1951. A new translation of the Bible in a special 2-volume edition in which every page alternates with a blank page for notes. Moes had the Bible rebound to include even more blank pages and allow for inserting loose sheets. Only Volume 2 containing Proverbs to Revelation has been found. This was well used by Moes in Manokwari and contains hundreds of sermon notes handwritten on the blank pages or handwritten or typed on pasted in pages or on loose sheets and cuttings of sermon illustrations, from the period 1952–1961, as well as notes in the margins. After her death this Bible went to Dick Groeneveld and is now in the possession of his daughter Ruth Groeneveld.

'Prekenboek 1936–1952' (Sermon Book) with 622 sermons. The first (unnumbered) 26 pages contain an alphabetic index of the sermons by title. The next 622 numbered pages, contain on each page the title of the sermon, a Bible reference, often followed by a few sentences about the content. Then remarks about where and when the sermon was delivered, often with details such as names of some present or absent, or remarks like 'no one from elsewhere', 'mixed service', 'suburb meeting'. Sermons 1–270 mostly start in the period 1936–1940. The part from page 271 seems to start from January 1941 and runs until 422 (1943) is mainly chronological, but the pages after that less so. From 619a until 622 all the notes are from Manokwari from May 1951 until February 1952. It would seem that after this Alt switched to making sermon notes in the Alt NBG Bijbel (see above). In Manokwari she no longer travelled extensively and therefore the sermon book was used less. After 1952 only two references, both from 1955, have been found. The book is in the possession of Ruth Groeneveld.

Kuyper, C. (translator). *Lichtstralen op den Levensweg* (*Light beams on the journey of life*). Amsterdam: Egelings Boekhandel, 1903, 800 pp. A morning and evening reading of Bible verses for every day. A gift from Marie Jansz to Alt on her first birthday (22 August 1911) at Taju. It contains 659 handwritten notes in the margin during the period 1919–1962, of which 88% are between 1921–1927.

Spurgeon, C.H. *Voor iederen morgen. Dagboek voor huisgezin of binnenkamer* (*Morning by Morning. Book for daily devotions for family or inner room*). Translation by D.P.M. Huet, sixth printing, originally Amsterdam: W.H. Kirberger, 1870. It contains 488 handwritten notes in the margins and on pasted in or loose sheets in the period 1921–1961, of which a quarter were made between 1921–1927 and over two third in the period 1950–1954.

Letters from M.A. Alt

Collection Evert van der Molen, 28 letters/postcards 1950–1953.
Collection Henk Sleebos, 7 letters 1954–1960.
Collection Dick Groeneveld, 9 letters 1949–1955.
Other letters, 6 letters 1910–1962.

Other publications Pinksterzending under auspices of M.A. Alt

Paul, J. *In Jezus' handen: Een ernstig woord tot genezingzoekenden (In Jesus' hands: A serious word for those seeking healing)*. Magelang: Theng Tjoen Gwan, [1937], 88 pp.; 2nd printing Surabaya: Pinksterzending/Assemblies of God in Indonesia, 1948, 60pp. In 1928 also as series in *Gouden Schooven*.

Series about Sanctification. Lawang: Pinksterzending.
1. [Paul, J.] *Geeft den Heiligen Geest plaats (Allow room for the Holy Spirit)*. Lawang: Pinksterzending, [1937], 35 pp.
2. [Paul, J.], *Pinkstervuur (Pentecostal Fire)*. Lawang: Pinksterzending, [1938], 27 pp.
3. Paul, J. *Hoe kan ik heilig leven (How can I live sanctified)*. Lawang: Pinksterzending, [1939], 35 pp.

New Series about Sanctification (previous one out of print).
1. Steinberger, G. *Het geheim van overwinning over de zonde (The secret of victory over sin)*. Surabaya: Pinksterzending/Assemblies of God [1948], 36 pp.; 2nd printing Velp: Pinksterzending, [1971], 36 pp.
2. Torrey, R.A. *De doop met den Heiligen Geest (The Baptism with the Holy Spirit)*. Surabaya: Pinksterzending/Assemblies of God [1948], 33 pp.
Uiteenzetting van Fundamentele Waarheden. Goedgekeurd Door de Algemene Raad van de Assemblies of God (Exposition of Fundamental Truths. Approved by the General Council of the Assemblies of God), Surabaya: Pinksterzending, 1948, traktaat.

Voor U (For You). Klein traktaat, [1948], [not found]. Probably the same as 'Voor U' in *Gouden Schoven* July 1953, p. 20, a conversation between Jesus and a believer.

Brasch, M. von. *Volkomen Verlossing in Christus (Full Deliverance in Christ)*. Surabaya: Pinksterzending, n.d., stencil, 103 pp. Translation by M.A. Alt of M. von Brasch, *Völlige Erlösung in Christo!* Brokstedt Holstein: Verlag Rotensande, [1939]. On page 3 of the original Moes writes in the margin: 'This book has been to me an unlimited blessing and revealed to me the full deliverance of spirit, soul and body'. On 25 May 1955, she writes in her diary that the book by Baroness von Brasch has been a rich blessing.

BIBLIOGRAPHY

'Het aantal Christenen in Nederlandsch Oost-Indië', *Nederlands Zendingsblad* 20 (1937), pp. 153-54.

Abell, F.A. 'Verslag', *GS* 11.4 (February 1938), p. 11.

Abkoude, F. van, 'Uit den Arbeid', *Pinksterkracht* 3.10 (October 1927), p. 11

Alt, M.A., 'Gedichtenbundel 1899-1906' (Poem Book).

—'Geachte heer Velthuijsen', *De Boodschapper* (February 1909), p. 31.

—'Uit Insulinde', *De Boodschapper* (September 1909), p. 165.

—'Dagboek 1910-1919'.

—'Het Spiritisme', *De Boodschapper* (February 1910), pp. 25-27.

—'De doop van Zr. Alt', *De Boodschapper* (May 1910), pp. 87-88.

—'Mijn vrede geef Ik u', *De Boodschapper* (October 1910), pp. 182-87.

—'Goede tijding', *De Boodschapper* (March 1911), pp. 31-32.

—'Uit een brief van Zr. Alt', *De Boodschapper* (March 1915), p. 60.

—'Uit Gambang Waloh', *De Boodschapper* (February 1916), pp. 45-46; 40 (April 1917), pp. 142-45; 45 (February 1921), pp. 36-37; 47 (March 1922), pp. 48, 62-64; 47 (April 1922), pp. 92-96.

—'Een blik op het werk van Zr. Alt', *De Boodschapper* (May 1916), pp. 134-35.

—'Van Zr. Alt', *De Boodschapper* (August 1916), pp. 238-39.

—'Goed nieuws uit Gambang Waloh', *De Boodschapper* (June 1918), pp. 205-206.

—'Brief van Zr. Alt', *De Boodschapper* (February 1919), p. 54.

—'Een treffend schrijven van Zr. Alt', *De Boodschapper* (May 1919), pp. 144-47.

—'Een brief van Zuster Alt over de plaats der vrouw in de gemeente', *De Boodschapper* (June 1920), pp. 156-57.

—'Een brief van Zuster Alt', *De Boodschapper* (November 1921), pp. 281-83.

—'Gambang Waloh', *Pinksterkracht* 3.2 (February 1927), pp. 15-16.

—'Gambang Waloh,' *Spade Regen* 20.2 (May 1927), pp. 31-31.

—'Java', *Spade Regen* 20.4 (July 1927), pp. 63-64.

—'Correspondentie', *Pinksterkracht* 4.1 (January 1928), pp. 8-9.

—'Onze Conferentie', *Pinksterkracht* 4.6 (June 1928), pp. 3-8.

—'Aan de lezers en lezeressen van ons blad', *GS* 4.9 (September 1928), p. 2.

—'Waarom ik mij bij de Pinkstergemeente heb aangesloten', *GS* 5.4 (April 1929), pp. 3-6.

—'Uit de correspondentie', *GS* 5.4 (April 1929), pp. 23-24.

—'Kennisgeving', *GS* 5.4 (April 1929), pp. 37-38; 8.22 (November 1932), p. 19; 10.14 (July 1934), p. 14; 10.22 (November 1934), p. 19; 19.3 (March 1950), p. 15; 20.5 (May 1951), p. 24; 22.1 (January 1953), p. 11.

—'Gambang Waloeh', *GS* 5.6 (June 1929), pp. 17-19.

—'Opwekkingsdiensten te Bandjermasin, Zuid-Borneo', *GS* 5.12 (December 1929), pp. 30-37.

—'En 't was avond geweest – en 't was morgen geweest – een nieuwen dag', *GS* 6.1 (January 1930), pp. 16-17.

—'De Pinkstergemeente', *GS* 6.2 (January 1930), pp. 19-20.

—'Onze verhuizing', *GS* 6.10 (March 1930), pp. 17-18; 9.10 (May 1936), p. 20; 9.13 (July 1936), p. 16.

—'De heilige Theresia', *GS* 6.14 (April 1930), pp. 14-16.

—'De inwijding van ons huis', *GS* 6.15 (April 1930), p. 17.

—'Aan onze Roomsch-Katholieke broeders en zusters', *GS* 6.17 (May 1930), pp. 7-8.

—'Voor nadenkende geloovigen', *GS* 6.18 (June 1930), pp. 12-13.

—'Groote overgang', *GS* 6.19 (June 1930), pp. 3-4.

—'Bandjermasin', *GS* 6.19 (June 1930), pp. 15-17.

—'Muziek', *GS* 6.27 (October 1930), pp. 4-5.

—'Opwekkingsdienst te Paree', *GS* 6.28 (November 1930), pp. 10-11.

—'Onze Vader in den hemel, Die de gebeden, verhoort', *GS* 7.1 (January 1931), pp. 18.

—'Soemobito', *GS* 7.4 (February 1931), pp. 11-12.

—'Broeder Frits IV', *GS* 7.6 (March 1931), pp. 10-12.

—'Het merkteeken van het Beest', *GS* 7.6 (March 1931), pp. 16-17.

—'Nieuwe opwekking te Gambang Waloeh', *GS* 7.7 (April 1931), pp. 11-12.

—'Een evangelist bij de gratie Gods: Br. Daniel Wilkens', *GS* 7.8 (April 1931), pp. 9-11.

—'Aanvragen om opwekkingsdiensten', *GS* 7.10 (May 1931), p. 24.

—'Doopdienst te Kediri', *GS* 7.11 (June 1931), p. 11; *GS* 7.13 (July 1931), pp. 12-13.

—'Ngoro', *GS* 7.11 (June 1931), p. 12.

—'Tegal', *GS* 7.12 (June 1931), p. 10.

—'Onze jonge werkers', *GS* 7.12 (June 1931), pp. 19-20.

—'De ontplooiing van het vrouwelijk kunnen', *GS* 7.13 (July 1931), p. 20.

—'Teekenen des Tijds', *GS* 7.14 (July 1931), pp. 16-18; *GS* 14.2 (January 1941), p. 11.

—'Geestelijke gaven in verband met onze persoonlijkheid', *GS* 7.16 (August 1931), pp. 4-5.

—'Verwachten wij de groote opwekking of eerst het Duizendjarig Rijk?' *GS* 7.16 (August 1931), pp. 11-12.

—'Onze reis naar Makasser', *GS* 7.22 (November 1931), pp. 8-12.

—'De melaatschen-kolonie Dana Radja', *GS* 8.8 (April 1932), pp. 4-7.

—'Hoe God de vrouwen gebruikt voor Zijn dienst', *GS* 8.9 (May 1932), p. 16.

—'Bruiloft in de desa', *GS* 8.13 (July 1932), pp. 15-17.

—'Inspiratie', *GS* 8.16 (August 1932), pp. 5-6.

—'De bevolking van Elim', *GS* 8.16 (August 1932), pp. 16-17.

—'Het swastica-kruis', *GS* 8.18 (September 1932), p. 4.

—'Correspondentie', *GS* 8.20 (October 1932), 18; *GS* 11.21 (November 1938), p. 17.

—'De Joden-vervolgingen', *GS* 8.21 (November 1932), pp. 9-10.

—'Bij intrede 1933', *GS* 9.2 (January 1933), pp. 16-17.

—'Mag de vrouw spreken in de gemeente?' *GS* 9.6 (March 1933), pp. 4-7.

—'Aan het einde van 't jaar', *GS* 9.24 (December 1933), pp. 23-24.

—'Berichten van het arbeidsveld', *GS* 10.1 (January 1934), p. 7; 10.15 (1937), p. 17; 16.3 (March 1947), p. 12; 16.11 (November 1947), p. 2; 17.5 (May 1948), p. 9; 17.9 (September 1948), pp 13; 17.11 (November 1948), p. 23; 18.1 (January 1949), p. 18; 19.6 (June 1950), p. 17; 20.2 (February 1951), p. 20; 20.4 (April 1951), p. 20.

—'Eén doop' *GS* 10.5 (March 1934), pp. 12-13.

—'Bijbelschool voor Javaansche jongens', *GS* 10.9 (May 1934), p. 23.

—'Vrijheid', *GS* 10.12 (June 1934), pp. 5-7.

—'Wat de Pinkstergemeente (over de gehele wereld), pp. gelooft en leert', *GS* 10.15 (August 1934), pp. 4-6.

—'Onze Broederbond', *GS* 10.16 (August 1934), pp. 7-8.

—'De bediening van den Heiligen Doop', *GS* 10.17 (September 1934), pp. 4-7.

—'De Tienden', *GS* 10.19 (October 1934), pp. 4-6.

—'De lofzang des Geestes', *GS* 10.23 (December 1934), pp. 4-6.

—'Ik geloof in één heilige algemeene kerk', *GS* 10.23 (December 1934), pp. 7-8.

—'De Pinksterzending', *GS* 11.4 (February 1935), pp. 18-19.

—'Het spreken van de vrouw in de gemeente', *GS* 11.5 (March 1935), pp. 4-6.

—'Bezoek van de Brs. Howard Carter en Sumrall', *GS* 11.9 (May 1935), pp. 14-15.

—'Afscheidsmeeting van de Brs. Carter en Sumrall', *GS* 11.11 (June 1935), pp. 9-11.

—'Onze cosmopolitische Pinksterkringen', *GS* 11.23 (December 1935), p. 11.

—'Wat is het teeken van den Geestesdoop?' *GS* 11.24 (December 1935), pp. 14-16.

—'De Pinksterzending in België', *GS* 9.2 (January 1936), p. 8.

—'Gedachten over de Sabbat', *GS* 9.3 (February 1936), pp. 4-6.

—'Onze Pinksterzending-school', *GS* 9.3 (February 1936), p. 14.

—'Iets over Pa van der Steur', *GS* 9.5 (March 1936), pp. 17-18.

—'Vragen-Beantwoording', *GS* 9.9 (May 1936), p. 13.

—'Afscheidssamenkomst te Kediri', *GS* 9.12 (June 1936), pp. 19-20.

—'Voor het dagelijksch leven: Zenuwachtigheid', *GS* 9.18 (September 1936), pp. 12-13.

—'Drieënvijftig jaren', *GS* 9.18 (September 1936), pp. 14-15.

—'Inwijding nieuwe zaal in Lawang', *GS* 9.21 (November 1936), pp. 9-10.

—'Het charisma der extase', *GS* 9.24 (December 1936), pp. 11-13.

—'Gedachten over gebedsgenezing', *GS* 10.2 (January 1937), pp. 4-6.

—'Genezing door het geloof', *GS* 10.8 (April 1937), pp. 5-7.

—'Onze Japansche evangelist', *GS* 10.18 (September 1937), p. 17.

—'Een wonderbaar resultaat', *GS* 10.20 (October 1937), pp. 15-16.

—'Aansluiting bij den Zendingsstudieraad', *GS* 10.20 (October 1937), p. 18.

—'Worden alle geloovigen opgenomen?' *GS* 10.22 (November 1937), pp. 12-13.

—'Ons ziele-leven', *GS* 10.23 (December 1937), pp. 4-5,

—'Bekeert U!' *GS* 11.5 (March 1938), pp. 20-21.

—'Waarom heb ik geen contact meer met God?' *GS* 11.7 (April 1938), pp. 4-5.

—'Het bewijs van den Geestesdoop', *GS* 11.8 (April 1938), pp. 10-11.

—'Naschrift Redactie', *GS* 11.11 (June 1938), p. 10.

—'Vragenrubriek', *GS* 11.12 (June 1938), pp. 6, 13-14; *GS* 16.10 (October 1947), p. 9; *GS* 16.10 (October 1947), pp. 9-10; 16.12 (December 1947), p. 12.

—'Gambang Waloeh', *GS* 11.12 (June 1938), p. 11.

—'De Waterdoop', *GS* 11.13 (July 1938), pp. 6-8; 13.18 (September 1940), p. 7.

—'Nogmaals de Waterdoop', *GS* 11.17 (September 1938), pp. 19-21.

—'Br. S. Miyahira', *GS* 11.16 (August 1938), p. 6.

—'Worden in de Pinksterzending ook de ambten gehandhaafd?' *GS* 11.19 (October 1938), p. 10.

—'Kan een kind Gods verloren gaan? ' *GS* 11.20 (October 1938), pp. 16-17.

—'Naschrift van de Redactie *G.S*', *GS* 11.23 (December 1938), p. 10.

—'Bruiloft te Gambang Waloeh', *GS* 12.20 (October 1939), pp. 18-19.

—'Onze Kerstvieringen', *GS* 13.2 (January 1940), pp. 4-7.

—'John Sung en zijn boodschap VI', *GS* 13.1 (January 1940), pp. 9-10.

—'Ons auto-ongeval', *GS* 13.6 (March 1940), pp. 7-8.

—'Hebt gij den Heiligen Geest ontvangen als gij geloofd hebt?' *GS* 13.9 (May 1940), pp. 4-5.

—'Rouw en droevenis', *GS* 13.11 (1 June 1940), p. 4.

—'Het profetisch woord dat zeer vast is. Tijdsprediking', *GS* 13.12 (June 1940), pp. 4-5.

—'De Wederkomst van Christus', *GS* 13.15 (August 1940), pp. 4-7.

—'De vervulling met den Heiligen Geest', *GS* 14.2 (January 1941), pp. 4-5.

—'In welk opzicht verschilt de Pinksterzending van de Protestant-sche Kerk?' *GS* 14.3 (February 1941), p. 13.

—'Opwekking onder Javanen', *GS* 14.12 (June 1941), pp. 5-6;

—'De Openbaring van Johannes XIV', *GS* 14.15 (August 1941), pp. 16-18.

—'Vrouw en de Kerk', *Indische Courant* 9 October 1941, referring to 'Vrouw en kerk' in *Indische Courant* (3 October 1941).

—'Vragenrubriek: Mag de vrouw spreken in de Gemeente?' *GS* 14.22 (November 1941), pp. 16-17.

—'Autobiografie 1943'.

—'Dagboek 1945-1961'.

—'Kerstviering in vrijheid', *GS* 19.1 (December 1946), pp. 1-2.

—*Van hart tot hart,* 1947. Reprint of 1934.

—'De eerste en de tweede zalving', *GS* 16.1 (January 1947), pp. 2-3.

—'Opdat zij allen een zijn', *GS* 16.2 (February 1947), pp. 1-2.

—'Kom Heilige Geest!' *GS* 16.3 (March 1947), pp. 1-3.

—'Onze Feestdag', *GS* 16.10 (October 1947), p. 5.

—*Ons Kampleven gedurende de Japansche en Rupublikeinsche bezetting* (Surabaya: De Pinksterzending – Assemblies of God in Indonesië, [1948]).

—*Mag de vrouw spreken in de Gemeente?* (Surabaya: Pinksterzending, 1948).

—*Wat gebeurt er met ongeboren kinderen?* (Surabaya: Pinksterzending, 1948).

—'Wedergeboren', *GS* 17.2 (February1948), p. 3.

—'Van Sabbat tot Pinksteren 1-3', *GS* 17.2 (February 1948), pp. 6-7; *GS* 17.3 (March 1948), pp. 4-6; *GS* 17.4 (April 1948), pp. 4-5.

—'Asal moelanja dan riwajat berdirinja The Assemblies of God (preface)', *Gandoem Mas* 10.1 (May 1948), p. 9.

—'Hoe Gods Geest op Gambang Waloeh viel 1-4', *GS* 17.5 (May 1948), pp. 4-6; 17.6 (June 1948), pp. 3-5; 17.7 (July 1948), pp. 4-5; 17.8 (August 1948), pp. 3.

—*Het Innerlijk Licht: Gedachten en Meditatieën* (Surabaya: Assemblies of God, [1949]).

—'Hebben wij de overwinning over de zonde?' *GS* 18.5 (May 1949), p. 10.

—'Pemberian Tahoe', *Gandoem Mas,* 10.1 (May 1948), p. 16.

—'Gezegende samenwerking', *GS* 17.6 (June 1948), p. 12.

—'Overgave', *GS* 17.9 (September 1948), p. 2.

—'Heerlijke berichten van Gambang Waloeh', *GS* 17.10 (October 1948), p. 8.

—'Goede tijding van Gambang Waloeh', *GS* 18.9 (September 1949), p. 16.

—'Jaarwisseling', *GS* 19.1 (January 1950), pp. 3-4; 28.1 (January 1959), pp. 3-4.

—'Nieuw-Guinea', *GS* 19.4 (April 1950), p. 15.

—'Makasser', *GS* 19.4 (April 1950), p. 16.

—'Onze Indonesische gemeenten', *GS* 19.6 (June 1950), pp. 16-17.

—'Moet de gelovige bidden om de Heilige Geest?' *GS* 19.7 (July 1950), pp. 3-4.

—'Hoe Jezus te volgen?' *GS* 19.8 (August 1950), pp. 22-23.

—'Een vijfdaagse Evangelisatie-Conferentie', *GS* 19.10 (October 1950), pp. 17-18.

—'Onze Evangelisatie-reis door West- en Midden-Java', GS 19.11 (November 1950), pp. 3-5.

—*Bijbel-Studie voor zelf-onderricht* (Surabaya: Pinksterzending, [1951]).

—'Br. Th. Den Daas', *GS* 20.2 (February 1951), p. 21.

—'Paas-Opwekkingsdienst te Soerabaja', *GS* 20.6 (June 1951), p. 14.

—'Reisbrieven', *GS* 20.9 (July 1951), pp. 22-24.

—'De Doop met de Heilige Geest', *GS* 21.3 (March 1952), pp. 3-6.

—'Wettisch Christendom', *GS* 21.4 (April 1952), p. 13.

—'Brieven uit Nieuw-Guinea', *GS* 21.6 (June 1952), pp. 22-24; 21.10 (October 1952), pp. 19-21; 22.6 (June 1953), pp. 20-22; 22.12 (December 1953), pp. 17-19; 23.6 (June 1954), pp. 21-22; 23.7 (July 1954), pp. 20-21; 27.9 (September 1958), pp. 22-23; 27.11 (November 1958), pp. 20-21; 27.12 (December 1958), pp. 22-23; 30.5 (May 1960), pp. 22-23.

—'Allerlei uit Israël. De Bijbel als aanklager', *GS* 21.8 (August 1952), p. 10.

—'Noot van de redactie', *GS* 21.11 (November 1952), pp. 20-21.

—'De zalving met olie volgens Jakobus', *GS* 21.12 (December 1952), pp. 17-18.

—'Gevraagd: Hartelijke voorbede voor Glorieklokken', *GS* 22.5 (May 1953), pp. 21-22.

—'En zij werden allen vervuld met de Heilige Geest', *GS* 23.6 (June 1954), pp. 3-4.

—'De twaalf geloofs-artikelen', *GS* 23.11 (November 1954), p. 6.

—*Mag de vrouw spreken in de Gemeente?* (Manokwari: [Pinksterzending], 1956).

—'Mogen christenen wijn drinken?' *GS* 25.6 (June 1956), pp. 13-14.

—'Brieven uit Manokwari', *GS* 24.7 (July 1955), pp. 21-22.; 26.1 (January 1957), pp. 20-21; 28.1 (January 1959), pp. 22-23; 32.5 (May 1961), pp. 21-23; 32.6 (June 1961), pp. 22-23; 32.7 (July 1961), pp. 22-23.

—'Pinksterzegen als in de dagen der Apostelen', *GS* 25.5 (May 1956), pp. 3-4.

—'Israël het Wondervolk', *GS* 26.4 (April 1957), pp. 12-13.

—'Bezoek aan Gambang Waloeh', *GS* 26.11 (November 1957), pp. 18-21.

—'Kerstfeest te Gambang Waloeh', *GS* 28.6 (June 1959), pp. 18-21.

—'Predikantenvergadering Nederlands Hervormde Kerk', *GS* 28.6 (June 1959), pp. 22-23.

—*In het volle licht: Dagboekje voor het huisgezin* (Manokwari: Pinksterzending, 1960).

—'Wat verwacht de Gemeente Gods voor 1960?' *GS* 30.1 (January 1960), pp. 3-5.

—'De wereld van heden', *GS* 30.10 (October 1960), pp. 10-11.

—'De Kerk en de Pinkstergroepen', *GS* 32.3 (March 1961), pp. 6-8.

—'Broeder Johannes de Heer. In Memoriam', *GS* 32.5 (May 1961), p. 24.

—'Onze reis met M.S. Zuiderkruis', *GS* 32.12 (December 1961), pp. 20-22.

—'Hoe kan ik gezond worden?' *GS* 33.1 (January 1962), pp. 7-8.

—'Ons maandelijks verslag', *GS* 33.2 (February 1962). pp. 16-17; 33.4 April 1962), pp. 16-17.

—'In Memoriam Moe Graafstal-van der Steur', *GS* 33.3 (March 1962), p. 23.

—'Berichten uit Indonesië en Nieuw-Guinea', *GS* 33.4 (April 1962), p. 19.

—*Glorieklokken. Liederen voor solo en samenzang* (Gorinchem: Kracht van Omhoog, 1963).

—*Herinneringen uit mijn leven.* Velp: Pinksterzending, 1963.

Anderson, Allan, *Spreading Fires: The Missionary Nature of Early Pentecostalism* (London: SCM, 2007).

Aritonang, Jan S. and Karel Steenbrink (eds.), *A History of Christianity in Indonesia* (Leiden: Brill, 2008).

Andes, F., 'Getuigenissen', *GS* 13.13 (July 1940), p. 20.

Andes, P., 'Getuigenissen', *GS* 13.9 (May 1940), p. 20.

Baarbé, C., *Dr. Sung: Een réveil op Java* (Lichtstralen op de akker der wereld 50.3. The Hague: Voorhoeve, [1949]).

Bakker, A., 'Pieter Hendrik Fonds', *De Boodschapper* (January 1909), p. 11.

Barfoot, Charles H. and Gerald T. Sheppard, 'Prophetic vs. Priestly Religion: The Changing Role of Women Clergy in Classical Pentecostal Churches', *Review of Religious Research* 22 (1980), pp. 2-17.

Barrett, David B., George T. Kurian and Todd M. Johnson, *Word Christian Encyclopedia 1* (Oxford: Oxford University Press, 2001).

Beek, W.A. van, 'In memoriam Zr. M.A. Alt', *Pinksterboodschap* 3.4 (April 1962), pp. 4-5.

'Begrooting van Nederlandsch-Indie voor het dienstjaar 1921, 4.10', *Handelingen der Staten-Generaal. Bijlagen 1920-1921*, appendix B, p. 77.

'Belangrijk nieuws uit Indië', *De Boodschapper* (November 1910), p. 212.

Bender, Harold S., W.F. Golterman and Leo Laurense, 'Doopsgezinde Zendingsraad' (1990), in *Global Anabaptist Mennonite Encyclopedia Online* (http://gameo.org/index.php?title=Doopsgezinde_Zendingsraad).

Berg, H.W. van den, 'De Pinkstergemeente,' *De Opwekker* 79 (1934), pp. 136-52.

'Bericht uit Nieuw-Guinea', *GS* 38.1 (January 1967), pp. 19-20.

Bernard, Wm., 'Brief', *Spade Regen* (November 1922), p. 128.

—'Java has never had a revival', *Things Old and New* 3.1 (April 1923), pp. 7-9.

—'Letter from Wm. Bernard', *Spade Regen* 16.4 (July 1923), p. 63.

—'Letter from Wm. Bernard', *Things Old and New* 3.3 (August 1923), p. 7.

—'Pentecost in Java', *The Latter Rain* 20.6 (March 1928), pp. 22-23.

'Een bezoek aan Sitiardjo', *Nederlandsch Zendingsblad* 19 (1936), p. 57.

Bilkes, Rosa, *De Spinazieacademie: 125 jaar Haags huishoudonderwijs* (The Hague: Haags Historisch Museum, 2012).

Biografie F.G. van Gessel (Amsterdam: Bride Tidings International, n.d).

Bo, Liem Hong, 'Kan God niet wonderen van genezing doen?', *GS* 14.12 (June 1941), pp. 15-16.

Boddy, A.A., 'Pentecostal Items', *Confidence* 5.2 (February 1912), p. 43.

Boissevain, H.D.J., *De zending in Oost en West: Verleden en Heden 2* (Zeist: Zendingsstudie-Raad, 1945).

'Bond voor Evangelisatie in Ned. O.-Indië', *Ons Orgaan* 18.280 (August 1923), pp. 268-69.

Bosma, Ulbe, Remco Raben and Wim Willems, *De geschiedenis van de Indische Nederlanders* (Amsterdam: Bert Bakker, 2008).

Brakkee, C.H.G.H., *Pa van der Steur vader van 7000 kinderen* (Eindhoven: B.O.S., 1981).

Brandl, Bernd, *Die Neukirchener Mission: ihre Geschichte als erste deutsche Glaubensmission* (Keulen: Rheinland Verlag, 1998).

Brasch, M. von, *Völlige Erlösung in Christo!* (Brokstedt Holstein: Verlag Rotensande, [1939]).

Brink, J.E. van den, 'Bij het heengaan van Zuster M.A. Alt', *Kracht van Omhoog* 25.19 (6 April 1962), p. 10.

Brodland, R.G., 'Bethel Temple Seattle's Missionary Church,' *Pentecostal Power Anniversary Edition* (1989), pp. 6-8, 14.

Brouwer, Melattie, *History of the Salvation Army in Indonesia 1 1894-1949* (Hawthorn, Victoria: Citadel Press, 1996).

Carlblom, Harold, 'History of Pentecostal/Assemblies of God Missions in Indonesia' (1979). Present in Assemblies of God World Missions Archive.

Carlos, Poldi, *Johannes van der Steur. Een Haarlemse diamant in de Gordel van Smaragd* (n.p.: [1998]).

Carter, Howard, *New York ... Tokyo ... Moscow ... When Time Flew By* (London: Hampstead Publications, 1936).

Colijn, Helen, *De kracht van een lied: Overleven in een vrouwenkamp* (Franeker: Van Wijnen, 1989).

Cooley, Frank L., *Indonesia: Church & Society* (New York: Friendship Press, 1968).

Delden, Mary C. van, *De republikeinse kampen in Nederlands-Indië oktober 1945-mei 1947: Orde in de chaos?* (Kockengen: by the author, 2007).

Descoeudres, 'Camp d'Internement Tawangsari à Lawang', Report of a visit on behalf of the International Red Cross, dated 13 February 1946.

Devin, R.M., 'Netherlands East Indies', *Pentecost* 8 (June 1949), p. 6.

—'Pendahoeloean Kata', *Gandoem Mas* 10.1 (May 1948), pp. 2-3.

Dharmowijono, W., *Van koelies, klontongs en kapiteins: het beeld van de Chinezen in Indisch-Nederlands literair proza 1880-1950* (PhD Dissertation, Faculty of Humanities, University of Amsterdam, 2009. http://dare.uva.nl/record/1/319403).

Direktori Gereja-Gereja, Yayasan, Pendidikan Agama dan Keagamaan Kristen di Indonesia 2013 (Jakarta: Kementerian Agama Republik Indonesia, Direktorat Jenderal Bimbingan Masyarakat Kristen, 2013).

Djaja, Theophilus Karunia, *Sejarah Gereja Pantekosta di Indonesia* (Semarang: GPdI, 1993).

Djie Chen Chu, Francesca and Westa Kwee Oen Hwie, 'Hian Ting Djie: Our Beloved Opa', in *To Tjhoe Khee Pok: Djie Family Reunion* (Kediri: private publication, 2014).

[Djie, Th.], *Verkondigt de pinkstergemeente het gansche evangelie en wat gelooft en leert de pinkstergemeente* (Kediri: Pinkstergemeente in Nederlandsch-Indië, 1933).

Doel, H.W. van der, *Afscheid van Indië: De val van het Nederlandse imperium in Azië* (Amsterdam: Prometheus, 2000).

'Donker Java', *De Boodschapper* (July 1914), p. 109.

'Doopbediening door een vrouw', *De Boodschapper* (January 1906), pp. 17-19.

Drost, J.D., 'De Pinksterbeweging en wij', *Kerkbode van de ECK te Hollandia* 2.9 (1 October 1957).

'A Dutch University Student's Pentecost', *Cloud of Witnesses to Pentecost in India* 8 (August 1908), pp. 25-26.

Dumas, Ch., *Waar Hagenaars kerkten: geschiedenis van de Haagse kerken gebouwd voor 1900* (The Hague: Boekencentrum, 1983).

Eeden, Frederik van, *Dagboek 1878-1923 Volume 4 1919-1923* (ed. H.W. van Tricht; Culemborg: Tjeenk Willink/Noorduijn, 1971).

Ekkart, R.E.O., 'Het geslacht Wigleven in Nederland', *Gens Nostra* 20 (1965), pp. 353-66.

End, Th. van den, ed., *Bladen uit mijn levensboek: Autobiografie van Ds. C.J. Hoekendijk (1873-1948)* (The Hague: Boekencentrum, 1993).

—*De Nederlandse Zendingsvereniging in West-Java 1858-1963* (Oegstgeest: Raad voor de Zending, 1991).

End, Th. van den and J. Weitjens, *Ragi Carita 2: Sejarah Gereja Di Indonesia 1860-an-Sekarang* (Jakarta: BPK. Gunung Mulia, 1999).

Fulton, J.E., 'A Letter', *North Pacific Union Gleaner* 3.39 (20 January 1909), p. 2.

Gabriël. J.C., 'Opwekkingsdiensten in Kediri en omstreken', *GS* 6.24 (1930). pp. 10-11.

Gee, Donald, 'Het Apostel-ambt: Heeft het opgehouden te bestaan?' *GS* 13.11 (June 1940), pp. 15-16.

'De geestdrijver Thiessen', *Sumatra Post* (5 June 1924).

Gelder, H.E. van, *'s-Gravenhage in zeven eeuwen* (Amsterdam: Meulenhof, 1937).

'De Gemeenten van God', *Indische Courant* (16 March 1935).

Gereja Gerakan Pentakosta. *Api Yang Tak Pernah Padam: Jubileum 90 tahun Gereja Gerakan Pentakosta (Pinksterbeweging)* (Jakarta: Gereja Gerakan Pentakosta, 2013).

Gonggryp, G.F.E. (ed.), *Geïllustreerde Encyclopaedie van Nederlands-Indië* (Leiden: Leidsche Uitgeversmaatschappij, 1934).

Graafstal, Marie, 'Zuster Slagter's feestdag', *Indische Courant* (5 November 1930).

Graafstal-van der Steur, S.M., 'Christelijke Philanthropie', *Nieuws van den dag voor Nederlandsch-Indië* (7 October 1939).

Groeneveld, D., 'Hoe het gebeurde', *GS* 33.5 (May 1962), pp. 17-18.

—'Wat lezers schreven over Zuster Alt', *GS* 33.10 (October 1962), pp. 21-23.

—'In Memoriam', *GS* 56.3 (March 1985), p. 4.

—*Naar onbeperkte ruimte: Memoires van D. Groeneveld* (Duiven: GMI Music, 2007).

Groot, A.K. de, 'Een Chineesch Opwekkingsprediker te Batavia', *Nederlands Zendingsblad* 22 (1939), pp. 123-25.

G[rullemans-V[elthuijsen], S., 'Gambang Waloh', *Soerabaijasch Handelsblad* (25 January 1921).

[Haeften, G.A.], ed., *Koninklijk Conservatorium voor Muziek te 's-Gravenhage, 1826-1926* (The Hague: Mouton, 1926).

Hananot, Ongkie, *Pdt. Jetro Bunjamin: Dari Gambarsari ke Batu Tulis* (Jakarta: n.p., 1995).

'A History of the Pentecostal Movement in Indonesia', *Asian Journal of Pentecostal Studies* 4.1 (2001), pp. 131-48.

Heek-de Graaf, A.J.C. van, 'Vergeet ons niet', *GS* 53.11 (November 1982), pp. 14-16.

Hildering, H.A.C., 'John Sung', *Nederlandsch Zendingsblad* 23 (1940), pp. 16-18.

Hook, Milton, *An Oriental Foster Child: Adventism in South-East Asia before 1912* (Wahroona, Australië: Adventist Education, n.d.).

Hoon, Chang-Yau, 'Between evangelism and multiculturalism: The dynamics of Protestant Christianity in Indonesia', *Social Compass: International review of sociology of religion* 60.4 (December 2013), pp. 457-70. http://jounals.sagepub.com/doi/abs/10.1177/0037768 613502758.

Jansz, M., 'Een veilige weg', *De Boodschapper* (August 1893), pp. 155-56.

—'Aan de Gemeente', *De Boodschapper* (November 1904), pp. 465-66; (July 1905), pp. 622-23.

—'Pangoengsen', *De Locomotief* (13 December 1902).

—'Van Pangoengsen', *De Boodschapper* (July 1904), pp. 382-83; (November 1905), p. 706; (March 1906), p. 49; (November 1907), pp. 209—210; (January 1908), p. 7.

—'Pangoengsen', *Bataviaasch Nieuwsblad* (19 July 1904); (15 August 1904); (20 December 1905).

—'Pangoengsen', *Soerabaijasch Handelsblad* (24 December 1908).

—'Een oude bekende aan het hoofd van Pangoengsen', *Bataviaasch Nieuwsblad* (27 December 1910).

—'Donker Java', *De Boodschapper* (October 1911), p. 150.

—'Pangoengsen', *Pniël: Weekblad voor het christelijk gezin* 28.1416 (25 February 1919). pp. 49-56.

—'Zorg voor Inl. weezen', *Nieuws van den dag voor Nederlandsch-Indië* (18 October 1922).

—'Javaansche Weezenkolonie', *Bataviaasch Nieuwsblad* (20 October 1922).

Jansz, M. and M.A. Alt, 'Pangoengsen', *Bataviaasch Nieuwsblad* (16November 1912).

Jansz, Pieter, 'Een pleidooi voor den Zondag', *De Boodschapper* (December 1893), pp. 236-38.

Jensma, Th.E., *Doopsgezinde zending in Indonesië* (The Hague: Boekencentrum, 1968).

Johnson, Robert A., 'A Bibliography of Hymnals Published by American Pentecostal Denominations', *The Hymn* 38.1 (1987), pp. 29-30.

Jong, Chr.G.F. de, *De Gereformeerde Zending in Midden-Java 1931-1975* (Zoetermeer: Boekencentrum, 1997).

Jongeling, Maria Cornelia, *Het Zendingsconsulaat in Nederlandsch-Indië 1906-1942* (Arnhem: Van Loghum Slaterus, 1966).

Kamma, F.C., ed., *Kruis en korwar: Een honderdjarig vraagstuk op Nieuw-Guinea* (The Hague: Voorhoeve, 1953).

Kamma, F.C., 'Pinksterbeweging en heidendom (De Beweging op Nieuw-Guinea)', [1959].

—*'Dit wonderlijke werk': Het probleem van de communicatie tussen Oost en West gebaseerd op de ervaringen in het zendingswerk op Nieuw-Guinea (Irian Jaya), pp. 1855-1972. Een socio-missiologische benadering* (Oegstgeest: Raad voor de Zending der Ned. Hervormde Kerk, 1976).

Keil, Klara, 'De Uittocht uit Gambang Waloh', *De Boodschapper* (June 1922), pp. 155-58.

Kennedy, Nancy. 'The Story of Walter Erikson and Edward Tritt', *CIU Connection* (Spring 2010), pp. 16-20.

'Kerstfeest in de Pinkstergemeente', *Soerabaiasch Handelsblad* (19 December 1934).

Klaver, Miranda, 'Glorieklokken: Spiegel van geleefd geloof', *Parakleet* 33.125 (2013), pp. 13-15.

Klaveran [sic], D. van and C.L. van Klaveran. *Messengers of the Cross to the Peoples, Tribes, Nations of the Dutch East-Indies* (Seattle, Washington: Bethel Temple, [1926]).

Koetsier, Gerrit, 'Goede tijding uit een ver land', *GS* 19.4 (April 1950), p. 20.

Kooi, C. van der, 'Theologie in de gloria: Opmerkingen bij de Bijbelstudie voor zelfonderricht van Moesje Alt', *Parakleet* 32.124 (2012), pp. 12-14.

Kooi, Rijn van, *Bermain dengan Api, Relasi antara Gereja-gereja Mainstream dan kalangan Kharismatik den Pentakosta* (Jakarta: BPK Gunung Mulia, n.d.).

Kossmann, E.H., *The Low Countries 1780-1940* (Oxford History of Modern Europe; Oxford: Clarendon Press, 1978).

Kraemer, H., *De strijd over Bali en de zending. Een studie en een appèl* (Amsterdam:. H.J. Paris, 1933).

Kraft, A.J.C., 'Een bezoek aan Bali', *Nederlandsch Zendingsblad* 5.11 (1922), pp. 168-69.

Kusardy, R., *De Pinksterbeweging 70 jaar 29 maart 1923-29 maart 1993* (The Hague: De Pinksterbeweging, 1993).

Kuyper, C., trans., *Lichtstralen op den Levensweg* (Amsterdam: Egelings Boekhandel, 1903).

Laan, Cornelis van der, *Sectarian Against His Will: Gerrit Roelof Polman and the Birth of Pentecostalism in the Netherlands* (Studies in Evangelicalism 11; Metuchen, NJ: Scarecrow, 1991).

—'Johan Thiessen, Margaretha Alt and the Birth of Pentecostalism in Indonesia', *PentecoStudies* 11.2 (2012), pp. 149-70.

—'Mutual Influences of Indonesian and Dutch Pentecostal Churches', *Gemi Teologi: Jurnal Teologi Kontekstual* 36.1 (April 2012), pp. 95-125.

Laan, P.N. van der, *The Question of Spiritual Unity: The Dutch Pentecostal Movement in Ecumenical Perspective* (PhD thesis, University of Birmingham, 1988).

'De levensloop van Zuster Alt', *GS* 33.4 (April 1962), pp. 6-7.

Lewis, P., 'Indonesia', in Stanley Burgess, ed., *New International Dictionary of Pentecostal and Charismatic Movements* (Grand Rapids: Eerdmans, 2001), pp. 126-31.

Lessen, A.H. van, 'Ter herdenking: Prof. ir. J. de Koning Knijff', *De Ingenieur* 40 (1925), pp. 363-64.

Lindenborn, M., *West-Java als zendingsterrein der Nederlandsche Zendingsvereeniging* (Onze Zendingsvelden III; Utrecht: Zendingsstudieraad, [1922]).

Loo, Vilan van de, *Johannes 'Pa' van der Steur (1865-1945): zijn leven, zijn werk en zijn Steurtjes* (The Hague: Stichting Tong Tong, 2015).

Lijkles, S., *Verslag omtrent het Gouvernements Krankzinnigengesticht Lawang (Residentie Pasoeroean) vanaf de opening op 23 Juni 1902 tot ultimo 1905* (Batavia: Landsdrukkerij, 1906).

Lyall, Leslie T., *A Biography of John Sung: Flame for God in the Far East* (London: China Inland Mission, 4th edn, 1961).

Marcus, R.E.H., *Van eeuwigheid tot Amen* (1996). http://www.papuaerfgoed.org/files/Marcus_nd_eeuwigheid%202.pdf.

Meijer, Hans, *In Indië geworteld: De twintigste eeuw* (Amsterdam: Bert Bakker, 2004).

Miedema, Jelle, *De Kebar 1850-1980: Sociale structuur en religie in de Vogelkop van West-Nieuw-Guinea* (Dordrecht: ICG Printing, 1984).

Ministerie van Binnenlandse Zaken, *Rapport inzake Nederlands-Nieuw-Guinea over het jaar 1960* (The Hague: MBZ, n.d.), appendix IVA.

'Minutes of the First General Conference of the Assemblies of God in Indonesia (Bethel Indies Mission)' (Jakarta, 1-5 January, 1951), pp. 1-2.

Molen, Evert van der, *Herinneringen* (Private publication, n.d.).

Moorhead, Max Wood, 'Clouds of Latter Rain Gathering Over Island of Java', *The Bridegroom Messenger* (1 February 1913), p. 4.

Nederlandsch Zendingsjaarboek voor 1937-1939. Zeist: Zendingsstudie-Raad, 1938.

Nieuwstraten, J.A., *Geschiedenis van de Zevendedags Baptiste Gemeenten in Nederland* (Haarlem: ZDB Gemeente, 1977).

Nijs, T. de and J. Sillevis (eds.), *Den Haag Geschiedenis van de stad 3: Negentiende en twintigste eeuw* (Zwolle: Waanders, 2005).

Nitisastra, Widjoje, *Population Trends in Indonesia* (Jakarta: Equinox, 2006).

Offiler, W.H., *God and His Bible* (Seattle: Bethel Temple, 1946).

Offiler, W.H., *God and His Name: A Message for Today* (2nd edn, 1932; reprint Bethel Fellowship Int., 2001).

Palmier, Leslie, *Indonesia* (London: Thames & Hudson, 1965).

'Pangoengsen', *Utrechts Nieuwsblad* (1 March 1927). Citing from *De Locomotief.*

Patoir, H., *De waarheid omtrent de Pinksterbeweging in Nederlands-Indië* (Bandung: De Pinksterbeweging, [1926]).

Paul, Jonathan, *Die Göttlichen Gaben* (Mülheim: Emil Humburg, 1908).

Pearson, Stuart, *Bittersweet: The Memoir of a Chinese-Indonesian Family in the Twentieth Century* (Singapore: National University of Singapore, 2008).

Pieter-Hendrikfonds, 'Donker Java' (October 1912).

'De Pinksterbeweging', *Bataviaasch Nieuwsblad* (6 June 1924).

'Pinksterbeweging', *Nieuws van den Dag voor Nederlandsch-Indië* (22 December 1924).

'De Pinksterbeweging', *Ons Orgaan* 18.282 (October 1923), pp. 282-83; 18.283 (November 1923), pp. 290-91; 19.285 (January 1924), pp. 308-309; 19.286 (February 1924), pp. 315-16.

Een Pinksterbroeder (A Pentecostal brother), 'Scheiden', *GS* 8.19 (October 1932), p. 16.

'De Pinkstergemeente', *Indische Courant* (10 August 1934).

'De Pinkstergemeente te Bandoeng', *Indische Courant* (22 July 1924).

'De Pinksterzending', *Soerabaiasch Handelsblad* (4 February 1935).

Pol, D., *Midden-Java ten zuiden* (Onze Zendingsvelden IV; Utrecht: Zendingsstudieraad, 1922).

Polman. G.R., 'Uit den arbeid', *Spade Regen* 15.3 (June 1922), p. 46; 18.1 (April 1925), p. 14.

298   Margaretha A. Alt

'Portugeesche Kerk bestormd', *Bataviaasch Nieuwsblad* (2 March 1939).

Pym, T.W., *Moderne psychologie en het leven van de christen* (Amsterdam: H.J. Paris, 1926).

Randwijck, M.C. Graaf van, *Handelen en denken in dienst der zending: Oegstgeest 1897-1942* (2 vols.; The Hague: Boekencentrum, 1981).

De Redactie, 'Donker Java', *De Boodschapper* (December 1922), p. 326.

Reenders, H., *De Gereformeerde Zending in Midden-Java 1859-1931* (Zoetermeer: Boekencentrum, 2001).

'Roomsche martelaren uit onze dagen', *GS* 6.22 (August 1930), p. 13.

S., M. v.d., 'Jaarverslag van de Gemeente van Zevendedags Baptisten te Haarlem over 1922', *De Boodschapper* (March 1923), p. 42.

'Sabbath-school Department Report', *Australasian Record* 15.48 (4 December 1911), p. 6.

Scanzoni, Letha Dawson and Susan Setta, 'Women in Evangelical, Holiness and Pentecostal Traditions', in Rosemary Radford Ruether and Rosemary Skinner Keller, eds., *Women & Religion in America 3 1900-1968* (San Francisco: Harper & Row, 1986), pp. 223-65.

Schotborgh, Ch., 'Verslag', *GS* 12.4 (February 1939), pp. 22-24.

Schouten, John P., 'Donker Java', *De Boodschapper* (April 1902), pp. 70-71.

—'Inzegening en Afvaardiging van Zuster Cornelia Slagter', *De Boodschapper* (October 1905), pp. 674-81.

Senduk, H.L., *Sejarah GBI. Suata Gereja Nasional Yang Termuda* (Jakarta: GBI, n.d.).

Sejarah Gereja Pentakosta di Indonesia (Jakarta: GPdI, n.d.).

Short, Kenneth G., 'Report of the Dutch East Indies' (Missionary Conference held at Springfield, MO, 16-18 March 1943).

Sigmond, J., 'Ingezonden Getuigenissen', *GS* 16.5 (May 1947), p. 12.

Simpson, Carl A., *A Critical Evaluation of the Contribution of Jonathan Paul to the Development of the German Pentecostal Movement* (PhD Thesis, Glyndŵr University, Wrexham, 2011).

Skadsheim, P.T., 'Pangoengsen, Tajoe, Java', *Union Conference Record* 11.19 (13 May 1907), pp. 2-3.

—'Country Life in Java', *The Signs of the Times* 22.20 (20 May 1907), pp. 314-15.

—'More News from Java', *Union Conference Record* 11.21 (27 May 1907), pp. 5-6.

Slagter, C., 'Een vrucht van "De Boodschapper"', *De Boodschapper* (October 1905), pp. 683-85.

—'Van Lawang', *De Boodschapper* (August 1908), pp. 147-49.

—'Van Zr. Slagter', *De Boodschapper* (February 1907), pp. 32-34; (January 1909), p. 10; (February 1909), p. 29; (April 1909), p. 90.

—'Hoe het thans gaat op Gambang Waloh ', *De Boodschapper* (April 1917), pp. 113-16.

—'Zeer verblijdend nieuws uit Gambang Waloh', *De Boodschapper* (February 1918), pp. 53-54.

—'Een aandoenlijke ontboezeming en een roepstem', *De Boodschapper* (November 1928), pp. 159-63.

Sleebos, H.C., 'In Memoriam', *Parakleet* 17 (Winter 1985), pp. 27-28.

Smit, C., *De liquidatie van een imperium: Nederland en Indonesië 1945-1962* (Amsterdam: Arbeiderspers, 1962).

Soekamto, Harsanto Adi, *Gereja Gerakan Pentakosta (Pinksterbeweging)* (Jakarta: Gereja Gerakan Pentakosta, 2005).

'Soerabaja's Bevolking', *Het Dagblad* (28 December 1947)

Spurgeon, C.H., *Voor iederen morgen. Dagboek voor huisgezin of binnenkamer* (transl. D.P.M. Huet, 6th edn; originally: Amsterdam: W.H. Kirberger, 1870).

Stefanus. S., 'Bezoek aan Gambang Waloeh', *GS* 26.11 (November 1957), pp. 18-20.

—'Indonesië: Een brief van br. S. Stefanus', *GS* 33.7 (July 1962), pp. 19-20.

—'Opwekking in de dessa', *GS* 38.8 (August 1967), pp. 17-18.

—'Uit het leven van Br. Stefanus', *GS* 49.4 (April 1978), pp. 8-10.

—'Brief van Br. Stefanus', *GS* 53.11 (November 1982), p. 18.

—'Over de kerkinwijding in Gambangwaluh', *GS* 54.11 (1983), pp. 24-25.

Stevens, Th., *Vrijmetselarij en samenleving in Nederlands-Indië en Indonesië 1764-1962* (Hilversum: Verloren, [1994]).

Sumrall, Lester, 'A Visit to a Javanese Kampong', *Redemption TidinGS* 11.14 (15 July 1935), p. 7.

—'How the Gospel Triumphed in Java', *Redemption Tidings* (28 July 1939), pp. 7-8.

—'How the Sorcerer's Power was Broken', *Pentecostal Evangel* (17 February 1940), p. 4.

—*Adventuring with Christ* (London: Marshall, Morgan and Scott, 1938; reprint South Bend, Indiana: LeSea, 1988).

Sumual, Nicky J., *Pantekosta Indonesia Suatu Sejarah* (Menado: 1981).

Suryadinata, Leo, Evi Nurvidya Arafin and Aris Ananta, *Indonesian Population: Ethnicity and Religion in a Changing Political Landscape* (Indonesian Population Series 1; Singapore: Institute of South East Studies, 2003).

Swijnenburg, J. (scribe), 'Notulen van de zesde bijeenkomst van de Commissie voor het Sektewezen' (Amsterdam, 24 April 1959).

Talumewo, Steven H., *Sejarah Gerakan Pentakosta* (Yogyakarta: ANDI, 2008).

Tapilatu, Mesakh, *Gereja-Gereja Pentakosta di Indonesia: Suatu Studie Tentang Sejarah, Organisasi, Anggota, Ibadah, Kegiatan, Ajaran dan Sikap Terhadap Gereja-Gereja Lain* (ThM Thesis, Sekolah Tinggi Theologia, Jakarta, 1982).

Teasdale, G., 'Java', *Union Conference Record* 11.14 (8 April 1907), p. 2.

—'Our Mission to Sourabaya', *The Signs of the Times* 24.17 (26 April 1909), p. 268.

'De teraardebestelling van Zr. M.A. Alt', *GS* 33.4 (April 1962), p. 10.

Theijs, C.J.H., 'Sitoebondo', *GS* 9.9 (May 1933), p. 16.

Thiessen, J., *Pakantan: Een belangrijk gedeelte van Sumatra* (Apeldoorn: J. Thiessen, 1914).

—'Brief, Bandung, 20 August 1922', *Spade Regen* 15.8 (November 1922), pp. 126-27.

—'Brief, 30 September 1922', *Spade Regen* 15.9 (December 1922), p. 143.

—'Brief, 1 November 1922, *Spade Regen* (January 1923), pp. 159-60.

—'Brief', *Spade Regen* 16.3 (June 1923), pp. 33-45.

—'Dit is het', *Dit is Het* 1.1 (July 1923), p. 69.

—'De Dienst der Vrouw in de Gemeente', *Dit is Het* 3.1 (July 1925), pp. 324-26.

—'Verklaren van moeilijke teksten', *Dit is Het* 15.11 (November 1938), p. 9.

Thiessen, H., *Het gouden jubileum van De Pinkster-Beweging* (The Hague: De Pinksterbeweging, 1973).

Tunheim, P., 'Java Mission', *Union Conference Record* 12.36 (7 September 1908), p. 25.

—'Back to Pangoengsen', *Union Conference Record* 13.7 (15 February 1909), p. 3.

Thomassen, K. (ed.), *Alba Amicorum. Vijf eeuwen vriendschap op papier gezet* (The Hague, 1990).

Ukur, Fridolin and Frank L. Cooley, *Jerih dan Juang: Laporan Nasional Survai Menyeluruh Gereja di Indonesia* (Jakarta: Lembaga Penelitan dan Studi-DGI, 1979).

Van onzen correspondent, 'Zuster M.A. Alt', *Indische Courant* (24 August 1937).

Van onzen correspondent, 'Zuster Alt en de Pinksterzending', *Indische Courant* (21 April 1938).

Velden, D. van, *De Japanse burgerkampen* (Franeker: T. Wever, 2nd edn, 1977).

Velthuijsen Jr., G., 'De inzegening van Joh. van der Steur als zendeling onder de kolonialen in Indië', *De Boodschapper* (December 1892), pp. 189-92.

—'Belangrijk bericht', *De Boodschapper* (February 1911), p. 28.

—'Donker Java', *De Boodschapper* (August 1911), pp. 113-14; (January 1915), p. 6.

—'Vragenbus: Mogen vrouwen in de gemeente voorgaan?', *De Boodschapper* (February 1916), pp. 62-63.

—'Laat het U een blijdschap zijn te helpen dragen!', *De Boodschapper* (May 1920), pp. 121-25.

—'Een waarlijk vruchtbaar leven en de gevaren die het bedreigen', *De Boodschapper* 48 (March 1923), p. 42.

—'Nadere berichtgeving van het Indische Arbeidsveld', *De Boodschapper* (January 1927), pp. 150-51.

Vizjak, G. 'Ein Brief aus Java von Kapitän Vizjak', *Der Kriegsruf* (14 March 1914); (3 July 1915).

—'Reisebericht der kapitäne Vieverglet und Vizjak aus Java', *Der Kriegsruf* (20 September 1913).

Volkstelling 1930: Deel VIII Overzicht voor Nederlands-Indië (Batavia: Landsdrukkerij, 1936).

'Voortgaande propaganda', *Bataviaasch Nieuwsblad* (15 June 1923).

Vrij, Bartje de, 'Getuigenissen', *GS* 13.13 (July 1940), pp. 19-20.

Wacker, Grant, *Heaven Below: Early Pentecostals and American Culture* (Cambridge: Harvard University Press, 2001).

Wal, Hans van de, *Een aanvechtbare en onzekere situatie: De Nederlandse Hervormde Kerk en Nieuw-Guinea 1949-1962* (Hilversum: Verloren, 2006).

Weatherhead, Leslie D., *Psychologie en leven* (Utrecht: Erven Bijleveld, 1936; Originally published as *Psychology and Life*. Hodder & Stoughton, 1934).

Weenink van Loon, D., 'Doorbraak te Tjepoe naar Joël 2 en Hand. 2 en10', *Spade Regen* 16.3 (June 1923), pp. 38-41. Reprinted from *Vredebode* and dated 4 April 1923.

—'Korte uiteenzetting van mijn uittreden uit den Bond van Evangelisatie', *Dit is Het* 1.1 (July 1923), pp. 12-13.

Wehl, Nannie van, *Verhalen van mijn jongen* (Arnhem: H. ten Brink, 1922).

Wertheim, Wim F., *Indonesië van vorstenrijk tot neo-kolonie* (Meppel: Boom, 1978).

—'Koloniaal racisme in Indonesië: Ons onverwerkt verleden?' *De Gids* 154 (1991), pp. 367-85.

'Het werk der liefde', *Bataviaasch Nieuwsblad* (1 October 1907).

Winarko, Andi, *Gereja Pinkster Zending Gambang Waluh Sebagai Cikal Bakal GSSJA di Jawa Tengah* (B.Th. Thesis, Satyabhakti Advanced School of Theology, Malang, Indonesië, 2001).

Winckel, A., 'Br. Hoekendijk', *Ons Orgaan* 17.271 (1 November 1922), p. 191.

Wiratno, Paulus, 'The beginning of Assemblies of God in Indonesia' (Term paper, Baguio City, Asian Pentecostal Theological Seminary, 1993).

Wijers, D.J.B., 'Mijn Brief IX', *De Vredebode* 8.339 [October or November 1921], p. 3.

Wiyono, Gani, *A Sketch of the History of the Assemblies of God of Indonesia (Gereja Sidang-sidang Jemaat Allah)* (Master Thesis, Baguio City, Filipijnen: Asia Pacific Theological Seminary, 2004).

—'Pentecostals in Indonesia', in Allan Anderson and Edmond Tang, eds., *Asian and Pentecostal: The Charismatic Face of Christianity in Asia* (Baguio City: Regnum Books, 2005), pp. 307-28.

—*Gereja Sidang-Sidang Jemaat Allah dalam lintasan sejarah: Sebua Sketsa*. Malang: Penerbit Gandum Mas, 2007.

'The Work in the Australasian Field', *Australasian Record* 15.13-14 (27 March 1911), p. 13.

Zevendedags-Baptiste Gemeente, *Zevendedags-Baptiste Zending* (Haarlem: ZDB-gemeente, 1935).

Zeijl-Versluis, Nathalie, *Zing voor de Heer. Onderzoek naar de hoofdthema's in liederen van de honderjarige pinksterbeweging in Nederland* (Bachelor Thesis, Azusa theologische hogeschool, Amsterdam, 2007).

'De z.g. "Pinkster-gemeente" en hare gevaren', *Nieuws van den Dag voor Nederlandsch-Indië* (13 December 1924).

'Zuster C. Slagter: Een onderscheiding', *Indische Courant* (2 March 1936).

Zijlstra, G., 'Historie der Zevendedags-Baptiste Gemeenten' (Lecture for the Annual SDB-Conference at Haarlem 7 July 1951).

INDEX OF BIBLICAL REFERENCES

Index of Names

www.ingramcontent.com/pod-product-compliance
Lightning Source LLC
Chambersburg PA
CBHW060040100426
42742CB00014B/2651